ENDORSE
Joyous Encounters

"Exploring the original Greek texts of Luke in great detail, Joyous Encounters powerfully reveals how Luke's paired books exalt the great joy and unbounded love from God as the fulfillment of the Christian message, life, and salvation, and how faith communities can learn and flourish."
—**David J. Theroux**, President, C.S. Lewis Society of California, and Founder/President, Independent Institute

I have long thought that the scholarship of the church has lacked ways to explore the emotional side of faith. Scholars promote the goal of critical thinking, as if the emotions will thus take care of themselves. This book takes a valuable step towards redressing this imbalance by a careful, scholarly treatment of perhaps the key emotional response to the gospel in the New Testament: joy.

In both a broad survey and careful attention to detail, Lyle Story takes us through Luke's account of the gospel, and demonstrates the ubiquitous presence of the one response which is genuinely congruent to the Luke-Acts narrative. Of course, such a study raises numerous pastoral questions, many of which are treated in the final chapter. One in particular I would paraphrase thusly:

Given that the early church was saturated in this positive emotion, why does joy often seem rather a faint feature in contemporary church life? Why have churches which historically emphasized the charismatic signs of faith too often found themselves under the pressure of exhortations by pastors and musicians to experience a state of joy, when in the primary texts of faith, as Story ably demonstrates, joy is a natural, not a coerced response to good news?

May this careful study contribute to helping the church attend to the source of joy, and help it worry less about its manufacture or fabrication.
—**Roger J. Newell**, Professor Emeritus, George Fox University, and author of *The Feeling Intellect: Reading the Bible with C.S.Lewis*

In Joyous Encounters Dr. Story reveals the relational connection of joy between God and humanity. This new presentation of joy shows how central it is to Luke's writing about Christ and the Church in Luke-Acts. We then see how joy is God's purposeful outcome of the new covenant.

The way Luke describes Jesus' ministry announcement is breath-taking to me. I can only imagine the fire ignited when he repeated the prophetic words first recorded in Isaiah 61:1. Then Dr. Story narrates Luke's explanation of how

Jesus was introducing the "purposeful and powerful agenda of a joyful ministry." When I read those words, I realized I had not thought seriously enough about Jesus' own excitement of what he was setting out to do. We also learn about the energy of Jesus in his days on earth and how joy was his and for everyone who connected with it.

"In highlighting God's activity, Luke suggests that the nascent community, in joyous celebration, catches up with God's purposeful activity in joyous celebration." This statement is certainly worth underlining and memorizing as a communal call for those of us in this generation who choose the with-God life: What would happen if we did the same? It certainly would affect the current state of today's church.

I love this book.

—**Rev. Kerrie L. Palmer**, Founding Pastor, Red Door Community Church, and blogger at FaithFamilyCreativity.com

"Joy, I believe, is the emotion of union. Moltman describes it as the very meaning of life. In this scholarly and very accessible book, Lyle Story argues for putting the emotional music back into Scripture. He focuses on Joy in Luke-Acts and makes the case that joy is a passionate reaction of elation over something very good that has happened, is occurring, or will take place—like being able to remain in the love of the Trinity, right now and forever."

—**Gary W. Moon**, M.Div., Ph.D. Executive Director Martin Institute and Dallas Willard Center, Westmont College, Author, *Apprenticeship with Jesus*, and *Becoming Dallas Willard: The Formation of a Philosopher, Teacher and Christ-Follower*.

"Luke's Gospel and the book of Acts, both written by Luke the physician, come alive with affect in Joyous Encounters by J. Lyle Story. Reading the two New Testament books in concert with the author's treatise on joy reminded me of the words of Indonesian educator and emancipator Raden Adjeng Kartini: "Those who cannot feel pain are not capable, either, of feeling joy." J. Lyle Story details Luke's emotion-filled recounting of painful experiences of doubt and loss by Jesus' followers, and the lives of the sick, wounded, and broken who cross paths with Jesus, are then miraculously touched by his divine healing and filled with unexpected, deepening joy."

—**Roger A. Marum**, Ph.D., psychologist, and lecturer, Middlebury College, and author of blog:www.yourreluctantdisciple.com

JOYOUS
ENCOUNTERS

ALSO BY THE AUTHOR

Greek to Me: Learning New Testament Greek through Memory Visualization
(with Cullen I.K. Story)

JOYOUS ENCOUNTERS

DISCOVERING THE HAPPY AFFECTIONS IN LUKE-ACTS

J. LYLE STORY

A Herder & Herder Book
The Crossroad Publishing Company
New York

A Herder & Herder Book
The Crossroad Publishing Company
www.crossroadpublishing.com

The text of this book is set in 12/15 Adobe Garamond Pro.
Composition by Absolute Design
Cover design by Sophie Appel

Library of Congress Cataloging-in-Publication Data
available upon request from the Library of Congress.

ISBN 978-0-8245-9930-0 paperback
ISBN 978-0-8245-9929-4 cloth
ISBN 978-0-8245-9931-7 ePub
ISBN 978-0-8245-9932-4 mobi

Books published by The Crossroad Publishing Company may be purchased at special quantity discount rates for classes and institutional use. For information, please e-mail sales@CrossroadPublishing.com.

CONTENTS

To my wife, Sherri, who has brought such joy into my life.

FOREWORD

Over forty-five years have elapsed since Lyle Story and I began our studies at Fuller Theological Seminary. Our paths have crossed too seldom since then, yet I readily remember with warm gratitude Lyle's fine gifts and his earnest pursuit of the things of Christ. Both of these are manifest in this volume, the mature fruit of his scholarship, teaching, and discipleship.

The book is especially timely in a season when not joy but suffering, rage, self-interest, and despair drive so much public discourse, even among Christians. There seems to be a pervasive, frustrated helplessness and hopelessness, along with a laudable determination not to wound the injured further, that has led to the divorce of the whole idea of Christian joy from anything resembling ordinary human happiness. Now, almost no one, least of all Story and I, would deny that there is a self-centered, sinfully self-indulgent "happiness" that deserves censure, not embrace. Nor can one deny that true joy has an eschatological thrust, that the day when all tears will be wiped away has not arrived, and that meanwhile there are many pressing needs calling for comfort, sustenance, and the vigorous pursuit of justice. The point is surely not to punish or doubt the faith of those overwhelmed by suffering. Scripture contains much lament spoken by the faithful; and not all biblical writers emphasize joy.

However, Luke in particular—both in his Gospel and in Acts—does give remarkable and too-often-overlooked attention to the emotionally positive concomitants of the Spirit's work in and among God's people. Story has done ordinary Christians hungry for the goodness of the Christian life a favor in reminding us all that the good Lord does will joy for his people, and that the Spirit can bring it, sometimes miraculously, in circumstances both good and bad. Furthermore, by his close reading of Luke's narratives, scrupulously annotated and carefully engaging scholarly debates, he challenges the academic community to reconsider the too-tidy disconnect between joy and happiness; and to engage the affective character of the Lukan narratives and its implications for the Christian life as lived, even in the midst of trials and persecution. I can only hope that this book might open our eyes to what has long been before us if we were willing to look honestly, and that it may encourage us yet again to "taste and see that the Lord is good" (Ps. 34:8).

Marguerite Shuster
Harold John Ockenga Professor Emerita of Preaching and Theology
Fuller Theological Seminary

PREFACE

During my seminary days as an M.Div. student, I embarked on a journey for the presence and power of the Holy Spirit, which extended well over a year. During this period of time, a pastor-friend, Rev. Bob Whitaker, took me to any number of home prayer meetings or services and I was struck and attracted by the atmosphere of joy that characterized such gatherings. This feeling was far different from my upbringing in a mainline denominational tradition. Simply put, I sought an experience with God that touched all aspects of my Christian experience, including the affections, not just the rational aspect of my Christian faith. I ended up teaching and working with small prayer group leaders in Southern California and was encouraged by the vibrancy of student life with their experiences, ethos, and contagious vitality of Christian witness.

Over the years of teaching biblical studies, biblical languages, and hermeneutics, I explored more of the relational nature of the Trinitarian fellowship of love and joy. As I explored biblical texts, wrote journal articles, dictionary articles, and book chapters, it became abundantly clear to me that not only is God affective, but that the Trinitarian fellowship wills joyous affection for the people of God, in their experience and communal life-together. Our Western world and Western exegesis has an inbuilt tendency to interpret texts in a purely rational manner, leading to propositional preaching.

Am I saying that propositions are unimportant? Certainly not. Paul's teaching about justification through trust is solid and must be constantly communicated to the people of God. However, emotions are a vital aspect of human experience and must not be denied or denigrated. For example, as we look at the Psalter, we discover the full gamut of human experience and human emotions, from the deepest grief and sorrow to ecstatic joy, and everything in between. There is an ongoing dialogue between the poets and God as well as an ongoing conversation with the people of God, and their communal exchange with God. Emotions belong to the very fabric of biblical texts and need to be factored into the holistic interpretation of Scripture.

Over the years I have been drawn to the topic of emotions in the biblical texts. The writers of the sacred texts wish to draw their readers into the emotions of the Scriptures. In particular, I became fascinated with the topic of joy as I worked with Luke-Acts. Luke's vocabulary is replete with full and rich nuances of joy, both explicit and implicit. As I worked with commentaries and journal articles, I was struck by the lack of scholarly attention to the emotion of joy that permeates the stories that Luke tells. No mention is made of the emotions inherent in the narratives. I will argue that Luke makes the case for a lived theology of joy.

Is this book only for the biblical scholar? Surely not. Luke wants his readers to be people who are affected by the stories he tells. Luke intends that his readers experience joy in personal and communal life. For pastors, this means that when they preach the good news that their people are moved with joy; joy is the implicit and expected response to good news. When my oldest son sent an email about the birth of their daughter, my immediate response was that of joy, and a joy, which is contagious and must be shared. Indeed, something is inherently wrong when good news is met with a joyless response.

When people experience God in any number of incursions, they experience joy. Indeed, the constant refrain in both testaments is, "Do not be afraid, but rejoice." God is a joyful God who wills joy for his people. I have been unimpressed by scholars who make a false distinction between an "inner joy" and an "external happiness," as if God is uninterested in external happiness. The Bible makes no such distinction between the two. This imbalanced attitude represents the Western proclivity to downgrade human emotions as if they're not to be trusted or are merely transitory and fleeting. Sometimes we hear the negative epithet, "That's just emotionalism." Yet, we live within our emotions and our relationships with others and with God include the human and God-given affections.

Joy is one emotion among many feelings that we as humans experience. Indeed, the fruit of the Spirit that Paul lists in Gal 5:22-23 includes joy that follows love in his inventory. These are not only privatized emotions but are also communal in nature, and are to be experienced and expressed in the full range of Christian life. God created people with emotions, to be experienced and expressed in the here and now, which will be eclipsed by the joyous bliss of the Eschaton. Luke wants his readers to be impacted by his stories in a powerful and life-giving manner.

I trust that as you read through the exegesis of Luke's stories that they will affect you in a new way and that you will be drawn into the joyous emotions of the stories that Luke recounts. May these stories elicit joyous affection for the very nature and being of God, his Son, and the Holy Spirit; may you be genuinely receptive to divine incursions into your life. And may that joyous affection spill over into your expressions in your faith communities and witness to the world in an attractive and winsome manner—this leads to effective and appealing evangelism and missional expression.

CHAPTER 1

JOYFUL ENCOUNTERS

"Joy is the meaning of human life, joy in thanksgiving and thanksgiving as joy. In a way, this answer abolishes the intention of such questions as: For what purpose has man been created? For what purpose am I here? For the answer does not indicate ethical goals and ideal purposes but justifies created existence as such."[1]
–JÜRGEN MOLTMAN

Any list of emotions characterizing true Christian spirituality must include joy. In his two volumes, Luke summons his audience to joy-filled living in personal and community life. This study aims to supplement a dearth of biblical and theological attention devoted to the topic of joy, specifically in relationship to the global Pentecostal and charismatic experience. Luke's paired volumes emphasize the importance of joy in narrative form, showing people encountering the numinous (supernatural) world through a plethora of charismatic experiences with the divine. These experiences include angelic visitations, visions, healings, and baptism in the Spirit. Within the broad canon of Scripture, Luke draws his readers into the affective experiences of others.

In examining biblical texts, interpreters must not ignore important features like the *emotional atmosphere, the charismatic experiences of individuals and groups, and their expressions of joy.* Embracing these features supports the reality that God wills joy for his people.

I

Affective language is inextricably woven into the very fabric of Scripture and cannot be separated from the cloth of Scripture in favor of more propositional or theological threads to be highlighted. For this monograph, the word, "affection" refers to emotion, not "fondness." Writers of the biblical texts draw readers into the stories, and invite the audience to experience the events, including the emotional responses. Thus, readers can sympathize with their expressions, whatever the genre might be. For example, Luke describes an incident when Jesus was critiqued for his disciples' non-fasting practice. Through parabolic language, Luke points to joy as the only appropriate response to Jesus' presence. Jesus uses images of a wedding and groom, a patch and garment, and wine and wineskin to underscore the truth that the only natural and correct response to the groom is joy. Fasting and related mourning do not belong to a wedding celebration—like "wet-blankets," they are out of order at a wedding (Luke 5:33-39). Jesus' shared life with his disciples and God's people should inspire joy. Furthermore, joyous emotion is an important part of Christian spirituality, identified by Paul as a fruit of the Spirit (Gal 5:22).

This study will show that Luke links charismatic encounters with the Christian affection of joy, confirmed by the repeated references to joy in Luke-Acts in his narratives. Numerous texts reflect an atmosphere, experience, and expression of joy, all intended to attract readers, then and now, to joyful living, as persons and communities of faith. Thus, Luke argues for a "lived theology" of joy when people encounter the supernatural world.

From a statistical standpoint, Luke emphasizes the "joy" word-family much more than the other gospels. He continues this emphasis in Acts. For the purpose of this monograph, I pay attention to explicit passages in Luke-Acts where joy is associated with some event of divine intervention, invasion or charismatic experience from the supernatural world. I will discuss these passages seen through this lens.[2]

The Motif of Joy in Luke-Acts

I propose that joy is a key motif in Luke-Acts. According to William Freedman, "A motif, then, is a recurrent theme, character, or verbal pattern, but it may also be a family or associational cluster of literal or figurative references to a given class of concepts or objects . . . It is generally symbolic—that is, it can be seen to carry a meaning beyond the literal one immediately apparent . . . ."[3]

Thus, when Luke uses the emotional language of joy, he propels his readers beyond the actual recorded events. Certainly, he informs his readers. He invites them to reflect upon the atmospheres, experiences and expressions of joy in the narrative. But he also elicits joy from his readers, as they are drawn into the emotions of the text, and he invites them to sympathize with certain events and key figures. He communicates, "This is the way life can be lived," and he intends for his readers to embrace this thrust in personal and community relationships, as people encounter the divine. Luke indicates that joy should characterize the new people of God.

For example, in Acts 15 Luke compares what Cornelius and others experienced with the same joyous encounter that Peter and others enjoyed on the initial Day of Pentecost. Luke's narrative includes Peter's statement: "And God who knows the heart bore witness to them (Cornelius and others), giving them the Holy Spirit *just as* he did to us" (Acts 15:8). Acts 15 shows that feelings shaped deliberations by members of the Jerusalem Council. Such Lucan texts of joy express Christian affection and lead to a communal solidarity.

I intend to demonstrate that Luke emphasizes joy in the context of various encounters with the numinous. To this end, I will probe the joy-vocabulary and repetition of the joy word-family in Luke-Acts in comparison/contrast with the other gospels, themes and Luke's special material (*Sondergut*). The text includes other occurrences of the joy-vocabulary in connection with other teachings of Jesus, e.g., "rejoicing and leaping for joy" in suffering and persecution (Luke 6:22-23)[4]; these passages will not be covered, since they are not immediately linked with charismatic experience. Further, Luke does describe other healings or exorcisms, which do not contain words from the joy-vocabulary. While I am unable to argue or exegete from silence, I also assume that such miraculous actions did produce joy from various individuals and witnesses to a powerful event.[5] The fact that Luke does not draw from the joy-vocabulary in these events does not mean that joy was not present. I suggest that Luke assumes such acts of liberation would produce joy, and he did not feel compelled to express it in specific language. Certainly, Luke would assume a natural "spill-over" between paragraphs. My selected texts bear upon Luke's theological and pastoral agenda of joy as a vital aspect of Christian experience and Christian affections in the human encounter with the other-worldly.

The Nature of Joy

I propose that joy is a term that serves as the broader umbrella covering the numerous vocabulary words that express nuances of the joy-vocabulary, e.g., delight, happiness, ecstasy, pleasure, gladness, blessedness, peace, celebration, excess, even laughter. The various Greek cognates all contain emotional content. As Marianne Meye Thompson argues, other texts express the ways joy replaces conditions of sorrow, grieving, affliction,[6] which directly relate to the distressed conditions of ill or possessed persons in Luke-Acts.

In contrast to many scholars who devalue emotion in biblical texts, I suggest that joy is an emotion of elation over something good that has happened, is occurring, or will take place. In this study, joy is a vital part of various charismatic experiences. As an emotion, joy has an object, and it is felt for a positive reason, deemed so by a person. For example, Luke refers to a healed leper, who is overjoyed at his healing. He is no longer an outcast, is set free, and returns to Jesus to give thanks to God and to Jesus for his healing (Luke 17:11-19). Something would be strangely amiss if he was joy-less. Here, joy is felt and expressed for the right reasons. Conversely, joy can be felt and expressed for the wrong motivation. Luke also notes the delight of religious leaders at Judas' offer to betray Jesus (Luke 22:4-6), or Herod Antipas' misguided joy, "rejoiced exceedingly" (ἐχάρη λίαν 23:8), followed by the explanation for his excessive joy: "for a long time he wanted *to see him*" "hoping *to see some sign* performed by him" (23:8). Clearly, Herod's "joy" is a sham, a far cry from the genuine joy believers experience when they encounter the miraculous.

Joy is a similar emotion, felt and experienced both by the leper, the religious leaders, and Antipas. However, the reasons for the emotion are poles apart. Thus, the same emotion is right in one instance and wrong in the other. This is what Matthew Elliott labels as "the cognitive content" associated with the emotions.[7] Thus, we find the rich fool, whose reason for joy is altogether immoral, because he lives only for himself without regard for God or others in his community (Luke 12:19). On the other hand, Jesus directs his disciples to the real grounds for their joy, "your names have been written in heaven"—not successful exorcisms alone (Luke 10:20). Occasions for a felt-joy can be grounded or motivated by both right and wrong reasons.

Matthew Elliott makes a solid case that "many New Testament scholars have taken their theology and defined emotion words by drawing on these beliefs. In other words, emotional vocabulary has often been redefined to mean a theological concept devoid of its emotional meaning. This method is the wrong way around; the cart is before the horse!"[8] This is why he counters the notion that "theological 'joy' is held to be important while the significance of how a Christian should feel is rarely mentioned . . . The word 'inner' provides a way to assert that it is not an emotion while maintaining the claim that joy is present."[9]

Many scholars draw a misleading distinction between "joy" and "happiness," "inner joy" and "outward happiness," "religious joy" and "secular joy." These divisions can minimize, trivialize or even delete the emotional content of joy. Examples of this approach are numerous. For example, Bultmann dismisses the affective content of Luke's statement that Jesus *rejoiced with exuberance in the Holy Spirit*" (ἠγαλλιάσατο [ἐν] τῷ πνεύματι τῷ ἁγίῳ Luke 10:21); he regards this merely as "inspiration."[10] Jesus' emotional response is occasioned by the seventy [two] returning from their successful short-term mission-trip. The verbs, "I exult, I am overjoyed, I am filled with exuberant joy" (ἀγαλλιάω ἀγαλλιάομαι)[11] suggest a joyous and ecstatic condition, since it is "in the Holy Spirit."

Similarly, in his article on "Joy," Creath Davis argues that "Joy is a gift of God . . . a quality of life and not simply a fleeting emotion."[12] Thus, for Davis, if joy is God's gift and a quality of life, then the emotional or personal component is absent. The only time Davis uses the word "emotion" in his article, he frames it in a negative expression. Dorothy Harvey's article on "Joy" begins with the statement, "The experience of joy, as related to praise and thanksgiving in public worship, or to the quiet confidence of the individual in God, or to the proclamation of God's saving power . . . ."[13] She draws attention to corporate worship, quiet confidence, and public proclamation, all without addressing emotion in her article.

Eric Beyreuther and Günter Finkenrath provide extensive and solid reasons for joy in the NT, but the word *emotion* is found only once in their nine-page article, and then, it is used in a pejorative expression, "the joy of the festive company, not the subjective emotion of an individual."[14] How can joyous festivity not touch emotions? Similarly, Gerald Hawthorne consistently argues that joy is something "inner" and not "outer," and he distinguishes between "joy" and "happiness." Hawthorne continues his demeaning premise, "Further, these writers do not appear to equate joy with happiness, as happiness is commonly understood today (this in spite of the fact that *makarios* is translated as "happy" in numerous versions), nor can any of them be termed advocates of what might be called "holy laughter" or other such ecstatic, visible expressions of joy."[15] He minimizes expressions of joy and happy feelings and points to something "more profound . . . akin to faith . . . a settled state of mind, marked by peace . . . an attitude toward life."[16] In his work, *Joy in the New Testament*, William Morrice also points to "this inward state of joy to the Christians."[17] In John Painter's article, "Joy," the words *emotion* or *feeling* do not appear.[18] However, the NT writers do not distinguish joy from happiness.[19] Thus, Wolfgang Bilner begins his article on "Joy" with the statement, "Joy, as a basic emotion, corresponds to the state of happiness."[20]

Experienced joy—an anticipatory (proleptic) celebration of the untold joy of the future

The delight that Luke's characters experience in the present anticipates the untold joy they will experience in the future. People who are freed from illness or troubling demonic spirits experience joy, but their emotional response foreshadows the sheer delight awaiting them in the *eschaton*, "a reality that transcends the world's horizons . . . that anticipates the fullness of God's remaking the world."[21] Emotions of joy are orientations to the present world, and also the future world. For example, the joy of the shepherd finding a lost sheep, or a woman finding a lost coin is contagious—it must be shared with others. Jesus clearly indicates that such joy is matched by the joy of heaven or the angels of God (Luke 15:8, 10). Human joy is concurrent with divine joy. When people discover God's miraculous power, they experience wonder, gratitude, and joy. They serve as contagious witnesses to God's unexpected grace. Their response is not anchored in duty or obligation. Their lives have been touched by God's charismatic power. From Luke's perspective, their joy is eschatological, a foretaste of the final consummation. As Karl Barth says, a Christian finds election in Jesus Christ who is the "incarnate gratitude of the creature . . . the original of this representation and illustration of the gracious God which is free of all self-will and therefore joyful, the true imitator of his work."[22]

With reference to Miriam's song of "wild delight" (Ex. 15), N.T. Wright is certainly on target when he states, "*Something has happened* as a result of a new world opened up. The thing that has happened is simultaneously an act of 'judgment' and an act of 'rescue.' God has put things right, to put a stop to evil, and to deliver his people from their enslaving enemy."[23]

He also points to a contrast between an emphasis upon "hope" in Second Temple Judaism, juxtaposed with the dominant note of joy by early Christians,[24] that is both theological and eschatological in nature.[25] Joy and communal celebration are "brought into a startling new focus because of Jesus. I have suggested that in the key passages we see the early Christian belief that in Jesus there has come about a new union between heaven and earth, with the celebrations of one spilling over necessarily into the celebrations of the other."[26]

N.T. Wright then grounds joy, "The *fact* of the resurrection and exaltation of the crucified Jesus opens up a new world, launches the new creation, over which Jesus himself is sovereign; that is the root cause of joy."[27] At the same time, Wright stops short, not taking into account the affirmation by Peter that subsequent to Jesus' exaltation at God's right hand, "he received the promised Holy Spirit from the Father, and has poured forth what you see and hear" (Acts 2:33). This is why the last days have already begun (Acts 2:17; Joel 2:28-32) in both a present and anticipatory celebration. The joyful experience in the initial Day of Pentecost is both participatory and proleptic.

The various charismatic incursions through powerful verbal proclamation of God's kingdom, along with healings, exorcisms, and other deliverances, all highlight God's will for life in the fullest sense. Thus Jesus fights against sickness which impairs life. By its very nature, the experienced joy of a new life seeks continuance, not only in this life, but in the age to come. This joy is not a means to an end, but it is an end in itself. Jesus clearly conveys this to the dying criminal, "Today, you will be with me in Paradise" (Luke 24:43).

Gratitude is the flip-side of joy—they are so often paired in Luke. An outcast Samaritan leper receives healing on his journey to a Jewish priest and what is his response? He expresses gratitude to the giver Jesus, and he does so with great joy (Luke 17:15-16). Gratitude completes the circuit of joy. And what is Jesus' response? "Your faith has saved you" (Luke 17:19). He pairs gratitude with trust.

Joy is passive, in that it is a response to some grand occurrence in the life of a person in deep need and distress, such as this outcast leper. At the same time, joy is active, also expressed by the leper in spontaneous gratitude. This is why Charles Matthews argues for the "middle voice—that is, a reality that is not purely passive, happening to us, nor simply active, something we do; but partaking of both receptivity and dynamism."[28] People can be summoned to joy, and they have a choice of feeling and expressing joy, "Rejoice that your names are written in heaven" (Luke 10:20). Similarly, the experienced joy of the shepherd, the woman, and the father upon finding lost things or a lost son pointedly leads to the active summons, "Rejoice with me" (Luke 15). The joy of Jesus and the joy of God in the unconditional acceptance of the toll-collectors and sinners (Luke 15:1-2) should also characterize God's people. In experiencing joy, they share in both the joy of Jesus and the joy of

God. This joyful response is neither shared by the religious critics or the older brother—they are joy-less and stand aloof from the celebration.

The affective language of joy

Commentaries on Luke-Acts present a famine of attention for the important emotion of joy.[29] The same holds true for some systematic theologies.[30] Joy belongs to the broader category of experiential language from narratives that are not propositional in nature, clearly defined, which easily lend themselves to theological or systematic correctness. Experiential language in narrative form expresses the mood or atmosphere for reading and interpreting biblical texts. As to the language of religious experience, Luke Timothy Johnson writes, "It occurs everywhere in the earliest Christian writings and points to realities and convictions of fundamental importance to both writers and readers of these writings. Yet precisely this register of language is least recognized or appreciated by the academic study of early Christianity."[31] The quote comes from Johnson's chapter, "What's missing from Christian origins?" in which he supports the legitimacy and importance of religious experience,[32] as "both elusive and disputable."[33]

> The difficulty of analyzing and speaking about religious experience must be taken seriously. But the category of religious experience, for all its elusiveness and ambiguity, remains necessary if we are not to deny or neglect certain important forms of human discourse and behavior. We need the category to account for people whose behavior, otherwise perfectly within the range of what we consider normal, appears in other respects to be organized around what they claim are convictions and experiences concerning powers that are neither reducible to immanent causes nor verifiable by neutral observation.[34]

Sarah Maitland suggests, "It is the very nature of this joy, born out of risk and uncertainty, that it is very difficult to pin any concrete solid meaning on to it, let alone stabilize it long enough to take a hard look at it."[35] Joy is one such religious experience, atmosphere, or expression, wherein people are invaded by the other-worldly (numinous), which involves whole persons and communities of faith in an intensive way.

Numerous texts from Luke-Acts describe joy as spontaneous and contagious. People who experience joy also feel a compulsion to share the experience, thus engaging the community. Joy belongs to the broader context of expressive language, helping the writer capture emotions and elicit feelings from the audience. Readers can draw near to the narratives with sympathy and shared experiences, or they may distance themselves from certain events or people, e. g. meanness by Jesus' joyless critics who are unable to celebrate the joy of a healing on the Sabbath.[36] With affective language, readers may gravitate between attraction and repulsion. G. B. Caird says, "For one half of the religious mind is utilitarian and regards all things, including life itself as raw material to be used in the service of purpose, while the other half is experiential, looking on all things as gifts to be enjoyed, objects of delight and wonder, signposts to the greater wonder of their Creator."[37]

Affective language provides the emotional climate of various stories and must be taken seriously if texts are to be understood in their fullness. Luke encases the truth he wishes to express within the emotional atmosphere of various accounts. He uses the joy-vocabulary, paired with his readers' imagination to feel the atmospheres, experiences, and expressions of joy, drawing his audience into the stories, and inviting them to feel fully alive as they experience the emotions of the text.[38] For example, Gabriel's announcement to an aged Zechariah infuses Luke's readership with a joyous expectation of what will follow in the narrative(s). Listeners and readers become not only spectators, but participants in the joyous narratives. Luke anticipates that his readers both accept and embrace such joyful experiences as people encounter the other-worldly. Such joyful encounters prompt spontaneity and contagion—joy must be shared by individuals in the narrative and by Luke's readers. Joy is completed when it is communicated with others in communal celebrations.

Joy and witness

When Pentecostal scholars view Luke-Acts, they frequently latch on to the important themes of empowered or inspired witness,[39] and the charismatic community in mission,[40] particularly in the book of Acts. Yes, Luke-Acts is concerned with the widening spheres of witness. At the same time, Luke's interpreters often minimize or ignore the experience or atmosphere of joy. If God grants charismatic experiences for missional purposes alone, then God becomes utilitarian in terms of how he views people and wants to use them. Thus, the meaning of their existence is bound up with the divine purpose, so that individuals and communities become "purpose-driven." To be sure, Acts 1 directs the Pentecostal community to the purpose of mission, subsequent to their baptism in the Holy Spirit (Acts 1:8). Yet their experience yields so much more than simple functionality or purpose. God does not relate to people as mere automatons, created to complete a task.[41]

Haya-Prats initially notes, "I recognize that the gift of the Holy Spirit in Acts has predominantly utilitarian-historical effects, whether kerygmatic or ethical: an impulse to testimony and evangelization, wisdom and fearlessness. This is natural, since Luke wishes to present the development of the church and sees in it a sign of divine assistance."[42] Yet, Haya-Prats goes on to affirm "rapturous effects . . . celestial fullness, joy . . . and exultant praise."[43] As unfolded in Acts 2, the actual experience is that of joy. God is not primarily interested in people because of a job he gives them to perform.[44] In a similar manner, Robert Tannehill argues that the "second noteworthy emphasis in Luke-Acts is the surprising link between repentance and joy rather than mourning, the traditional expression of repentance . . . to the joy of a restored relationship, a joy that excludes the demonstrations of sorrow normally associated with repentance."[45] For example, when the risen Jesus confronts Saul on the Damascus Road, he does so with grace; there is no catalogue of sins that Saul must own up to and then confess. It is as if the risen Jesus says to Saul, "Look, this chapter of your life is over. Here is the new direction and orientation for your life. Get up and go . . . ." (Acts 9:6).

As Moltmann looks at the Western Church, he launches a broad-side attack on a "purpose-driven" God. As he argues, God becomes oppressive, demanding, "the supreme projected Father-figure, an abuser, whose primary concern is the human response of ethics, duty, usefulness and a burdensome slave morality."[46] He traces the Western pathology to Augustine and his view of the human person, leading to sickness and morbidity.[47] The charismatic experience of joy is primary, and then it yields purpose. This negates the idea that doing leads to being, indicating instead that being leads to doing. "Man is not liberated from his old nature by imperatives to be new and to change, but he rejoices in the new which makes him free and lifts him beyond himself. Where repentance is understood as a spiritual return to the evil and rejected past, it deals in self-accusation, contrition, sackcloth and ashes. But when repentance is a return to the future, it becomes concrete in rejoicing, in new self-confidence and in love."[48]

Again, joy is proleptic. This is precisely what happens to Saul in his encounter with the risen Jesus. Purpose-free rejoicing in God may then take the place of the uses and abuses of God. Moltmann cites Karl Barth's statement related to God and joy, "Karl Barth was the only theologian in the continental Protestant tradition who has dared to call God 'beautiful' . . . Another corresponding term is love, a love which does not merely manifest itself ethically in love to the neighbor but also aesthetically in festive play before God."[49]

Works on joy

Pentecostal scholar James Shelton provides a chapter in *Mighty in Word and Deed*, which discusses joy in the context of "Prayer and Praise."[50] He takes note of some of the joy-vocabulary words and concentrates on Jesus' rejoicing in the Holy Spirit (Luke 10:21), subsequent to the powerful mission of the seventy [two]. S. Paulo J Bernadicou's dissertation, *Joy in the Gospel of Luke*, explores some of the Lucan vocabulary of joy, specifically in the communitarian dimension, noted especially in the Lucan banquet scenes, but he fails to explore the relationship between joy and numerous charismatic invasions in both Luke and Acts.[51] John Navone provides a chapter on joy in his book *Themes of St. Luke*, however his treatment does not express thorough analysis of various texts.[52] Building upon his dissertation, William Morrice has written two books on the theme of joy: *Joy in the New Testament,*[53] and *We Joy in God.*[54] Given the breadth of his approach, he provides no exegesis of texts, only nine pages devoted to Luke-Acts,[55] little interest in miraculous encounters, and a distinction between *happiness* and *joy.*[56] He bases his argument upon four main doctrines, without really dealing with the Christian emotion of joy as something to be felt.

Recently, Kindalee Pfremmer De Long has written a fine monograph, *Surprised by God: Praise Responses in the Narrative of Luke-Acts* in which she accentuates the praise-responses to divine visitation in Luke-Acts.[57] She does investigate numerous texts in her treatment in which she links joy and praise, or joyous praise, notably in the birth narratives in Luke 1-2. However, in doing so, the language of emotions and feelings is notably absent. She says very little about the joyous atmosphere that leads individuals to experience joy. She also does not address how these affective experiences lead to spontaneous and contagious expressions of joy, voiced through praise. Charismatic experiences of supernatural events receive minimal or no attention, e.g. the various Pentecosts in Acts. I will interact with her contributions through the course of this monograph.

In the last two decades, more attention has been given to the emotions and their role in understanding biblical texts. Robert C. Roberts work, *Spirituality and Human Emotion*[58] argues that emotions are "construals" or "ways of seeing things," including one's own circumstances.[59] He states, "Emotion-dispositions are concerns, and concerns of a special type which can be called passions constitute our character, our inmost self."[60] In his work, he draws attention to the particular fruit of the Spirit, gratitude, hope, and compassion, all built upon the emotion of humility. However, Roberts does not specifically address the affection of joy.

In his book, *Faithful Feelings: Rethinking Emotion in the New Testament,* Elliott, builds upon Roberts' arguments in terms of his emphasis upon the cognitive element, associated with Christian affections. He argues against an "anti-emotion bias in modern scholarship."[61] In his work, he analyzes the emotions of love, joy, and hope, in particular. His analysis of joy in the diverse writings of the NT is solid as he points to the cognitive element of joy, and provides numerous reasons for the human emotion of joy. Although he devotes fourteen pages to the Christian affection of joy in the NT, he does not discuss joy-texts. While he draws attention to Luke as the "gospel of joy,"[62] the companion volume of Acts is unaddressed. Certainly I sympathize with his basic thrust and argument; however, he provides no interpretation of texts in his treatment of emotions in the context of charismatic encounters.

The emotional language found in the gospels and Acts expresses Jesus' joyous involvement with people. The Church has long argued for a Trinitarian-fellowship, a fellowship of love in mutuality and communication. Traditionally, the Church has focused upon orthodoxy (right doctrine) and orthopraxis (right practice), but in recent years, attention has been given to orthopathos (right affections). Thus, Steven Land argues, "Orthodoxy (right praise-confession), orthopathy (right affections) and orthopraxy (right praxis) are related in a way analogous of the Holy Trinity. God, who is Spirit, creates in humanity a spirituality which is at once cognitive, affective, and behavioral, thus driving toward a unified epistemology, metaphysics, and ethics."[63] Land carefully develops the progression of thought from John Wesley, Jonathan Edwards, Karl Barth, Jürgen Moltmann, to the Methodist theologian T. H. Runyon—to pave the way for a fresh understanding and appreciation for the vital role of Christian affections.[64] And most certainly, the Holy Spirit is the vital aspect for Christian spirituality and the related affections.[65]

Land quotes from Runyan, "[It is] feelings that focus our energies, enlist us, motivate us, and give us passion. Who will fight against injustice, prejudice, and corruption who does not have feelings of justice and outrage against injustice?"[66] From his Latin American and Pentecostal perspective, Samuel Solivan makes a solid case for orthopathos (right affections) that he calls an "interlocutor between North American Protestant orthodoxy and praxis-oriented liberation theologies."[67] Such contributions build upon Abraham Heschel, in his two-volume work,

The Prophets, more specifically in Vol. 2.[68] In his book, Land argues in a similar way to Elliott, but he highlights the Christian affections of gratitude, compassion, and courage.[69] He does narrate the experiences of early Pentecostals and emphasize, "The joy of the fullness of the Spirit was strength and encouragement to believers as they walked in the Spirit and not after the flesh."[70] He also affirms that the Christian life "is a pattern of deep emotions, which are the fruit of the Spirit . . . and are the definition of Christian spirituality."[71] He affirms the integration of beliefs, affections, and actions (of knowing, being, and doing)."[72] However, when Land makes a chart of "Pentecostal Affections," he does not mention joy.

Thus, in the last two decades, some more scholarly attention has been devoted to the affections and their import for Christian spirituality. Fraser Watts, Rebecca Nie, and Sarah Savage summarize that "recent theories of emotion have emphasized the close intertwining of cognition and emotion, that emotion can be an integral part of human understanding, rather than an impediment to it. The phrase, 'emotional intelligence' captures well this new view of emotion."[73]

Still, there has been no exegetical approach to Luke-Acts taking into account the plethora of joy-vocabulary terms that are used to set the stage for a charismatic event, which express the emotional experience of the people of God, or narrate their affective responses, such as gratitude, thanksgiving, or praise, or glorifying God.

Paul Elbert's recent article highlights Luke's use of Pauline material, and his expression of similar themes through his narrative examples and precedents.[74] Since Paul himself has an extensive *joy* vocabulary,[75] is it not possible that Luke provides stories of examples and precedents of Paul's theological statements as a *lived-theology*?[76]

To be sure, many detractors object to emotional experiences and expressions, often with the statement, "They're just emotional," in a negative manner. Roberts interprets this epithet, "We mean that he is not quite in possession of himself. He is weak, immature, hollow, shallow, flabby, 'not-together.'"[77] Land responds, "The Enlightenment view of the opposition of reason and emotion, as well as the fundamentalist emphasis on their 'balance', combine to produce a cultural suspicion, if not outright derogation, of 'Holy Rollers.'"[78] He then applies this attitude to persons who perceive others through the lens of socio-economics, race, socio-politics and education. Christians can be discounted as "emotional" and in need of a proper "balance" in their lives, with the presupposition that reason trumps emotion. One example of such a dismissive response is Calvin Miller, who entitles a full chapter, "Happiness—Mind over Mood."[79]

People who experience a supernatural incursion into their lives express emotion in praise and thanksgiving with affective language. God's grace-gifts affect people deeply, eliciting spontaneous response to the giver. If Christians receive a supernatural answer to prayer, the only reasonable response is spontaneous joy and gratitude. Something vital is missing without expressive and shared gratitude. For example, Mary's excited "haste" to see Elizabeth (Luke 1:39) reflects a spontaneous and contagious joy as does the mention of "singing and dancing" in a father's house (Luke 15:25). To be sure, the Christian life is not a series of emotional outbreaks, but Christian affections are integrated in the whole of life, beliefs, practices, theological reflection, relationships with God and the community—within the broader umbrella of the kingdom of God, expressed in love and power.

Certainly, joy is not the conclusive emotion; it is but one fruit of the Spirit. This affection can be both elevated and discounted in importance; this emotion needs to be integrated into the whole of one's person and faith-community. This is what Luke does in his two volumes. Joy is an important affection and does reveal the truth about what Christians believe and value. Luke highlights the Christian emotion of joy as he describes the response of people experiencing a divine incursion.

Organization of this study

Why should we pay attention to Luke's vocabulary of joy? In this monograph, Chapter 2 compares the word-frequencies of joy-related terms in the gospels and Acts, with reference to the standard lexicons and theological dictionaries. Luke uses forty-seven terms of the joy-vocabulary. More specifically, he taps into nine unique words, not used by the other evangelists. Often Luke records a miracle story shared by the other gospels, but Luke alone narrates the account with an expression of joy. Frequently his miracle stories lead to the climax of joy. Luke's rich joy-vocabulary draws his readers into affective reading, interpretation, and application to their own faith-communities.

Chapter 3 of this monograph describes how Luke begins his gospel. He uses a clear link between charismatic activity and joy in the annunciation and birth narratives (Luke 1-2), through his narration of divine incursions (in numerous modes) to various individuals (Zechariah, Mary, Elizabeth, John the Baptist (in utero), shepherds, Simeon, Anna, neighbors). Luke intends to draw his readers into charismatic events of joy, so they feel the expressions of joy, e.g., "Behold I bring you good news of *great joy*" (Luke 2:10). Joy is voiced through various songs of joyful praise, fulfilled prophecy. Luke paints a word picture showing joy as spontaneous, contagious, and meant to be shared. He communicates this through extensive affective vocabulary.

Chapter 4 of this study features Luke's description of the beginning of Jesus' ministry. Luke highlights the Spirit, Jesus' agenda, and joy (Luke 4:16-30), empowered by "the descent of the Spirit in bodily form as a dove." Luke prods his community to ponder Jesus' personal Pentecost that prepares him for his purposeful and powerful agenda of a joyful ministry in so many life-giving ways.

How do people respond to Jesus' ministry, and how does Jesus respond to others? Chapter 5 will show that joy is integral to the whole of Jesus' miraculous activity (healings, exorcisms, and mighty works, the joyous short-term mission-trips of his disciples, and Jesus' affective response to their mission). Luke notes the atmosphere, experiences and expressions of joy that are a vital part of these narratives, expressed through extensive emotive language. Through these expressions, Luke invites his readers to embrace Jesus' powerful ministry with attendant joy.

How do people respond to the resurrected Jesus? Chapter 6 focuses on Luke's post-resurrection stories (Luke 24:1-53) including angelic visitations, experiences with an unrecognized Jesus and a recognized Jesus, the promise of the Spirit, and the ascension. Throughout these encounters, Luke notes how people are in-process as they discover the joyful wonder of the risen Jesus. All of these numinous events are positioned within contexts of joy. Luke includes the climax of "great joy" at the end of his narrative, which matches the announcement of "great joy" to the shepherds at the beginning of his narrative of Jesus. Luke's readers should ponder the wonder of these appearances to individuals or groups, further reflecting and joyfully receiving the "promise of my Father" when they are "clothed with power from on high" (Luke 24:49). Joyous anticipation and experience of the Holy Spirit are intended for the initial community, with the intention of extending beyond, moving far and wide through Luke's communities.

Chapter 7 describes how people respond to the Jesus-event and gift of the Holy Spirit through the book of Acts. In numerous miraculous encounters, Luke pairs joy in conversion and baptism in the Holy Spirit. Luke's initial Pentecost story is followed by several other Pentecostal stories, recounting a powerful witness and mission with attendant joy. He encourages his audience to visualize joy-propelled witness through the courageous witness of Peter, Philip, and Paul, coupled with the happy and ecstatic response of people experiencing God's power. Luke also records three vignettes in which the apostles confront demonic powers and magic. Through numerous climaxes of joy, Luke anticipates that his readers feel and experience the joy of a Spirit-filled life and community.

What about life-together in the nascent church? Chapter 8 examines Luke's interjected "narrative summaries," in which he pairs joy with miraculous activity, making a case for the reader to see the recorded events as illustrating the joyous and powerful way that the Christian life is meant to be lived. These short summaries are more than stops in the narrative, for they serve Luke's case for a lived-theology of joyful encounter through charismatic experience. In life-together, how does the community go about making important decisions? Luke tells the story of the Jerusalem Council (Acts 15), which constitutes a call to celebrate the inclusionary purpose of God. Luke couples numinous aspects with joy, indeed great joy. Luke emphasizes the joyful and joint involvement of the divine (numinous) and human—seeking to discern God's will in changing circumstances.

How does the community respond to threatening circumstances? Chapter 9 examines Luke's stories of how individuals (Peter, Paul) deal with threats, including abuse, imprisonment, even a shipwreck. Charismatic power trumps threats and even within these stories, Luke records the language of joy. Luke intend for his readers to experience joyous affection in their threatening circumstances?

Finally, chapter 10 examines the implications of Luke's pairing joy with charismatic power. Luke makes the case that Christian joy is a vital aspect of life in the Spirit and is a vital part of biblical narratives. As such, it is a fitting subject for proper interpretation of biblical texts. Luke summons the Christian community, then and now, to appreciate the wonder that God is a God of great joy, who encounters people in numerous charismatic experiences, who seeks to elicit joy. God wills joy for his people. It is hoped that the scholarly community and the Church would pay more attention to the affective language of joy in the sacred texts. This is an important part of the exegetical process. Narrative theology is just as important as some of the propositional theology that we may find in the Pauline letters. Scholars and faith-communities need to be open and receptive to charismatic experience (whatever form that may take), and discover joy in such encounters.

NOTES

1   Jürgen Moltmann, *Theology and Joy* (London: SCM Press LTD, 1973), 42.
2   Thus, my primary purpose does not include extensive source-critical or historical work on Luke-Acts or full exegesis of select passages.
3   William Freedman, "The Literary Motif: A Definition and Evaluation," *Novel* 4 (1970/71): 131, cited also by Robert J. Karris, *Luke: Artist and Theologian* (Eugene, OR: Wipf & Stock, 1985), 5. In this study, the motif of joy can be discerned by: 1) The frequency and repetition of the extensive joy-vocabulary in Luke-Acts as compared with the other gospels, 2) The significance of the joy-vocabulary in charismatic contexts, 3) How the atmosphere, experience and expression of joy is consistent within the whole of Luke-Acts, 4) The instances where Luke uses the joy-vocabulary, while the other evangelists do not include this vocabulary when referring to the same event, 5) Uses of the joy-vocabulary in distinctly Lucan texts, 6) Negative attitudes (suspicion, indignation, jealousy, anger, lying in wait, murderous intent, rejection), "the deep gloom which hangs over the 'good,'" to highlight a celebration of joy.

Günther Bornkamm, *Jesus of Nazareth* (trans. Irene and Fraser McLuskey; New York: Harper & Row Publishers, 1960), 85.

4   Marianne Meye Thompson labels her third kind of joy as "a *joy notwithstanding* one's condition, state, or circumstances, joy when one's circumstances seem not to warrant it." Marriane Meye Thompson, "Reflections on Joy in the Bible" in *Joy and Human Flourishing* (ed. Miroslav Volf and Justin E. Crisp; Minneapolis: Fortress Press, 2015), 20.

5   For example, Luke's paragraph on the healing of the leper makes no explicit mention of joy (Luke 5:13-16), although it may be assumed in the growing popularity of Jesus (Luke 5:15-16).

6   Marianne Meye Thompson, 19.

7   Matthew A. Elliott, *Faithful Feelings: Rethinking Emotion in the New Testament* (Grand Rapids: Kregel, 2006).

8   Elliott, 128.

9   Elliott, 165-166. He also cites evidence for the bifurcation of theological words and emotional content, seen in several articles in *TDNT*, e.g. "a distinctive religious joy which accrues to man from his share in the salvation of the kingdom of God.", 165, F. Hauck, "μακάριος," *TDNT*, 4:367.

10   R. Bultmann, "ἀγαλλιάομαι, ἀγαλλίασις," *TDNT* 1:21.

11   BDAG, 3-4, "a demonstrative joy." LS, 5, "express great joy, exult, pay honor to a god."

12   Creath Davis, "Joy" *Evangelical Dictionary of Theology* (ed. Walter A Elwell; Grand Rapids: Baker Academic, 2001), 636.

13   Dorothy Harvey, "Joy, *IDB* E-J (ed. George A. Buttrick; Nashville: Abingdon Press, 1962), 1000.

14   Eric Beyreuther, Günther Finkenrath, "Joy, Rejoice," *NIDNTT*, Vol. 2 (ed. Colin Brown; Grand Rapids, Zondervan Publishing House, 1971), 355.

15   Gerald Hawthorne, "Joy" *Dictionary of the Later New Testament & Its Developments* (ed. Ralph P. Martin, Peter H. Davids; Downers Grove, IL: InterVarsity Press, 1997), 604. Donald Hagner also argues for an "inner joy." Donald A. Hagner, *Matthew 1-13* (Nashville: Thomas Nelson Publishers, 1993), 91.

16   Hawthorne, 604.

17   William Morrice, *Joy in the New Testament* (Grand Rapids: William B. Eerdmans Publishing Company, 1984), 75.

18   John Painter, "Joy" *Dictionary of Jesus and the Gospels* (ed. Joel B. Green, Scot McKnight, I. Howard Marshall; Downers Grove IL; InterVarsity Press, 1992), 395-396.

19   A further example of such a division between *joy* and *happiness* is voiced through Calvin Miller, *The Taste of Joy* (Downers Grove IL: InterVarsity Press, 1983). He argues from Webster's Dictionary, not a sound Greek lexicon, "The word *happiness* has the same root as the word *happening. Happiness happens.*" 12.

20   Wolfgang Beilner, "Joy" *Encyclopedia of Biblical Theology* (ed. Johannes B. Bauer; New York: Crossroad, 1981), 438.

21 Thompson, 33.

22 Karl Barth, *Church Dogmatics* II/2, 413-414.

23 N.T. Wright, "Joy, New Testament Perspectives and Questions" in *Joy and Human Flourishing* (ed. Miroslav Volf and Justin E. Crisp; Minneapolis: Fortress Press, 2015), 41-42.

24 N.T. Wright, 46.

25 N.T. Wright, 47.

26 N.T. Wright, 59.

27 N.T. Wright, 59.

28 Charles Matthews, "Toward a Theology of Joy" in *Joy and Human Flourishing* (ed. Miroslav Volf and Justin E. Crisp; Minneapolis: Fortress Press, 2015), 66.

29 e.g. Fitzmyer's introduction in his critical commentary provides extensive discussion of Luke's theology (115 pages), with hardly a mention of joy. Joseph A Fitzmyer, *The Gospel According to Luke (I-IX)*, (Garden City: Doubleday & Company, Inc. 1979), 143-258. In Richard Pervo's commentary on Acts, under theology, there is no mention of joy. Richard I. Pervo, *Acts* (ed. Harold W. Attridge; Minneapolis: Fortress Press), 22-25.

30 Millard J. Erickson, *Christian Theology* (Grand Rapids: Baker Books, 1998). Wayne Grudem, *Systematic Theology* (Grand Rapids: Zondervan Publishing House, 1994).

31 Luke Timothy Johnson, *Religious Experience in Early Christianity* (Minneapolis: Fortress Press, 1998), 12.

32 Johnson, 1-37.

33 Johnson, 55.

34 Johnson, 59.

35 Sarah Maitland, *A Joyful Theology* (Minneapolis: Augsburg Books, 2002), 125.

36 Luke 6:6-11; 13:10-17; 14:1-6.

37 G. B. Caird, *The Language and Imagery of the Bible* (Philadelphia: The Westminster Press, 1980), 32.

38 Luke's stories resemble the *ekphrasis* of Greek rhetoric, in which an orator/writer recounts, "A speech that brings the subject matter vividly before the eyes." Ruth Webb, *Ekphrasis, Imagination and Persuasion in the Ancient Rhetorical Theory and Practice* (Burlington, VT: Ashgate Publishing Company, 2009), 1. More broadly, the term, *ekphrasis* can refer to pictorial or sculptural works of art. Ekphrasis falls under Greek rhetorical principles found in the *Progymnasmata*, which are rhetorical exercises designed to lead practitioners in their speech (both oral and written), which find formal expression in the second and third centuries CE. For a historical overview of this discipline, see Vernon K. Robbins, "Socio-Rhetorical Interpretation," *The Blackwell Companion to the New Testament, Journal of Theological Studies* (April 2012) (ed. David Aune), 192-219. See also George A. Kennedy, *Progymnasmata: Greek Texbooks of Prose Composition and Rhetoric* (Atlanta, GA: Society of Biblical Literature, 2003), 47.

39   Gonzalo Haya-Prats, *Empowered Believers: The Holy Spirit in the Book of Acts* (ed. Paul Elbert; trans. Scott A. Ellington; Eugene, Oregon: Cascade Books, 2011); Robert Menzies, *Empowered for Witness: The Spirit in Luke-Acts* (London, New York: T & T Clark, 2006); Cecil M. Robeck, "Baptism in the Holy Spirit: Its Purpose(s)," *Pneuma* 7 (Fall, 1985).

40   Roger Stronstad, *The Charismatic Theology of St. Luke* (Peabody, Mass.: Hendrickson Publishers, 1984).

41   Miller denigrates such joyous charismatic encounters, "Perhaps the greatest weakness of the charismatic movement is this unfortunate yen to titillate the sensors of Christians by seeking to put more fireworks in their faith", 15.

42   Haya-Prats, 68.

43   Haya-Prats 68.

44   Moltmann, 15.

45   Robert C. Tannehill, *The Shape of Luke's Story* (Eugene OR: Cascade Books, 2005), 93.

46   Moltmann, 17.

47   Moltmann, 7-10.

48   Moltmann, 20.

49   Moltmann, 10.

50   James B. Shelton, *Mighty in Word and Deed*, (Eugene, OR: WIPF and STOCK Publishers, 2000), 85-101.

51   Paulo J. Bernadicou, *Joy in the Gospel of Luke* (Rome: Pontificiae Universitatis Gregoriannae, 1970).

52   John Navone SJ, *Themes of St. Luke* (Rome: Gregorian University Press, 1971), 71-87.

53   William Morrice, *Joy in the New Testament* (Grand Rapids: William B. Eerdmans Publishing Company, 1984).

54   William Morrice, *We Joy in God* (London: SPCK, 1977).

55   Morrice, *Joy in the New Testament*, 91-99.

56   "Such joy . . . is not something emotional and superficial." Morrice, *We Joy in God*, 80.

57   Kindalee Pfremmer De Long, *Surprised by God* (Berlin: Walter de Gruyter, 2009).

58   Robert C. Roberts, *Spirituality and Human Emotion* (Grand Rapids, MI: William B. Eerdmans Publishing Co., 1942). See also Robert C. Roberts, Mark R. Talbot, *Limning the Psyche: Explorations in Christian Psychology* (Grand Rapids MI: William B. Eerdmans Publishing Company, 1997).

59   Roberts, *Spirituality*, 15.

60   Roberts, *Spirituality*, 19.

61   Elliott, 127-128.

62   Elliott, 167.

63   Steven Jack Land, *Pentecostal Spirituality: A Passion for the Kingdom* (Cleveland TN: CPT Press, 2010), 31.

64   Land, 28-34.

65   In his argument, Land probes the various ways in which word and Spirit have been related in different church traditions and dogma (Protestant and Catholic).

66   Land, 33; *Aldersgate Reconsidered* (ed. R. MaddoxNashville: Abingdon Press, 1990), 93-108.

67   Samuel Solivan, *The Spirit, Pathos, and Liberation: Toward an Hispanic Pentecostal Theology* (ed. John Christopher Thomas, Rickie D. Moore, Steven J. Land; Sheffield: Sheffield Academic Press, 1998), 68.

68   Abraham Heshchel, *The Prophets* in his chapters on "The Philosophy of Pathos," and "Religion of Sympathy."

69   Land, 135.

70   Land, 126.

71   Land, 130.

72   Land, 30.

73   Fraser Watts, Rebeca Nie, Sarah Savage, *Psychology for Christian Ministry* (London: Routledge, 2002), 17.

74   Paul Elbert, "Progymnasmatic Examples in Luke-Acts of Salvation Experience—Necessary Persuasion from Jesus Tradition and History that Clarifies Paul," Formation of Luke-Acts Section SBL, Chicago, 2012.

75   William Morrice provides a chart of the various words for joy in the NT. *Joy in the New Testament*, 80.

76   I assume that Luke is more interested in "an experience of the Spirit" than the soteriology and sanctification by the Spirit (Paul). See Haya-Prats, 155-162; Stronstad, 75-83; Robert Menzies, *Empowered for Witness: The Spirit in Luke Acts* (Sheffield, England: Sheffield Academic Press, 1994), 237-243. All three authors make the solid argument that Luke should stand in his own right as a theologian and not be interpreted through a Pauline lens; this means that Pauline theology should not "trump" Luke's theological narratives.

77   Roberts, 14-15.

78   Land, 116

79   Miller, 9-24.

CHAPTER 2

LUKE'S JOY-VOCABULARY

Words are known by the company they keep. [80]
–J LYLE STORY

Work with a concordance can be both misleading and helpful. Certainly, we can assume that "words are known by the company they keep"—the context of each word is all-important. However, the concordance does reveal Luke's extensive joy-vocabulary. Many texts contain Luke's "special-material" (*Sondergut*), which accentuates the affection of joy. Although the nouns and verbs suggest nuances, they all embody emotions, felt for something good that has happened, is occurring, or will follow. Luke taps several words in the joy-vocabulary that are exclusive to him:

"I thank (in public expression), ἀνθομολογέομαι,

"I announce/preach the good news,"[81] εὐαγγελίζομαι,

"Honored, distinguished, glorious in terms of a splendid deed," ἔνδοξος,

"I am glad" or "gladness," εὐφραίνω, εὐφροσύνη,

"I cheer, take delight or courage," εὐθυμέω, εὔθυμος,

25

"I leap, spring about as a sign of joy," σκιρτάω,

"Wonderful, remarkable" παράδοξος,

"I rejoice with, feel joy with someone, 'because of something,'"
συγχαίρω,

The preponderance of the language of the "grace" word-family, χαρ—.[82]

Luke employs additional terms of joy more frequently when compared
to the other gospels:

"I praise God, I praise (extol) the Lord" or "praise," αἰνέω, αἶνος,

"Peace, welfare, wholeness," εἰρήνη,

"I speak well of, praise, give thanks, bless" or "blessed/praised,"
εὐλογέω, εὐλογητός.

Other expressions of the joy-vocabulary resonate with Luke's peers.
Certainly, the joy-vocabulary permeates the annunciation and birth
narratives of Luke 1-2 and the trilogy of parables in Lk. 15. Several
paragraphs in Luke, which are common to Matthew and/or Mark,
contain words of joy, not found in parallel texts (e.g. Lk. 18:43; Matt.
20:34; Mk. 10:52). Other expressions of joy are certainly implicit, e.g.
"singing and dancing" (Lk. 15:25) or Luke's frequent banquet-scenes with
joyful table-fellowship.

Explicit words of Luke's joy-vocabulary compare with the other
evangelists:

ἀγαλλιάω ἀγαλλιάομαι: "I exult, I am overjoyed, I am filled with
exuberant joy."[83]
ἀγαλλίασις: "exultant or exuberant joy." [84]

	Matt.	Mk.	Lk.	Jn.	Acts
ἀγαλλιάω ἀγαλλιάομαι	1	0	2	2	2
ἀγαλλίασις	0	0	2	0	1

αἰνέω: "I praise God," "I praise the Lord, I extol."[85]
αἶνος: "praise."[86]

	Matt.	Mk.	Lk.	Jn.	Acts
αἰνέω	0	0	4	0	3
αἶνος	1	0	1	0	0

ἅλλομαι: "I leap, spring up, used of quick movement."[87]

	Matt.	Mk.	Lk.	Jn.	Acts
ἅλλομαι, ἐξάλλομαι	0	0	0	1	3

ἀνθομολογέομαι: "I thank (public expression)."[88]

	Matt.	Mk.	Lk.	Jn.	Acts
ἀνθομολογέομαι	0	0	1	0	0

δοξάζω: "I praise, honor, magnify, glorify (generally of the Father)."[89]
δόξα: "brightness, splendor, majesty, glory, fame, renown, honor."[90]
ἔνδοξος: "honored, distinguished, glorious in terms of a splendid deed."[91]
παράδοξος: "contrary to opinion or expectation, strange, wonderful, remarkable."[92]

	Matt.	Mk.	Lk.	Jn.	Acts
δοξάζω	4	1	9	22	5
δόξα	8	3	13	19	4
ἔνδοξος	0	0	2	0	0
παράδοξος	0	0	1	0	0

εὐδοκέω: "I consider good, be well pleased, take pleasure in."[93]
εὐδοκία: "good will, good pleasure, favor."[94]

	Matt.	Mk.	Lk.	Jn.	Acts
εὐδοκέω	3	I	2	0	0
εὐδοκία	I	0	2	0	0

εἰρήνη: "peace, associated with *shalom*, in the sense of welfare and is an essential characteristic of the Messianic kingdom."[95] Wholeness of life includes joy.

	Matt.	Mk.	Lk.	Jn.	Acts
εἰρήνη	3	I	14	5	7

ἐκπλήσσω: "I amaze, astound, overwhelm, strike out of one's senses."[96]

	Matt.	Mk.	Lk.	Jn.	Acts
ἐκπλήσσω	4	5	3	0	I

ἐξίστημι: "I drive one out of one's senses + weakened sense of 'I am amazed, astounded.'"[97]
ἔκστασις: "amazement, trance, ecstasy."[98]
ὅραμα: "vision."
ὀπτασία: "vision." The nouns associated with "vision" are included because of their links with "amazement" and "ecstasy," in contexts of joy

	Matt.	Mk.	Lk.	Jn.	Acts
ἐξίστημι	I	4	3	0	8
ἔκστασις	0	2	I	0	4
ὅραμα	I	0	0	0	II
ὀπτασία	0	0	2	0	I

ἐξομολογέω: "I admit, confess, agree, praise."[99]

	Matt.	Mk.	Lk.	Jn.	Acts
ἐξομολογέω	2	I	2	0	I

εὐαγγελίζω: "I preach the good news," frequently linked with "the presence of the kingdom that means joy."[100]

εὐαγγέλιον: "good news" for "repentance means joy and gives joy."[101]

	Matt.	Mk.	Lk.	Jn.	Acts
εὐαγγελίζω	1	0	10	0	15
εὐαγγέλιον	4	8	0	0	2

εὐθυμέω: "I cheer, cheer up, delight, take courage."[102]

εὔθυμος: "cheerful, in good spirits."[103]

	Matt.	Mk.	Lk.	Jn.	Acts
εὐθυμέω	0	0	0	0	2
εὔθυμος	0	0	0	0	1

εὐλογέω: "I speak well of, praise, give thanks, bless."[104]

εὐλογητός: "blessed, praised."[105]

	Matt.	Mk.	Lk.	Jn.	Acts
εὐλογέω	6	6	14	1	1
εὐλογητός	0	1	1	0	0

εὐφραίνω: "I gladden, cheer, enjoy oneself, rejoice," often in the context of meals.[106]

εὐφροσύνη: "joy, gladness, cheerfulness."[107]

	Matt.	Mk.	Lk.	Jn.	Acts
εὐφραίνω	0	0	6	0	2
εὐφροσύνη	0	0	0	0	2

εὐχαριστέω: "I give thanks, feel obligated to thank, return thanks."[108]

εὐχαριστία: "thankfulness, gratitude, rendering of thanks."[109]

	Matt.	Mk.	Lk.	Jn.	Acts
εὐχαριστέω	2	2	4	3	2
εὐχαριστία	0	0	0	0	1

θαμβέω: "I am astounded, wonder, am surprised."[110]
θάμβος: "amazement, astonishment," sometimes associated with fear.[111]

	Matt.	Mk.	Lk.	Jn.	Acts
θαμβέω	0	3	0	0	1
θάμβος	0	0	2	0	1

θαρρέω: "I am confident, draw courage."[112]
θαρσέω: "I am cheerful, draw courage," used as an antidote to fear.[113]

	Matt.	Mk.	Lk.	Jn.	Acts
θαρσέω	3	2	1	1	1
θάρσος	0	0	0	0	1

θαυμάζω: "I wonder, marvel, am astonished."[114]

	Matt.	Mk.	Lk.	Jn.	Acts
θαυμάζω	8	6	13	6	5

μακαρίζω: "I call or consider one blessed, fortunate or happy."[115]
μακάριος: "blessed, fortunate, happy, privileged recipient of divine favor."[116]

	Matt.	Mk.	Lk.	Jn.	Acts
μακαρίζω	0	0	1	0	0
μακάριος	13	0	15	2	2

μεγαλύνω: "I exalt, glorify, praise, extol."[117]

	Matt.	Mk.	Lk.	Jn.	Acts
μεγαλύνω	1	0	2	0	3

παρακαλέω: "I appeal, urge, exhort, encourage, cheer up."[118]
παράκλησις: "encouragement, exhortation, consolation, comfort."[119]

	Matt.	Mk.	Lk.	Jn.	Acts
παρακαλέω	10	9	7	0	21
παράκλησις	0	0	2	0	4

σκιρτάω: "I leap, spring about as a sign of joy."[120]

	Matt.	Mk.	Lk.	Jn.	Acts
σκιρτάω	0	0	3	0	0

χαίρω: "I rejoice, am glad" often followed by the reason for joy.[121]

χαρά: "joy, pleasure," often used an experience of joy and the joyous result of someone or something."[122]

συγχαίρω: "I rejoice with, feel joy with someone," because of something.[123]

	Matt.	Mk.	Lk.	Jn.	Acts
χαίρω	6	2	12	9	7
χαρά	6	1	8	9	5
συγχαίρω	0	0	3	0	0

χαρίζομαι: "I give freely or graciously as a favor, remit, forgive, pardon."[124]

χάρις: "graciousness, attractiveness, grace, favor."[125]

χαριτόω: "I bestow favor upon, favor highly, bless."[126]

	Matt.	Mk.	Lk.	Jn.	Acts
χαρίζομαι	0	0	3	0	4
χάρις	0	0	8	3	16
χαριτόω	0	0	1	0	0

The Joy-Vocabulary in Charismatic Experience

Luke establishes that Jesus and his disciples were fully charismatic, recognizing their direct dependence upon the empowering Spirit for miracles that led to religious enthusiasm, self-transcendence, well-being, celebration, and joy. Encounters with the other-worldly (numinous— *mysterium tremendum* Rudolf Otto), whatever the various agency might be, all "spill over" into human affections. In many paragraphs, Luke sets the stage for charismatic encounters of individuals and groups, highlighting the joyful experience and recording joyful expressions for gracious encounters. He knits together communal enthusiasm and group ecstasy with climaxes. Through stories, Luke visualizes numerous charismatic invasions (e.g. angels, a "voice," signs and wonders, prophecy, healing, exorcism), without creating any hierarchy of charismatic experience.[127] Luke intends that his readers be drawn into such joyful and effusive charismatic encounters. The term *charismatic* is more appropriate, rather than Menzies' terms, "prophecy" or "spirit of prophecy,"[128] for, the term, "charismatic," expresses the atmosphere, experience, and expressions of speaking and acting for God. Luke frequently alternates terms as he recounts charismatic experience, e.g. a "trance" (ἔκστασις) falls upon Peter (Acts 10:1) in which a "voice" (φωνή) speaks to him three times. The first time, Peter responds to the voice with the term "Lord" (κύριε v. 14), and subsequently "the Spirit" (τὸ πνεῦμα v. 19) speaks to Peter about the meaning of the "vision" (ὅραμα twice in vss. 17-18).

In his joy-vocabulary, Luke highlights the personal, effusive, communal, tangible, and emotional expressions of joy when participants and onlookers encounter the numinous. Through his stories, Luke documents how Jesus and his community wage war on various forces or conditions that undermine life and joy in their fullest sense. Along with his community, he possesses the eschatological Spirit,[129] works miracles, experiences the miraculous, and is filled with a personal and communal enthusiasm. All of this is reflected in various terms for spontaneous and contagious joy. Joy does not privatize but embraces the participants, witnesses, and Luke's readership. "In addition, the significance of the cures and other prodigies worked by the Savior on earth was to . . . anticipate and provide a glimpse of the proportions of this final and complete salvation."[130] Joyous experiences anticipate the *eschaton*.

NOTES

80   A personal motto of the author.
81   One occurrence in Matthew.
82   The noun "grace" χάρις, is only found in John; 32 references in Luke-Acts to the word-family.
83   BDAG, 3-4, "a demonstrative joy." LS, 5, "express great joy, exult, pay honor to a god."

84 BDAG, 3-4; Bultmann, "ἀγαλλιάομαι," *TDNT,* I, 20-21, "a jubilant and thankful exultation . . . an individual joy . . . In the cultus the community actually celebrates and acknowledges the divine act of salvation." Bernadicou emphasizes a "demonstrative joy," 14. LS, 5, "transport of joy."

85 BDAG, 23. LS, "praise, approve."

86 BDAG, 23; Schlier, "αἰνέω, αἶνος," 177. Bernadicou, "the inner experience of joy in an externalization of grateful and worshipful praise of God and his saving works," 16. MM, 13, "the praise of God."

87 BDAG, 67. MM, 23, "spring forth, quiver." LS, 79, "leap upon, leap over."

88 BDAG, 67. MM, "acknowledge, formally admit." LS, 140, "make a mutual agreement, covenant, return thanks to a god freely."

89 BDAG, 204. MM, 169, "to make glorious, adorn with lustre." LS, 444, "think, imagine, entertain opinions."

90 BDAG, 203-204. A far cry from secular Greek usage, "I think, have an opinion, I count as." Kittel, "δοξάζω, δόξα, κτλ." *TDNT,* 2:233-234. MM, 169, "sometimes applied to the sun." LS, 444, "expectation, notion, opinion, judgment."

91 BDAG, 263; Kittel, *TDNT,* 2:254. In the Fourth Gospel, most of the uses of the δόξ-word-family concern God's glory, Jesus' glory or the disciples' glory—with no real reference to the human response of people as a result of an act of power. MM, 212, "become illustrious." LS, 561, "honored, distinguished, held in esteem."

92 BDAG, 615. MM, 483, "wonderful, remarkable," and is applied to an athletic victor. LS, 1309, "contrary to expectation, incredible."

93 BDAG, 319. Gottlob Schrenk notes, "Of all the terms for election . . . εὐδοκεῖν brings out most strongly the emotional side of the love of Him who elects." "εὐδοκέω, κτλ." TDNT, 2:740-741. MM, 260, "to please one well." LS, 719, "be pleased, content, happy, satisfied."

94 BDAG, 319. Schrenk notes that in Lk. 2:14, "We have thus to understand by εὐδοκία, the unfathomably gracious and sovereign good pleasure of God in the sense of His decree as a decree of free grace and favor." "εὐδοκέω," *TDNT,* II, 750. MM, 261, "good pleasure, good will." LS, 710, "good pleasure."

95 BDAG, 277. The noun is used in contexts of praise and blessing. MM, 185-186, "tranquility enjoyed under one." LS, 490, "peace often following a war, treaty, often in contexts of greeting."

96 BDAG 244, often with the reason given. MM, 198, "be dazzled by." LS, 517, "strike out of, drive away, drive out of one's senses by a sudden shock, amaze, astound." LS, 595, "change, alter utterly, drive out of one's senses."

97 BDAG, 276. MM, 224, "bewilder, confound."

98 BDAG, 245. MM, 198, "outbursts of frenzy." LS, 520, "displacement, distraction of mind, from terror, astonishment, anger, entrancement."

99 BDAG, 277. Luke alone uses the verb as "I praise," in Lk. 10:21, parallel with the verb, "I publicly give thanks" (ἀνθομολογέομαι) in Anna's public praise (Lk.

2:38). The verb is frequent in the Psalter, used in Lk. 1-2. Michael, "ὁμολογέω," *TDNT*, 5:213-215. MM, 224, "acknowledge, avow openly, praise." LS, 597, "confess, acknowledge, give thanks, express praises."

100 BDAG, 317; Friedrick, "εὐαγγελίζομαι," *TDNT*, 2:718. As Friedrick notes, 707, "In all Semitic languages . . . the sense of 'joy' is contained in the stem," e.g. bringing news of a victory brings joy to the recipients. It is frequently noted in Dt. Isa. in contexts of joyous anticipation, expectation, joy and the announcement of peace and salvation. The proclamation of "good news" elicits joy from the messengers' report. MM, 259, "full of joy to bring an annunciation of marriage." LS, 704-705, "bring or preach good news."

101 BDAG, 317; Friedrick, "εὐαγγέλιον," *TDNT*, 2:729. MM, 259, "bring good tidings" leading to joy. LS, 705, "good news"

102 BDAG, 320. MM, 261, associated with joy and health in epistolary expressions. LS, 715, "be of good cheer, delight."

103 BDAG, 320. MM, 261, "cheerful." LS, 715, "cheerfulness, contentment."

104 BDAG. 322. MM, "praise, bless." LS, 720, "speak well of, praise."

105 BDAG, 322; Beyer, "εὐλογέω, *TDNT,* 2:761-765. LS, 720, "blessed."

106 BDAG, 327. Bultmann, "εὐφραίνω," *TDNT*, 2:772-775. MM, 267, "merrymaking at a feast." LS, 737, "cheer, gladden, make merry, enjoy oneself, take pleasure in."

107 BDAG, 328. MM, 267, "being glad." LS, 737, "mirth, merriment, good cheer, festivity."

108 BDAG, 328. MM, 267, "do a good turn to, be grateful, thank, pray." LS, 738, "bestow a favor on, oblige, often connected with the gods."

109 BDAG,328. The word family relates to the "grace word-family" (χαρίζομαι, χάρις). MM, 267, "gratification, contentment, pleasure." LS, 738, "thankfulness, an expression of gratitude, thank-offering."

110 BDAG, 350. MM, 283, "blind, dazzle." LS, 783, associated with θαμβαίνω, "be astonished, terrified, astounded"

111 BDAG, 350. The response of fear is often associated with religious dread. See Bertram, "θαμβέω, κτλ." *TDNT,* 3:4-7. LS, 783, "terror, object of wonder, astonishment."

112 BDAG, 352. MM, 284, used interchangeably with θαρσέω, "have confidence."

113 BDAG, 352; Grundman, "θαρρέω, θαρσέω," *TDNT,* 3:25-27. MM, 284, "take courage, speak encouragingly." LS, 784-785, "take courage, fear not, have confidence in."

114 BDAG, 352; Bertram, "θαυμάζω κτλ.," *TDNT,* 3:37, "often used in the context of miracle stories." MM, 284, "incredulous surprise, astonishment, sometimes associated with the verb, 'I believe.'" LS, 785, "wonder, marvel, honor, admire, worship."

115 BDAG, 486. MM, 386, "deem happy." LS, 1073-1074, "to declare to be blessed."

116 BDAG, 486; "distinctive religious joy which accrues to man from his share in the salvation of the kingdom of God," Hauck, "μακάριος," *TDNT*, 4:367. Seven

beatitudes in Matt. 5, 4 in Luke. MM, 386, "a state of true well-being." LS, 1074, "blessed, fortunate."

117   BDAG, 497; Grundmann, "μεγαλύνω κτλ.," *TDNT*, 4:543. The adjective "great," is often used with joy, "great joy," e.g. in Lk. 2:10; 24:52; Acts 8:8; 15:3 or "great grace" in Acts 4:33; frequent uses of the adjective "great" (μέγας) in terms of a "loud voice," in contexts of thanksgiving and praise (e.g., Acts 15:3). MM, 392, "get glory or praise." LS, 1083, "make great or powerful, make great by word, extol, magnify."

118   BDAG, 617. MM, 484, "ask, beseech, please, extend good will." LS, 1311, "call in, summons, appeal, encourage."

119   BDAG, 618. Schmitz, "παρακαλέω, παράκλησις," *TDNT*, 5:793-799. He notes, "παρακαλεῖν occurs especially in Ac. and Pl. for exhortation by the Word proclaimed in the power of the Holy Ghost." 794. MM, 485, "appeal, exhortation, comfort." LS, 1313, "calling to one's aid, summons, appeal."

120   BDAG, 755. MM, 578, "leap, bound." LS, "leap, bound of young horses."

121   BDAG, 873. A few occurrences of a joyful greeting. BDAG, 874; Bernadicou notes, "the word-family includes both the subjective feeling as well as the objective reality on which it is based, 15. MM, 682, "rejoice often in greetings and farewells—in contexts of joy." LS, 1969, "rejoice at, take pleasure in."

122   BDAG, 875-876. Conzelmann, Zimmerli, "χαίρω κτλ.,*TDNT*, 9:359-372. In Luke, "this mood of joy persists throughout the Gospel as joy at the acts of Jesus," 367. MM, 683, "joy, making a manifestation of joy, fullness of joy." LS, 1976, "joy, delight."

123   BDAG, 775. LS, 1668, "rejoice with, congratulate."

124   BDAG, 876-877. Used in a word-play with the verb "I rejoice" (χαίρω). MM, 684, "double meaning of show kindness and graciously bestow or favor." LS, 1978, "say or do something agreeable to a person, show him favor or kindness, give graciously or cheerfully."

125   BDAG 877. MM, 684, "grace, graciousness, favor, thanks, gratitude." LS, 1978, "outward grace or favor, beauty, grace, kindness to someone."

126   BDAG, 879. Conzelmann, Zimmerli, "χαρίζομαι, κτλ." *TDNT*, 9:392. The authors note several nuances in the Lukan texts and summarize, "Luke wants to bring out the element of divine 'good pleasure.'" MM, 685, "bestow favor." LS, 1980, "show grace or favor with graceful import."

127   Luke counters some of the "magical" abuses (e.g., Acts 8:9-13, 18-24).

128   e.g. Menzies distinguishes between "Spirit" (πνεῦμα) associated with "prophetic speech" and "power" (δύναμις) associated with exorcisms and miracles of healing," 126. Such distinctions cannot be supported in Luke-Acts.

129   Haya-Prats lists 10 verbs that Luke uses to signify the various comings of the Spirit and provides a helpful chart, detailing the various tenses of the 10 verbs. 54-56.

130   Pietro Dacquino, "Human Joy and the Hereafter in the Biblical Books," *The Gift of Joy* (ed. Christian Duquoc; New York: Paulist Press, 1968), 29.

CHAPTER 3

CHARISMATIC ACTIVITY AND JOY IN THE ANNUNCIATION/ BIRTH NARRATIVES

*For behold, I am bringing you good news of great joy
which shall be for all the people.*
–LUKE 2:10

In the joyous atmosphere of two annunciation and birth stories, Luke attunes his readers to hear a choir of emotional voices, male and female, youthful and elderly, earthly and heavenly, humble, righteous, lowly. These voices all sing of the joyous events of Luke 1-2. This choir sings its melody and harmony through the full "musical score," in which God "visits" (ἐπισκέπτομαι[131]) his people through supernatural ways and brings "redemption" (λύτρωσις).

Luke narrates the drama of the incarnation through intertwined stories that accentuate charismatic incursions—all bound together in joyous praise for two miraculous conceptions and births, those of John the Baptist and Jesus. He presents a movement from heaven to earth, the human to the divine, the old to the new, as well as the new to the old. The miraculous conception of God's Son, along with his precursor, reveal that God's activity is not only for Jews but for Gentiles as well. The supra-historical enters the mainstream of limited human history in the atmosphere of emotional, spontaneous, and contagious joy. The resulting joyful expressions erupt notably in praise. Luke majors on the atmosphere, experiences and expressions of joy. Clearly he intends his readers and their communities to feel similar affections of effusive joy upon reading these astonishing experiences.

Joy in Angelic Encounter

Luke's story contains three angelic[132] encounters with Zechariah (Luke 1:5-25), Mary (1:26-37), and a group of shepherds (2:8-21). In each encounter, the angel suggests such an appearance should not elicit "fear" (religious dread[133]) but "joy." This is further explained through angelic reassurances, so the resulting joy spreads effusively. Thus, the appearance of one angel to the shepherds is complemented by "a multitude of the heavenly host" (2:13) and "angels" (2:15). Luke mentions Gabriel in the first two angelophanies (1:19, 26). Then he mentions an unnamed angel of the Lord in 2:9.[134] In comparison with Matthew's narrative (Matt 1-2), Shelton comments, "Matthew concentrates on events that emphasize Jesus' messianic royalty and the fulfillment of prophecy, while Luke highlights the major themes of salvation, praise, joy and the Holy Spirit."[135] These experiences mean untold joy for those experiencing them in the moment, and also for those experiencing them vicariously through reading Luke's account.

Zechariah: To the aged Zechariah, fulfilling his duties in the Temple, Gabriel explains why ("because" διότι) he is summoned to joy rather than fear. His specific petition has been heard, his wife Elizabeth will bear a son, and Zechariah is to name the child "John," meaning, "God has been gracious" (Luke 1:13). The pronouncement occurs despite human impossibility, for Luke mentions the couple's advanced age even as he introduces them (1:7). He also records Zechariah's objection to the angel's promise: "I am an old man and my wife is advanced in years" (1:18). Later, Elizabeth makes a similar response—that her shame [of childlessness] has been taken away (1:25). Gabriel then underscores what this miraculous birth will mean for Zechariah (and Elizabeth), "joy and joyful exuberance for you" (χαρά σοι καὶ ἀγαλλίασις 1:14) and joy's impact for the "many who will rejoice at his birth" (πολλοὶ ἐπὶ τῇ γενέσει αὐτοῦ χαρήσονται 1:14). According to Luke's account, joy is not simply the gift of parenthood, but "it is the joy of eschatological fulfillment,"[136] which is also communal in nature.

Gabriel then promises that this miracle-child will be filled[137] with the Spirit even within Elizabeth's womb (1:15), and he will go forth, "in the Spirit and power of Elijah" (1:17). This promise leads to a partial fulfilment when the pre-natal John "leaps with joy" (1:44). Gabriel declares the course of the miracle-child's life as the way-preparing messenger (1:16-18; MT Mal 3:23; LXX Mal 4:5-6). The entire encounter is summed up, "I was sent to speak to you and to preach the good news of these things to you" (ἀπεσιάλην λαλῆσαι πρὸς σὲ καὶ εὐαγγελίσασθαί σοι ταῦτα Luke 1:19). The verb, "I preach the good news" (εὐαγγελίζομαι) certainly elicits the "sense of 'joy' that is contained in the stem."[138] The people waiting for Zechariah to emerge after fulfilling his responsibilities at the Temple "were marveling" (ἐθαύμαζον), and they understood that Zachariah had seen a "vision" (ὀπτασία 1:21-22). However, Zechariah's emotional expression of joy will be delayed,[139] due to the disciplinary sign of becoming mute (Luke 1:20, 22) and deaf (Luke 1:62)

Mary: Joy permeates Gabriel's greeting and announcement, "Rejoice, O highly favored one.[140] The Lord is with you" (Χαῖρε, κεχαριτωμένη, ὁ κύριος μετὰ σου 1:28).[141] Luke alliterates the imperative "rejoice" (χαῖρε), the perfect passive participle, "highly favored one" (κεχαριτωμένη), and the noun, "grace" (χάρις) that Mary has found with God (1:30). Gabriel accentuates joyful emotions for Mary's miraculous conception of Jesus, followed by the pronouncement concerning the name, identity, significance and role of a second miracle-child to be born to Elizabeth.[142] The second miraculous conception of John serves to buttress Mary's trust-response.

To reinforce Mary's faith-response, Gabriel directs Mary to the miraculous conception experienced by her relative Elizabeth, now six months pregnant (1:36). The statement implies, "God has already accomplished a miraculous conception." Gabriel's final comment, "for nothing shall be impossible with God" (οὐκ ἀδυνατήσει παρὰ τοῦ θεοῦ πᾶν ῥῆμα 1:37), also alludes to Sarah's miraculous conception of Isaac in the LXX of Gen. 18:14, "Shall anything be impossible with the

Lord?" (Μὴ ἀδυνατήσει παρὰ τῷ θεῷ ῥῆμα); the wording is nearly exact.[143] Thus, Sarah's example joins with Elizabeth's case to elicit Mary's response of trust (1:38, 45).

The shepherds: The radiating angel of the Lord encounters several shepherds in the dark countryside, causing a sense of panic. The text says, "they feared a great fear" (ἐφοβήθησαν φόβον μέγαν—cognate accusative 2:9). The angelic appearance should not spell religious dread, but it should invite the shepherds to respond with "great joy," "For behold, I bring you good news of great joy, which shall be for all the people" (ἰδοὺ γὰρ εὐαγγελίζομαι ὑμῖν χαρὰν μεγάλην ἥτις ἔσται παντὶ τῷ λαῷ 2:10—the same words of joy that characterize Zechariah's angelophany (1:14, 19). Great fear is contrasted with great emotional joy. While the first two angelophanies relate to the future conception, this encounter confirms something already fulfilled, "Today" (σήμερον 2:11). Their great joy will also be inclusive, "for all the people." Fitzmyer notes, "The note of joy is struck again (see 1:14); such is the atmosphere that surrounds the dawn of the messianic age."[144] Personal and communal joy affects both Zechariah (1:14) and the shepherds (2:10).

To the shepherds, the angel explains why there will be such great joy— the birth of the savior, Christ, the Lord. Luke connects the narrative concerning the "manger" (2:7), with the angel's pronouncement of a confirming sign of the "manger" (2:12), with the realization of the manger-sign when the shepherds discover the truth for themselves (2:16). This prophetic sign confirms both the joy and the identity of the Messiah child (savior, Christ, the Lord). Joy progresses with the declaration of the "multitude of the heavenly host," who "praise God" (αἰνούντων τὸν θεὸν 2:13) with a doxology replete with Luke's "joy-vocabulary": "glory" (δόξα), "peace" (εἰρήνη) and "[God's] good pleasure" (εὐδοκία)[145]:

Glory to God in the highest

and

peace on earth for people who are recipients of God's goodpleasure (2:14).

The announcement parallels "glory" with "peace," "in the highest" with "on earth," and "God" with "people who are recipients of God's 'good pleasure." The doxology brings together the sphere of the heavenly and earthly—all united in emotional experiences of joy at the birth of the Messiah-child. A joyous God takes pleasure in his people. Luke draws his readers into the emotional language of the narrative. The shepherds' emotional excitement radiates through the participle, "having made haste" (σπεύσαντες) and coordinates with the verb, "they came" (2:16).

Similarly, the people in Bethlehem rejoice with the shepherds, who report on the "manger-sign" and the identity of the Messiah-child; "they marveled" (ἐθαύμασαν) at the shepherds' report (2:17) as well as the shepherds' fulfilled "sign." In the conclusion, the shepherds return to their flocks in the same emotional glow, "glorifying and praising God" (δοξάζοντες καὶ αἰνοῦντες τὸν θεὸν) at what they heard, saw, and the confirming sign, "just as it was spoken to them [by the angels]" (2:20). Through angelic appearances and a fulfilled sign, Luke combines angelic joy with the shepherds' joy, the joy for all the people, and the joy of the people in Bethlehem—all centered in upon the good news of the Messiah-child and his significance, "Messiah, the Lord" (2:11).

Joy and the Holy Spirit
(expressed in prophecy and hymnic praise).

John: Gabriel declares the source of John's prophetic inspiration through a contrast between alcohol and the Holy Spirit, sharpened with the pronouncement that John "will be filled with the Holy Spirit, even from his mother's womb" (1:15). Even before John begins his adult prophetic ministry, Gabriel states that John's Spirit-filling occurs now within Elizabeth's womb. Luke introduces this promise to prepare for the later prophetic experience when the pre-natal John "leaps with joyful exuberance" in Elizabeth's womb (ἐσκίρτησεν ἐν ἀγαλλιάσει τὸ βρέφος ἐν τῇ κοιλίᾳ μου (1:44); John joyfully defers in his witness to Jesus. Gabriel also announces that John "will go before him [the Lord] in the Spirit and power of Elijah" (1:17).[146] John will be "great before the Lord" (1:15), a way-preparing messenger before the Messiah, and a prophet of eschatological significance, who fulfills the prophecies of Malachi.[147]

Mary: To Mary, Gabriel features the crucial and dynamic role of the Holy Spirit. In response to Mary's question about this miraculous conception, Gabriel grounds Jesus' holiness and sonship with two parallel statements:

> "The Holy Spirit shall come[148] upon you
> Πνεῦμα ἅγιον ἐπελεύσεται ἐπὶ σε
>
> and
> καὶ
>
> "the power[149] of the most high shall overshadow you"
> δύναμις ὑψίστου ἐπισκιάσει σοι (1:35).[150]

Luke specifies that the invasive Spirit/power is responsible, "for that reason" (διό), not only for the conception, but for the identity and significance of Jesus as "the holy one—the Son of God," and the subsequent promises (Davidic throne, reign over an endless kingdom 1:32-33), and the later growth-statement. Grace (χάρις) and wisdom (σοφία) characterize the two growth statements (2:40, 52). [151]

Elizabeth and Mary. Effusive joy dominates the encounter between Elizabeth in which the Spirit and prophecy converge with Luke's vocabulary of joy; joy is an emotion that is felt and expressed by both women:

"Mary went "with haste" (μετὰ σπουδῆς 1:39),

"the pre-natal child leaped (ἐσκίρτησεν 1:41) within Elizabeth's womb,""Elizabeth was filled with the Holy Spirit" (ἐπλήσθη πνεύματος ἁγίου ἡ Ἐλισάβετ 1:41),

"She cried out with a loud voice" (1:42)

"Blessed (εὐλογημένη) are you among women" (1:42),

"Blessed (εὐλογημένη) is the fruit of your womb" (1:42),

"the pre-natal John leaped with joyful exuberance in my womb" (ἐσκίρτησεν ἐν ἀγαλλιάσει τὸ βρέφος ἐν τῇ κοιλίᾳ μου 1:44).

"How fortunate[152] (μακαρία) is she who believed" (1:45)

De Long rightfully draws attention to the chain-like contagion of joy from Mary (1:28) > Mary's greeting (1:40) > John's response in the womb (1:41) > Elizabeth's response (1:42-44) > Mary's response (1:45-46) in which she voices both joy and praise.[153]

In this tender scene, Luke attaches the two mothers, who miraculously conceive sons in humanly impossible conditions (Luke. 1:39-45). Without angelic direction, Mary travels to see Elizabeth and share in the joy of two miraculous conceptions. Certainly, Mary's joyous excitement emanates in her journey, made "with haste" (μετὰ σπουδῆς 1:39), setting the stage for the actual encounter. Luke unites the two stories with a clear interdependence.[154]

In the ensuing dialogue, Elizabeth is the primary speaker; Mary only greets Elizabeth, setting off numerous statements of blessing, joy, and beatitude. They affirm Mary's superiority over Elizabeth, despite the age-difference, and the superiority of Jesus over John the Baptist.

Luke reveals that "knowing" revelation and prophetic speech are the immediate effects of the Holy Spirit. At the precise moment of Mary's greeting,[155] the pre-natal John leaps for joy[156] in Elizabeth's womb and Elizabeth "is filled with the Holy Spirit" (ἐπλήσθη πνεύματος ἁγίου—1:41); this is how Elizabeth interprets the significance of John's leaping in her womb.

Just as Mary "knows" of Elizabeth's pregnancy (now six months) through Gabriel's revelation (1:36), so Elizabeth "knows" of Mary's pregnant status through Elizabeth's being filled with the Holy Spirit and the action of the unborn John, leaping in her womb.[157] Luke has already informed the reader of the action of the Holy Spirit in the future role of the Baptist (1:15-17). Now, the unborn John begins his prophetic ministry through his joyful jumping in Elizabeth's womb. Elizabeth not only "knows" of Mary's pregnancy through the revelation of the Holy Spirit, but she also "knows" of Mary's favored condition, the significance of her unborn child, and Mary's previous trust-response (1:45). The Holy Spirit also inspires[158] her two statements of blessing[159] (1:42), an identification of Mary (1:43), and a beatitude pronounced over Mary (1:45).

Elizabeth recognizes that the child is her "Lord" (κύριος—1:43), expressed also as, "from the Lord" παρὰ κυρίου (1:45). Mary's believing response contrasts with Zechariah's unbelief (Luke 1:20).

Mary's Song of Joy (Magnificat). For Luke, Mary's joyful Magnificat is the direct effect of Elizabeth's prophecy and Gabriel's joyous pronouncement about the source of her miraculous conception (1:35). Although Luke does not state that Mary is filled with the Holy Spirit until Pentecost, the atmosphere of the passage surely argues that the Holy Spirit inspires her joyous song. As Shelton argues, "one must ask: How is it that Mary, the mother of the Lord, is seen as less under the influence and guidance of the Holy Spirit than John, Elizabeth, Zechariah, or Simeon?"[160] In the previous paragraph, Elizabeth praises Mary, the mother of the Lord. Now in Mary's song, she not only recognizes her blessed condition, but transfers her praise to God as the ultimate benefactor of her miraculous conception.

As Brown notes, the Magnificat follows a structured hymn of praise from the OT: "a) an *introduction* praising God, b) *the body of the hymn* listing the motives of praise . . . often begun by a "because" clause . . . c) the *conclusion*."[161] Brown also provides OT texts that support Mary's Magnificat as a "mosaic" of OT texts, most notably from Hannah's song of the "humble poor" (*Anawim* I Sam. 1:11; 2:1-10).[162]

In Mary's song, the joy-vocabulary is used twice in Mary's praise of God, and once in a "because"-clause, which explains why Mary bursts forth with joy:

Introduction	My soul *magnifies* the Lord and my spirit *rejoices* in God, my Savior (1:46)	Μεγαλύνει ἡ ψυχή μου τὸν κύριον καὶ ἠγαλλίασεν τὸ πνεῦμά μου ἐπὶ τῷ θεῷ τῷ σωτῆρί μου.
"Because" clause	Because he has regarded the low estate of his handmaid, for behold, henceforth, all generations *will call me fortunate* (1:48)	ὅτι ἐπέβλεψεν ἐπὶ τὴν ταπείνωσιν τῆς δούλης αὐτοῦ. ἰδου γὰρ ἀπὸ τοῦ νῦν μαρκαριοῦσιν με πᾶσαι αἱ γενεαί.

Synonymous parallelism links the verbs "magnify" and "rejoice"; "my soul" matches "my spirit."[163] Furthermore, Mary's emotional statement of gratitude, "all generations shall call me fortunate," is paired with joyful emotion. Barth notes, "Joy is really the simplest form of gratitude."[164] Mary's Christian affections of joy and gratitude correspond to divine affection and activity. Her joyous gratitude spills over into a song of joy, as a witness of the unexpected and spontaneous grace of God in which she becomes a willing partner. This is well expressed in the repetition of her "bond-servant" language: "Behold the bond-servant of the Lord (ἡ δουλή κυρίου), may it happen to me according to your word" (1:37); "he has looked upon the humble condition of his bond-servant (τῆς δούλης αὐτοῦ 1:48). As God rejoices in himself, he also privileges Mary with her partnership in divine joy.

She voices her emotions with spontaneous and Spirit-filled delight through a song of enjoyment for this unheard-of event of a virginal conception. Her song affirms that "the **power**ful one" (ὁ δύνατος 1:49) has done great things." Her language reiterates Gabriel's twin affirmations: "the **power** of the most high" (δύναμις ὑψίστου 1:35) and "nothing **shall be impossible** with God" (οὐκ ἀδυνατήσει παρὰ τοῦ θεοῦ πᾶν ῥῆμα 1:37). When Mary experiences God's graceful love as highly favored (1:28-29), she also learns of the powerful Holy Spirit, and thereby can only respond with joyful and grateful partnership. Barth notes:

> For the other partner in the covenant to whom God turns in this grace, the only proper thing, but the thing which is unconditionally and inescapably demanded, is that he should be thankful. How can anything more or different be asked of man? The only answer to χάρις is εὐχαριστία ("grace is thanksgiving" writer's addition). Grace and gratitude belong together like heaven and earth. Grace evokes gratitude like lightning and thunder."[165]

*The birth and naming of John and Zechariah's hymn of joy
(Benedictus).*

Joyous emotion pervades John's birth and naming, along with Zechariah's
resultant joyous hymn. Elizabeth gives birth to a son in impossible
circumstances. Her friends and relatives would not have known of her
pregnancy since she had kept herself in seclusion (1:24). Thus, they
recognize that "the Lord had magnified (ἐμεγάλυνεν) his mercy to her
and they were rejoicing with her" in a communal way (συνέχαιρον
αὐτῇ 1:58).

Luke focuses upon the miraculous naming of the son at the time of
his circumcision. Gabriel's previous announcement (Luke 1:14) of "joy
and exuberant joy" (χαρά καὶ ἀγαλλίασις 1:14) and generational
joy ("many will rejoice" χαρήσονται) is initially fulfilled in the
shared joy of their relatives and friends. The second part of Gabriel's
announcement concerns the naming of the child, "you will call his
name, 'John'" (1:13), for Luke devotes the majority of the paragraph to
John's miraculous naming (1:59-66). Friends and relatives are unaware
of Gabriel's announcement of the son's name (1:13), and Elizabeth does
not know of Gabriel's command, for her husband is both dumb (1:20-
22) and deaf (1:62). Perhaps they had communicated through writing,
but for Luke, the naming of the child is miraculous. The community
discovers that Zechariah has selected the same unexpected name,
"John," as Elizabeth did. "Zechariah's regaining his power to speak is
understandable to the reader because now the things predicted by the
angel have happened (1:20: unable to speak *until the day that these
things will happen*)."[166] The birth of the miracle-son and the miraculous
naming of the child lead to the emotional astonishment of all
(ἐθαύμασαν πάντες 1:63).

Zechariah needs divine healing for his deaf and dumb condition
before he can speak. Thus, at the very moment when Zechariah's mouth
was opened and his tongue at last freed, "he began[167] to speak blessing
God" (ἐλάλει εὐλογῶν τὸν θεὸν 1:64).[168] The adverb, "immediately"
(παραχρῆμα) highlights Zechariah's spontaneous joy, which will be
repeated in other miraculous events in Luke-Acts,[169] leading to joy and

joyful expression. The entire event (miraculous conception, naming, healing, prophetic speech) emerges within an atmosphere of fulfilled and effusive joy (Luke 1:14). Thus, supernatural events and emotional language are threads, woven into the fabric of the text, in the atmosphere, experience and expressions of reverential fear, and wonderment for the infant John (1:65-66).

Luke notes that Zechariah's hymn of joy (*Benedictus* (Luke 1:68-79) is occasioned by the Holy Spirit, expressed through the parallel statements, "Zechariah . . . was filled with the Holy Spirit" (Ζαχαρίας . . . ἐπλήσθη πνεύματος ἁγίου) and "he prophesied" (ἐπροφήτευσεν 1:67). Luke's readers connect the Holy Spirit and prophecy with both Elizabeth (1:41-45) and Zechariah (1:67).

His hymn follows the similar structure of Mary's *Magnificat*. The introduction contains joyful language, "Blessed (εὐλογητὸς) be the God of Israel" (Luke 1:68), followed by numerous "because of" clauses, which explain why Zechariah blesses God. The hymn celebrates the continuity between God's past and present activity,[170] including the Baptist's role as a way-preparing messenger (1:76-79).[171] Luke accents God's "feeling-involvement" or "compassion" with his people, "on account of the heartfelt compassion of our God" (διὰ σπλάγχνα ἐλέους θεοῦ ἡμῶν 1:78). The noun, "bowels" (σπλάγχνα), e.g. the "bowels of mercy," conveys the idea of the human viscera (heart, lungs, liver, etc.), which pairs with activity that leads one to do something for another.[172] In the *Benedictus*, "compassion" is attributed to God,[173] in which he graciously "visits" (ἐπισκέψεται 1:78) his people. The concluding line affirms John's way-preparing-messenger role (also "prophet of the Most High" 1:76), who will "guide our feet into the way of peace" (τοῦ κατευθῦναι τοὺς πόδας ἡμῶν εἰς ὁδὸν εἰρήνης 1:79).[174] Luke's concluding "growth-statement," "the child grew and became strong in the [Holy] Spirit" (ηὔξανεν καὶ ἐκραταιοῦτο πνεύματι 1:80), echoes previous language connecting John with the Holy Spirit (1:15, 41).

Simeon and Anna (2:25-38). Luke then narrates the joyous response of two aged people who encounter the infant Jesus and his parents at the Temple (Luke 2:25-38). Both of these older adults know the identity and significance of Jesus. Luke introduces the two figures in the same way.[175] Before Simeon prophesies the significance and future role of Jesus, Luke highlights the role of the Holy Spirit in Simeon's life through three statements:

"The *Holy Spirit* was upon him" (πνεῦμα ἦν ἅγιον ἐπ᾽ αὐτόν)—2:25,[176]

"It had been revealed to him by the *Holy Spirit*" (ἦν αὐτῷ κεχρηματισμένον ὑπὸ τοῦ πνεύματος τοῦ ἁγίου)—2:26,

"he came in the *Spirit*" (ἦλθεν ἐν τῷ πνεύματι)—2:27.

Since the Holy Spirit is upon him and reveals his certainty of seeing Yahweh's Messiah, he enters the Temple in the sphere of the Spirit; thereby he is both able to "know" and attest the importance of this child; the verb "revealed" (χρηματίζω) signifies "something revealed or prophesied."[177] Luke explicitly labels Anna as a "prophetess" (προφῆτις—2:36).

In terms of their prior revelation, both figures are joined together, along with others who look forward with joyful hope to the Messianic age:

Simeon: "expecting the consolation[178] of Israel" (προσδεχόμενος παράκλησιν τοῦ ᾽Ισραήλ)—2:26

Anna: "to all those who were expecting the redemption of Israel" (τοῖς προσδεχομένοις λύτρωιν ᾽Ιερουσαλήμ)—2:38

Simeon had been informed that he would live to see "the Lord's Messiah" (τὸν χριστὸν κυρίου-2:26). François Bovin notes, "The divine oracle is fulfilled not only by 'seeing' (vss. 26, 30), but in 'touching,'[179] the infant when Simeon receives him into his arms (2:28) and "blesses God" (εὐλόγησεν τὸν θεὸν 2:28). Luke highlights the time of joyous fulfillment[180] for both Simeon and Anna in another tender scene. When Simeon prays for his personal release from life "according to your word in peace" (κατὰ τὸ ῥῆμά σου ἐν εἰρήνῃ—2:29), Luke forges the connection with his previous revelation about seeing the Lord's Messiah prior to his death (2:26). Simeon's prophetic awareness emerges from OT Scripture (Isa. 52:9-10; 49:6; 46:13; 42: 6; 40:5).[181]

Luke features that "at just the right time," when Jesus' parents present their son, Simeon and Anna are here in the Temple, which occasions their prophetic knowledge and expressions. What does Simeon now know? The child Jesus (τὸ παιδίον Ἰησοῦν—2:28) is identified through several terms and expressions:

"your salvation" (τὸ σωτήριόν σου), which shall be for all the peoples (2:30),

"light" (φῶς) for revelation to the Gentiles (2:32),

"glory/splendor" (δόξα) for your people, Israel (2:32).

Fulfilled joy is contrasted with Simeon's ominous prophecy of the child's future. Simeon embraces the paradox of the child's blessing with the somber and divisive nature of this infant. "This child is appointed for":

"the fall and rising of many in Israel" (πτῶσιν καὶ ἀνάστασιν ἐν τῷ Ἰσραὴλ)—2:34,

"for a sign[182] provoking contradiction" (εἰς σημεῖον ἀντιλεγόμενον)—2:34,

"and a sword[183] will pierce your own heart" (σοῦ [δὲ] αὐτῆς τὴν ψυχὴν διελεύσεται ῥομφαία)—2:35,

The upheaval, noted in 2:34 will "result in the exposure of the thoughts from many hearts (ὅπως ἂν ἀποκαλυφθῶσιν ἐκ πολλῶν καρδιῶν διαλογισμοί)—2:35.[184]

Likewise, Anna "arrives at just the right time" (αὐτῇ τῇ ὥρᾳ ἐπιστᾶσα—2:38). Although Luke does not provide her actual speech, he states that she was praising God in a public manner,[185] and was speaking concerning the child to all those who were expecting the redemption of Israel. As a prophetess, she "knows" and communicates the identity and significance of the child to others, which confirm Simeon's prophecy. Once again, Luke characterizes the joy of this scene as personal, effusive, communal, and contagious.

In the two paragraphs of joyous fulfillment, Luke joins several expressions that highlight joy, the Spirit's role, prophecy, prophet(ess), particular revelation, "knowing," both positive and negative—all in the context of a paradoxical "blessing," praise to God and "omen." Simeon's prophetic "eyes" foresee "the salvation that this child will bring to the Gentiles and Israel alike; but as a true prophet, he also sees the rejection and the catastrophe."[186] Verheyden notes, "The child Jesus . . . is solemnly announced . . . with a plethora of titles reflecting a high Christology, as king and Son of the Most High, Son of God . . . also labeling John as 'his' prophet."[187]

Thus, Luke links the Holy Spirit to OT fulfillment, and inextricably weaves the OT into narratives of the new, in the language of "today" (Luke 2:11). In Luke's thinking, such joyful encounters with the numinous are not limited to various Pentecosts but comprise the sub-strata of Luke's landscape in the events of Luke 1-2. Luke's panorama does not square with Conzelmann's three-fold division of history into three distinct epochs: 1) period of Israel, 2) Jesus, 3) the Church).[188] From Luke's perspective, all persons described in Luke 1-2 do not simply herald the new, but they joyously participate in God's new activity of prophecy and fulfillment. Shelton argues, "This goes back to Luke's tendency to blur the epochs of salvation history. To him, salvation history is progressive, something like slowly turning up the volume on a radio. Just as it is difficult to pinpoint the precise moment that the radio gets loud, so it is hard to pinpoint the precise moment of the arrival of the new age. Luke does not even try."[189]

In the parallel stories, Luke highlights the affective emotions of joy, grace, exuberance, praise, being fortunate, leaping for joy, grace, divine pleasure, gratitude, marvel, wonder, and blessing as he provides two annunciations, two birth narratives, and the witness of so many to the two births. Joy is emotional, personal, effusive, and communal—the correlative of the "good news," which must be voiced in a spontaneous and contagious fashion; people flourish in such charismatic incursions.

NOTES

131 Luke's two volumes contain 7 occurrences of the verb, "I visit" (ἐπισκέπτομαι) of 10 uses in the NT (Luke 1:68, 78; 7:16; Acts 6:3; 7:23; 15:14, 36); 1 of 4 references of the noun, "visitation" (ἐπισκοπή Luke 19:44). Visitation couples with "redemption" (λύτρωσις), twice in the annunciation/birth narratives (Luke 1:68—by Zechariah; 2:38—by Anna the prophetess).

132 Raymond Brown dismisses the reality of angels, and interprets them as "a way of describing God's visible presence among men." Raymond E. Brown, *The Birth of the Messiah* (New York: Doubleday, 1993), 260. Further, he argues "that the Christology once attached to the resurrection (and later to the ministry) has been moved back to the conception and birth of Jesus," by the Early Church. 272.

133 Zechariah: "was troubled" (ἐταράχθη), "fear fell upon him" (φόβος ἐπέσεν ἐπ᾽ αὐτόν), "stop fearing" (μὴ φοβοῦ) Luke 1:12-13); Mary: "was troubled and was wondering" (διεταράχθη καὶ διελογίζετο), "stop fearing" (μὴ φοβοῦ) 1:29-30; the shepherds: "they feared a great fear" (ἐφοβήθησαν φόβον μέγαν— cognate accusative), "stop fearing" (μη φοβεῖσθε) 2:9-10.

134 In two angelophanies, Luke provides a parallel structure: a) introduction to parents, b) angelic appearance, c) response of fear, d) promise of a miracle-son, e) question/objection, f) answer, g) sign, h) angel's departure. The angelophany to the shepherds in Luke 2:8-20 mentions no "question or objection" on their part (Luke 2:8-20).

135 Shelton, 15. Menzies mentions the joy vocabulary in Luke 1-2, but does not follow through with other joyful texts in Luke-Acts. Robert Menzies, *The Development of Early Christian Pneumatology* JSOT: Series 54 (Sheffield, England: Sheffield Academic Press, 1991), 118.

136 John Nolland, *Luke 1-9:20* WBC 35A, (Waco, TX: Nelson Reference & Electronic, 1989), 35.

137 The verb, "I fill/fulfill" (πίμπλημι) in Luke 1:15, paired with the Spirit, is found in Lukan texts, often linked with "power" (δύναμις): 1:41—Elizabeth; 1:67—Zechariah; Acts 2:4—the 120; 4:8—Peter; 4:31—the believers; 9:17—Saul; 13:9—Paul; 13:52—believers in Iconium—also filled with "joy." See further discussion by Menzies, 119.

138 Friedrich, 707; the noun/verb is used extensively in Dt. Isa. and the Psalter (e.g., Isa. 40:9; 52:7; 61:1; Psa. 40:10; 68:11) and in secular Greek; joy comes to listeners when the good news is proclaimed.

139 De Long, 138.

140 See De Long's well supported argument for interpreting, "rejoice" (χαίρε), instead of a simple greeting., 139-141. Contra Brown, 332-325.

141   Several Zion texts (Joel 2:19-27; Zeph. 3; Zech. 9:9-10; Isa. 66:7-11) in Mary's *Magnificat.* De Long, 156-157

142   Luke underscores Mary's virginity (1:27, 34).

143   De Long alludes to seven references to barren women in the OT. 170-173.

144   Fitzmyer, 409.

145   See Fitzmyer for the appropriate translation, "good pleasure" (εὐδοκία) as "God's good pleasure." 411-412.

146   After Jesus' inaugural address in Nazareth, Jesus alludes to the parallels between his powerful ministry to the outsiders and those of Elijah and Elisha (Luke 4:25-27). See also Shelton, 18-19.

147   2:6-7; 3:1, 18; 4:5-6; see also ben-Sirach 48:10.

148   The verb "I come upon" (ἐπέρχομαι) is used in Acts 1:8 with the Spirit and "power" (δύναμις).

149   Menzies argues that the term "power" (δύναμις) is understood to be linked with healing and exorcism, 126.

150   Barrett interprets the verb, "overshadow" (ἐπισκιάζω) with the first creation narrative in which the Spirit of God is likened to a bird that "broods or hovers" מְרַחֶפֶת Piel participle Gen. 1:2) over the chaos. "The life is not in the chaos; it is in the Spirit (or breath, or wind). C. K. Barrett, *The Holy Spirit and the Gospel Tradition* (London: SPCK, 1970), 18. This link suggests that the conception of Jesus reflects the language of the new creation. See Menzies, 122-128 for an extended treatment of Luke 1:35—and his clear counter to Barrett's approach.

151   Expressed later with Jesus' wisdom when he interacts with the religious authorities in Jerusalem (2:41-50).

152   Comparative is used as a superlative here BDF 245§ 245.3.

153   De Long, 143. She connects several stories of a "greeting" (ἀσπάζομαι verb; ἀσπασμός noun) in which one greeting leads to another (1:29, 40, 41, 44)., 143.

154   De Long connects this story with Joel 2:21-26. 173.

155   Three occurrences of the "greet" word-family (ἀσπάζομαι I greet; ἀσπασμός greeting) in this narrative: "she greeted Elizabeth"-1:40; "Mary's greeting"-1:41; "the sound of your greeting"-1:44.

156   Two mentions of the verb, "leap" (σκιρτάω): "the unborn child leaped"-1:41; "the unborn child leaped in joy"-1:44. Joy is to be understood as an eschatological joy of the Messianic salvation.

157   Christopher Forbes links the figures of Elizabeth, Zechariah, Simeon and Anna in terms of their prophetic inspiration, whether the term "prophecy\prophet(ess)" is used or not. Christopher Forbes, *Prophecy and Inspired Speech in Early Christianity and its Hellenistic Environment* (Tübingen: J.C.B. Mohr (Paul Siebeck), 1995), 51-52.

158   Luke says that Elizabeth "cried out with a loud cry" (Luke 1:42), understood by Plummer as "a cry of strong feeling." Alfred Plummer, *A Critical and Exegetical Commentary on the Gospel According to S. Luke*, (Edinburgh: T & T Clark, 1969), 29.

159   A later corrective to the beatitude in Luke 11:27.

160   Shelton, 20; see 20-21 for a fuller argument.

161   Brown, 355-356.

162   Brown 357-365 for other OT texts that are part of Mary's mosaic. De Long alludes to Psa. 97:1-3, 160.

163   Partitive language, which divides the human person is inappropriate here.

164   Karl Barth, *Church Dogmatics* II (ed. G. W. Bromiley, Thomas F. Torrance; Edinburgh: T & T Clark, 1956-1975), 376.

165   Barth, IV/1, 41. Contra De Long, who argues that "the writer of Luke-Acts prefers praise over joy." Her argument is countered by numerous references to joy in the narrative.

166   Brown, 375.

167   ἐλάλει is an inceptive imperfect, "he *began* to speak."

168   De Long alludes to the LXX of Psa. 125:1-2, "Then *our mouth* (τὸ στόμα ἡμῶν) was filled with *joy* (χαρᾶς) and our *tongue with rejoicing* (ἡ γλῶσσα ἡμῶν ἀγαλλιάσεως). Then they will say among the nations, 'The Lord *has done great things* for us'" (ἐμεγάλυνεν)., 153-154. This miraculous event may be an expression from Isa. 35:5-6, which is elsewhere used in Luke (7:22).

169   Luke 5:25; 13:3; 18:43; Acts 3:7-8.

170   Brown suggests numerous parallels with the OT, 386-389.

171   Luke introduces the beginning of John's adult ministry, in the language of the prophetic call genre, "the word of the Lord came to . . . " (ἐγένετο ῥῆμα θεοῦ ἐπὶ . . . Luke 3:2; see LXX of Jer. 1:1;13:3; Isa. 38:4.

172   The Samaritan's "compassion," moves him to do help the half-dead victim in practical ways (Luke 10: 33-34).

173   For the noun, "compassion" see *Testament of Zebulun* 7:3; 8:2 and *Naphtali* 4:5 for similar language.

174   Mention of "peace" may allude to the angelic words to the shepherds, "and peace for those who are favored by God" (2:14).

175   "Now there was a man in Jerusalem, whose name was Simeon" (καὶ ἰδοὺ ἄνθρωπος ἦν ἐν Ἰερουσαλὴμ ᾧ ὄνομα Συμεών—2:25); "And there was a prophetess, Anna"(καὶ ἦν" Αννα προφῆτις—2:36).

176   Luke anticipates the same expression by Jesus in his synagogue sermon, when he reads from Isa. 61:1-3.

177   BDAG, 885. See also Bo Reicke, "χρῆμα κ.τ.λ." *TDNT*, vol. IX, 481.

178   Plummer connects several "consolation/comfort" promises (Isa. 40:1; 49:13; 51:3; 61:2; 66:13). 66.

179   François Bovin, *Luke 1: A Commentary on the Gospel of Luke 1:1-9:50* (ed. Helmut Koester; trans. Christine M. Thomas; Minneapolis: Fortress Press, 2002), 101.

180   De Long alludes to Psa. 97:2-3, 164-165.

181   See Brown for more extensive explanation, 459.

182   On "sign," see Isa. 7:14; 8:14, 18.

183   A sword of "discrimination" not simply judgment. See Ezek. 14:17; Luke 12:51-53.

184   The antecedent should not be understood as the sword piercing Mary, which will lay bare such thoughts; the antecedent should be the first part of Simon's oracle (2:34b-c). See Fitzmyer, 430. The conjunction, ὅπως should be understood, "with the result that." Perhaps Luke suggests a preliminary fulfillment when Jesus dialogues with the teachers in the Temple precincts (Luke 2:41-52). He is noted for his "understanding and answers" (2:47). Relative to his parents, the youth Jesus knows the will of God and not his parents, "Do you not know that I must be in my Father's house?" (2:49). The noun, "thought" (διαλογισμός) is consistently used in negative contexts in Luke.

185   Bovin notes that the verb "praise" (ἀνθομολογέομαι) means "to ratify an agreement" or "to recognize something," 106, noted in BDAG as a "public expression."

186   Brown, 460.

187   Verheyden, 181.

188   Hans Conzelmann, *The Theology of St. Luke* (transl. G. Buswell; New York: Harper & Row, 1961).

189   Shelton, 25.

CHAPTER 4

THE SPIRIT, JESUS' AGENDA, AND JOY (LUKE 4:16-30)

The Spirit of the Lord is upon me because
he has anointed me to bring good news to the poor.
—LUKE 4:18 (ISAIAH 61:1) (NRSV)

How does Jesus begin his ministry? Luke highlights the Holy Spirit's role in Jesus' joyous agenda (Luke 4:16-30). He describes Jesus' empowerment through "the descent of the Spirit in bodily form as a dove." Luke invites his community to ponder Jesus' personal Pentecost that prepares him for his purposeful and powerful agenda of a joyful ministry.

Emotional language encases Jesus' inaugural address and his initial ministry. Luke sandwiches the Nazareth[190] event between two summaries (Luke 4:14-15; 4:42-44) of Jesus' life-giving ministry and the joyous response from participants. Before the Nazareth episode, Luke notes Jesus' popularity in the widespread *report* (φήμη 4:14) and Galilean response, explaining that "he was being glorified by all" (δοξαζόμενος ὑπὸ πάντων 4:15).[191] Later in 4:42-44, Luke describes the joyous content of the "good news," using the term "kingdom of God" (4:44). Jesus is attractive, emotive, and winsome. People are delighted with Jesus, responding to the joyous "good news" evident in Jesus' words and actions.

Luke highlights Jesus' personal Pentecost[192] (Luke 3:21-22), signaled by "the descent of the Spirit *in bodily form* as a dove" (τὸ πνεῦμα τὸ ἅγιον σωματικῷ . . . ὡς περιστερὰν ἐπ' αὐτόν). This charismatic event prepares Jesus for his purposeful agenda in so many jubilant and vibrant ways. Luke clearly accentuates the progressive role of the Spirit through four expressions:

- "Now, Jesus, *full of the Holy Spirit*" ('Ἰησοῦς δὲ πλήρης πνεύματος ἁγίου 4:1),
- "was led *by the Spirit* in the wilderness" (ἤγετο ἐν τῷ πνεύματι ἐν τῇ ἐρήμῳ 4:1)
- "Jesus returned *in the power of the Spirit* into Galilee" (ἐν τῇ δυνάμει τοῦ πνεύματος εἰς τὴν Γαλιλαίαν 4:14),
- "*The Spirit of the Lord is upon me*, because he anointed me" (Πνεῦμα κυρίου ἐπ' ἐμέ οὗ εἵνεκεν ἔχρισέν με 4:18).

Luke's opening expression, "full of the Spirit" (Luke 4:1), emerges in Luke's two volumes.[193] The Spirit which anointed Jesus at his baptism is the same agent by which Jesus "is led into the wilderness" (4:1). The Spirit then empowers Jesus to return from the wilderness-temptation "in the power of the Spirit into Galilee" (4:14).[194] Jesus, who has been baptized with the Spirit and subsequently defeated temptation, now begins his ministry in the power of the Spirit. His powerful deeds[195] elicit a joyous response from the people. Joyous emotion surfaces in Jesus' declarations from Isaiah (Isa 61:1-3; 58:6) and also in the crowd's initial response (Luke 4:22).

Luke places Jesus' visit to Nazareth at the outset of Jesus' ministry.[196] Verheyden states, "Jesus is now explicitly linked to the figure of a prophet, and this in a two-fold way. First, he selects, reads and comments upon two passages from Isaiah, on what seems to be a description of the appointment and the task of a prophet. And second, he answers his critics with a saying about a prophet and his hometown and by calling to mind the activities of the prophets."[197]

In comparison to the other Synoptic gospels, Luke's piece contains much more of what Jesus said and how his hometown responded with joy.

	Matt 13:53-58	Mark 6:1-6a	Luke 4:16-30
Place	His own country–synagogue (v. 54)	His own country–synagogue (vss. 1-2)	Nazareth and synagogue (v. 16)
Jesus' activity	Taught (v. 54)	Began to teach (v. 2)	He stood up to read (v. 16) from Isaiah (v. 17)
OT text(s) with declaration	—	—	Isa. 61:1-3; 58:6 with Jesus' declaration, "Today this Scripture has been fulfilled in your hearing."
People's initial response	They were astonished (v. 54) and took offense (v. 57)	Many were astonished (v. 2) and took offense (v. 6a)	All spoke well of him and wondered at the gracious words which proceeded out of his mouth (v. 22)

Jesus' Declaration from Isaiah

Jesus' "sermon," highlights a major Old Testament quotation, a commissioning statement, and a preview and review of the narrative's course,[198] which proceeds in Luke's narrative.

> "The Spirit of the Lord is upon me,
>   because he has anointed me
> He has sent me: to announce good news[199] to the poor
>   to preach release to the captives,
> recovery of sight to the blind,
>   to send in release those who are in an oppressed condition
> to proclaim the favorable year of the Lord" (Isa. 61:1-3; 58:6).[200]

The "resting" of the Spirit upon him is due[201] to his "anointing," "he anointed me,"[202] ἔχρισεν με (4:18a). Since the Spirit rests upon Jesus, he is sent ("he has sent me" ἀπέσταλκεν με 4:18b), for four explicit purposes[203]: "to announce good news" εὐαγγελίσασθαι; "to preach" (twice) κηρύξαι; "to send/release" ἀποστεῖλαι.

Four groups benefit from Jesus' concern: "to the poor" (πτωχοῖς), "to the captives" (αἰχμαλώτοις), "to the blind" (τυφλοῖς), "those who are oppressed" (τεθραυσμένους). Jesus concludes with a proclamation of the favorable year of the Lord, which covers all persons of divine concern. "Release"[204] or "forgiveness of sins" (ἄφεσις) is proclaimed to both the captives and the oppressed, while recovery of sight (ἀνάβλεψις) is promised to the blind. First and foremost is the proclamation of "good news to the poor." The various terms that characterize the needy can be understood in both literal and figurative ways, e.g. physical and spiritual blindness.[205] Jesus' purposeful agenda evokes the affection of joy, e.g. certainly the joyful emotion of a blind person who now sees.

The annunciation and birth narratives highlight that joy is the co-relative of the verb, "I preach the good news" (εὐαγγελίζομαι Luke 1:19; 2:10). Here, the verb expresses the joyous atmosphere and experience of Jesus' self-declaration. Luke coordinates verbs of speaking:

- "I teach" (διδάσκω—Jesus "was teaching" (ἐδίδιασκεν) in their synagogues, leading to the joy of all (4:14-15),
- "I preach" (κηρύσσω—twice in v.18b) and the supplementary participle, "he was teaching" (ἦν κηρύσσων) in the synagogues,
- "I send" (ἀποστέλλω), paired with "I preach the good news (εὐαγγελίζομαι), with an infinitive of purpose, "he has sent me" ἀπέσταλκέν με), "to announce good news" (εὐαγγελίσασθαι 4:18a; 4:43), with the joyous message of the kingdom of God.

Beyond the immediate reference to Isa. 61:1-3; 58:6,[206] other Old Testament texts[207] support Isaiah's pronouncement, which include affections of joy and exuberance—the joy of God and the joy of his needy people who will experience relief. Emotional expressions are full:

- Isa 26:18: "The dead shall rise and they that are in the tombs shall be raised, and they that are in the tombs shall be raised, and they that are in the earth *shall be gladdened*: for the dew from you is healing to them" (ἀναστήσονται οἱ νεκροὶ καὶ ἐγερθήσονται οἱ ἐν τοῖς μνημείοις, καὶ *εὐφρανθήσονται* οἱ ἐν τῇ γῇ. ἡ γὰρ δρόσος ἡ παρὰ σοῦ ἴαμα αὐτοῖς)

- Isa 35:5-6: "Then the eyes of the blind shall be opened, and the ears of the deaf shall be unstopped. Then shall the lame man leap as a deer, and the tongue of the dumb *shall sing for joy.*"[208]

- Isa 29:18-19: "And in that day shall the deaf hear the words of the book and the eyes of the blind shall see out of obscurity and out of darkness. *And the poor shall rejoice in gladness because of the Lord* (καὶ *ἀγαλλιάσονται πτωχοὶ διὰ κύριον ἐν εὐφροσύνῃ*) and they that had no hope among men *shall be filled with gladness* (ἐμπλησθήσονται *εὐφροσύνης*),

- Isa 65:19: "Behold, I make Jerusalem *an exuberance*, and my people *a gladness*" (ἰδοὺ ἐγὼ ποιῶ *ἀγαλλίαμα* Ἱερουσαλὴμ καὶ τὸν λαόν μου *εὐφροσύνην*),

- Zeph 3:17f.: "He *will rejoice* over you with *gladness*, he will renew you in his love; he will *exult* over you with loud singing as on a day of festival, and I will gather your afflicted ones" (ἐπάξει ἐπὶ σε *εὐφροσύνην*, καὶ καινιεῖ σε ἐν τῇ ἀγαπήσει αὐτοῦ, καὶ *εὐφρανθήσεται* ἐπὶ σὲ ἐν τέρψει ὡς ἐν ἡμέρᾳ ἑορτῆς. καὶ συνάξω τοὺς συντετριμμένους σου).

In particular, the entire paragraph of Isaiah 35 expresses the effusive emotions of the coming age in the mood, experience, and celebratory expressions. Though Isa 35:5-6 does not contain a Messianic figure, the text does describe the return of God's people to Zion, with all the accompanying blessings and celebration. Luke's vocabulary of joy mirrors Isaiah's language:

- "to *gladden* oneself" (εὐφραίνω) in Isa 35:1.
- "*gladness*" (εὐφροσύνης) in 35:8 "*gladness* of birds" 35:10, "*gladness* and *eternal gladness* shall be upon their heads"; "*gladness* shall take possession of them."
- "I am filled with *exuberant joy*" (ἀγαλλιάω, ἀγαλλιάομαι), 35:1 (twice)—"the desert and desert places will be filled with *exuberant joy*" in 35:1.
- "*exuberant joy*" (ἀγαλλίαμα), "on their head there shall be *exuberant joy*,"
- "*praise*" (αἴνεσις) in 35:10, "*praise* shall be over their head."
- "the *glory* of the Lord" (ἡ δόξα κυρίου) in 35:2.
- "*encourage*" (παρακαλέω) in 35:4.

The coming age will be characterized by joy for all who are in a needy condition. Luke's gospel provides other lists of needy persons who are relieved from their distress (Luke 7:22[209]). He describes people who are elated over good things that will happen for them. Their feelings are full and expressive. Jeremias cogently remarks:

> Like all the three Isaiah passages, it has the character of a list. The images that they use, light for the blind, hearing for the deaf, shouting for joy by the dumb, etc., are all age-old phrases in the east for the time of salvation, when there will be no more sorrow, no more crying and no more grief . . . . Even now, *the consummation of the world is dawning.* The six fold list merely picks out examples of the fullness of its gifts; it could continue endlessly, as the continuation of the three Isaiah passages shows. It should be noted that the lepers and the dead are not mentioned in the three lists in Isaiah. That Jesus mentions them means that the fulfillment goes far beyond all promises, hopes, and expectations.[210]

The climax of the list in Luke 7:23 is found in the statement, *the poor are having good news preached to them* πτωχοὶ εὐαγγελίζονται, which corresponds to the first item in Jesus' inaugural address (Luke 4:18).[211] Jesus announces the eschatological presence of the kingdom realized in the proclamation of good news to the poor and oppressed (NEB "society's broken victims"). Weakened and vulnerable persons have always been high on God's agenda. The poor surface again in Luke's Beatitudes, "Blessed are you poor, for yours is the kingdom of God" (Luke 6:20).[212] Correspondingly, Luke's version promises to the ones who weep, "you will laugh" (γελάσετε 6:21b). Weeping will give way to joyful laughter. Nolland notes, "Laughter is the release of joy as tears are the release of sorrow."[213]

Luke features the anointing Spirit directing Jesus' agenda, thus bringing untold joy and holistic relief to so many in needy circumstances. His readers should appreciate that Jesus is doing what Isaiah prophesied that the Spirit-anointed and royal Messiah would do (Isa 42:1; Ps 2:7).

Initially, the townspeople receive this full announcement in a most positive light.[214] Even before Jesus announces the fulfillment of Isaiah's promises ("Today"), Luke notes that the eyes of all the villagers "were staring at him" (ἦσαν ἀτενίζοντες αὐτῷ 4:20). Fitzmyer understands this as, "a steadfast gaze of trust and esteem."[215] Luke's comment builds up tension in the narrative, leaving the reader asking, "What is going to happen next since Jesus is on center-stage and all eyes are riveted upon him?" When Jesus announces the fulfillment of Isaiah's promise ("Today"), Luke states that all the villagers "were bearing witness to him and were marveling at the words of grace which were proceeding from his mouth" (πάντες ἐμαρτύρουν αὐτῷ καὶ ἐθαύμαζον ἐπὶ τοῖς λόγοις τῆς χάριτος ἐκπορευομένοις ἐκ τοῦ στόματος αὐτοῦ 4:22). What are these "words of grace?" Surely the joyful emotions of Isaiah's fulfilled prophecy about the life-giving and joy-producing activity of the Spirit-anointed royal Messiah.

Some interpreters understand the clause, "they were witnessing to him," (ἐμαρτύρουν αὐτῷ) in a negative light, "they all bore witness *against* him."[216] However, this construal strains the text. The translation, "they spoke well of him" or "they praised him,"[217] is more appropriate to the context. The combination of the two verbs, "they spoke well of him" and "they were marveling" (ἐθαύμαζον) "by the words of grace" (τοῖς λόγοις τῆς χάριτος), surely suggests a response of initial admiration of Jesus. Luke seems to reveal something attractive and winsome in the exchange. His words convey divine favor and joyous fulfillment, also revealed by the expression, "the Lord's year of favor."[218]

To be sure, the remainder of the narrative expresses anger and murderous rage from the villagers. However, this fury is occasioned by Jesus' prophetic awareness of the residents' jealous exclusiveness, when Jesus points to the respective missions of Elijah and Elisha for recipients outside of Israel (widow of Zarephath, and Namaan the Syrian Luke 4:25-27). Nevertheless, this rage does not diminish the initial and joyful response of Nazareth's townspeople. Even their question, "Is this not Joseph's son?" is occasioned by Jesus' interpretation of Isaiah and its fulfillment, "Today." As such, their question conveys an amiable surprise and respect. Jesus stirs their feelings. Luke's Nazareth paragraph coordinates Jesus' identity as the Spirit-anointed and royal Messiah, his message of preaching "good news," his beneficent activity (e.g. healing and exorcism), and the fulfillment ("today") of Old Testament prophecy. Luke positions all of these affirmations within an atmosphere, experience and expression of joy, with the full engagement of emotions.[219]

NOTES

190   With others, it is assumed that Luke ignores Matthew and Mark's chronology, wherein Jesus first ministered in Capernaum and then Nazareth, since the Nazareth story occurs much later (Mark 6:1-6a; Matt 13:53-58).

191   Luke highlights the universal reaction of "all" in other places: 5:26; 7:16; 9:43; 18:43; 19:37.

192   Haya-Prats, 231.

193   Luke 4:1; Acts 6:3; 6:5, 8; 7:55; 11:24. Menzies suggests that Luke adds the expression, "full of the Holy Spirit" to "bring out the continuity between Jesus' experience of the Spirit and that of the early church . . . just as Jesus was empowered by the Spirit at the Jordan, so it was also for the early church at Pentecost and beyond; and so it must be for the church to which Luke writes," 157.

194   "power exerted by or through the divine Spirit," Barrett, 76. Luke uses other similar expressions of the "power of the Spirit" (Luke 1:17; 1:35—conception of

Jesus; also 4:36; 5:17; 6:19; 8:46); see also Acts 10:38 and the Pentecostal promise in Acts 1:8. See Menzies, 160-161 for a discussion on Jesus' commitment to his messianic task, "his worthiness to be a man of the Spirit." 160.

195   This also coheres with the powerful exorcism of the Capernaum demoniac and the "wonder" of the witnesses, "with authority and power he commands the unclean spirits and they depart" (ἐν ἐξουσίᾳ καὶ δυνάμει ἐπιτάσσει τοῖς ἀκαθάρτοις πνεύμασιν καὶ ἐξέρχονται Luke 4:36).

196   Veryheden argues that this pericope is a variant of Mark 6:1-6a and a "product of Luke's compositional artistry." Joseph Verheyden, "Calling Jesus a Prophet, as Seen by Luke," *Prophets and Prophecy in Jewish and Early Christian Literature* (Tübingen: Mohr Siebeck, 2010), 184

197   Verheyden, 184. At the same time, he argues against his two statements, 184-186.

198   Tannehill, 61.

199   I. Howard Marshall rightly suggests that the verb, "I send" (ἀποστέλλω) is followed by the four infinitives of purpose for the sending, also based upon a link with 4:43, where sending precedes the purposeful announcement of the good news (εὐαγγελίσασθαι με . . . ὅτι ἐπὶ τοῦτο ἀπεστάλην). Further, this punctuation agrees with both the MT and LXX. I. Howard Marshall, *The Gospel of Luke* (Grand Rapids: William B. Eerdmans Publishing Company, 1978), 183. This explains the changed word order of "he has sent" (ἀπέσταλκεν) in 4:18b.

200   Noteworthy absence of "the day of vengeance of our God" (Isa. 61:62).

201   οὗ εἵνεκεν "on account of," BDAG, 226.

202   Jesus' self-identification is emphasized by the three-fold repetition of the personal pronoun, "me" (με). Also, the same verbal form, "he anointed" (ἔχρισεν) is found in Acts 10:38. Luke views Jesus' entire ministry, as well as his anointing (as Luke 4:18-19 indicates), in prophetic terms. Anointing is expressed in charismatic language of speaking and acting for God.

203   Infinitives of purpose.

204   In the LXX of Leviticus, the Jubilee Year is the "year of release" (ἐνιαυτὸς ἀφέσεως Lev. 25:10. For Luke, "release" from bondage may also include Jesus' exorcisms of those who are "bound" by Satan, e.g., Luke 13:10-17, Acts 10:38.

205   e.g., Luke 7:22—literal; 1:78-79; 2:30-32; 3:6—figurative. Also figurative in Acts 13:47; 26:17-18.

206   See Menzies for an extensive discussion of tradition and redaction in the use of Isaiah 61 and Isaiah 58, 162-177.

207   Also a plethora of identical or similar terms in the inter-testamental literature, e.g., Test. Zeb. 9:8.

208   MT-רָנַן "shall sing\shout for joy"; LXX "the tongue of the dumb shall speak clearly (τρανὴ ἔσται γλῶσσα μογιλάλων).

209   "Proclaim to John what you see and hear, blind receive sight, lame walk, lepers are being cleansed, deaf hear, dead are being raised, poor are having the good news proclaimed to them (πτωχοὶ εὐαγγελίζονται)." Luke accentuates Jesus'

life-giving activity more than Q (Matt 11:5), for Jesus' pronouncement follows John's question when his messengers come "in that hour" (ἐν ἐκείνῃ τῇ ὥρᾳ). What is "that hour?" It is the time when Jesus heals and exorcises people that are specified in the "needy-list" in v. 22, "he healed many from their diseases and plagues and evil spirits and he graciously gave eyesight to many who were blind" (ἐθεράπευσεν πολλοὺς ἀπὸ νόσων καὶ μαστίγων καὶ πνευμάτων πονηρῶν, καὶ τυφλοῖς πολλοῖς ἐχαρίσατο βλέπειν).

210   Joachim Jeremias, *New Testament Theology*, (New York: Charles Scribner's Sons, 1971), p. 104.

211   In Luke 14, a four-fold list of needy persons is highlighted twice (Luke 14:13, 21)

212   Matthew spiritualizes Luke's "the poor," with "poor in spirit" (Matt 5:3).

213   Nolland, 284.

214   Neither Matthew nor Mark contain a positive response from the villagers; instead they note that the townspeople "took offense at him" (ἐσκανδαλίζοντο ἐν αὐτῷ Mark. 6:3; Matt 13:57), which is due to "unbelief" (ἀπιστία Mark. 6:6a; Matt 13:58).

215   Fitzmyer, 533.

216   Joachim Jeremias, *Jesus' Promise to the Nations* (Naperville: Allenson, 1958), 44-46. Jeremias understands "at him" (αὐτῷ) as a dative of disadvantage instead of the more natural dative of advantage.

217   John Martin Creed, *The Gospel According to St. Luke* (London: Macmillan and Co., Limited, 1950), 67.

218   Fitzmyer, 534.

219   De Long makes no comment on the Nazareth event.

CHAPTER 5

JOYOUS HEALINGS, EXORCISMS AND MIGHTY WORKS

Today (December 28) in 1843, an unclean spirit cried
"Jesus is victor!" as it departed from a young girl
in Möttlingen, Germany.[220]
–JOHANN BLUMHARDT

Luke's narratives reveal how people respond to Jesus' charismatic ministry and how Jesus responds to the people. Luke links joy to Jesus' miraculous activity (healings, exorcisms, and mighty works) and also to his disciples' joyous short-term mission trips, including Jesus' affective response to their reports upon their return. Through his generous language, Luke invites readers to embrace Jesus' powerful ministry, including the attendant joy. Numerous paragraphs express the atmosphere, experience and expression of joy, giving Luke rich opportunity to invite his readers to feel similar emotions as they share in Jesus' charismatic mission.

The Capernaum Demoniac
(Luke 4:31-37; Mark 1:21-27)

The accounts of Jesus' exorcism of the Capernaum victim in Luke and Mark are very similar. They include the worshippers' "amazement" (ἐξεπλήσσοντο) before the exorcism[221] and their "astonishment" after the exorcism ("they all were astonished," ἐθαμβήθησαν Mark 1:27; "astonishment came (*fell*) upon all," (ἐγένετο θάμβος ἐπὶ πάντας

Luke 4:36). Both versions narrate the widespread report of this exorcism. Mark's statement links "teaching" with "authority" (Mark 1:22). Luke's narrative accentuates that Jesus ministered "with power and authority" (ἐν ἐξουσία καὶ δυνάμει Luke 4:36),[222] and he highlights the verb, "I command" (ἐπιτάσσω) in Luke 4:36.[223] Luke's link of *power* (δύναμις) with *authority* (ἐξουσία) returns his readers to Luke 4:14 describing Jesus' return to Galilee "in the power of the Spirit" (ἐν τῇ δυνάμει τοῦ πνεύματος), following his baptism in the Spirit and ensuing temptation.

Luke shows Jesus fulfilling his life-giving and joy-producing agenda, noted in his address recorded earlier in this same chapter: "to release the captives and to send in release those who are in an oppressed condition" (Luke 4:18b). According to Luke, Jesus effected this exorcism through the Spirit's power. That overwhelming power prompted an astonished response within the synagogue, and a widespread report in the region. Luke's presentation underscores the progression from a charismatic event to a spontaneous and contagious witness and joyful declaration.[224]

Peter's Miraculous Catch of Fish
(Luke 5:1-11; Matt 4:18-22; Mark 1:16-20)

The narratives of Matthew and Mark describe the call of two paired brothers, using two historical progressions, each of which builds towards the climax, "they followed him" (Matt 4:20, 22; Mark 1:18, 20). Luke's story focuses upon Simon, the miraculous catch of fish and his call,[225] with the similar climax, "they followed him" (Luke 5:11).

However, Luke's story is set within the context of Jesus' departure from Capernaum, in which Jesus states that he was "sent to announce the good news" (ἐπι τοῦτο ἀπεστάλην εὐαγγελίσασθαι Luke 4:43). Luke's account links the declaration of the "good news" with "the kingdom of God" (ἡ βασιλεία τοῦ θεοῦ Lk 4:43). The author also paired the declaration with the verb, "I preach" (κηρύσσω Luke 4:44). Luke's combined vocabulary reminds his readers of the verbs in Jesus' inaugural address (εὐαγγελίσασθαι Luke 4:18b; κηρύξαι, twice in Luke 4:18b). These references are followed by a similar statement in Luke 5:1, which notes, "the crowd pressed upon him to hear the 'word of God'" (τὸν λόγον τοῦ θεοῦ). Thus, the announcement of "good news" (4:43) parallels "preaching" (4:44), the "kingdom of God" (4:43), and "the word of God" (5:1). Jesus engages his stated life-giving agenda, and then Luke's narrative describes how it "spills-over" into his departure from Capernaum (4:42-43) and the crowd's physical response of pressing upon Jesus (5:1). Surely Luke describes an atmosphere of joy and receptivity.

In this life-giving context, Jesus' prophetic knowledge of the "catch of fish" (Luke 5:4) emerges in the "great shoal of fish" (5:6). However, Simon must obey Jesus' seemingly absurd command. Peter, an experienced fisherman, has been frustrated by empty nets through the entire night (Luke 5:5). His response might be paraphrased, "Lord, we've come up empty—all night. What will one more cast of the nets do?" Luke accentuates the "great shoal of fish" with other clauses, "breaking of the nets" (5:6), "beckoning of their partners in the other boat" (5:7) and the "filling of both boats and their sinking" (5:7). Clearly, Luke wants his readers to see this event as miraculous.

In Simon's initial response to Jesus' prophetic knowledge and the miraculous catch, he distances himself from Jesus, followed by an explanation for why (ὅτι) Jesus should depart, "for I am a sinful man" (5:8). Luke further explains (γάρ) Simon's response by including the response of the other fishermen, "for astonishment had seized him and all that were with him" (θάμβος γὰρ περιέσχεν αὐτὸν καὶ πάντας τοὺς σὺν αὐτῷ 5:9). Just as Gabriel replaced "fear" with "joy" for Zechariah (Luke 1:13), Mary (1:30) and the shepherds (Luke 2:10), so Jesus replaces "fear" with the announcement, "from now on you will be catching people alive" (ἀπὸ τοῦ νῦν ἀνθρώπους ἔσῃ ζωγρῶν 5:11).

Luke's intentional word-play in the compound verb, "catch alive" (ζωγρέω) includes the adjective, "alive" (ζωός)[226] and the verb, "I catch/ seize" (ἀγρέω). In this context, the verb relates to the "catch" (ἄγρα 5:4, 9), noted in 5:6 as a "great shoal of fish." Implicitly, Luke intends for his readers to understand that Jesus had been "catching people alive" in 5:1, as they pressed upon him to hear the word. The same activity will characterize Simon's future. As Tannehill notes, "Jesus' call of a sinful man to share his life and work is equivalent to a declaration of forgiveness."[227] Jesus gives life

and touches the affections through his miraculous activity: healing Peter's
mother-in-law of a great fever (Luke 4:30-31), prophetic knowledge of a
miraculous catch (Luke 5:4), forgiving sins, and demonstrating life-giving
activity ("catching people alive" 5:11). Simon's new role is a promising and
joyful vocation.

Healing a Paralytic
(Luke 5:17-26; Matt 9:1-8; Mark 2:1-12)

The account, preserved in the triple-tradition, focuses on Jesus' authority
to "forgive sins" (four times in Mark and Luke; three times in Matt). The
healing of the paralytic substantiates Jesus' authority to forgive[228]
sins, "But in order (ἵνα) that you may know that the Son of Man has
authority on earth to forgive sins . . . " (Luke 5:24; Matt 9:6; Mark 2:10).
This is the story's central message.

However, Luke's account contains features not found in parallel
accounts. First, Luke provides expressions that highlight the numinous
encounter. Luke introduces the story with a reference to the numinous
atmosphere, "and the power of the Lord was with him to heal" (καὶ
δύναμις κυρίου ἦν εἰς τὸ ἰᾶσθαι αὐτόν Luke 5:17),[229] which parallels
Jesus' agenda, "the Spirit of the Lord is upon me" (Luke 4:18a). Barrett
notes that *power* (δύναμις) in 5:17 means miraculous power,[230] almost
"as a physical fluid transferable to others . . . ."[231] Luke portrays Jesus
as a *pneumatic* person, working under a numinous authority, who
can prophetically know people's inner thoughts (Luke 5:22), release
people from their sins (5:20) and heal (5:25). The adverb *immediately*
(παραχρῆμα) highlights the instantaneous healing and joyful expression.

Luke highlights Jesus' *power* (δύναμις) in his preface to the Sermon
on the Plain, "for power came forth from him and healed them all" (ὅτι
δύναμις παρ' αὐτοῦ ἐξήρχετο καὶ ἰᾶτο πάντας 6:19). Before the
Sermon, Luke highlights *healing* with three statements:

- "to be healed" (ἰαθῆναι 6:18);
- people who were *troubled* (ἐνοχλέω 6:18) by unclean
  spirits "were being healed" (ἐθεραπεύοντο);
- the power "was healing" (ἰᾶτο 6:19) all.

While a joyful response is not mentioned with respect to healing and exorcism, it is at least implicit in the expression, "all the crowd was seeking to touch him" (6:19). Nolland suggests that Luke continues to clarify "what it means for Jesus to have become through the descent of the Spirit, the repository of the power of God (3:22; 4:1; 14, 18-19; 6:19; 8:44). If anything varies, it will be the use to which the power of God is to be put."[232] Luke associates *power* (δύναμις) and *authority* (ἐξουσία) with healing and exorcism.

Luke alone highlights the numinous character of the paralytic's healing and the onlookers' parallel responses of joy and praise:

- "And astonishment seized them all and they were glorifying God"
- (καὶ ἔκστασις ἔλαβεν ἅπαντασ καὶ ἐδόξαζον τὸν θεὸν Luke 5:26))
- "and they were filled with awe, saying, 'we have seen a wonderful event[233]'"
- (καὶ ἐπλήσθησαν φόβου λέγοντες ὅτι εἴδομεν παράδοξα σήμερον 5:26)

Luke alone records the paralytic's joyful response, noting that "he went home glorifying God" (ἀπῆλθεν εἰς τὸν οἶκον αὐτοῦ δοξάζων τὸν θεόν, 5:26). Yes, the triple-tradition does include the "joyful" (δοξάζω) response of the onlookers,[234] but Luke includes the healed paralytic's joyful expressions. Surely the man's emotional response includes gratitude. For Luke, emotional elation is part of a charismatic event, felt by the paralytic and the community in response to forgiveness and physical healing. In addition to describing the experienced and expressed joy, Luke also contrasts that image with the joy-less religious critics who can only accuse (Luke 5:21).

The Raising of a Widow's Son at Nain
(Luke 7:11-17)

Luke alone includes a story of the resuscitation of a widow's only son from death. In the broader context of Luke 7, the author recounts

Jesus' tampering with the religious, racial, and social taboos of Jewish particularism: healing a Gentile Centurion's servant (7:1-10), interrupting a funeral, touching a coffin, and raising a son (7:11-17),[235] table-fellowship with unclean persons (7:34), and affirmation of an unclean woman (7:35).

The pericope of the son's raising narrates the feeling-involvement of Jesus (7:13) and God (7:16) in the widow's gloomy plight, the powerful raising of the widow's *only* son (7:14-15), the joyous response of the many onlookers (7:16), and a joyful and spontaneous witness (7:17). Jesus' feeling-involvement is expressed, "the Lord felt compassion" (ἐσπλαγχνίσθη, 7:13) for the widow's hopeless condition. She had lost her husband and her only son. Now she also would be bereft of financial support. As a result of Jesus' compassion and resuscitation of the widow's son, God's feeling involvement is proclaimed by the mourners, "God has visited his people" (ἐπεσκέψατο ὁ θεὸς τὸν λαὸν αὐτοῦ, Luke 7:16). The verb *I visit* conveys the idea of an actual visit, but more importantly, it holds the idea of care, compassion and concern.[236] Beyer notes that the verb means "always 'to be concerned' about them, with a sense of responsibility for others."[237]

Subsequent to the son's resuscitation,[238] Luke combines the mourners' *fear* (φόβος) that seized all (Luke 7:16) and their *joyful response*, "they were glorifying God" (ἐδόξαζον τὸν θεὸν 7:16). Although Luke does not mention the widow's response (7:15), readers certainly assume she reacted with overwhelming joy. The mourners highlight Jesus' prophetic status, noting, "A great prophet has arisen in our midst" (Προφήτης μέγας ἠγέρθη ἐν ἡμῖν 7:16). Jesus already alluded to his role as prophet (Luke 4:25), linking himself with Elijah (4:26).[239] Although the people vaguely understand Jesus and his identity, surely their response is positive. For the moment, they understand Jesus as a "great prophet," substantiated by his mighty miracle of raising the widow's son from the dead, which they interpret as God's gracious and compassionate visitation.

Luke describes how this joyful and powerful event leads to a spontaneous and joyful witness: "And this report (λόγος)[240] concerning him spread through the whole of Judea and all the surrounding country" (Luke 7:17). A joyful report of experienced power is naturally effusive and contagious. In such a case, suppressing the resulting joy and wonder would be unnatural.

The Good News and Grateful Women
(Luke 8:1-3)

Luke alone narrates the presence of many women, along with the twelve,[241] accompanying Jesus in his itinerant mission. Luke summarizes Jesus' activity in cities and villages, "preaching and announcing the good news of the kingdom of God" (κηρύσσων καὶ εὐαγγελιζόμενος τὴν βασιλείαν τοῦ θεοῦ Luke 8:1). Here, as in 4:43-44, the two verbs *I preach* (κηρύσσω) and *I announce the good news* (εὐαγγελίζομαι) refer to the same activity. Both passages also include the content of the message, "the kingdom of God" and joy. Further, Luke links "the good news" with "the kingdom of God," contextualizing verbal proclamation within Jesus' miraculous activity. Luke notes the women's healed condition[242] "from evil spirits" (ἀπὸ πνευμάτων πονηρῶν) and "illnesses" (ἀσθενειῶν). Although some women are named,[243] Luke highlights Mary called Magdalene, "from whom seven demons had gone out" (ἀφ᾽ ἧς δαιμόνια ἑπτὰ ἐξεληλύθη 8:2).

Luke also mentions women who footed the bill for Jesus' itinerant ministry.[244] Because Luke highlights Jesus' powerful healings and deliverances, he intimates that their financial outlay is motivated by gratitude for their healed condition. Indeed, the paragraph preceding this inclusion of women among Jesus' supporters conveys the gratitude of one sinful woman "who loves much" (i.e. "is so grateful"), for she has been forgiven much (Luke 7:47). The gratitude of one forgiven woman spills over into the gratitude of many women who have experienced Jesus' mighty acts of deliverance and healing. Thus, these women freely give of their financial resources. Joy is implicit in the good news, the kingdom of God, and the grateful response from these women who have experienced Jesus' power.

Healing a Demon-Possessed Boy
(Luke 9:37-43a; Mark 9:14-29; Matt 17:14-21)

The story of Jesus' healing/exorcism of a father's epileptic only son is found in the triple-tradition, and it follows the narrative of Jesus' transfiguration.[245] There are many points of similarity and dissimilarity, e.g. the extended conversation between Jesus and the father in Mark's story (Mark 9:21-24). The evangelists draw readers into the emotional pain of a father who pleads with Jesus for his demon-possessed son, trapped in the direst circumstances.

After the successful exorcism, Luke alone narrates Jesus' giving the boy back to the father (Luke 9:42)[246] and the joyful response of the people to the healing (Luke 9:43), "And all were astonished at the majesty of God" (ἐξεπλήσσοντο δὲ πάντες ἐπὶ τῇ μεγαλειότητι τοῦ θεοῦ, Luke 9:43). In the triple-tradition, the disciples' failure to effect a cure/exorcism (Luke 9:40)[247], along with the description of a faithless and perverse generation (Luke 9:41), create a contrast to highlight Jesus' powerful healing of a son in desperate circumstances (spirit seizes, convulses, foams, grinds teeth, will hardly leave Luke 9:39). Luke underscores the crowd's joyful astonishment at God's majesty, so manifest in the powerful deliverance. Luke records the reason for their amazement, "the majesty of God" (or "God's grandeur"[248], juxtaposing it with the disciples' inability to exorcise the son.

Luke provides another joyous response, noting, "all are marveling at everything which Jesus was doing" (πάντων δὲ θαυμαζόντων ἐπὶ πᾶσιν οἷς ἐποίει Luke 9:43b); this introduces Jesus' second passion pronouncement.[249] This leads to the astonishment at "everything which Jesus was doing,"[250] including the previous exorcism and "mighty works" that Luke has included so far in his narrative. Privately, Jesus wants the significance of his passion "to sink into your ears" (θέσεσθε ὑμεῖς εἰς τὰ ὦτα ὑμῶν Luke 9:44a), i.e. his disciples' ears. Nolland notes, "the whole clause underlines the importance and solemnity of Jesus' coming statement."[251] While previous stories might orient the disciples to power and prestige, Jesus speaks of his impending suffering and the need for disciples to desist from their in-house rivalry ("Who is the greatest?") and their need to become the "least" of all of these (Luke 9:46-48).

The Joyful Mission of the Twelve[252] and Seventy (-two)[253] with Jesus' Joyful Response to their Mission[254]
(Luke 9:1-6; 10:1-24)

The triple-tradition contains the twelve's mission, but Luke alone contains the mission of the seventy (-two), coupled with their joyful success and "report-back," eliciting Jesus' ecstatic reaction. Luke wants readers to feel joyful emotion in the charismatic mission of both groups. Certain facets link the two narratives:

First, Luke records that Jesus' sent (ἀποστέλλω)[255] both groups: "*he sent* them" (9:2); "*he sent* them" (10:1); "*I am sending* you" (10:5).[256] From the Hebrew perspective, the *sent one* (*shaliach*) represents the sender, in this case, Jesus. The "advance-party" will represent Jesus in terms of message (i.e. God's kingdom) and mighty works including healing and exorcism.

Second, both groups *announce the good news of God's kingdom*. For Donald Senior and Carroll Stuhlmueller, the kingdom of God is the "starting point and context for mission." [257] Luke contains four expressions:

- 9:2, "to preach the kingdom of God" (κηρύσσειν τὴν βασιλείαν τοῦ θεοῦ);
- 9:6, "announcing the good news" (εὐαγγελιζόμενοι);[258]
- 10:9, "you are to say, 'the kingdom of God has approached you'" (λέγετε αὐτοῖς Ἤγγικεν ἐφ᾽ ὑμᾶς ἡ βασιλεία τοῦ θεοῦ)."
- 10:11, "know that the kingdom of God has arrived"[259] (γινώσκετε ὅτι ἤγγικεν ἡ βασιλεία τοῦ θεοῦ).

In this context, the kingdom of God refers to the dynamic and Spirit-filled reign of God, expressed through the person, words, and works of Jesus—God's ruling power fulfilled in him. This factor has an already-but-not-yet tension, still awaiting glorious consummation. As David Burnett notes, "Both the words and works of Jesus are the beginning of the new age—the kingdom of God. The casting out of demons signals God's invasion of the kingdom of Satan and foretells his future destruction."[260] God's reign is holistic, touching all dimensions of human existence, including the emotions. It is to be received with trust and joy. Evangelical and Pentecostal communities often see God's kingdom only in a reductionistic manner, limited to forgiveness of sins and release from guilt. Jesus and Luke see God's kingdom with a larger view.

Luke pairs the kingdom of God (with its verbal proclamation of the joy-eliciting "good news") with a ministry of healing and exorcism. More than the other evangelists, Luke highlights the verb, "I preach the good news" (εὐαγγελίζομαι), which implies a joyful response.[261] The disciples both heal the sick and exorcise demon-possessed people, thereby communicating in word action, "a God committed to saving his people, a God intent on destroying pain, sickness, evil, and death."[262] Since God's reign is both present and future, the healings and exorcisms are proleptic anticipations of the grand consummation in the *eschaton*. The references to miracles are numerous in both sendings:

- 9:1, "he gave them power[263] and authority over all demons and *to heal diseases*" (ἔδωκεν αὐτοῖς δύναμιν καὶ ἐξουσίαν ἐπὶ πάντα δαιμόνια καὶ νόσους θεραπεύειν);
- 9:2, Hand in hand with their joyous proclamation, they are "to heal [the sick]" (ἰᾶσθαι [τοὺς ἀσθενεῖς]);
- 9:6, Luke's narrative includes their travels through the villages, "announcing the good news and *healing everywhere*" (εὐαγγελιζόμενοι καὶ θεραπεύοντες πανταχοῦ);
- 10:9, *Healing* the sick is again paired with the announcement that the kingdom of God has drawn near (θεραπεύετε τοὺς ἐν αὐτῇ ἀσθενεῖς καὶ λέγετε αὐτοῖς Ἤγγικεν ἐφ' ὑμᾶς ἡ βασιλεία τοῦ θεοῦ);
- 10:17-20, There are three references to *exorcisms* by the seventy (-two):
- 10:17, "the *demons* are subject[264] to us in your name" (τὰ δαιμόνια ὑποτάσσεται ἡμῖν ἐν τῷ ὀνόματί σου),
- 10:19, "I have given to you the authority to tread upon *snakes and scorpions* and over all the *power of the enemy*" (δέδωκα ὑμῖν ἐξουσίαν τοῦ πατεῖν ἐπάνω ὄφεων καὶ σκορπίων, καὶ ἐπὶ πᾶσαν τὴν δύναμιν τοῦ ἐχθροῦ),
- "the *spirits* are subject to you" (τὰ πνεύματα ὑμῖν ὑποτάσσεται 10:20).

The kingdom of God, paired with healing and exorcism, leads to Jesus' statement in the following chapter, "But if it is I by the finger of God[265] cast out demons, then the kingdom of God has come upon you" (Luke 11:20). Thus, the unique combination of the distinctive person of Jesus and the Spirit of God, along with the evidence of exorcisms, leads to the presence of God's kingdom. God's reign is holistic, charismatic, compassionate, transforming, and joy-producing, when people are set free. This mission is realized through the "sent ones."

In the "report-back" session, the twelve apostles narrate to Jesus "all the things they did" (ὅσα ἐποίησαν Luke 9:10), including verbal proclamation, healings, and exorcisms. Luke also prepares for Jesus' feeding the 5000, highlighting Jesus' declaration of the kingdom of God and his healing: ". . . he was speaking to them [the crowd] concerning the *kingdom of God* and was *healing* those in need of healing" (ἐλάλει αὐτοῖς περὶ τῆς βασιλείας τοῦ θεοῦ, καὶ τοὺς χρείαν ἔχοντας θεραπείας ἰᾶτο 9:11). Thus, Luke sandwiches Jesus' verbal proclamation and miraculous healings in between the short-term missions trips of the twelve (9:1-6) and the seventy-two (Luke 10:1-12). They follow Jesus' example, announcing the good news of God's kingdom in both word and miraculous activity—all in joyous settings.

Both groups receive instruction about what to take and what not to take (Luke 9:3; 10:4). In sum, Jesus tells his "sent ones" to pack lightly and trust God and the hospitality of others, thus leaving room for God and others to act. Both groups also receive directions of what to do in the face of reception and rejection (Luke 9:4-5; Luke 10:6-8).

The mission of both groups is followed by a *report-back session* (Luke 9:10 and 10:17-20). Overall, Luke infuses the joy-vocabulary into the two short-term mission trips and report-back sessions, thus pairing joy with charismatic experiences. Joy, which is implicit in the sending of the twelve, becomes explicit in the mission of the seventy (-two), expressed through variations of the joy-vocabulary.

In Luke 9:6, the disciples announce the good news, with the implicit response of joy. The narrative includes three references to *peace* (εἰρήνη) (Luke 10:5-6). This word *peace* (εἰρήνη 10:5-6) reflects the Hebrew understanding of wholeness or well-being. In his discussion of the parallel Hebrew word *shalom*, Spicq states that "the sense of the root is 'be well, complete, safe and sound . . . it is euphoria with security.' Nothing better can be desired for oneself and for others."²⁶⁶ Peace as *wholeness* or *well-being* is almost tangible. Foerster notes, "The greeting which they give on entering a house is not a wish. It is a gift which is either received or rejected as such. So real is this that if rejected it returns to the disciples."²⁶⁷ The wholeness conveyed by the missionaries certainly includes their joyful proclamation, whether by verbal announcement or miracles, paired with the gift of peace to recipients.

When the seventy (-two) return for their report-back session, they do so "with joy" (μετὰ χαρᾶς Luke 10:17). Jesus responds to their joyful report with two contrasting imperatives of joy, "do not rejoice . . . but rejoice" (μὴ χαίρετε . . . χαίρετε δὲ Luke 10:20).

After instructing the disciples, Jesus "rejoiced with exuberance in the Holy Spirit" (ἠγαλλιάσατο [ἐν] τῷ πνεύματι τῷ ἁγίῳ Luke 10:21). The verbs, ἀγαλλιάω ἀγαλλιάομαι mean, "I exult, I am overjoyed, I am filled with exuberant joy,"²⁶⁸ and in this context, the verb suggest an ecstatic condition, since it is "in the Holy Spirit." Jesus' joy in the Holy Spirit leads him to articulate a prayer of joy to the Father, "I praise you" (ἐξομολογοῦμαι σοι Luke 10:21), "your good pleasure" (εὐδοκία . . . σου Luke 10:21). Jesus turns to the disciples and speaks of their blessed and joyous condition: "How blessed/how fortunate are your eyes" (Μακάριοι οἱ ὀφθαλμοὶ Luke 10:23).

Joy dominates the return of the seventy (-two) in Luke 10:17-20. Their immediate report of successful exorcisms is expressed "with joy" (μετὰ χαρᾶς Luke 10:17). They are flush with excitement that even the demons submit to them in Jesus' name.²⁶⁹ Initially, Jesus interprets their joyful success through his visionary experience, "I was beholding Satan falling like lightning from heaven" (Ἐθεώρουν τὸν Σατανᾶν ὡς ἀστραπὴν ἐκ τοῦ οὐρανοῦ πέσοντα 10:18). The subjugation of Satan's subordinate "demons" (10:17) or "spirits" (10:20) to the missionaries surely signifies Satan's defeat, as falling from heaven, i.e., "at the height of his influence."²⁷⁰ Jesus' declaration, "I was beholding" (ἐθεώρουν) suggests a continued visionary occurrence²⁷¹ that Jesus experienced while the missionaries were absent.²⁷² Jesus' vision summarizes their successful activity in healings and exorcisms. Barrett notes that v. 18 is "an eschatological saying expressed in a visionary form, possibly resting upon a real visionary experience, and formulated by Is. 14:12."[273] God's triumphant reign is not only present in Jesus, but also in his missionaries who joyfully proclaim it through word and deed. Certainly their emotional joy is matched by the emotional experience of those who have been set free.

Jesus grounds their joyous victories in his previous gift of authority and power prior to their actual mission, "Behold I have given to you the authority to trample upon snakes and scorpions and over all the power of the enemy" (ἰδου δέδωκα ὑμῖν τὴν ἐξουσίαν τοῦ πατεῖν ἐπάνω ὄφεων καὶ σκορπίων καὶ ἐπὶ πασαν τὴν δύναμιν τοῦ ἐχθροῦ 10:19).[274] "The disciples as representatives of Jesus (10:16) and as ones sent on ahead of him (10:1) have been able to confront evil in its various manifestations."[275] In this paragraph, mention of "snakes and scorpions" appears to coordinate with "demons" (10:17) or "spirits" (10:20), while the term "Satan" (10:18) matches "the enemy" (10:19).

While Jesus affirms and grounds their successful exorcisms, he also qualifies their joy through a contrast, introduced by the adversative, "Nevertheless" (πλήν), "in this 'do not rejoice' (μὴ χαίρετε)[276] that the spirits are subject to you, 'but rejoice' (χαίρετε δὲ) that your names are written in heaven" (10:20). Marshall comments, "The saying should probably be interpreted in terms of Semitic idiom to mean, 'Do not rejoice primarily that . . . but rather that . . . .'"[277] Jesus affirms their joy in successful exorcisms, but he focuses their joy, stating it is not found in doing, but in their condition and being. They are enrolled in the heavenly book—that is their condition.[278] Luke contrasts "Satan's fall *from heaven*" (10:18) and the missionaries' names that are written *in heaven*" (10:20). If Jesus intended rebuke, it is only slight, for Jesus himself proceeds to rejoice with exuberance (Luke 10:21). In their mission, the disciples recognize the divine visitation—an important theme for Luke. The miracles (αἱ δυνάμεις) accomplished in their trip "are signs pointing to visitation of God through Jesus".[279]

Luke introduces Jesus' thanksgiving-prayer with an explicit link with the missionaries' joyous report. His exuberant joy in the Holy Spirit occurs "in the very[280] hour" (ἐν αὐτῇ τῇ ὥρᾳ Luke 10:21) of their joyful return (Luke 10:17).[281] Matthew's introduction is less specific, "in that time" (ἐν ἐκείνῳ τῷ καιρῷ Matt. 11:25) and is followed by the verb, *he said*, while Luke's narrative is followed by the statement, "he rejoiced with exuberance[282] in the Holy Spirit" (ἠγαλλιάσατο τῷ πνεύματι τῷ ἁγίῳ).[283] Jesus' charismatic joy in the Holy Spirit (10:21b) parallels both the joyful witnesses in the annunciation/birth narratives in Luke 1-2 and the witnessing community in the Book of Acts. Matthew's thanksgiving-prayer directly follows Jesus' denunciation of Chorazin and Bethsaida (Matt. 11:20-24), while Luke's thanksgiving-prayer directly follows the return of the missionaries (Luke 10:17-20). In Luke's narrative, the denunciation of the two cities precedes the return of the missionaries (Luke 10:13-16).

Jesus' exuberant joy spills over into praise ("I praise" ἐξομολογοῦμαι Luke 10:21) of the Father, followed by the reason (*because* ὅτι) for his praise. Jesus' praise is grounded in the paradoxical double-contrast in which the Father "*hid* these things[284] from the *wise and intelligent*" and "*revealed* these things to *infants*" (10:21). This reflects his immediate (non-mediated) knowledge of the Father, and the way Jesus mediates the knowledge/revelation of the Father to them (Luke 10:22).

Who are these "infants" or "minors" (νήπιοι 10:21), serving as objects of divine revelation and pleasure? Clearly, they are contrasted with the *wise* (σοφός) and *intelligent* (συνετός) members of society. In Luke's context, the infants/minors are those who have been "unspoiled by learning,"[285] also identified as the missionaries who have been sent and have returned with joy.

The paradoxical hiding and revealing, understood as God's *pleasure* (εὐδοκία 10:21), falls within Luke's emphasis upon reversal. While Matthew's thanksgiving prayer[286] is followed by Jesus' invitation as revealer to his own (Matt. 11:28-30), Luke's thanksgiving prayer is followed by a joyful beatitude pronounced over the disciples, "How blessed/fortunate" (Μακάριοι Luke 10:23), which is grounded in their utterly privileged position.[287] The basis for their immense joy and privilege is explained (*for* γάρ) in 10:24, "*For* I say to you that many prophets and kings desired to see the things which you see and they did not see, and to hear what you hear and they did not hear." This paragraph includes several reversal statements,[288] highlighting the points of contrast and also affirming the blessed condition of the disciples' privileged and joyful condition:

	Contrasting Clauses	
10:21 10:24	"you hid these things" ἀπέ κρυψας ταῦτα "did not see" οὐκ εἶδαν "did not hear" οὐκ ἤκουσαν	"you revealed these things" ἀπεκάλυψας αὐτὰ "you see" βλέπετε "you hear" ἀκούετε
10:21 10:22	"from the wise and intelligent" ἀπὸ σοφῶν καὶ συνετῶν	"to infants\minors" νηπίοις and "to whomever the Son chooses to reveal" καὶ ᾧ ἐὰν βούληται ὁ υἱὸς ἀποκαλύψαι
10:23-24	"many prophets and kings wished to see" πολλοὶ προφῆται καὶ βασιλεῖς ἠθέλησαν ἰδεῖν	"you, i.e., disciples," "Blessed are your eyes, which see" Μακάριοι οἱ ὀφθαλμοὶ οἱ βλέποντες

Part of their privilege is participation in God's kingdom as co-laborers with Jesus. The urgency of harvest requires more missionaries, and thus Jesus tells them to pray for more fellow-laborers (Luke 10:2). "What was for the best men of the past only an object of faith and hope is now a matter of present experience."[289] They have been joyful participants in the declaration and charismatic expression of the holistic kingdom of God. They have been privileged with Jesus' name, endowed with power and authority, verbal declaration, exorcisms, and healings. Their experience as eyewitnesses of Jesus and their joyful mission in word and deed is understood as an immeasurable privilege. Their joyful experiences match Jesus' exuberant rejoicing "in the Holy Spirit."[290] In Luke 11, Jesus explains that they can ask for the Holy Spirit with full assurance that the good-natured Father will attend to their request (Luke 11:13). This promise finds initial fulfillment on the Day of Pentecost.

Luke intends that his readers feel the atmosphere, experience, and expressions of joy when the disciples are sent and return in their life-giving and joyous mission. Joyous effusion grips Jesus, the missionaries, and their beneficiaries. Most certainly, Luke draws no distinction between "external happiness" and "inner joy." All are elated over a charismatic incursion into human existence that spells new life and wholeness, when the good news of the kingdom of God is proclaimed in word and deed. Joyous affection is spontaneous, contagious, communal, and a proleptic celebration of a joyous future:

> Someone who knows that God will one day wipe away all tears, cannot with resignation accept the tears of those who suffer and are oppressed now. If we believe that one day all disease will vanish, we cannot but begin to anticipate here and now the victory over disease in individuals and communities. If we accept that the enemy of God and man, the devil, will ultimately be completely conquered, we cannot but begin at once to unmask his stratagems in the individual, family, and society.[291]

Healing a Crippled Woman on the Sabbath
(Luke 13:10-17)

Luke alone narrates the story of the hunch-backed woman, including it as a Sabbath-controversy story.[292] Luke subdivides the story into two historical progressions, each building to the climax of joy, first expressed by the healed woman, "she was glorifying[293] God" (ἐδόξαζεν τὸν θεόν 13:13), and then expressed by the crowd, "And all the crowd was rejoicing[294] at all the glorious/splendid things that were being done by him" (καὶ πᾶς ὁ ὄχλος ἔχαιρεν ἐπὶ πᾶσιν τοῖς ἐνδόξοις γινομένοις ὑπ᾽ αὐτοῦ 13:17).[295] Luke expresses a cause-effect relationship between the healing and joyous response (13:10-13) and the complaint and joyous response (13:14-17).

To this end, Luke mentions the Sabbath five times (13:10, 14—twice, 15, 16). He varies his description of the woman's condition: "having a spirit of disability"(πνεῦμα ἔχουσα ἀσθενείας 13:11), "for eighteen years she was doubled over and was unable to fully stand erect" (ἔτη δεκαοκτὼ καὶ ἦν συγκύπτουσα καὶ μὴ δυναμένη ἀνακύψαι εἰς τὸ παντελές 13:11, eighteen years in 13:17), "disability" (ἀσθενεία 13:12), "from this bond" (ἀπὸ τοῦ δεσμοῦ 13:16), "whom Satan has bound" (ἣν ἔδησεν ὁ Σατανᾶς 13:16). Luke underscores the woman's pitiful condition so his readers will feel the pathos of her long-standing disability, "to increase sympathy for those whom he heals."[296] Her plight also accentuates Jesus' power, enabling Luke to establish that Jesus is "Lord" (13:15) over the Sabbath. This appears to be a case of healing rather than an exorcism per se, yet her condition is attributed to a spirit (13:11) or Satan (13:16).[297] In a tender way, Jesus makes a radical statement about her as a woman, "this is a daughter of Abraham," a term that cannot be found elsewhere in the New Testament or Jewish writings.

Jesus assumes the initiative when he calls her front and center" (13:12). Her healing is immediate[298] and is mediated by Jesus' word, "Woman, you are released from your disability" (Γύναι ἀπολέλυσαι τῆς ἀσθενείας σου 13:12), along with his physical touch, "he laid his hands upon her" (ἐπέθηκεν αὐτῇ τὰς χεῖρας 13:13).[299] The effect of Jesus' words and touch is expressed by the verbal form, "she stood erect" (ἀνωρθώθη 13:13). Twice, Luke gives evidence that the synagogue president understood her restoration as a healing ("Jesus healed" ἐθεράπευσεν ὁ Ἰησοῦς 13:14), and "Come and be healed" (ἐρχόμενοι θεραπεύεσθε 13:14). Luke also describes the healing as a "release" or "loosing," or "freeing," using words based on the "I loose" root (λύω): "*you are released*" (ἀπολέλυσαι 13:12), "do *you* not *loose/untie* your cattle and donkey from the feeding trough" (οὐ λύει τὸν βοῦν αὐτοῦ ἢ τὸν ὄνον ἀπὸ τῆς φάντης 13:15), "was it not necessary[300] *to be released* from this bond" (οὐ ἔδει λυθῆναι ἀπὸ τοῦ δεσμοῦ τούτου 13:16).[301]

Jesus poses two rhetorical questions (with the negative, "not" οὐ οὐκ), which both expect the positive response, *of course*: "*Of course*, you untie your animals and lead them to drink!" (13:15), "*Of course*, it stands under the divine must that this woman be healed on the Sabbath!" (13:16). Luke intends that his readers agree with Jesus' logic and force. For Jesus and Luke, wholeness of life takes precedence over the Sabbath command.

Both the synagogue president and Jesus appeal to Scripture: the president appeals to the Sabbath command for people (Exod 20:9; Deut 5:13), while Jesus appeals to the thrust of Deut 5:14 relative to animals. In effect, the president affirms that animals are to be treated better than humans.

Further, Luke wants his readers to feel the force of his minor-major form of argument,[302] which exposes the hypocrisy ("You hypocrites Ὑποκριταί 13:15) of the synagogue president and all the opponents (13:17)[303]: "Since you untie your animals and lead them to drink on the Sabbath, how much more should you agree with the release of this woman, 'a daughter of Abraham' on the Sabbath!" The president cannot deny the miracle; however, he tells the people to come for healing on a different day—not the Sabbath. Luke also presents a temporal contrast between an animal that is "not loosed/tied/bound" for one day, while this woman has been bound for eighteen years. Luke pairs the female, "daughter of Abraham" (Luke 13:15) with the male Zacchaeus as a "son of Abraham" (Luke 19:9).[304] Jesus exposes their hypocrisy by their inconsistency—they are not playing by the same rules. Since they cannot deny the woman's healing and cannot contest Jesus' logic, "all of his opponents are shamed" (κατῃσχύνοντο πάντες οἱ ἀντικείμενοι 13:17), a strong expression in the first century. Those who seek to shame Jesus are themselves shamed.[305]

Luke's narrative purpose goes beyond simply describing Jesus' joy-less[306] opponents and the angry president (13:14, "becoming indignant" ἀγανακτῶν), along with the opponents' humiliation (13:17). The author uses the contrast to highlight the joyous response of both the woman and the crowd. Onlookers are won over not just by the healing, but also by the force of Jesus' argument. It is striking that the synagogue official directs his complaint to the crowd rather than to Jesus. He seems to want to draw them into shaming Jesus for his Sabbath-healing (13:14). By way of contrast, the crowd doesn't buy into the president's complaint. Instead, the crowd was rejoicing (ἔχαιρεν 13:17), not only for this healing but for all of the splendid things that Jesus was doing (ἐπὶ πᾶσιν τοῖς ἐνδόξοις τοῖς γινομένος ὑπ᾽ αὐτοῦ Luke 13:17); emotional language drowns out the petty complaints and "religious" shaming.

A Trilogy of Parables
(Luke 15)[307]

Joyous emotion flows through the entire chapter of Luke 15, in its setting (Luke 15:1-2) and the following trilogy of parables. The parables' primary feature is the "new union between the heaven and earth, with the celebrations of the one spilling over necessarily into the celebrations of the other."[308] The first parable is similar to Matt 18:10-14,[309] while the next two parables are unique to Luke. There are eleven explicit references to joy and almost as many implicit indications, e.g. singing and dancing. In Luke 14, the invitation to table-fellowship with Jesus embraces the socially and economically disadvantaged (Luke 14:13, 14, 21). In Luke 15:1-2, we find that table-fellowship with Jesus includes the religiously ostracized, which Luke emphasizes by the adjective *all* as he notes, "Now *all* the toll-collectors and sinners[310] were coming near to listen[311] to him" (15:1)—such joy is without conditions. This occasions the grumbling of the religious leaders[312] who say, "This fellow welcomes[313] sinners and eats with them," (Οὗτος ἁμαρωλοὺς προσδέχεται καὶ συνεσθίει αὐτοῖς 15:2). Jesus' hospitable and joyous welcome to the religiously marginalized is paired with his inclusive table-fellowship, "he eats with them." Luke's readers would appreciate the sacred and communal nature of table-fellowship. Luke provides three compound verbs that include the preposition, "with" (σύν) that underscore the effusive and communal atmosphere:

- "he eats *with* (συνεσθίει) toll-collectors and sinners" (15:2),
- "he calls *together* (συγκαλεῖ) his friends and neighbors" (15:6),
- "rejoice *with* me" " (Συγχάρητέ μοι 15:6)
- "she calls *together* (συγκαλει) her friends and neighbors" (15:9)
- "rejoice *with* me" " (Συγχάρητέ μοι 15:6)

The shared celebration by "friends and neighbors"[314] (Luke 15:6) opens up to the grand celebration in the third parable. Since the father is an authority figure, he barks out orders to the slaves to prepare for a joyous banquet: "bring out the best robe," put a ring and sandals" (15:22), "bring out the fatted calf and kill it, let us eat and celebrate" (15:33). The hortatory subjunctive, "let us eat" (εὐφρανθῶμεν 15:23) highlights the community celebration. Although the third parable does not explicitly include the compound verb, "rejoice with me, "nonetheless it is readily apparent in the various commands of the father, especially in the father's last statement, "Yet it was necessary[315] to be glad and to rejoice" (εὐφρανθῆναι δὲ χαρῆναι ἔδει 15:32).

The divine will corresponds to what "anyone of you would do" when faced with the loss of a sheep, coin, or son. The first two parables are introduced by rhetorical questions, that combine with the negative, "not" (οὐ, 15:4; οὐχί 15:8). This negative, "not," points to the certain and appropriate reaction, "Of course, this is that way that anyone of would act in the face of a found sheep or coin—and this will lead to the inevitable celebration of joy." The finding of things (sheep, coin) is then eclipsed by the finding of a son whose worth is beyond compare. In the third parable, the father's response to the younger son's return constitutes a communal and contagious invitation to share in the joy.

To fraternize and eat with toll-collectors and sinners implies hospitality, even camaraderie and acceptance around a common table. Jesus not only eats with them, but he extends an invitation of hospitality towards them, i.e., he accepts them where they are, without conditions. Eta Linnemann suggests, "This man takes pleasure in tax-collectors and sinners and eats with them."[316] Manson notes, "Morality prescribed that one could not even approach a wicked man to teach him the laws of God, much more was the close company of a meal ruled out."[317] The Pharisees and lawyers simply cannot accept Jesus' joyous and inclusive behavior. They operate on the maxims that "you can't touch tar without being tarred," or "birds of a feather flock together." The very word, "Pharisee," often implies one who is separatist and aloof from cultic defilement and societal outcasts; therefore, Jesus' joyful fellowship with the religiously marginalized leads to the joy-less grumbling of the religious leaders.[318] The older brother expresses his joy-less existence through legalist and slavish activity, "these many ways I've been slaving for you" (τοσαῦτα ἔτη δουλεύω σοι 15: 29). This attitude and behavior characterizes Jesus' critics in 15:2.

Thus, Jesus' three parables constitute Jesus' answer to the charge that he has crossed over boundary lines. Therein he justifies his behavior and interprets the joy of his table-fellowship with the marginalized. The compulsion of the shepherd, woman and father to share their joy with others matches the joyous table-fellowship that Jesus shares with the religious outcasts (15:1) and the corresponding joy in heaven.

Luke 15 is included in this study because of its preponderance of joy and its link with "joy in heaven" (χαρὰ ἐν τῷ οὐρανῷ 15:7), "joy in the presence of God's angels" (χαρὰ ἐνώπιον τῶν ἀγγέλων τοῦ θεοῦ 15:9)[319], and the manifest and contagious joy of the father who surely represents God as Father. These three parables point to joy in heaven, joy in the presence of angels, and the joy of the heavenly Father—the joy of the *eschaton*. Luke has already introduced angels in the annunciation and birth stories of John and Jesus. From Luke's perspective they are real and personal beings who belong to the numinous. Thus, we find that Jesus' joyous activity in v. 1 mirrors what takes place in heaven, in the presence of angels and the Father. Human expressions of joy parallel joy in the sphere of the numinous, as celebrations of the future.

Each parable presents a common structure progressing from the introduction of a central figure to the climactic celebration of joy:

- A central figure (shepherd, woman, father),
- Something or someone of value related to the central figure is lost (sheep, coin, younger son),
- A search (go after until it is found, lighting of lamp/ sweeping the floor/search carefully, father is in the memory of his youngest son and scans the horizon [from afar]),
- The object or person is found (he finds, she finds, was found),

- The recovery of what is lost must be celebrated with joy in community (shepherd's friends and neighbors, woman's friends and neighbors, the father's entire household).

The third parable is different in both length and detail, and in the discordant voice of the older brother. Neither the shepherd nor the woman in the previous parables faced dissenting voices complaining that joyous celebration is ill-founded. Once again, Luke contrasts the joy-less attitude of Jesus' critics (and the older brother) to highlight the major motif of joy through the atmosphere and words of joy that portray the merging of human and divine joy.

Ten expressions from the joy-vocabulary saturate these parables:

- "on his shoulders *rejoicing* (χαίρων 15:5),
- "*rejoice with* me" (Συγχάρητε μοι 15:6),
- "*joy* in heaven" (χαρά ἐν τῷ οὐρανῷ 15:7)
- "*rejoice with* me" (Συγχάρητε μοι 15:9),
- "*joy* in the presence of God's angels" (χαρά ἐνώπιον τῶν ἀγγέλων τοῦ θεοῦ 15:9),
- "*let us be celebrate*" (εὐφρανθῶμεν 15:23),
- "they began *to celebrate*" (ἤρξαντο εὐφραίνεσθαι 15:24),
- the father "*exhorts*" (παρακαλεῖ) the older brother to come in and celebrate (15:28)
- "in order that *I might celebrate* with my friends" (ἵνα μετὰ τῶν φίλων μου εὐφρανθῶ 15:29),
- "it was necessary *to celebrate* and *rejoice*" (εὐφρανθῆναι δὲ καὶ χαρῆναι ἔδει 15:32).

Other expressions in the third parable implicitly emphasize the joyous atmosphere: "the father saw the son from afar, felt compassion (ἐσπλαγνίσθη) and ran, fell on his neck and kissed him" (15:20), the father's interruption of the son's "canned" in that the father does not allow the son to complete his planned speech, the father's numerous commands that stress urgency ("quickly" ταχυ 5:22-23), "singing and dancing" (15:25). The divine necessity for celebrating is a fitting climax

(15:32, not only of the third parable, but it embraces the other two parables as well. It highlights the divine will for personal and communal joy; human joy is matched by heavenly joy.

Just as the joy-less older brother refuses to come in "out of the cold," is angry and disrespectful to his father, so Jesus' critics (15:2) can only respond with grumbling to the joy of Jesus' table-fellowship with toll-collectors and sinner (15:1). As such, they are bitter just as the older brother is bitter ("you never gave" 15:29). There is a clear contrast between the older brother's refusal to "go in" (15:28a) to the grand celebration and the father who "goes out" to plead with the recalcitrant brother (15:28b).

While repentance is mentioned in the first two parables (15:7, 10), repentance is not singled out as the event that occasions the finding or acceptance into the family fold. The text does affirm that the son "came to himself/his senses," (εἰς ἑαυτόν δὲ ἐλθών 15:17). [320] However, the son's return is motivated by his destitute condition. Out among the swine, he has indeed come to the end of his rope. As the son's' monologue continues, Luke reveals the son is not thinking with remorse about how he has injured God, divided and lost the family inheritance, violated his father, or given himself to prostitutes (mentioned by the older brother 15:30). Rather, he is motivated by his empty stomach, coupled with the memory of abundant provision of his father's servants. Even in his intended confession, his approach is pragmatic.

However, we may find more in the text. Severe hunger and abject poverty begin to make the son wise, even in his self-concern, and that initial motivation may become purified on his return journey home. Luke doesn't explicitly describe this change in attitude. However, the son's confession begins with the address, "Father," [321] which may explore the relationship which the son once enjoyed. He is open about his sin, above and below, "against heaven" and before his father. It is well known from rabbinic writings that heaven often substitutes for God. Biblical texts reveal their own supporting evidence, including the surrogate "kingdom of heaven" (Matt.) for "kingdom of God" (Mark, Luke).[322] Perhaps the light of repentance, incomplete as it may be, filters through his words. The concluding statements of the first two parables do include such mention, "joy in heaven or joy before the angels of God over one sinner who *repents*" (15:7, 9).[323] Certainly, the repentance motif is not uppermost, since sheep or coins don't repent. The father's compassion, grace, and joy over the recovered and re-instituted son reign supreme. The young man was lost and is now found, and he has been dead but now is alive. His worth is beyond compare. Thus, the communal joy is directly related to his new condition as "found" and "alive."

The son "plans to live in the village as a hired servant. With such a position his status will be secure. He can perhaps fulfill his responsibility to his father, and the problem of any relationship to his brother is eliminated. The village with its mockery will have to be faced. He will have to pay this bitter price in order to get home. He must go home because he is starving."[324]

The parable aims to justify Jesus' reception of publicly acknowledged sinners by emphasizing the fundamental principle that "God loves the sinner before he repents; and that it is this divine love that makes the sinner's repentance possible."[325] This is an occasion of the greatest joy.

For first-century Judaism, repentance prepared for the coming kingdom of God as a pre-condition for grace and joy. It provided away for a righteous man to prove his righteousness. Bornkamm notes, "So little is repentance a human action preparing the way for grace, that it can be placed on the same level as being found. Salvation and repentance have, however, now changed places. While to the Jewish ways of thinking repentance is the first thing, the condition which affords the sinner the hope of grace, it is now the case that repentance comes by means of grace . . . The tax collectors and sinners with whom Jesus sits at meat are not asked first about the state of their moral improvement, any more than is the prodigal when he returns home."[326]

The invitation to share in the joy is open-ended, for Luke doesn't reveal how the religious leaders responded after the trilogy of parables, nor how the parabolic older brother might have reacted after the father issued his invitation. The entire chapter serves as an invitation to joy, set in the context of the joyous reality part of the numinous. Heaven, the angels, and the Father celebrate in the joyous atmosphere of Jesus' table-fellowship with the religious outcasts (15:1). Luke intends that his readers participate in the communal and joyous celebration. Later in Acts, Luke will describe the early Christian church and mission, revealing a summons to celebrate the influx of Gentiles into the new people of God. More boundary lines will be crossed. Jesus' example of joyous and inclusive behavior in 15:1-2 will later see even broader fulfillment as Jews and Gentiles experience joy, once Gentiles are accepted among God's people (Acts 15:3). For Luke, Jesus' outward-looking approach models how the Christian community should be inclusive and joyful.

The Grateful Samaritan Leper
(Luke 17:11-18)

Luke alone narrates the story of ten healed lepers, contrasting the nine thankless Jewish lepers with the joyous gratitude and expression of one Samaritan leper.[327] Initially, the story accords with other narratives of Jesus healing individuals. Ten leprous men "stood at a distance" (ἔστησαν πόρρωθεν Luke 17:12)[328] from Jesus on a town's outskirts. All ten cry out for mercy[329] and address Jesus as "Jesus Master" (Ἰησοῦ ἐπιστάτα 17:13). Perhaps they had heard reports about Jesus' healing power. Instead of providing an immediate healing, Jesus tells them to follow the Mosaic prescription of going to a priest (a "health-inspector"), who would certify their healing so they could live as full-members of the community.[330] Luke says they were healed "as they were going" (ἐν τῷ ὑπάγειν αὐτοὺς 15:14), not when they were present with Jesus. Some level of faith was operative in them, for they leave Jesus without an actual healing.

Luke then focuses one leper and his joyous response:

- "seeing that he was healed" (ἰδὼν ὅτι ἰάθη 17:15),
- "returned with a loud voice[331] glorifying God" (ὑπέστρεψεν μετὰ φωνῆς μεγάλης δοξάζων τὸν θεόν 17:15),
- "he fell upon his face at his [Jesus'] feet giving thanks to him" (ἔπεσεν ἐπὶ πόδας αὐτοῦ εὐχαριστῶν αὐτῷ 17:16).

Luke suspends the shock-factor of this account until after the leper's healing and subsequent expressions of joy and gratitude. The shock is felt in the brief statement, "Now the man was a Samaritan" (17:16). This unexpected statement alters the force of the paragraph. Only the Samaritan, a religious and social outcast, returns with joyous gratitude. Extensive literature highlights the long-standing and bitter relationship between Jews and Samaritans.[332]

Luke accentuates the "other" condition of this leper: 1) Jesus was between Samaria and Galilee (17:11), 2) "Now this man was a Samaritan" (17:16), 3) "this foreigner" (ὁ ἀλλογενὴς οὗτος 17:18). Earlier, Luke records a similar shock in his story of the compassionate Samaritan (Luke 10:25-37, esp. v. 33). In the context of that story, the audience would have expected some other person, e.g. a Pharisee (layman), to act with compassion. Instead, the hated Samaritan traveler provides numerous acts of compassion for the half-dead victim, while the Jewish religious leaders pass by on the other side of the road.

In Luke 17, the other nine lepers (all Jewish) went merrily on their way to the priest for certification. The Samaritan leper, on the other hand, disobeys Jesus' command to go to the priest. Instead, he returns to Jesus, "praising God" (δοξάζων τὸν θεόν 17:15) and "thanking" (εὐχαριστῶν) Jesus (17:16).[333] Now he no longer "stood from a distance" (17:12), but he came into Jesus' very presence, prostrate at Jesus' feet. He drew close to Jesus with heartfelt gratitude for his healing from leprosy's scourge and bitter isolation. Luke accentuates his joyous affection. By way of response, Jesus asks three agonizing and rhetorical questions:

- "Were not ten cleansed/healed?" (17:17).
- "Where are the nine?" (17:17).
- "Was none of them found to return and give praise to God except this foreigner?" (17:18).

Luke's readers fill in the answers: Yes, ten lepers were healed. Obviously the other nine are somewhere else, but not here with Jesus; they've gone their way. Not one of them returned to praise God or thank Jesus for their healing.

Inextricably related to gratitude, joy is emotional, spontaneous, and contagious. Luke uses the joy-less attitude and behavior of the nine healed Jewish lepers to highlight the Samaritan's joyous return and joyous gratitude. Unexpressed joy is inherently wrong, or at least incomplete. No doubt, the other nine felt joy for their healing, but they chose not to express it in gratitude to God and Jesus.

At the conclusion, Jesus tells the healed Samaritan, "Get up and go your way. Your faith has saved you" (17:18). What constitutes the Samaritan's "faith"? In this context, trust means gratitude. Luke links Jesus' mighty acts to joy and gratitude; it is not merely a relationship of reciprocity, but it is like the flow of the circulatory system with its ongoing activity. The circular flow between a physical healing and grateful expression is destroyed when gratitude ceases to exist (the nine Jewish lepers). Joyous gratitude must be expressed. The healed Samaritan is a friend of the forgiven woman in Luke 7:36-50, who loves more, i.e. she is so grateful for the many sins that Jesus has forgiven (Luke 7:47). Her actions in the Pharisee's home vulnerably express her extreme gratitude for what Jesus has meant to her. Without gratitude, the circuit of joy is incomplete. We can ask the question about a Lukan connection between the Samaritan's joyous response with the Samaritan response of joy in Acts 8; is this something that Luke pre-figures?

Healing a Blind Beggar
(Luke 18:35-43; Matt. 20:29-34; 9:27-31; Mark 10:46-52)

The basic story, with variations, is found in the triple-tradition. In terms of geography, Matthew and Mark narrate the story as Jesus departs from Jericho (Matt. 20:29; Mark 10:46), while Luke informs his readers that Jesus was drawing near Jericho (Luke 18:35). Luke prepares the readers for Jesus' arrival in Jericho, where he will encounter Zacchaeus (Luke 19:1-10). The account of this meeting is unique to Luke.

In terms of biography, Luke notes one nameless blind man (18:35), Mark provides the name "Bartimaeus" (10:46), and Matthew speaks of two nameless blind men (Matt. 20:30). Matthew also doubles the story with another incident of Jesus healing two nameless blind men (Matt 9:27).[334] Mark and Luke describe the blind man as a beggar (Mark

10:46; Luke 18:35), while Matthew makes no mention of begging. Other variations occur:

- Luke includes the blind man's inquiry about what was happening with the movement ("noise"?) of the multitude (Luke 18:36);
- Mark alone mentions Bartimaeus' throwing his mantle aside as he responds to the crowd's report of Jesus' charge, "he is calling you" (Mark 10:49-50);
- Matthew's two accounts note Jesus' physical touch of their eyes (20:34; 9:29), while Mark and Luke only record Jesus' word of healing (Mark 10:52; Luke 18:42).

Aside from the variants, the stories are similar, e.g. the intensification of the plea, "Have mercy upon me/us,[335] Son of David," coupled with the attempt to silence the blind man (men).

More importantly, Luke provides a progression of events building to the joyous climax, expressed by the beggar "glorifying God" (δοξάζων τὸ θεόν Luke 18:43), and the crowd's joyous emotional response, "and all the people, when they saw it [the healing of blindness] gave praise to God" (καὶ πᾶς ὁ λαὸς ἰδὼν ἔδωκεν αἶνον τῷ θεῷ Luke 18:43). The blind man's joyful response parallels the healed Samaritan leper's grateful joy (Luke 17:15-16). Matthew's two stories and Mark's story find their climax in the healing of blindness, while Luke highlights the dual response of joy, both from the man and the people. For Luke, joyous affection is an important piece of the story.

This story is a fulfillment of the Spirit-anointed Messiah's agenda of "announcing good news to the poor" and "recovery of sight to the blind" (Luke 4:18).[336] The man is both a beggar and blind (Luke 18: 35). Jesus' healings and exorcisms are fueled by the Spirit's anointing. The man's joy is the direct effect of his immediate[337] healing, but there is more than the restoration of sight. His elation is also grounded in his growing insight into Jesus' identity. Luke offers a clear progression of terms by which he identifies Jesus: "Jesus the Nazorean"[338] (18:37), "Jesus Son of David"[339] (18:38), "Son of David" (18:39), "Lord" (18:41).[340] His happiness is also grounded in Jesus' statement, "your faith has saved you" (ἡ πίστις σοῦ σέσωκέν σε 18:42[341]), for Jesus honors the man's persistence in the face of an opposing group of travelers who try to squelch his cry for a compassionate healing. Luke does not explain why this crowd tried to silence the blind man. At the very least, this group[342] regarded the man and his cry as unimportant (18:39).[343] Instead of being silenced by the group's rebuke, the man's cry becomes stronger and more forceful (18:39).

Tannehill draws parallels with other Lucan stories wherein an obstacle is overcome in finding a cure (e.g. Luke 5:17-26; 8:41-56), "these obstacles also increase the readers' involvement in the experience of the person in need."[344] Luke draws his readers into the pathos of such texts and propels them to sympathize with the joyous cure at several levels. He intends for his audience to feel the man's persistence in the same vein. "Luke's version of the story creates a strong contrast between the immobile, dependent blind man and the mobile, assertive, privileged individuals who lead the procession as it approaches Jericho."[345] By way of contrast, persons such as the blind man "go beyond accepted and polite behavior to obtain what Jesus can offer."[346]

Luke uses the verb *I cry out* (βοάω) for the man's first cry, "he cried out" (ἐβόησεν 18:38) and also in the application of the Parable of the Widow and Unjust Judge (Luke 18:1-8), "for his chosen ones, who *cry out* to him day and night" (τῶν ἐκλεκτῶν αὐτοῦ τῶν βοώντων αὐτῷ ἡμέρας καὶ νυκτός 18:7). Just as the widow refuses to be put off by the recalcitrant judge, so the blind man refuses to be dismissed by the opposition. Further, the once-blind man does not return to his community in his healed condition, but "he was following"[347] (ἠκολούθει 18:43) Jesus in discipleship.[348] Luke contrasts this healed man with the rich young ruler, who sadly couldn't give up his exceeding riches to follow Jesus and learn from him (Luke 18:22-23). Since the healed beggar has nothing to leave behind, he follows Jesus in joyful discipleship.

The Triumphal Entry

(Luke 19:28-40; Matt 21:1-9; Mark 11:1-10; John 12:12-19)

Commentaries provide detailed analysis[349] on the four gospels' accounts of the event. Luke's version expresses a joyful theology in the explicit atmosphere of joy, joyful responses, and praise in Jesus' entry that are the direct result of Jesus' mighty acts (Luke 19:37).[350]

In terms of setting, Luke prefaces the Triumphal Entry by linking it to the previous Parable of the Pounds (Luke 19:11-26), with the expression, "after saying these things." The two units are analogous. Several items surface in this parable that bear upon the Triumphal Entry. For instance, in this parable, Jesus repeats kingly language:

- Jesus will correct the notion that the "*kingdom of God* was to immediately appear" (παραχρῆμα μέλλει ἡ βασιλεία τοῦ θεοῦ ἀναφαίνεσθαι 19:11).

- "a nobleman went into the far country to receive *the kingdom* and then to return" (ἐπορεύθη εἰς χώραν μακρὰν τοῦ λαβεῖν ἑαυτῷ βασιλείαν καὶ ὑποστρέψαι 19:12;

- the hatred of citizens (19:14) that is expressed by their delegation, "we do not wish this king *to rule* over us" (Ου θέλομεν τοῦτον βασιλεῦσαι ἐφ᾽ ἡμᾶς),

- "these enemies of mine who do not want me *to rule* over them" (τοὺς ἐχθρούς μου τούτους τοὺς μὴ θελήσαντάς με βασιλεῦσαι ἐπ᾽ αὐτοὺς 19:27).

Luke contrasts the citizen's hatred of the king and his subsequent rule with the joyful acclamation of the multitude of disciples during the Triumphal Entry, "Blessed is the *king* who comes in the name of the Lord" (εὐλογημένος ὁ ἐρχόμενος ὁ βασιλεύς ἐν ὀνόματι κυρίου Luke 19:38). When Jesus comes as a pilgrim to Jerusalem, "he is hailed as a king and prepares for his destiny, his passion, his transit to the Father."[351]

Though the crowd rejoices and pronounces blessing upon Jesus as their king, some joy-less Pharisees command Jesus to rebuke his numerous disciples for their celebratory blessing of his kingship (19:39). Thus, Luke describes an interchange between the citizen's hatred of a king (19:14, 27), the positive affirmation of Jesus' kingship by the multitudes (19:38), and the Pharisees' negative response, ordering Jesus to silence the multitude's joyful declaration of Jesus' kingly status (19:39). The hateful response of the citizens in the parable parallels the Pharisees' silence-command. Hatred will intensify when the religious leaders seek to kill Jesus (Luke 19:47) after he cleanses the Temple (Luke 19:45-47). For Luke, their joy-less prohibition serves as a foil to highlight the positive experiences and expressions of joy

The killing of the hostile citizens in Luke's parable (Luke 19:27) is later expressed in the judgmental language of Jesus' lament over Jerusalem, when he envisions the destruction of Jerusalem and its inhabitants:

- "your enemies will cast a bank upon you" (19:43).
- "surround you" (19:43).
- "hem you in on every side" (19:43).
- "dash you to the ground, you and your children within you" (19:44).
- "will not leave one stone upon another in you" (19:44).

The stone-imagery ("the very stones would cry out" 19:40; "not one stone upon another" 19:44), will be further developed in the conclusion of the Parable of the Wicked tenants ("the rejected stone has become the head of the corner" 20:17; "everyone who falls on that stone will be broken but when it [the stone] falls on any one it will crush him" 20:18).[352] Luke also mentions the destructive stone-imagery in the introduction to the apocalyptic discourse ("beautiful stones" 21:5; "not one stone upon a stone will be left which will not be destroyed" 21:6).

In Luke's introduction to the Triumphal Entry,[353] he highlights Jesus' prophetic directive to two of his disciples to find a colt,[354] its owner, and what to say to the owner (Luke 19:28-34; Matt. 21: 1-6; Mark 11:1-6). Several details comprise Jesus' prophetic knowledge:

- the geographical place where the colt will be found.
- its tied condition.

- its fresh condition (never been ridden).
- an upcoming question related to taking the animal.
- the confidence that the owner(s) will grant the request.

Matthew simply states that "the disciples did as Jesus directed them" (Matt. 21:6). Mark states that "they found a colt tied at the door . . . and they told them what Jesus said" (Mark 11:4, 6). However, Luke explicitly connects Jesus' prophetic knowledge and its fulfillment, "So those who were sent, went away and 'found it *just as he had told them*'" (εὗρον καθὼς εἶπεν αὐτοῖς 19:32).[355] The use of the colt for Jesus' triumphal entry no doubt alludes to Zechariah the prophet, in which great joy is linked with the king's arrival on a new colt.[356] Joy is the only appropriate response to such a visitation, which must not be silenced by the joy-less religious critics (Luke 19:39).

Luke alone highlights the atmosphere and expressions of joy, loud joy, based upon Jesus' mighty acts. He notes, "... all the multitude of the disciples began to rejoice and praise God with a loud voice for all the mighty works that they had seen" (ἤρξαντο ἅπαν τὸ πλῆθος τῶν μαθητῶν χαίροντες αἰνεῖν τὸν θεὸν φωνῇ μεγάλῃ περὶ πασῶν ὧν εἶδον δυνάμεων 19:37).[357] Luke uses hyperbole with the repetition of *all*: "*all* (ἅπαν) the multitude," or "the entire multitude," coupled with "*all* (πασῶν) the mighty works." The multitude surely includes recipients of Jesus' powerful benefaction, eyewitnesses, and others who have heard of his miracles.

Luke alone highlights the joyous atmosphere and expressions of joy in an explicit manner with the use of the verbal forms, "they began to rejoice" (ἤρξαντο . . . χαίροντες)[358] and "to praise God" (αἰνεῖν τὸν θεὸν), and the very public expression of joy and praise, "with a loud voice" (φωνῇ μεγάλῃ), and the physical act of placing garments on the colt and spreading the garments along the road (Luke 19:35-36).[359] Thus, Luke's atmosphere and expressions of joy are not only related to the joyful Triumphal Entry, but they are grounded in Jesus' "mighty-works," which are retrospective—looking back to the whole of Jesus' ministry, "now drawing to a close."[360] Luke establishes that "this is not a group encountering Jesus for the first time but witnesses of Jesus' previous ministry who have accompanied him for some time."³⁶¹ The various disciples have been the recipients or witnesses of Jesus' mighty works in some manner and now express their joy.

Luke draws explicit attention to Jesus' identity as king, "Blessed is the king who comes³⁶² in the name of the Lord" (εὐλογημένος ὁ ἐρχόμενος ὁ βασιλεὺς ἐν ὀνόματι κυρίου Luke 19:38). Matthew mentions "Hosannah to the Son of David" (Matt. 21:9); Mark does not refer to the king but does include a blessing upon the kingdom of our father David that is coming (Mark 19:28); John notes, "Blessed is the one who comes in the name of the Lord, even the king of Israel" (Jn 12:13).

Luke's declaration of Jesus' kingship is expressed through the language of one of Israel's Hallel Psalms (Ps 118:26 MT; Ps 117:25 LXX). The psalm is classified as an individual song of thanksgiving, in which the speaker (royalty) calls upon the community or pilgrims to join a festive procession to the house of the Lord in gratitude to God for delivering him (them) from some dangerous crisis. The Psalm features fifteen references to the joy vocabulary: "I praise" (ἐξομολογέω) in the LXX of Ps 117:1, 19, 21, 28, 29; "exuberance" (ἀγαλλίασις 117:15), "I rejoice with exuberance" (ἀγαλλιάω) in 117:23; "I celebrate" (συνίστημι 117:27); "I am glad" (εὐφραίνω 117:24); "song" (ὕμνησις 117:14); "I bless" (εὐλογέω 117:26-twice); "marvelous" (θαυμάστος 117:23); "I exult" (ὑψόω 117:16, 28).

Further, there are two references to "power" (δύναμις Ps 117:15, 16). The power (δύναμις) of God that leads to deliverance (Psa. 117:15) is consonant with the reference to "all of Jesus' mighty works" (πασῶν δυνάμεων Luke 19:37). The atmosphere and expressions of joy between Ps 117 (LXX) are analogous to the Triumphal Entry. The same Hallel Psalm that speaks about the rejected stone that becomes the arch-stone (Ps 117:22-23) surfaces in the Parable of the Wicked Tenants (Luke 20:17). As a whole, Ps 117 affirms the inseparable link between personal and communal gratitude and joy, which also finds a home in the communal and joyous response from the multitudes in the Triumphal Entry. In commenting on Psa. 118 (Psa.117 LXX), Hassell Bullock states, "Gratitude . . . throws the door . . . open and liberates the soul to thank God for what he has done and to share this spirit of grateful elation with fellow human beings."³⁶³

The joyous blessing of Jesus as king is further expressed by Luke's doxology[364] that echoes the earlier doxology, pronounced by the angels to the shepherds:

"Glory to God in the *highest*
    and
Peace upon *earth*, peace among
men who are objects of God's
good pleasure"
 	
Δόξα ἐν ὑψίστοις θεῷ
    καὶ
ἐπὶ *γῆς* εἰρήνη ἐν ἀνθρώποις
εὐδοκίας
 	
Luke 2:14
	"Peace in *heaven*
	    and
	glory in the *highest*"
	
	ἐν *οὐρανῷ* εἰρήνη
	    καὶ
	δόξα ἐν ὑψίστοις
	
	Luke 19:38

The first doxology pairs heaven and earth in celebration, while the second doxology is oriented to heaven—not earth. While the angels celebrated *"peace"* (εἰρήνη) on earth (Luke 2:14), now that very welfare appears to be restricted to heaven, for in the forthcoming lament over Jerusalem, the city and its inhabitants did not know "the things that make for *peace*" (τὰ πρὸς εἰρήνην 19:42). The seventy (-two) extended the gift of *peace* (Luke 10:5-6) to various households. Zechariah's song (Benedictus) concludes with the affirmation that John's birth will find its purpose, "to guide[365] our feet into the path of *peace*" (τοῦ καταθύναι τοὺς πόδας ἡμῶν εἰς ὁδὸν εἰρήνης Luke 1:70). In Jesus' lament, the expression, "the things that make for *peace*" (19:41)[366] is coordinated with the expression, "the time of your visitation" (τὸν καιρὸν τῆς ἐπισκοπῆς 19:44). Both "the things that make for peace" and "the time of your visitation"[367] are things that Jerusalem does not recognize: "Would that even *today you would know*" (εἰ ἔγνως ἐν τῇ ἡμέρᾳ ταύτῃ 19:41); "because you did not know" (ἀνθ' ὧν οὐκ ἔγνως 19:44).

Tannehill states, "These links make it highly likely that the narrator intends to connect the arrival in Jerusalem with the birth narrative in order to highlight the tragic turn which the narrative is now taking."[368] Simeon's prophetic word in 2:34 stated that the infant Jesus would become "for a sign to be opposed" (εἰς σημεῖον ἀντιλεγόμενον); thus Jesus will not mean *peace* for everyone (Luke 12:51—"Do you think that I came to give peace on earth?"). Jerusalem and its inhabitants should have recognized the things that make for peace and God's gracious visitation; however, in their deliberate rejection, "these things were hidden from your eyes" (ἐκρύβη ἀπὸ ὀφθαλμῶν σου 19:42).

The joy of the Triumphal Entry leads to tragic pathos, both in the silencing charge of some of the Pharisees, who seek to squelch the joy (Luke 19:39-40) and further in Luke's narrative of Jesus weeping over Jerusalem (Luke 19:41-44). Through his tears and verbal complaint, Jesus is emotionally involved in Jerusalem's tragic rejection of him and their subsequent demise.[369] Jesus' concern is not primarily related to his personal fate, but the city's fate. In addition to the repeated second person singular of the verbal form, "would that *you* knew"[370] (εἰ ἔγνως 19:42); "*you* did not know" (οὐκ ἔγνως 19:44), there are twelve forms of the second person singular pronoun, *you* (σύ) in only three verses.[371] Jesus weeps over Jerusalem and addresses the whole of Jerusalem in the singular, *you*. David Tiede links Jesus' sorrowful weeping with several OT prophets, "It is finally the sympathy of the suffering prophet, of Deuteronomy's Moses, of Jeremiah, Isaiah, and Hosea, caught up in the rage, anguish, frustration, and sorrow of God for Israel that constitutes the pathos of the story."[372]

This lament over Jerusalem echoes Jesus' earlier grief (Luke 13:31-35) expressed when he addressed the city, "Oh Jerusalem, Oh Jerusalem" (Luke 13:34). Jesus compared himself with a mother hen who desires to gather her chicks under her wings, all to no avail; the chicks scatter off and do their own thing. The passage includes two poignant uses of the verb *I desire* (θέλω): "How often *I desired*" (ποσάκις ἠθέλησα 13:34) to gather you," followed by the indicting statement, "you were not *desiring*" (οὐ ἠθελήσατε 13:34), which is also expressed in the Parable of the Pounds: "*we do not wish* (οὐ θέλομεν 19:14) this man to rule over us";

"these my enemies who *did not wish* (μὴ θελήσαντας) that I would rule over them" (19:27).

Joy courses through the Triumphal Entry, but the account tragically leads to willful and accountable rejection of Jesus and his kingly-status. The joy-less response of some Pharisees (19:39) will intensify in their murderous plot (19:47) and its execution, portrayed so vividly in the Parable of the Wicked Tenants ("let us kill him [the beloved son]" 20:14; "they killed him" 20:15). Sadly, expressions of joy and praise with a *loud voice* in the Triumphal Entry (19:37) are followed by the *loud voice* of those seeking Jesus' execution (23:23), with their *loud voice* prevailing in Jerusalem (κατίσχυον αἱ φωναὶ αὐτῶν 23:23). The welfare (peace) and joy Jesus offers through his life-giving mighty works are met with tragic rejection and the life-taking attitude and behavior of the religious leaders. Judgment will follow Jerusalem's willful rejection of her king (Luke 19:43-44; 21:20-23; 23:28-31). Joy and praise will be silenced in the following passion events; however, a Gentile centurion will break that silence at Jesus' death (Luke 23:47).

The Roman Centurion
(Luke 23:47)

In the crucifixion narrative, Luke joins the numinous dimension with a response of praise to God, voiced through the lips of the Roman Centurion. The climactic crucifixion scene moves towards its pinnacle in the responses from: 1) the Roman Centurion (Luke 23:47), 2) the crowd (23:48) and 3) Jesus' acquaintances, most notably from the women (23:49). Luke structures the three responses in a similar fashion:

	v. 47	v. 48	v. 49
Witness(es)	Roman Centurion	The assembled crowd	Acquaintances[373] & women,[374] following from Galilee
Verb of seeing	"when he saw" ἰδὼν	"when they saw" θεωρήσαντες	"seeing" ὁρῶσαι

	v. 47	v. 48	v. 49
Object which is seen	"what had happened" τὸ γενόμενον	"the spectacle" θεωρίαν "the things that had happened" τὰ γενόμενα	"these things" ταῦτα
Response to what is seen	"he praised God and said, 'Truly this man was righteous (innocent)'" ἐδόξαζεν τὸν θεὸν λέγων ὄντως ὁ ἄνθρωπος οὗτος δίκαιος ἦν.	"returned home, beating their breasts" τύπτοντες τὰ στήθη ὑπέστρεφον	"stood from a distance" εἱστήκεισαν . . . ἀπὸ μακρόθεν

A few questions are in order: What is the antecedent of "this thing which has happened" (v. 47), "these things which have happened" (v. 48) and "the spectacle" (v. 49) or "these things" (v. 49)? Why does the soldier respond with praise to God, coupled with his identification of Jesus as the righteous one?

If the antecedent, "this thing which has happened" only refers to Jesus' prayer of commitment in death, [375] following the language of Ps 31:5, then it is difficult to explain why the Centurion would praise God in the death of a righteous (innocent) man. The object of what the next two groups observe emerges in the plural form of the verb, "happen" (γίνομαι) and in the feminine plural participle, "seeing" linked with "these things" (ὁρῶσαι ταῦτα). Surely, the antecedent embraces the whole of the crucifixion event as narrated by Luke, including his special material— which the Centurion has witnessed. [376] Various elements of the story lead to the Centurion's declaration of praise:

- Jesus' prayer to the Father for the forgiveness of Jesus' enemies coupled with an explanation for why they should be forgiven, i.e. their ignorance ("they do not know what they are doing" (Luke 23:34).[377]
- The theme of Jesus' innocence that permeates the trial and execution (voiced by Pilate in 23:4, 14, 22[378]; by Pilate and Herod in 23:15; by the second criminal in 23:40-41[379]; by the Centurion in 23:47[380]) for a total of seven affirmations of Jesus' innocence. Jesus' innocence is highlighted by numerous responses of silence or near silence to the civil and religious authorities and the various mockers (Pilate v. 3; Herod v. 9; religious leaders v. 35; soldiers v. 37; the first criminal v. 39).
- Jesus' promise of companionship to the second criminal and the offer of Paradise—today (23:43), as this criminal owns up to his guilt and pleads that Jesus will remember him when Jesus enters his kingdom (23:42).
- A supernatural darkness lasting three hours in the middle of the day (v. 45) points to the numinous.[381]
- The tearing of the Temple's veil raises the narrative to cosmic proportions (v. 45).[382]
- Jesus' self-entrustment to the Father (v. 46 from Psa. 31:5).[383]
- Jesus' death, "breathed his last" (23:46).

While Luke mentions two explicit statements about the numinous (a supernatural darkness, rending of the Temple veil), there are other implicit references to the other-worldly nature of Jesus' responses. Who is able to pray for forgiveness for one's indirect and direct executioners and then follow with an explanation as to why God should forgive them (Luke 23:34)? Who is able to be silent without cursing or maligning his executioners? Given the repeated affirmations of Jesus' innocence, who can respond without self-defense? The other-worldly nature of Jesus' response is also evident in Jesus' joyful affirmation to the second criminal; in contrast to this criminal's statement about the future, "*whenever* you should come into your kingdom," Jesus states the language of the present *today*, "*today* you will be with me in Paradise" (Luke 23:42). How does this promise impact the Centurion? Who is this Jesus who can make such a promise of a shared and joyous fellowship in Paradise to a criminal in the throes of dying such a gruesome death?

A somber response of joy is evident in the Centurion's praise of God[384] grounded in his recognition of Jesus' nature. With the use of the adjective, "righteous" (δίκαιος v. 47), Luke may well express a double-entendre in that Jesus is both "innocent" and "righteous." Luke's seven statements about Jesus' innocence certainly lead to a reiteration of his innocence of any political crime. However, the predicate adjective, *righteous* is also consistent with Luke's use of the adjective, *righteous* (δίκαιος) both in Luke and Acts, in that Jesus fulfills God's will. "Jesus and not the religious leaders stands in the right relationship with God."[385] Nolland argues that Luke never uses the adjective, *righteous* elsewhere with the sense of *innocence*.[386] It is noteworthy that in the following burial scene, Joseph is presented as "a good and *righteous* man" (ἀνὴρ ἀγαθὸς καὶ δίκαιος v. 50). Clearly the term *righteous* does not mean Joseph's *innocence*. Luke's adjective, *righteous* is also used in Acts in reference to Jesus:

- "you have rejected the holy and *righteous one*" (Acts 3:14),
- "about the coming of the *righteous one*" (Acts 7:52),
- "to see *the righteous one* and to hear a call from his mouth" (Acts 22:14).[387]

Thus, the Centurion's perception of Jesus' nature, seen through the various scenes, leads to his expression of praise to God.[388] This Gentile centurion may well pre-figure the positive response of the Gentiles in Luke's second volume, notably in the Cornelius story (Acts 10-11). Similarly Joseph of Arimathea's positive response to Jesus' death may well pre-figure the positive Jewish response in the book of Acts.

The Centurion is paired with the second criminal who *really sees* Jesus' nature, and to a lesser degree, the crowd (v. 48), the acquaintances and the women (v. 49). The crowd returns home with great remorse at the tragedy, while the acquaintances and women *stand from a distance* (εἰστήκεισαν . . . ἀπὸ μακρόθεν v. 49)[389] In particular, these women who have witnessed Jesus' cruel death will also witness Jesus' burial (Luke 23:55) and the two angels' testimony to the reality of Jesus' resurrection. They will try to explain the truth of Jesus' resurrection to the unbelieving disciples, even in the face of a demeaning response of "nonsense" (λῆρος 24:11).

Thus, while the gentile Centurion witnesses Jesus in the throes of death, and all of the attendant events, he is moved to a joyful doxology, coupled with the affirmation of Jesus' righteousness. The stage is set for Jesus' post-resurrection appearances in Luke 24.

NOTES

220   Johann Blumhardt, *The Awakening*.
221   Matthew's similar statement (Matt 7:28-29) locates the people's response at the conclusion of the Sermon.
222   Pairing of "power" and "authority" carries over in Jesus' commission of the twelve for their missions trip (Luke 9:1).
223   Luke links verbs of command in Luke 4: 4:36—the crowd's statement about Jesus' command; 4:39—rebuke of a fever; 4:41—rebuke of many demoniacs who confess Jesus' identity.
224   Spontaneous witness also occurs in the leper's healing, "the word about him was spreading more" (Luke 5:15).
225   Luke notes the more general, "all those that were with him" (Luke 5:9), followed by the particular names of James and John, with their response of "astonishment" (θάμβος Luke 5:9).
226   Liddell Scott, 760. ζῷον is the noun, "living thing." BDAG, 341.
227   Tannehill, 204. Similar to Levi's call and other tax-collectors—sinners called to a new future (5:27-32).
228   The verb, "I forgive" (ἀφίημι) also compares to the "release" of the fever from Simon's mother-in-law (Luke 4:39) and Jesus' stated purpose of "release" (ἄφεσις) in 4:18b (twice). The paralytic is "released" from his sins.
229   Other mss. read "was present to heal them."
230   Barrett, 76.
231   Barrett75.
232   Nolland, 234.
233   BDAG, 615.
234   Luke 5:26; Matt 9:8; Mark 2:12. De Long unconvincingly argues that the joyous response of "all," means the religious authorities, 186.
235   Touching a coffin incurs one day's defilement (Num 19:21-22); by touching a corpse, Jesus would contract uncleanness for a week (Numb. 5:2-3; 19:11-20).

236　See the repetition of the verb, "I visit" (ἐπισκέπτομαι) in Luke 1:68, 78—with "heartfelt mercy of our God").

237　Beyer, "ἐπισκέπτομαι," *TDNT*, II, 604. The OT is replete with many such references in which God is the concerned visitor, e.g., Gen 21:1; 50:24-25; Deut 11:12.

238　Luke links this event with Jesus' statement in 7:22, "the dead are being raised."

239　Specifically with reference Elijah's ministry to the widow of Zerephath with the loss of her only son (1 Kgs 17:8-24); similar references will occur later in Luke's gospel in terms of power, prophet, mighty deeds, and rejection (Luke 7:39; 8:55; 9:42; 13:32-33; 24:19). Luke links "prophet" with "mighty deeds" and/or rejection.

240　Elsewhere, joyous report links "news" (ἦχος Luke 4:36) or "report" (φήμη Luke 4:14). See 6:17-19 for a similar converging of the crowd upon Jesus, for "hearing," exorcism of demons and healing, explained by Luke, "for the power (δύναμις) of the Lord was going forth from Jesus and healing all" (6:19).

241　Luke frequently pairs men and women in his narratives, e.g. the Roman Centurion and the widow of Nain in Luke 7:1-11; the widow of Zarephath and Naaman in Luke 4:25-27.

242　The meaning of the perfect passive participle "had been healed" (τεθεραπευμέναι 8:2). Earlier, Luke paired Jesus' healings and exorcisms (Luke 4:40-41).

243　Joanna appears to be mentioned, because she is a person of means ("wife of Herod's steward"), who is able to contribute in financial ways (8:3); she is also mentioned along with Mary Magdalene as a witness of the empty tomb and the angelic pronouncement (Luke 24:3, 4, 10).

244　Luke does not clarify whether Jesus' financial backing came from all the women or only a smaller number.

245　Luke 9:28-36; Mark 9:2-13; Matt 17:1-13.

246　Similar to Jesus' giving the widow's son back to her after his resuscitation (Luke 7:15).

247　In 9:1-6, Jesus gave the twelve power and authority over unclean spirits; apparently they had were successful as the seventy (-two) (Luke 10:17). It raises the questions, "Why were they unsuccessful in this instance?"

248　BDAG, 496.

249　Luke 9:43b-45; Mark 9:30-32; Matt 17:22-23. Matthew and Mark provide geographical movement (Matt 17:22; Mark 9:30), which Luke does not mention.

250　The imperfect tense, "he was doing" (ἐποίει) covers a wider sweep of time than the preceding exorcism.

251　Nolland, 513.

252　Luke 9:1-6; Matt 10:5-15; Mark 6:7-13.

253　Luke 10:1-12. External and internal evidence for 70 or 72 missionaries is equally divided. See Bruce Metzger, *A Textual Commentary on the Greek New Testament* (London: United Bible Societies, 1971), 150-151.

254　Luke 10:17-22.

255   Luke intends that his readership think of Jesus' formal choice of the twelve, "whom he named 'apostles'" (οὓς καὶ ἀποστόλους ὠνόμασεν Luke 6:13).

256   Luke notes that they are sent as an "advance-party" (Luke 10:1) to prepare the way for Jesus' visit, similar to Luke 9:51-56 when the disciples are sent to Samaria.

257   Interspersed within the two trips is Luke's narrative about Jesus' announcement of the kingdom of God (Luke 9:11).

258   The verb "I preach" (κηρύσσω) is used synonymously with "I announce the good news" (εὐαγγελίζομαι) and is linked with the content, "the kingdom of God," in Luke 4:42-44.

259   I follow Johnson's translation; the verb, "has drawn near" (ἤγγικεν) is paired in Luke 10:9 with the prepositional expression, "upon you" (ἐφ᾽ ὑμᾶς) in 10:9; thus, the meaning "has arrived," Luke Timothy Johnson, *The Gospel of Luke* (Collegeville, Minnesota: The Liturgical Press, 1991), 166.

260   David Burnett, *God's Mission: Healing the Nations* (MARC Europe: Send the Light Books, 1984), 129.

261   The pairing of "preaching the good news" and "joy" is thoroughly Jewish in nature, e.g., Isa. 52:7-9.

262   Senior, Stuhlmueller, 145.

263   Luke links "power" (δύναμις) and "mighty works" (αἱ δυνάμεις), effected in Chorazin and Bethsaida (Luke 10:13).

264   It is possible that the "authority" (ἐξουσία) given to the twelve (Luke 9:1), carries over into the report-back session of the seventy (-two) with the repetition of the verb, "I subject" (ὑποτάσσω) in Luke 10:17, 20. The authority that Jesus gives to the seventy (-two) is expressed in the subjugation of the "demons/ [unclean spirits]" (Luke 10:17, 20).

265   In the similar statement, Matthew uses the term "Spirit of God" (Matt 12:28).

266   Ceslas Spicq, *Theological Lexicon of the New Testament* Vol. I (transl. James D. Ernest; Peabody, MASS: Hendrickson Publishers, 1994), 427. Luke's readers might remember the way in which "peace" comes at the climax of Zechariah's song (Luke 1:79) or the angelic pronouncement to the shepherds, "peace on earth for people who are recipients of God's good pleasure" (εὐδοκία Luke 2:14).

267   W. Foerster, "εἰρήνη," *TDNT*, II, 413.

268   BDAG, 3-4, "a demonstrative joy." LS, 5, "express great joy, exult, pay honor to a god."

269   Jesus directly casts out demons while his missionaries cast out demons "in Jesus' name." In Luke 9:49, an exorcist who does not belong to the twelve casts out demons in Jesus' name. Mention of Jesus' name will surface in Luke's second volume, Acts: Acts 3:6; 4:10, 17-18, 30:5:40; 9:27.

270   Fitzmyer, 860.

271   Use of the Greek imperfect tense.

272   Understood by R. Bultmann as a "report of a vision." Rudolf Bultmann, *History of the Synoptic Tradition* (transl. John Marsh; New York: Harper & Row Publishers),

108. The same verb, "I was beholding" (ἐθεώρουν) is used in the LXX of Daniel 7, as preparation for an apocalyptic vision.

273   C. K. Barrett, *The Holy Spirit and the Gospel Tradition* (London: S.P.C.K., 1947), 64.

274   Their report of successful exorcisms compares with the charge to the apostles in Luke 9:1. The use of "serpents and scorpions" refers to the dangerous and malevolent forces that seek to injure or kill and are frequently found in the OT and inter-testamental literarture, also linked with other animals (Gen 3:1-14; Ps 91:13; 58:4; 140:3; Num 21:6-9; Sirach 21:2; 39:30; 1 Kgs 12:11, 14; 2 Chr 10:11, 14). See also. W. Foerster, "ὄφις," *TDNT,* IV, 579.

275   Fitzmyer, 860.

276   The use of a negated present imperative may be expressed as "Stop rejoicing," which directly refers to their initial joy over their successful exorcisms (10:17).

277   I Howard Marshall, *Luke: Historian and Theologian* (Devon: The Paternoster Press, 1970), 430.

278   Use of the perfect tense, "are written," or "have been written" (ἐγγέγραπται) connotes an abiding condition. The idea of God's book is found in Exod 32:32-33; Isa 4:3; Enoch 47: 3; Dan 12:1; Mal 3:16-17.

279   De Long, 221.

280   Or "same," the meaning of the intensive pronoun here, noted by BDF: "The article is sometimes omitted." 150.

281   Contra Fitzmyer, who argues that the verb "I rejoice with exuberance," in 10:21, is "purely accidental." 871. The text includes the three-fold use of the "rejoice" (χαρ—word family) in 10:17-20.

282   The verb, "I rejoice with exuberance" (ἀγαλλιάομαι) and related noun are frequent in Luke-Acts.

283   Menzies alludes to several LXX uses from the Psalter, where the verb "I rejoice with exuberance," 158. Menzies also makes a case for Lukan redaction of the Q passage "Jesus answered and said" (Matt. 11:25b) with "he rejoiced in the Holy Spirit and said." Robert P. Menzies, *Empowered for Witness: The Spirit in Luke-Acts* (Sheffield: Sheffield Academic Press, 1991), 178-179.

284   The demonstrative pronoun, "these things" (ταῦτα 10:21) surely refers to the disciples' successful preaching and powerful activity (αἱ δυνάμεις) by the 72.

285   BDAG, 537.

286   There are numerous articles and chapters devoted to this thanksgiving-prayer, Q, its use by Matthew and Luke, and its interpretation, but lie outside the focus of this study, e.g., Joachim Jeremias, *New Testament Theology* (transl. John Bowden; New York: Charles Scribner's Sons, 1971), 56-61; T. W. Manson, *The Sayings of Jesus* (Grand Rapids, MI: William B. Eerdmans Publishing Company, 1957), 78-80; James D.G. Dunn, *Jesus and the Spirit* (Philadelphia: The Westminster Press, 1975), 27-34.

287   Matthew places this "blessing" in the context of parables of the kingdom of heaven (Matt 13:16-17).

288 I have modified Green's chart. Joel B. Green, *The Gospel of Luke* (Grand Rapids: William B. Eerdmans Publishing Company, 1997), 423.

289 Manson, 80.

290 Shelton understands the expression "inspired by the Holy Spirit," i.e. in an instrumental sense, "by means of." James B. Shelton, *Mighty in Word and Deed* (Eugene, OR: Wipf and Stock Publishers, 1971), 88. The expression may convey, "in the sphere of the Holy Spirit," or "under the influence of the Spirit," BDAG, 260-261.

291 Bosch, 247.

292 It parallels the story of Jesus' healing of a dropsical man (Luke 14:1-6). Again, Luke parallels female-male stories. The two stories are bound together by: 1) Sabbath setting (Luke 13:1; 14:1), 2) Introduction of person, "And behold" (καὶ ἰδού) a woman (13:1) man (14:2), 3) Description of their physical affliction (13:11; 14:2), 4) Controversial healing (13:13; 14:4), 5) The use of the verb, "I release" (ἀπολύω) for both healings (13:12; 14:4), 5) Opposition by a religious leader: synagogue president (13:14), Pharisees and experts in the law (14:1, 3), 6) Jesus' use of the minor-major form of argument using animals (minor) to support healing of humans (major) on the Sabbath (13:15; 14:5), 7) Shaming of the opponents (13:17; 14:4, 6). A similar Sabbath controversy occurs in Luke 6:6-11 with the healing of the man with the withered hand.

293 The imperfect tense suggests the continued response of joy. The same verb, "I glorify" (δοξάζω) as a response to miracles is found in Luke 2:20. 5:25-26; 7:16.

294 Again, the imperfect tense is linked with the present participle, "he was doing" (γινομένοις) to emphasize their ongoing joy.

295 "Glorious things" (ἔνδοξα) parallels "wonderful" (παράδοξα) in response to the healing and forgiveness.

296 Tannehill, 92.

297 Compare with Peter's sermon to Cornelius, "healing all who were oppressed by the devil" (πάντας τοὺς καταδυναστευομένος ὑπὸ τοῦ διαβόλου Acts 10:38) as well as the "prisoners" (αἰχμαλώτοις) in Jesus' inaugural address (Luke 4:18).

298 The instantaneous healing is noted by the adverb, "immediately" (παραχρῆμα Luke 13:13).

299 Other references to Jesus' touch are found in Luke 4:40—the healing and exorcism of numerous people; 5:13—the leper; 8:54—Jairus' daughter.

300 The "loose" (λύω) word-family is contrasted with the "bind" (δέω) word-family. Luke's audience might sense irony with the use of the impersonal verb, "it is necessary" (δεῖ, ἔδει). The official says "it is necessary" (δεῖ) to work on six days but not work on the Sabbath (13:14). By way of contrast, Jesus says, "it was necessary" (ἔδει) for this woman to be released from her bond (13:16)

301 "Loosing" is compared with the repetition of "release" (ἄφεσις) in Jesus' Nazareth address (Luke 4:18), as Jesus' stated purpose. Tannehill compares the "release" of this woman with the "release" from the personal force of a great fever

that had constrained (συνεχομένη) Simon's mother-in law (Luke 4:38), 84. This comports with Isa. 58:6, in Jesus' inaugural address (Luke 4:18): "to loose the bonds of wickedness, to undo the thongs of the yoke, to let the oppressed go free, and to break every yoke."

302 In Rabbinic terms, "light and heavy," lesser to the greater/more serious.

303 Understood by Nolland as "You and your kind," 723.

304 The Zacchaeus story also refers to "joy" with respect to Zacchaeus' warm reception of Jesus, "he received him joyfully" (ὑπεδέξατο αὐτὸν χαίρων Luke 19:6) which is joined by Zacchaeus' "haste" (σπεύσας 19:6), following Jesus' command, "make haste" (σπεύσας Luke 19:5).

305 The important motif of shame carries over into Luke 14:1-6 with the healing of the dropsical man. The religious authorities are unable to answer (Luke 14:4, 6) Jesus' two rhetorical questions (14:3, 6). Though Jesus exposes their hostile intent (14:1), they are strangely silent. In Luke 11:53-54, Luke piles words together—all of which suggest the idea of a "religious hunt or ambush," i.e. "bitterly have a grudge against him, to besiege him with questions, ambushing him to entrap him in a mistake in something he might say." There is a probable allusion to the LXX of Isa 45:16-17, which combines the idea of "opponents," who are" put to shame," since the vocabulary is the same: "All that are opposed (πάντες οἱ ἀντικείμενοι) shall be shamed (αἰσχυνθήσονται) and confounded by him and shall go forth in shame (ἐν αἰσχύνη)." By way of contrast, Israel "shall not be shamed (οὐκ αἰσχυνθήσονται) nor confounded for evermore." Luke sees that this healing event is a fulfillment of Isa 45:16-17. Nolland, 725.

306 There is no hint of joy in the president's response—only his angry response that a healing takes place on the wrong day.

307 Extensive bibliography exists on this chapter (books, major chapters, articles), but we can only deal with the theme of joy set within the context of the numinous, i.e. heaven, angels and the Father.

308 N.T. Wright, 59.

309 Matthew's Parable of the Lost Sheep (Matt 1810-14) does not accentuate the theme of joy; rather he uses the parable to stress the community's need for restoring a wandering brother ("one sheep should wander\stray," πλανηθῇ ἓν ἐξ αὐτῶν Matt 18:12). The entire chapter deals with community life and relationships. Both the intent and message of the parable are different from Luke's version.

310 This group of people are responsive either to John or Jesus (3:10-14; 5:27-32; 7:29, 34—"Jesus is a friend of toll-collectors and sinners").

311 See the use of the verb, "I hear" (ἀκούω) in the final statement of the previous paragraph, "He who has ears to hear, let him hear" (ὁ ἔχων ὦτα ἀκούειν, ἀκουέτω Luke 14:35b). Johnson points to numerous Lukan examples wherein hearing is a sign of conversion, 235.

312 Frequently, Luke depicts the Pharisees and scribes as Jesus' opponents, e.g., 5:17-6:11; 7:29-30, 14:1-6; 16:14; 19:1-10.

313   The verb, "I welcome" (δέχομαι), means a broad and inclusive hospitality (9:53; 10:8, 10; 16:4, 9).

314   See the parallel use of the expression in Luke 14:12.

315   Luke uses the impersonal verb, "it is necessary" (δεῖ) to signify God's will that must come to pass (19 times in Luke; 18 times in Acts), much more than the other evangelists.

316   Eta Linnemann, *Parables of Jesus* (London: SPCK, 1966), 69.

317   Manson, 574.

318   Luke provides other references that register their complaint against Jesus for his table-fellowship with toll-collectors and sinners (Luke 5:30; 7:29-30, 34; 19:7).

319   Gabriel in Luke 1:19, 26; angels in 2:13-15; 9:26; 12:8-9; Acts 10:3; 27:23.

320   In the Hebrew setting, we should expect a term like shub "turn, turn back, return." Bailey calls attention to the Codex Bezae with the identical words ἦλθεν εἰς ἑαυτὸν, which, in the context of the ungodly judge, does not mean repentance. "He merely wants to get rid of the woman who is giving him a headache, so he changes his mind." Kenneth Bailey, Poet & Peasant and Through Peasant Eyes (Grand Rapids: William B. Eerdmans Publishing Co., 1976), 175.

321   vocative case (15:18, 21).

322   Mark 10:30; Ezra 9:6; Rev 18:20; Matt 19:23-24.

323   Heaven's residents participate in the joy of recovery.

324   Bailey, 179.

325   Manson, 57.

326   Günther Bornkamm, *Jesus of Nazareth*, (New York: Harper & Row, 1960), 83-84. The concept that repentance is a work which people do prior to acceptance before God is consistently found in the Rabbinic writings. Bailey notes how the Rabbis made use of Lam 5:21 and Mal 3:7: Lam 5:21 "Restore us to thyself, O LORD, that we may be restored! Renew our days as of old!" Mal 3:7 "From the days of your fathers you have turned aside from my statutes and have not kept them. Return to me, and I will return to you, says the LORD of hosts.' But you say, 'How shall we return?'"
       While God's grace was apparent in the gift of repentance, the Rabbis viewed repentance as a human work which assured one of God's grace and favor. Indeed repentance became one of the chief human activities which replaced the whole of the sacrificial system.

327   There are several points of similarity between the Samaritan's healing and the Elisha-Namaan story in 2 Kgs 5:1-19a and its message of God's inclusive concern and care for outsiders.

328   Since lepers are "unclean," the texts of Lev 13:46 and Num 5:2-3 limit lepers to outside the camp.

329   Similar to the cry for mercy by the toll collector in Jesus' Parable of the Pharisee and Toll-Collector (Luke 18:13).

330   Lev 14:1-57 prescribes a complicated procedure that follows the certification of a healed leper (14:2-3).

331 All ten lepers "lifted up their voice" (ἦραν φωνὴν 17:13) while the one leper raises a loud voice

332 E.g. the statement by the woman of Samaria that Jews have no friendly dealings with Samaritans (συγχράομαι), "use [vessels for food and drink]" John 4:9. On the other hand, readers find that Jesus and his disciples were rejected in Samaria (Luke 9:51-56).

333 Contra De Long who diminishes the Samaritan's thankfulness to Jesus, 190.

334 Matthew has a proclivity for "two," e.g. two Gadarene demoniacs (Matt 9:28), Jesus sitting on two animals upon his triumphal entry (Matt 21:7).

335 The same expression, "Have mercy upon" is voiced by the ten lepers in Luke 17:13.

336 A fulfillment of Isaiah's prophecy (Isa 61:1-3; 58:6).

337 As Johnson notes, Luke's frequently uses the adverb "immediately" (παράχρημα) "to signal the sudden results of a miracle, e.g. 4:39; 5:25; 8:44." 284.

338 There is discussion in the commentaries on the spelling and meaning of the term, all of which is inconclusive.

339 The Davidic link was introduced earlier as a royal messianic title (Luke 1:27, 32; 2:4; see also Psalms of Solomon 17). Later the Davidic son is used in a controversy story (Luke 20:21-24); Acts contains 11 references to David, all of which are contained in sermons.

340 By way of contrast, Mark's version uses the term "my rabbi" (ῥαββουνί Mark 10:51). Luke's use of "Lord" (Κύριε 18:41) should be understood in the full sense (Luke 2:11; 5:8; 13:23, 25).

341 The same expression is found in Luke (7:50—the grateful prostitute; 8:48—the hemorrhaging woman; 8:50—with Jairus; 17:19—the healed Samaritan leper).

342 Luke identifies them as "the ones in front" (οἱ προάγοντες 18:39), which is ambiguous. Is this a group which is spatially in front, religious leaders or disciples?

343 In contrast, Jesus recognizes the man's worth.

344 Tannehill, 93.

345 De Long, 191.

346 Tannehill, 115.

347 The imperfect form may denote his following of Jesus or it may be an inceptive imperfect, "he began to follow."

348 Luke uses the verb "I follow" (ἀκολουθέω) in numerous passages which are linked with discipleship (Luke 5:11; 9:23, 57, 59, 61; 18:22, 28).

349 The commentaries are filled with analysis of source(s), interdependence, redaction and form criticism, the use of the Old Testament in all four accounts.

350 "mighty deed/act of power" (δύναμις) in Luke 4:14, 36; 5:17; 6:19; 8:46; 9:1; 10:13, 19, which will later be promised to the disciples (Luke 24:49).

351 Fitzmyer, 1246. This is also supported in Luke 9:31 in which Jesus speaks of his "exodus" (ἔξοδος), which he was to accomplish in Jerusalem, followed by the statement in 9:51, "Jesus set his face like flint to depart unto Jerusalem, which introduces Luke's Travel Narrative, culminating in Luke 19:28.

352 Nolland notes, "The description of what awaits the city is a pastiche of OT texts that describe the taking in siege of cities, and especially of Jerusalem . . . parallels in Isa 29:3; Ezek 4:1-3.," 933.

353 The verb, "I draw near" (ἐγγίζω) is a key verb for Luke, especially as the Travel Narrative closes (Luke 18:35; 19:11, 37, 41).

354 Both Matthew and John draw an explicit fulfillment from the announcement in Zech. 9:9 (Matt 21:5; John 12:14-15); in Mark and Luke the motif at best is implicit. Discussion abounds about the nature of this animal, since different terms are used by the evangelists. Nolland alludes to Gen. 49:11, which appears to be speculative, 924.

355 I argue for Luke's emphasis on Jesus' prophetic knowledge (not omniscience) in "If This Man Were a Prophet . . . ." in *Journal of Biblical and Pneumatological Research*. Luke records a similar story in the Passion narrative, highlighting Jesus' prophetic knowledge concerning the upper room for the Passover celebration (Luke 22:13).

356 Zech 9:9—"*Rejoice greatly*, O Daughter of Zion! See, *your king comes to you*, righteous and having salvation, gentle and riding on a donkey, *on a colt*, the foal of a donkey" (χαῖρε σφόδρα, θύγατερ Σιων, κήρυσσει, Θύγατερ Ἰερουσαλήμ, ἰδοὺ ὁ βασιλεύς σου ἔρχεταί σοι, δίκαιος καὶ σῴζων αὐτός, πραῢς καὶ ἐπιβεβηκὼς ἐπὶ ὑποζύγιον καὶ πῶλον νέον).

357 See the use of the verb, "I praise," (αἰνέω) in Luke 2:13, 20.

358 The participle may be translated as an adverb, "joyfully."

359 Also a link with royalty as in 2 Kgs 9:14.

360 Nolland, 928.

361 Tannehill, 158.

362 See the same participle in Luke 7:19, with a connotation from Mal. 3:1.

363 C. Hassell Bullock, *Encountering the Psalms* (Grand Rapids: Baker Academic, 2001), 162.

364 Luke alone contains the full doxology; Matthew's version only states, "Hosanna in the highest" (Matt 21:9).

365 An articular infinitive of purpose.

366 Fitzmyer argues for a play on words between "peace" (*shalom*) and "Jeru*salem*": "The city, whose very name is associated with peace, fails to recognize what makes for its own peace—fails to recognize the bearer of heaven's peace, fails to recognize its 'king' of peace.", 1256.

367 Note the use of the "visitation" language in Luke 1:68, 78; 7:16; Acts 15:14, 36 and earlier comments. The term "time" (καιρός) indicates a specific season or opportunity (Luke 4:13; 12:42, 56; 21:10). "The season of your visitation" not only includes both Jesus' Triumphal Entry but the whole of the Jesus event. Due to their willful rejection, Jesus' positive visitation will tragically become a visitation of judgment.

368 Tannehill, 160.

369 Jesus' tears over the city will be matched by the tears of Jerusalem's mothers (Luke 23:26-32).

370 "An unattainable or unfulfilled wish." BDF § 359.1.

371 See, Tannehill, 160.

372 David Lenz Tiede, *Prophecy and History in Luke-Acts* (Philadelphia: Fortress Press, 1980), 78.

375 The same prayer is expressed by the stoned Stephen at his death (Acts 7:59). Luke's prayer of self-entrustment is a marked contrast with synoptic traditions, expressing Jesus' cry of abandonment (Matt 27:46; Mark 15:34).

376 Obviously, the Centurion is at the site of the crucifixion, not a witness to the torn veil in the Temple. However, Luke wants his readers to sense the numinous at work, even outside of the crucifixion site.

377 We should note that the existence of other manuscript traditions that exclude v. 34. For the link between guilt and ignorance, see Hans Conzelmann, *The Theology of St. Luke* (transl. Geoffrey Buswell; New York: Harper & Row, Publishers, 1953), 90-92.

378 "no crime" (οὐδὲν αἴτιον v. 4), "no crime" (οὐθὲν αἴτιον 23:14), "nothing deserving death" (οὐδὲν ἄξιον θανάτου 23:15, "no crime deserving of death" (οὐδὲν αἴτιον θανάτου 23:22).

379 "this man *has done nothing wrong*" (οὐδὲν ἄτοπον ἔπραξεν 23:41) in contrast with the just penalty of death for the two criminals.

380 "this man was righteous (innocent δίκαιος 23:47)."

381 See the figurative use of the darkness in Luke 22:53.

382 It is beyond this study to investigate the Lukan possibilities for "darkness" and the exact "veil."

383 The use of Psa 31:5 in Luke 23:46 adds the personal address, "Father." As Nolland notes, "where the psalmist entrusts himself to God in the context of life, Jesus entrusts himself to God in the face of death." Nolland, 1160.

384 Luke uses the verb, "I glorify, praise" in similar contexts (Luke 2:20; 5:26-27; 7:16; 13:13; 17:15; 18:43). See also Acts 4:21; 11:18; 21:20.

385 Nolland, 1159.

386 Nolland, 1158-1159.

387 These texts should be regarded as co-texts with Isa 52:13-53:12.

388 In Mark's Gospel, the Centurion makes the confession that Jesus is "a Son of God," based upon how Jesus died (Mark 15:39); in Matthew's Gospel, the Centurion also affirms that Jesus is "a Son of God," based upon his fear, engendered by an earthquake (Matt 27:54).

389 Perhaps there is an allusion here to Psa 38:12 and/or Psa 88:9. Earlier, Peter followed Jesus *from afar* (Luke 22:54).

CHAPTER 6

JOY IN POST-RESURRECTION STORIES (LUKE 24:1-53)

Were not our hearts burning within us
as he was speaking to us . . . ?
—LUKE 24:32 (NRSV)

Luke's post-resurrection stories portray people transitioning from fear to great joy when they experience the joyful wonder of the risen Jesus. Luke includes descriptions of people experiencing angels. Some encounter Jesus without recognizing him. Others do recognize him. And then Jesus' faithful followers learn of the promised Spirit and witness his ascension.

Luke caps off the stories with the climax of "great joy," matching the announcement of "great joy" to the shepherds at the outset of the Jesus-story. Luke invites his readers to ponder the wonder of these appearances and to joyfully anticipate the "promise of my Father" when they will be "clothed with power from on high" (Luke 24:49). Joyous anticipation and experience of the Holy Spirit is not reserved only for the initial community, but God intends for it to extend far and wide through Luke's community. These narratives climax Luke's gospel, preparing the reader for the author's second volume, which will show the risen Jesus continuing "to do and teach" (Acts 1:1) through the Spirit-baptized community.[390] Luke accentuates the emotions of all the witnesses to this once-for-all event of Jesus' resurrection.

Luke records four inter-connected narrative[391] units in which persons are emotionally engaged as they witness the wonder and joy of the Easter-Day events:

- the appearance of the angels to the women at the empty tomb (Luke 23:56b-24:12).
- a "recognition story" in the appearance of the resurrected Jesus to two travelers (Luke 24:13-35).
- an appearance story to all the disciples (Luke 24:36-49)
- an ascension story of Jesus (Luke 24:50-53).[392]

Dillon remarks, "Luke is not primarily interested . . . in the external time-framework of the paschal happenings, but in their inner unity and totality . . . and editorially condensed . . . in the schema of a single day's course."[393]

Luke's language is strong and affective, expressed through nouns and verbal forms as people process the resurrection:

- Movement from hopelessness (imperfect tense, "we were hoping" in Luke 24:21) to a marveling and qualified joy ("still disbelieving and marveling because of their joy" in 24:41), then followed by their "worship" and "great joy" (24:52) and "worshipping and blessing God" (24:52-53).
- "Fear" ("I fear" [ἐμφοβέω] in Luke 24:5 of the women and the disciples who are "afraid" [ἔμφοβος] and "terrified" [πτοέω] in 24:37; "astounded" [ἐξίστημι] in 24:22 used to describe the effect of the women's report.
- "Hearts *burning*" [καίω] in Luke 24:32
- "Perplexity/at a loss" [ἀπορέω] of the women in Luke 24:4.
- "I trouble" [ταράσσω], describing the frightened disciples in Luke 24:38.
- "I marvel" [θαυμάζω] of Peter (Luke 24:12) and the disciples (24:41) in the ascension story.
- "I bless" [εὐλογέω] in which Jesus blesses the bread in Luke 24:30, followed by three statements of "blessing" in the ascension

story, referring twice to Jesus (24:50-51) and once to the disciples who continually "bless God" in the Temple (24:53).

The intertwined stories intensify as they unfold. Confusion gives way to clarity, despair changes into great joy, disbelief transforms into trust and certainty, blindness gives way to sight and insight. An ordinary trip on a specific road becomes an extra-ordinary experience. Through this progression, Luke shows eyewitnesses becoming empowered testifiers, individual experiences combining to become a communal story, all leading to the fulfillment of prophecies from the Old Testament and from Jesus himself. De Long notes, "And particularly germane to our topic, when revelation occurs, both the divine revealers and the human characters who see, voice praise of God."[394] At the same time, De Long gives little attention to the importance of Luke 24 as the culmination of Luke's gospel with the ascension story that climaxes the post-resurrection stories in Luke 24—specifically as the movement from sadness to "great joy."

Both females and males transition in Luke's connected narrative. As Johnson reminds us, Luke "shapes a shared narrative," which also "shows at the same time a community in the process of formation."[395] Luke establishes that a joyful community awaits the promise of the Father when its members will be "clothed with power from on high" (Luke 24:49). Yes, they will be given a witnessing task to do, beginning in Jerusalem (24:47), yet they will witness out of their reservoir of "great joy."

Numerous scholars accentuate the interpretive role played by the angels and Jesus, who both interpret the Torah and Jesus' earlier passion pronouncements, as if this is the major factor for their progress in faith. For instance:

- "This is disclosed through a new understanding of Scripture" (Tannehill).[396]
- "Note the *fact* of the empty tomb does not itself lead to faith. It must be interpreted" (Johnson).[397]

- "Jesus' role is not only that of a hermeut for his followers. He must enable them properly to read the Scriptures" (Green).[398]

Yet these sources fail to consider the numinous aspect of these experiences. Emotional and charismatic experiences with angels or the risen Jesus should serve as the base for interpretation. This foundation can then be augmented by the dynamic interplay of the Old Testament (which Jesus interprets for them), the promised Spirit, and the community of faith. Post-resurrection encounters lead Jesus' followers to understand the prophecies in community.

The Empty Tomb
(Luke 23:56b-24:12)

In the first paragraph, Luke hints at the unusual nature of the women's[399] visit to the empty tomb, with the initial contrast between what they found and what they didn't find: "they *found* the stone rolled away" (24:2) but "*didn't find* the body of the Lord Jesus" (24:3).[400] Although Luke makes no previous mention of the stone that sealed the tomb's mouth,[401] nonetheless his brief contrasting statements alert the reader that something curious will unfold in the narrative, expressed through their *wonderment* ("at a loss" ἀπορέω in Luke 24:4). Clearly the women did not know what to make of this anomaly, for while they expected an intact corpse, they found no body.

In Luke's account, their confusion prepares the reader for their encounter with an other-worldly group described as "young men in clothes that gleamed like lightning" that "suddenly came upon them" (Luke 24:4). Luke later identifies these men as angels (24:23). The author's mention of "dazzling clothes" (ἐν ἐσθῆτι ἀστραπούσῃ in 24:4) reminds Luke's readers of Jesus' dazzling clothes, "his clothes became as bright as a flash of lightning" (ὁ ἱματισμὸς αὐτοῦ λευκὸς ἐξαστράπτων Luke 9:29) in the transfiguration. It also previews the appearance of "two men dressed in white clothing" (ἄνδρες δύο . . . ἐν ἐσθήσει λευκαῖς Acts 1:10) in Jesus' ascension in Luke's companion volume. The other-worldly nature of the angels' appearance is also conveyed through the verb "I approach, appear" (ἐφίστημι), "often with the connotation of suddenness."⁴⁰²

The immediate and emotive effect of this dazzling appearance is the women's "fear" (ἐμφόβων) and their physical prostration before the dazzling angels ("bowed down their faces to the ground" κλινουσῶν τὰ πρόσωπα εἰς τὴν γῆν in Luke 24:5). The angels rebuked the women with a rhetorical question, "Why are you looking for the living among the dead?" (Luke 24:5). Their statement is foregrounded in the previous verses, where the women are looking for Jesus' corpse (24:2-3).⁴⁰³ After an initial rebuke for looking for Jesus in the wrong place, the angels proclaim that Jesus' body is not to be found in the tomb, because *he has risen* (ἠγέρθη 24:6). "That 'he has been raised' is both a proclamation of the Easter message and explanation of the empty tomb."⁴⁰⁴ The angels substantiate their claim by reminding the women of Jesus' previous passion pronouncements (Luke 9:22, 44; 17:25; 18:32-33), which included the final affirmation that he would be raised *on the third day* (24:7).⁴⁰⁵ Luke notes clear harmony between the angels' command, "remember" (μνήσθητε 24:6) and the women actually remembering ("they remembered" ἐμνήσθησαν 24:8).

This numinous encounter leads to the women's spontaneous and joyous proclamation to the eleven males of the totality of their experience ("all these things" ταῦτα πάντα (Luke 24:9⁴⁰⁶). They described the appearance of angels, and noted the angels' proclamation about Jesus' aliveness and the fulfilled passion pronouncements. Luke names three of the women, and he also mentions several other unnamed women,⁴⁰⁷ who witnessed to the eleven about their experience. The eleven males did not welcome this joyful and positive declaration. Instead, they countered the women with a demeaning and chauvinistic response. Luke notes "they did not believe the women, because their words seemed to be delirious" (24:11).⁴⁰⁸ Luke contrasts the believing witness of the women with the dismissive attitude of the male disciples. It is revealing that they do not believe the women, but they accept Peter's report of an unrecorded appearance of the risen Jesus to him ("It is true! The Lord has risen and has appeared to Simon," Luke 24:34). Clearly there is a double-standard.

Although Peter is one of the eleven disbelieving disciples, nonetheless he must have seen a ray of hope, for he ran to the tomb, stooped down, and saw the linen strips (Luke 24:12).[409] Evidently, something about the women's joyful report prompted him to satisfy his curiosity. This implies that, to some extent, he took the women's report seriously. Green notes, "His behavior portends at least the possibility of a more full understanding of Jesus' message on their part."[410] Certainly his response is less than the dismissal of the women's account. Luke then notes that Peter "was marveling" (θαυμάζων) at what had happened (24:12).[411]

The Emmaus Story
(Luke 24:13-35)

The second post-resurrection story is a "recognition scene" in which two disciples make both a physical and spiritual journey. Luke introduces this pair as "two of them," inviting his readers to link this duo with the unbelieving eleven mentioned previously (Luke24:11). Their facial expressions, "sad or downcast look" (σκυθρωπός Luke 24:17), are verbally expressed in their loss of hope: "we were hoping (ἠλπίζομεν) that he [Jesus] was the one who was to redeem Israel" (Luke 24:21).[412] Clearly their hopes have been crushed, since Jesus was crucified and presumed dead for three days (24:21).

Luke accentuates several supernatural occurrences in this dramatic and moving story, some of which are initially unnoticed by the two travelers: *The sudden appearance of Jesus on the Emmaus Road (Luke 24:15) and Jesus' sudden disappearance from the Emmaus home (24:31).* While the pair initially supposes that Jesus' appearance is a normal event (a fellow traveler catching up with them on the road), for Luke and his readers, this is not an ordinary event. Luke notes this with the emphatic, "Jesus himself" (αὐτὸς Ἰησοῦς), coupled with the participle, "after drawing near" (ἐγγίσας) and the verbal expression, "was walking along with them" (συνεπορεύετο αὐτοῖς 24:15). Another sudden appearance of the risen Jesus will occur in Luke 24:36, where the disciples gather, when "he himself" (αὐτός) appeared. The counterpart of Jesus' appearance is his sudden departure after he is recognized, "he was invisible from them" (αὐτὸς ἄφαντος ἀπ᾽ αὐτῶν 24:31), again noted by the pronoun, "he himself" (αὐτός). This charismatic experience prompts the Emmaus pair to reflect on Jesus' words as he interpreted the Scriptures, taking note of their reaction to Jesus' initial appearance (Luke 24:15).⁴¹³

Luke harmonizes their eyes, "their eyes were kept from recognizing him" (Luke 24:16) and the counter-part, "their eyes were opened and they recognized him" (24:31). The passive verbs, "were kept" (ἐκρατοῦντο 24:16) and "were opened" (διηνοίχθησαν 24:31), should be regarded as divine passives, i.e. "*God kept* their eyes from recognizing Jesus" and "*God opened* their eyes to recognize Jesus."⁴¹⁴ This paradox is similar to the passion pronouncement, which was "hidden from" the disciples.⁴¹⁵ Dillon notes, "Only personal encounter with the resurrected One could produce faith in his person, hence the moment of recognition in the Easter story was punctually determined by the Will which had charted Jesus' course."⁴¹⁶

*The Emmaus pair identifies Jesus, "This man was a prophet,*⁴¹⁷ *powerful in word and deed before God and all the people"* (ὃς ἐγένετο ἀνὴρ προφήτης δυνατὸς ἐν ἔργῳ καὶ λόγῳ ἐναντίον τοῦ θεοῦ καὶ παντὸς τοῦ λαοῦ, see Luke 24:19). Luke has consistently used the term "power(ful)" (δύνατος) or "power" (δύναμις) to emphasize the charismatic nature of Jesus' ministry.⁴¹⁸ A similar use of "word and deed" finds its antecedent in Moses, "powerful in words and deeds" (Acts 7:22; Deut 34:10-12; see Acts 2:22). Jesus' power will be later expressed in the ascension account, with Jesus promising that his disciples "will be clothed with "power" from on high (Luke 24:49).

The women's report of their encounter with angels and their declaration of the aliveness of Jesus (Luke 24:22-23) joins with the visit of numerous others to the tomb (24:24). Luke notes the emotional effect on the disciples, including the Emmaus pair. "They astonished us!" (ἐξέστησαν ἡμᾶς in Luke 24:22). Although the pair are profoundly disappointed, their report of the women's experience ("vision of angels" ὀπτασίαν ἀγγέλων 24:22) reveals their glimmer of hope, which also finds support in the witness of numerous others who found an empty tomb (24:24), though the text makes no mention of additional experiences with angels. The witness of the women had a profound effect: "they astonished us/ they caused us to lose our senses" (ἐξέστησαν).⁴¹⁹

The meal in the Emmaus home reveals that Jesus the guest, becomes the host of the meal, wherein "he took bread, gave thanks, broke it and began to give it to them" (Luke 24:30). Although the two men do not immediately perceive the meal's significance, Luke leads his readers to associate their experience with Jesus' miraculous feeding of the 5000. He does this by repeating four verbs: Jesus *took* (λαβὼν) the five loaves and two fish, *gave thanks* (εὐλόγησεν), *broke* (κατέκλασεν) the bread, followed by the imperfect verb, *he was giving* (ἐδίδου) it to the disciples (Luke 9:16).

In a secondary sense, the meal may allude to the Lord's Supper in Luke 22:14-20, described using the same four verbs. All three contexts of "breaking bread" possess revelatory significance.[420] While the meal itself is commonplace, for Luke, his frequent comments about meals in both Luke and Acts lift these events to a higher plane. Jesus' table-fellowship with toll collectors and sinners (Luke 15:1-2) is congruent with joy in heaven (Luke 15:7) or rejoicing in the presence of God's angels (15:10). Luke has already devoted chapter 14 to the banquet theme, thereby informing his readers of the close parallel between the earthly and heavenly banquet and its attendant joy, "How fortunate (μακάριος) is the person who will eat at the feast in the kingdom of God!" (Luke 14:15)[421] The kingdom of God is the source of joy (14:15) and remains a constant invitation to an experience that is simultaneously shared between earth and heaven. Navone states, "Thus there are two banquets simultaneously in progress. It is only for those who accept Jesus with faith that the first banquet suggests the second . . . The eschatological dimension of the second banquet appears in its correspondence to the banquets of the messianic prophecies in which the perfect reconciliation between God and man is expressed (Isa 55:1-3; 65:13)."[422]

The Emmaus pair use affective language to describe how they felt on the road, "our hearts were burning within us" (ἡ καρδία ἡμῶν καιομένη ἦν ἐν ἡμῖν in Luke 24:32). Even though they were not fully cognizant during the journey itself, upon further reflection, they remind themselves of the emotional impact of Jesus' conversation. Their previous exhilaration now becomes fully conscious and meaningful, in the light of their experience with Jesus at the meal. The pair now shares joy.

Luke knits the shared experience of the Jerusalem disciples, the Emmaus pair, and an unrecorded personal appearance of Jesus to Peter (Luke24:33-35). Although the day has drawn to a close, the pair must return to the disciples, gathered in Jerusalem (24:29). They cannot wait till the following day to share their experience with others. Their joy is both spontaneous and contagious. When they arrive at Jerusalem, they are met with the joyful affirmation, "The Lord is really risen" (ὄντως ἠγέρθη ὁ κύριος),[423] supported by Jesus' appearance to Simon (24:34). In response, the Emmaus pair share their experience with the risen Jesus, both during their journey, and specifically, how Jesus was revealed to them in the breaking of bread (24:35).[424] Witness joins witness in this effusive and contagious celebration. Luke describes the formation of a new community as various individuals tell their joyful stories.

The Appearance to the Full Community
(Luke 24:36-49)

The third post-resurrection story narrates Jesus' full appearance to the disciples in Jerusalem while they were sharing individual stories of Jesus' appearances, ("while they were speaking of these things," in Luke 24:36). The full group now shares the experience together. Luke's story combines numinous elements with a full gamut of affective language expressing the disciples' response to the risen Jesus, e.g. their qualified joy (Luke 24:41). The text notes several supernatural elements:

Jesus' sudden and emphatic appearance, "he himself (αὐτός) stood in their midst" (Luke 24:36), corresponds with his emphatic appearance to the Emmaus pair ("he himself" αὐτὸς Ἰησοῦς 24:15). It also contrasts with Jesus' sudden disappearance from the Emmaus home ("he himself disappeared" αὐτὸς ἄφαντος 24:31).

Luke explains the reason for the disciples' initial terror, for they initially perceive that they were seeing "a ghost" (πνεῦμα 24:37, 39). Jesus effectively counters their error. Eduard Schweizer notes that the term "ghost" (πνεῦμα) here "denotes a shadowy, non-corporeal existence."[425] Jesus contrasts their initial perception with his emphatic, "It is I myself" (ἐγώ εἰμι αὐτός 24:39).

Jesus then explains why he is not a ghost (Luke 24:39-43). He emphasizes his real body with both structure and form. He mentions "hands and feet" (24:39), "flesh and bones" (24:39), "hands and feet" (24:40). Other verbal expressions underscore his physicality: "look" (24:39), "touch and see" (24:39); "you perceive" (24:39); "he showed" (24:40); Jesus' action of eating grilled fish (24:42-43) in a shared meal, in their presence.[426] These combined expressions identify the risen Jesus as the same person they knew in his earthly existence.[427] Their eyewitness experience in a private room will assist their public witness, "you are witnesses of these things" (ὑμεῖς μάρτυρες τούτων in 24:48).

Luke highlights Jesus' "with-ness" with the disciples in a different way (Luke 24:44) through a paradox. On the one hand, Jesus underscores his own physicality, "It is I, myself" On the other hand, Jesus reminds them of his passion pronouncements, "when I was still with you" (ἔτι ὢν σύν ὑμῖν 24:44). Jesus helps the community understand that he is still with them, but now in a new way. The resurrection has occasioned the transition from his earthly existence to his resurrected state.

In the same setting, Jesus promises the Father's gift, the Holy Spirit. When the Spirit arrives, the disciples will "be clothed with power from on high" (Luke 24:49). He links this promise with a command. When Jesus describes their life of witness (24:48) and their preaching activity (24:47), he also affirms the empowerment of the Holy Spirit, which will lead to effective witness in his name (24:49).[428] The same empowerment for Jesus' ministry (Luke 4:14; 5:17) and the needed power for the short-term mission trips of the disciples (9:1-6; 10:1-20), will characterize the Pentecostal community in Acts 2. Jesus says "I am about to send[429] the promise of my Father upon you" (ἀποστέλλω τὴν ἐπαγγελίαν τοῦ πατρός μου ἐφ' ὑμᾶς 24:49). Jesus' mention of the *Father's promise* in Luke 24:49 is linked with "the *promise of the Father* which you heard from me" (Acts 1:4). Luke unites the Father's promise with "being clothed with power from on high"[430] and the identified Holy Spirit.[431]

The disciples' mission, beginning in Jerusalem, will only occur after they have received the promise of the Father (Luke 24:49; Acts 1:4), expressed as "the gift of God" (Luke 11:13), and described as something that Jesus is "about to send" (ἀποστέλλω). Through this gift, Jesus' followers will receive empowerment to preach and work signs and wonders. Shelton suggests that Luke's promise anticipates the Pentecost event, which "was the pneumatic catalyst for the disciples' ministry."[432] This promise/gift will empower the nascent community for effective witness, "you are witnesses of "these things" (ὑμεῖς μάρτυρες τούτων, see Luke 24:48). The antecedents for "these things" include Jesus' post-resurrection appearances, his explanation of the Old Testament, and his own passion prophecies, including his resurrection *on the third day* (24:7, 46), in which he would "enter his glory" (24:26). Luke knits together Jesus' crucifixion, his resurrection, post-resurrection encounters, subsequent exaltation, and the bestowal of the Spirit's power. Luke's companion volume begins with the promise and gift of the Holy Spirit (Acts 1:4-5, 8; 2:33), wherein there is a "centrifugal missionary movement,"[433] originating in Jerusalem:

- "to all the nations, beginning from Jerusalem" (Luke 24:47),
- "from Jerusalem to Judea, to Samaria, to the ends of the earth" (Acts 1:8).

The progression of the disciple's affective responses is striking, wherein the gathered community moves from "terror" (Luke 24:37) to a joy that is qualified by disbelieving and marveling (24:41):

- "they were terrified" (πτοηθέντες 24:37),
- "afraid" (ἔμφοβοι 24:37),[434]
- "troubled" (τεταραγμένοι (24:38),
- "doubts arise in your hearts" (διαλογισμοὶ ἀναβαίνουσιν ἐν τῇ καρδίᾳ ὑμῶν Luke 24:39),
- "still disbelieving and marveling because of their joy" (ἔτι δὲ ἀπιστούντων αὐτῶν ἀπὸ χαρᾶς καὶ θαυμαζόντων 24:41).[435]

For Luke, Jesus' blessing of "peace" (24:36) contrasts with the disciples' initial response of terror (24:37), due to the community's faulty assumption[436] that they were seeing a "ghost." Jesus' explains why they were wrong

(Luke 24:39-43), inviting them to see (ἴδετε twice in 24:39) and "touch" (ψηλαφήσατέ in 24:39).[437] He "demonstrates" (ἔδειξεν 24:40) his physicality, his emphatic self-identification, "It is I myself" (ἐγώ εἰμι αὐτός 24:39). These implicit and explicit references to Jesus' physicality climax when Jesus eats a piece of grilled fish "in their presence" (ἐνώπιον αὐτῶν 24:43). As a whole, Jesus tries to dispel their "doubts" (διαλογισμοί) "with many proofs" (ἐν πολλοῖς τεκμήριοις, see Acts 1:3).[438]

Luke highlights the community's emotional response, "still disbelieving and marveling because of their joy" (ἔτι δὲ ἀπιστούντων αὐτῶν ἀπὸ χαρᾶς καὶ θαυμαζόντων 24:41).[439] Luke pairs two participles,[440] "disbelieving" and "marveling" (ἀπιστούντων αὐτῶν . . . θαυμαζόντων). Then he qualifies them, "because of their joy" (ἀπὸ χαρᾶς). The mention of "disbelieving" takes the reader back to the demeaning male response to the women's joyful declaration (24:11), while the mention of "marveling" hearkens back to Peter's response to the empty tomb and linen clothes (24:12). Although Luke qualifies their joy, his readers would reflect on his positive use of "joy" elsewhere in his gospel, when people experience charismatic events. In current use, the paradoxical responses express the idiom, "too good to be true." Johnson suggests, "Luke is portraying an *emotional* response which is so powerful that they are too overwhelmed to really 'believe' it in the sense of committing themselves to its reality."[441]

The Ascension Story
(Luke 24:50-53)

The fourth story records Jesus' ascension story (Luke 24:50-53), which is filled out in greater detail in Acts 1:9-11. The story is expressed in numinous terms, for Jesus is physically "separated from them" (διέστη ἀπ' αὐτῶν) and "is taken up into heaven" (ἀνεφέρετο εἰς τὸν οὐρανόν Luke 24:51). His movement is both horizontal and vertical.[442] His superior status is marked by his upward movement. Johnson notes, ". . . the 'withdrawal' of Jesus is not so much an absence as it is a presence in a new and more powerful mode."[443] As a consequence of Jesus' ascension, he can provide his followers the surety of the Holy Spirit (Luke. 24:49; Acts 2:32-33). His release of the Holy Spirit's power is conditional, based upon his ascension, "Since[444] he has been exalted at the right hand of God, and since he has received the promise of the Holy Spirit, he has poured forth this which you see and hear" (Acts 2:33). Acts 1 includes four explicit references to Jesus' ascension.[445] At the same time, Luke's companion volume reveals a forty-day period in which Jesus appeared to his followers, "eating with them and speaking about the kingdom of God" (Acts 1:3), prior to the ascension.[446]

Luke's story contains three references to the verb, "I bless" (εὐλογέω), which belong with Luke's joy-vocabulary:

- Jesus "blessed them" (εὐλόγησεν αὐτούς Luke 24:50),
- "while he was blessing them" (ἐν τῷ εὐλογεῖν αὐτὸν αὐτούς 24:51)
- "blessing God" εὐλογοῦντες τὸν θεόν 24:53)

The first two forms affirm Jesus' blessing for the nascent community[447] while the last form communicates the communal blessing of God.[448]

Other affective language expresses the community's response: "they themselves were worshipping[449] him" (αὐτοὶ προσκυνήσαντες αὐτὸν 24:52); "they returned to Jerusalem with great joy" (ὑπέστρεψαν εἰς Ἰερουσαλὴμ μετὰ χαρᾶς μεγάλης 24:52). In essence, great joy eclipses their sadness for the physical loss of the risen Jesus. This occasions their discovery that Jesus will be "with them" in a different manner. Luke's gospel, which begins with a preponderance of joy-vocabulary (Luke 1:14, 68; 2:10, 20, 28) is similarly couched with joyful expressions in the ascension story. Luke hints at the joyous experience on the horizon.

Luke highlights the progression from "disbelief" (ἠπίστουν Luke 24:11) to a qualified mixture of, "still disbelieving and marveling because of their joy" (ἔτι δὲ ἀπιστούντων αὐτῶν ἀπὸ χαρᾶς καὶ θαυμαζόντων 24:41) to an unqualified "with great joy" (μετὰ χαρᾶς μεγάλης 24:52), when a full awareness of their future grips the community.[450] Luke's musical score of the narratives in Luke 24 builds to a crescendo in his fitting climax of "great joy." Why are the disciples filled with great joy upon seeing the risen Jesus removed from their eyes? As N.T. Wright suggests, "Something is happening—something has happened—as a result of which the world is a different place . . . a joy resting on a foundation that, it seems, no trouble or sorrow can shake."[451] The disciples have seen the world change before their eyes with the post-resurrected Jesus. In light of that, they discover great joy with the anticipated grand promise of the Holy Spirit, when they will be clothed with power from on high.

Just as Luke 24 serves as the climax of Luke's gospel, the ascension story is the peak of the progression, already noted in the four stories in Luke 24. The community transitions to readiness for ministry in an atmosphere of great joy and blessing. Easter faith is knit with an atmosphere of joy as the community anticipates the Pentecostal experience. Not only do the eyewitnesses know what they need to know, but they draw from the well of joy as they await the promised Holy Spirit. This joyous chapter is set within the larger drama of God's saving purpose for humanity, which will be expressed through the Acts-narrative. In the words of Tannehill, the appearance to the disciples and ascension story represent both a *closure* of the story of Jesus, which is now over and an *openness* to the broader saving purpose of God, expressed in the book of Acts.[452]

Summary Comments on Luke

In comparison with the Synoptic Gospels, Luke invites his readers to experience joyous affection as observe people experiencing charismatic dimensions or divine incursions. At the outset, Luke draws his readers into joyous encounters in the annunciation and birth narratives of both John the Baptist and Jesus; the language is fully emotive. In Luke 1-2, joy not only characterizes the experiences and responses of various people to the other-worldly, but Luke provides the emotional atmosphere of joyous effusion that is spontaneous and contagious. Luke reveals his commitment to charismatic experience in a plethora of means—all of which lead participants and Luke's readers to communal joy in word and hymn.

Luke highlights the role of the Holy Spirit in Jesus' own baptism, temptation and subsequent experience of power, which then leads to Jesus' joyous declaration of his Spirit-anointed agenda in a Nazareth synagogue (Luke 4:16-22). Readers discover that Jesus' initial ministry of preaching the good news is set within contexts and responses of joy, as Jesus fulfills Isaiah's (and others) statements about the coming Messiah and Messianic age. Joy is the result of a holistic message of the kingdom of God that embraces both verbal proclamation and relief to those who are in needy physical conditions. Emotional language of joy embraces Jesus' holistic ministry to countless individuals, who are in genuine need. Many of Luke's stories lead to a joyous climax by both recipients and onlookers. In these stories, expressions of joy are contrasted with the joy-less response of Jesus' critics.

Joy is accentuated in the successful short-term mission trips of the disciples (the twelve—Luke 9:1-6; the seventy-two—Luke 10:1-12), which includes joyful proclamation, healings and exorcisms—all are expressions of power. The missionaries' joy elicits both Jesus' ecstatic exuberance in the Spirit (Luke 10:21). In the parables of joy (Luke 15), Luke's readers learn of a simultaneous joy of God that is paired with the contagious human joy—a joy that must be shared with others; it is a joy of the coming *echaton*. Jesus' triumphal entry is celebrated by joyous participants (Luke 19:23-40) as a result of Jesus' mighty acts (Luke 19:37). A Roman centurion praises God in a somber moment at the time of Jesus' death (Luke 23:47), which is positioned within powerful cosmic events.

In the four post-resurrection stories of chapter 24, Luke's readers discover that charismatic experiences build to the joyful climax in the ascension story and its sequel. The same gospel that begins with "great joy," announced by the angels (Luke 2:10) concludes with the community's response of "great joy" (Luke 24:52). The experience, atmosphere and expression of "great joy" in the ascension story carries over into Acts 1-2 by the numerous persons who saw the risen Jesus and eagerly anticipate the fulfillment of the Holy Spirit, identified as the "Father's promise" (Luke 24:49; Acts 1:4).

Luke intends for his readers and their faith-communities to feel happy when they read his stories. As an emotion, joy is not to be marginalized or trivialized, because it is integral to Luke's accounts. The Christian affection of joy is integrally bound to proper exegesis. How can people not be happy when they experience a charismatic event? How can a healed Samaritan leper not be happy when he is healed of leprosy's scourge and bitter isolation from the community? Luke's miraculous and joyful stories of Jesus' full-orbed ministry are also proleptic anticipations of the joyful bliss of the coming age. Experienced joy in the present is certainly central; at the same time, present joy will be fully eclipsed by the joyful bliss of the coming *eschaton*. This is God's dream for his people. The same joy in Jesus' ministry will also influence Luke's second volume when the nascent community experiences the same emotions as they witness to the joyful Jesus-event and its implications for all of humanity.

NOTES

390   Green lays out several parallels between Luke 24 and Acts 1:4-11, 832-833. Tannehill suggests the terms, "review" and "preview," 277.

391   Luke provides several examples of inter-connection: 1) The women's positive witness to the empty tomb, angelic appearance, and pronouncement (Luke 24:3-10), reiterated by the two travelers in Luke 24:22-24; 2) Three references to Jesus' passion pronouncement (to the women in Luke 24:7; to the two travelers in Luke 24:25-26; to the gathered disciples (Luke 24:44-46); 3) The repeated verb, "I open" (διανοίγω: of the travelers' eyes that "were opened" Luke 24:31; of Jesus who "opened" the Scriptures to the travelers, Luke 24:33, and the minds of the gathered disciples, Luke 24:45); 4) All paragraphs emphasize Jesus' aliveness (to the women in Luke 24:5-6; to the gathered disciples in Jerusalem in Luke 24:34, to the appearance of the "material" Jesus in Luke 24:39-43 and the ascension story in Luke 24:50-53; 5) Verbs that express "cognition" ("I remember" [μνημονεύομαι] in Luke 24:6, 8); "I interpret " [διερμηνεύω] in Luke 24:27 of Jesus; in a "recognition" story, ("I recognize" [ἐπιγινώσκω] in 24:31 of the two travelers who "recognize" Jesus, who also narrate how Jesus "was made known" ("I know" [γινώσκω] in Luke 24:35.

392   Discussions abound concerning literary structure (chiasms), source, and redaction criticism. Nolland compares the Lukan stories with the other gospels and notes "different streams of similar material.", 1180. For analysis and comparison see Nolland, 1177-1188; Fitzmyer, 1536-1543. Richard Dillon approaches the chapter from tradition- and redaction-criticism and focuses upon the Emmaus-story "in the itinerant charismatic mission to households where the rigorous precepts of

Jesus' mission sayings were carefully observed." Richard J. Dillon, *From Eye-Witness to Ministers of the Word* (Rome: Biblical Institute Press, 19780, 225.

393   Dillon, 181.

394   De Long, 244.

395   Johnson, 404.

396   Tannehill

397   Johnson, 387.

398   Green, 835.

399   Dillon notes how the women are connected with the events of Luke 23:49—witnesses of the crucifixion, 23:55-56—witnesses of Jesus' burial and their preparation of spices, which was interrupted by the Sabbath (Luke 23:56b-24:1. Dillon, 9-11. Dillon also makes a case for the presence of the woman-sinner in Luke 7:36-50, 12-13. He Dillon suggests that "The integrity of the women's experience is guaranteed by the earlier Lucan mention of their scrutiny of the burial (Luke 23:55).

400   The idea of not finding the body is reiterated in Luke 24:24, "him they did not see."

401   Similar to John 20:1; Matt 28:2 and Mark 16:3 are more explicit.

402   BDAG, 330. Dillon makes a solid case for an intentional link between all three stories. Dillon, 22-23.

403   See Acts 1:11 for a similar question from the angels to the disciples who look up into heaven (Acts 1:11), looking for Jesus in the wrong place. See Paul Elbert, "An Observation on Luke's Composition and Narrative Style of Questions," *The Catholic Biblical Quarterly* 66 (2003), 98-109. The rhetorical question is then followed by explanation and instruction. In Luke 24, there are six such rhetorical questions, which are foregrounded in the preceeding narrative (Luke 24:5, 17, 19, 26, 32, 38).

404   Nolland, 1190.

405   Luke 9:22 and Luke 18:33 explicitly mention the raising on the third day.

406   See the similar expression of the Emmaus pair ("concerning all the things that had come together"—Luke 24:14 and "these things" (ταῦτα 24:21).

407   See Luke 8:1-3 for a fuller list.

408   Luke has previously mentioned the failure of the disciples to understand Jesus' passion pronouncements (ῥῆμα in Luke 9:45; 18:34).

409   Some MSS do not include v. 12. For extensive discussion on the inclusion of v. 12, see Dillon, 59-68.

410   Green, 836.

411   For Luke, the verb "I marvel" (θαυμάζω) is frequently associated with other numinous events: Luke 1:21 —of the people who marvel at Zechariah's delay in the sanctuary; 1:63—of neighbors who marvel at the miraculous naming of John; 2:18—of the people who marvel at the shepherds' experience of the angels and the fulfilled sign of the infant wrapped in linen strips, lying in a manger; 2:33—of Jesus' parents who marvel at Simeon's prophecy; 4:22—the people

of Nazareth who marvel at Jesus' words of grace; 7:9—Jesus' marvel at the Centurion's faith; 8:25—of the disciples who marvel at Jesus' effectual command to the storm. Tannehill notes, "The reference to Peter in 24:12, if it is original, would help bridge the gap between Jesus' promise of Peter's special role in 22:32 and the first sign of his new leadership in proclaiming the risen Messiah," 279. See similar comments about the use of verb, "I marvel" (θαυμάζω) in Luke, by Dillon, 67-68.

412   Dillon notes that Luke intends that his readers interpret "Israel" in the sense of "all peoples" (24:47), 127.

413   The numinous aspect of the appearance and invisibility of Jesus is downplayed by Nolland, "There is no reason to think of Jesus being in 'another form' as in the later ending of Mark 16:12, 1201. Dillon draws a link with a similar link between Philip's encounter with the Ethiopian Eunuch, 112.

414   Pace Dillon, 104-105. Contra Nolland who argues that this is a "Satanic blinding," 1201.

415   "this word was hidden from them" (τὸ ῥῆμα τοῦτο . . . ἦν παρκεκαλυμμένον ἀπ' αὐτῶν Luke 9:45); "this word was hidden from them" (ἦν τὸ ῥῆμα τοῦτο κεκρυμμένον ἀπ' αὐτῶν Luke 18:34), both in the context of the failure of the disciples to "understand with insight" (συνίημι 9:45; 18:34) the meaning of Jesus' passion pronouncements. See also Dillon in terms of concealment and disclosure, 133.

416   Dillon, 105.

417   See earlier discussion on the prophet motif in Luke 7:16, 19ff.

418   Luke 4:14, 36; 5:17; 6:19; 9:1—a transferred power and authority to the twelve in their short-term missions adventure; 10:13—disciples' power over the enemy; 19:37—response of the crowd to Jesus' acts of power.

419   BDAG, 276.

420   See Luke 9:20-Peter's confession; 22:14-23—wherein Jesus explains the meaning of the Lord's Supper; 24:31—wherein their eyes are opened to see Jesus with new insight.

421   See Lyle Story, "One Banquet with Many Courses Luke 14:1-24, *"Journal of Biblical and Pneumatological Research* (Fall 2012), 67-93.

422   Navone, *Themes of St. Luke* (Rome: Gregorian University Press, 1971), 27.

423   The adverb, "really," (ὄντως) was also used of the centurion's affirmation of Jesus' righteousness (Luke 23:47)

424   Parallels between the breaking of bread with the 5000 (Luke 9:22; 22:19; 24:30) and in Acts (2:46; 20:7, 11; 27:35).

425   Eduard Schweizer, "πνεῦμα κτλ." *TDNT* VI, 415.

426   Perhaps an allusion to the fish in the feeding of the 5000 (Luke 9:16), noted with the meal with the Emmaus pair (Luke 24:30). On the expression, "before them" (ἐνώπιον αὐτῶν Luke 24:43, Tannehill notes that it implies "a meal shared with those 'before' whom one eats." Tannehill, 291. The expression is found in Luke 13:26.

427 Pace Dillon, it is rather speculative to simply argue for an anti-gnostic thrust., 195.

428 Their message includes a call to repentance (μετάνοιαν εἰς ἄφεσιν ἁμαρτιῶν Luke 24:47). Tannehill notes the positive aspect of repentance in Luke-Acts, "there are other passages that relate repentance to the joy of a restored relationship, a joy that excludes the demonstrations of sorrow normally associated with repentance" Robert C. Tannehill, *The Shape of Luke's Story* (Eugene OR: Cascade Books, 2005), 93.

429 The verb, "I send" (ἀποστέλλω) is a futuristic present, similar to the Qal active participle in Hebrew.

430 Perhaps a conscious allusion to Elisha's succession from Elijah—the transfer of Elijah's mantle, Elisha's request for a double portion of the Spirit (II Kings 2:9-14), and Elijah's transfer to heaven in a whirlwind (2 Kgs 2:11.

431 See similar expressions in Luke 1:35, 4:14; Acts 1:8: 2:33.

432 Shelton, 118. "as a fulfillment of John's Pneumatological prophecy." 119. See Luke 9:51.

433 Green, 857.

434 Used of the women in Luke 24:5.

435 A translation suggested by Johnson, 402.

436 The verb, "I think, seem, consider" (δοκέω) is frequently used with the infinitive following and suggests a faulty supposition—something that needs correction.

437 "no 'visual deception' was involved," Nolland, 1213.

438 Fitzmyer, 1574.

439 The preposition "from" (ἀπό) can also express cause (Luke 21:26; 22:45; Acts 12:14).

440 Genitive absolutes.

441 Johnson, 402.

442 The ascension is to be linked with Jesus' "exodus" (ἔξοδος), which he was about to accomplish in Jerusalem (Luke 9:31) and the language of Luke 9:51, "As the time approached for him *to be taken up to heaven*." Just as Luke's gospel begins and concludes with Jerusalem, so the book of Acts begins in the Jerusalem setting.

443 Johnson, 406.

444 The participles, "having been exalted" (ὑψωθείς) and "having received" (λαβών) are causal and are assumed as true, thus the translation, "since."

445 "he was taken up" (ἀνελήμφη Acts 1:2), "he was taken up" (ἐπήρθη Acts 1:9), "This Jesus, the one who was taken up" (οὗτος ὁ Ἰησοῦς ὁ ἀνελημφθεὶς Acts 1:11), "he was taken up" (ἀνελήμφθη Acts 1:22).

446 Similar language is found in Acts 10:41.

447 Green notes the parallel "blessing" in other leave-takings, e.g., Abraham in Gen 49 or Moses in Deut 33, Green 861.

448 Several scholars point to the allusion and parallelism with Sirach 50:20-22, "he lifted up his hand . . . to give a blessing . . . in worship . . . bless God." Nolland,

1227. Luke's birth narratives link joy, blessing, and praise (Luke 1:14, 64, 68; 2:10, 20, 28, 37).

449   The first occurrence of "worship" in Luke that is used of the disciples.

450   The "certainty" (ἀσφάλεια) of Luke's prologue that is integral to Luke's purpose (Luke 1:4) is brought to its conclusion in the ascension story.

451   N. T. Wright, 40.

452   Tannehill, 298.

CHAPTER 7

JOYFUL ENCOUNTERS
IN ACTS

The power of the Spirit flooded my being and I
broke forth in tongues for the first time in my experience . . .
A definite experience of boundless love and joy filled me,
a joy I cannot express, a joy unspeakable and full of glory,
for I felt like singing and praising God continually.
–HOWARD CARTER (CITED BY VINSON SYNAN)

How does Luke frame his stories of people who experience the wonder of the Jesus-event and the gift of the Holy Spirit? Luke presents the initial Pentecost story, followed by several other Pentecostal stories, recounting a powerful witness with attendant joy. Acts invites the reader to visualize joy-propelled witness through the courageous and powerful witnesses of Peter, Philip, and Paul. Luke's text couples their words and actions with the happy and ecstatic responses of people who experience God's power in personal and communal life. Through numerous climaxes of joy, Luke anticipates that his readers will feel the joy of a Spirit-filled life, community, and witness.

The Initial Pentecost Story[453]
(Acts 1:1-2:47)
In preparation for the initial Pentecost story, Luke links Jesus' post-resurrection stories and ascension story in Luke 24 with the similar narrative in Acts 1, offering a variant account of the same event. Several scholars, notably Charles Talbert, call attention to parallels between the two accounts.[454] Certainly Luke is not adverse to repetition.[455]

Luke's readers would sense the broad movement of Acts 1:1-2:47 in terms of inter-connected events, speeches, and themes—a sequential progression from: Jesus' ministry > his crucifixion > resurrection > post-resurrection appearances > angels > ascension > exaltation > reception of the gift of the Holy Spirit > pouring forth > charismatic experience > witness > human responses of confusion, marvel, trust, reception, repentance, and joy, with attention to inclusion, unity, and shared meals. Individual pieces of the story cannot be understood apart from Luke's all-encompassing flow of events and themes that are dynamically interrelated. For example, the gift of tongues must be viewed against Luke's broad canvas.

In support of this progression, Luke mentions Jesus' crucifixion/ death three times[456] and refers to the resurrection five times.[457] He describes four post-resurrection appearances [458] and one appearance of angels.[459] Six times he refers to the ascension,[460] makes four comments about Jesus' exaltation,[461] refers twelve times to the Holy Spirit,[462] gives nineteen indications of charismatic experience,[463] and five references to "witness."[464] Luke also emphasizes the human responses of confusion and marvel,[465] reception/trust, repentance and the gift of the Holy Spirit.[466]

Happiness permeates the narrative in the experience, atmosphere and expressions of the nascent community. Luke draws attention to inclusion[467] and importance of true community,[468] also expressed in shared meals.[469] Luke also establishes sequential events that progressed in a causative manner. For example, because Jesus has been exalted, he is not only able to receive the promise of the Holy Spirit, but he also "pours forth what you see and hear" (2:33), i.e. the miracle of tongues. Events and themes are intertwined in the narrative and speech. Luke's progression is a complete package. He intends to draw his readers into the joyous atmosphere through their shared imagination. He invites them to experience the same encounter with the Holy Spirit and to express the same joyful emotions.

Joyously setting the stage for the ascension (Acts 1:1-11). In his introduction, Luke focuses on the unfolding of supernatural elements, which represent an "in-breaking of the divine,"[470] and lead to joyous anticipation and fulfillment. His mention of "all that Jesus began to do and teach" (Acts

1:1) certainly includes Jesus' miraculous activity in his pre-crucifixion ministry. But it also intimates that Jesus will "continue" *to do and teach* through the Spirit-led community, which is empowered to both speak and act for God. Jesus' instructions to the apostles are inspired "through the Holy Spirit" (Acts 1:2).[471]

Numinous post-resurrection appearances affirm Jesus' "aliveness" ("as living" ζῶντα 1:3; "appearing to them over a period of forty days" 1:3). In addition, these appearances are substantiated by his "many convincing proofs" (ἐν πολλοῖς τεκμηρίοις 1:3).[472] Such "proofs" surely include Jesus' post-resurrection physicality, emphasized in Luke 24:39-43, "It is I myself" (ἐγώ εἰμι αὐτός Luke 24:39). Per Luke, his physicality is also expressed by the "shared eating" ("eating with them"[473] συναλιζόμενος . . . αὐτοῖς Acts 1:4). In context, meals themselves are occasions of joy.

The participial expression "appearing to them" (ὀπτανόμενος αὐτοῖς 1:3) depicts a real appearance,[474] not a vision. In Luke 24, Jesus' post-resurrection appearances yield responses of "marvel" and "joy," even "great joy." Luke's mention of the ascension (Acts 1:2) previews the narrative in Acts 1:9-11. Surely he looks back to his gospel when he refers to instructions concerning God's kingdom (1:3). His previous work linked the kingdom of God with verbal proclamation, miraculous power, and joy (Luke 8:1-3—with women; 9:1-2—with the twelve; 10:8-9—with the seventy [two]). This passage at the beginning of Acts, which includes Luke's remark about the kingdom of God, "not only gives the content of the conversation but prepares for the disciples' question about the kingdom (v. 6)."[475]

A joyous and familial promise (Acts 1:4-5). Luke highlights the baptism in the Holy Spirit (1:4-5), first identified as "the promise of the Father" (τὴν ἐπαγγελίαν τοῦ πατρός Acts 1:4)[476] and the sphere of the community's baptism (1:5).[477] The words in Acts 1:5 directly relate to the Baptist's contrast between a present literal baptism and the future more-figurative baptism (Luke 3:16):

"I baptize you with water ... "
"... he himself will baptize you in the Holy Spirit and fire."

In Acts 1:5, the Baptist's earlier promise now becomes Jesus' promise, "which you heard from *me*" (ἥν ἠκούσατέ με Acts 1:4). This implies that Jesus made a promise during his ministry, but it was not recorded in the narratives about him. In his gospel, Luke links the Baptist's promise (Luke 3:16) with Jesus' own Pentecostal baptism (Luke 3:21-22; 4:1, 4, 18), and with Jesus' promise of the gift of the Holy Spirit to those who ask him (Luke 11:13). The promise is restated in Acts 1:5. The initial fulfillment is recorded in Acts 2:1-4 on the Day of Pentecost, but the promise is open-ended, reaching beyond this initial experience.[478] Tannehill states, "The importance of Luke 11:13 for the Lukan image of the Spirit is indicated by calling the Spirit the promise of the *Father* in Luke 24:49 and Acts 1:4 ... The importance of Luke 11:13 is also shown by the repeated references in Acts to the Spirit as God's 'gift' (2:38; 8:20; 10:45; 11:17; cf. 5:32)."[479]

Jesus' earlier promise was encased within the warm relationship of a father to a son; certainly, a human father will not give anything dangerous (snake, scorpion) to his son who asks for a life-giving fish or an egg (Luke 11:11-12). Within the happy, secure, and life-giving relationship between the Father and his son/daughter, the Father will give the promise and gift of the Holy Spirit. "The Spirit ... is more than the necessary means to fulfill a task ... is part of a close family relationship with God ... Thus the Spirit is not merely a means to an end but part of the blessings of salvation, and is listed as such in 2:38-40."[480]

Certainly, the theme of witness is prominent in Acts 1:8. The full picture, though, reveals an empowered witness flowing from a warm family relationship with the Father. This relationship is celebrated with a joyous community that anticipates (and will experience) supernatural events of Luke 24 and Acts 1-2. In both chapters, contagious joy must be shared. Specifically, the Holy Spirit is not an impersonal force. He is a gift/promise[481] for God's new family. Thus, the full picture reveals that God is not utilitarian, simply empowering people to get his task done. Rather, he is relational. This understanding paints the apostle's ministry as a contagious outgrowth of a dynamic, loving, and relational bond.

While Haya-Prats does recognize the utilitarian-historical aspect of the Holy Spirit, nonetheless he affirms, "Luke knows also some of the rapturous effects that anticipate celestial fullness—joy, glossolalia as exultant praise—and the reader can see at the very least in these joyous gifts a confirmation of the divine presence."[482] Further, he notes, "Perhaps it is possible to advance a step further and arrive at the deduction that the joyful, eschatological aspect is more important, even in Acts, than the utilitarian-historical aspect in spite of the author's insistence on the latter, owing to the practical character of his work."[483]

The promised Holy Spirit "in a few days" (Acts 1:5) occasions the disciples' expectation of an immediate and narrow restoration of the kingdom to Israel ("is it at this time?" Acts 1:6) 1:6). Jesus provides no direct answer to the disciples' immediate and narrow question.[484] Instead, he offers both a joyous promise and a command in 1:8: "but you will receive power, when the Holy Spirit comes *upon* you and you shall be my witnesses ..." (ἀλλὰ λήμψεσθε δύναμιν ἐπελθόντος τοῦ ἁγίου πνεύματος ἐφ ο ὑμᾶς καὶ ἔσεσθε μου μάρτυρες ...). Acts 2:1-4 records the initial fulfillment of that promise on the Day of Pentecost. The passage describes a community of people gathered in a room. In that context, tongues like fire rested *upon* each one of them" (ἐκάθισεν ἐφ᾽ ἕνα ἕκαστον αὐτῶν 2:3) when they were all filled with the Holy Spirit (2:4). The texts reiterate Jesus' earlier statements recorded in Luke 24:47-49:

- His promise ("the promise of my Father").
- His declaration ("you will be clothed with power from on high").
- His command to a progressive witness beginning in Jerusalem.[485]

The command to witness in Acts 1:8 finds initial fulfillment in Acts 2:32, wherein Peter and others tell of the resurrection and resulting exaltation.[486]

The promise of the Holy Spirit in Luke 24:49 elicits both "great joy and blessing" (Luke 24:52-53) and is intimated in Acts 1:8 as well. In support, Haya-Prats argues, "The promise of Acts 1:8 concerning the power of the Spirit for testimony does not contain the entire interpretation of Jesus concerning the sending of the Spirit, and, therefore, we cannot deduce from this one text the function of the Holy Spirit in Acts."[487] Interventions of the Spirit in Acts are multi-faceted in various settings.[488]

For Luke, *power* (δύναμις) is an important feature of Jesus' ministry and also of the witness of the nascent community.[489] Pervo states, "for Luke the essence of power is the miraculous so long as one understands that every manifestation of divine power is a miracle ..."[490] Thus, Acts 1-2 associates miraculous power with the gift/promise of the Holy Spirit and presents this power as an experienced reality received by the community (Acts 1:8). This gift aligns with Jesus' ministry, "with miracles and wonders and signs" (δυνάμεσι καὶ τέρασι καὶ σημείοις Acts 2:22).[491] "Luke regards miracle as a mode of authorization ... the author communicates theological views by showing rather than telling, through narrative rather than through exposition."[492] Miracles unite with verbal witness and authenticate the emissaries' good news in sensory and affective language and empirical experience.

As Keener notes, Luke's "narratives ... usually refer to reserve the language of 'receiving the Spirit' for his focus upon empowerment for mission (whether experienced at or after conversion), which for Luke, who references the Spirit's activity in mission, is central to the church's life."[493] Further, the Holy Spirit will orchestrate the various geographical spheres of evangelism (Jerusalem, Judea ...). Haya-Prats notes, "It could be said that Christ transmits to his apostles the presence of the Spirit that he received at the Jordan and in a joyous order, the anticipation of the eschatological gift that he received in his exaltation."[494]

Yes, restoration (ἀποκαθιστάνω 1:6) will occur (Acts 3:20-21[495]), but not in the manner that the disciples expect. Receiving the Spirit will also mean enjoying messianic blessings in Amos' prophecy and in the community's life-together (Acts 2:41-47; 4:32-37).

Joy in the ascension (Acts 1:9-11). The joyous promise and command of Acts 1:8 immediately spills over into the ascension narrative (1:9-11), "after saying *these things*," i.e. the antecedent promise and command (1:8). The numinous nature of the ascension scene is expressed through several verbal expressions: "he was taken up" (ἐπήρθη 1:9); "a cloud received/hid him from their sight" (νεφέλη ὑπέλαβεν αὐτὸν ἀπὸ τῶν ὀφθαλμῶν αὐτῶν 1:9); "as they were staring into heaven" (ὡς ἀτενίζοντες ἦσαν εἰς τὸν οὐρανόν 1:1), with three other references to "into heaven" (εἰς τὸν οὐρανόν all occurring in 1:11), and the participle, "the one who was taken up" (ὁ ἀναλημφθείς 1:11). Similar to Luke 24:51, Jesus' movement is expressed in both horizontal and vertical terms (horizontal: "from their eyes" (ἀπὸ τῶν ὀφθαλμῶν αὐτῶν 1:9), "from you" (ἀφ' ὑμῶν 1:11); vertical: "into heaven" (εἰς τὸν οὐρανόν 1:10, 11).

Luke highlights the numinous nature of the event by his description of the sudden presence of "two men/angels dressed in white, who stood beside them" (ἰδοὺ ἄνδρες δύο παρειστήκεισαν αὐτοῖς ἐν ἐσθήσεσι λευκαῖς 1:10). He also records their promise about Jesus' future return in the same manner in which he left (1:11). Luke's mention of "the appearance of two men dressed in white" corresponds with the similar description of "two men in dazzling white" who appeared to the women in Luke 24:4, later understood as "angels" (24:23 "a vision of angels" ὀπτασίαν ἀγγέλων). In both settings, the two angels raise similar rhetorical questions:

- "Why do you seek the living among the dead?" (Luke 24:5)
- "Why do you stand looking into heaven?" (Acts 1:11).[496]

These questions serve as rebukes for looking in the wrong places. Pervo notes, "Jesus is to be seen neither at the grave nor in the sky."[497]

Paul Elbert draws attention to Greek rhetoric, in which rhetorical questions are foregrounded in preceding narratives.[498] Thus, in Luke 24, the angels' rhetorical question is foregrounded in the women's previous search Jesus' body in the tomb (Luke 24:2-3). In Acts 1, the angels' rhetorical question is foregrounded in the ascension narrative when the disciples look up into heaven" (Acts 1:9-10).[499] Thus, Elbert argues "this author has a consistent purpose in mind ... Luke fully realized that appropriately composed narrative-rhetorical questions can have a direct bearing on the comprehension of future words that are to be recorded after them."[500] In both settings, the angels follow up on the rhetorical questions with further explanation and instruction.

The ascension event anticipates the joy-filled and Spirit-empowered ministry of Jesus' successors. In Peter's sermon, the ascension highlights the nature of Jesus' ministry ("miracles, wonders, signs" Acts 1:22). Those elements will now characterize the witnesses' ministry (2:17-21, 43). Although Luke offers no explicit joy-vocabulary in 1:1-11, the numerous parallels between Luke 24 and Acts 1 certainly give space to assume the reality of joy in the events recorded. The angels' description of Jesus' return "in the same manner" stresses the physicality of the returning Jesus, highlighted in Luke 24:36-43.[501] Similarly, just as the disciples "returned to Jerusalem with great joy ... blessing God" (Luke 24:52-53), so the disciples "returned to Jerusalem" following the ascension (Acts 1:12). The context for both statements is the same, for the return to Jerusalem follows the ascension narrative. The "great joy and blessing God" of Luke 24:52-53 is surely intimated in Acts 1:9-12. Joy can be assumed as an attendant emotion. Luke should not be pressed to provide exhaustive detail for each event.[502]

As Johnson notes, the opening portion of Acts "functions as a transition to a new stage in the story, a transition wherein the author does not provide new material but rather rewords and elaborates a portion of the story already told. The reader, I think, is meant to imagine the gestures and words in Acts 1:11(12) as an elaborate variant of those in Luke 24:36-53."[503] Thus, Acts 1 both reviews Luke 24 and previews what will occur in the Book of Acts.

Joyous anticipation (Acts 1:12-14). Prior to the choice of Judas' successor (Acts 1:15-26), Luke provides the atmosphere of anticipation, togetherness, and unity in the context of "devoted" (προσκαρτεροῦντες Acts 1:14[504]) prayer emanating from a community "of one accord" (ὁμοθυμαδὸν Acts 1:14[505]). Luke's narrative is inclusive, with the presence of women (1:14), specifically Mary, who will be one of Israel's "daughters" who will prophesy (2:17). Mary is important both in the beginning of Luke and Acts. The community is in a state of joyful anticipation of the promised baptism in the Holy Spirit, with its "experiential effects in the life of the church."[506]

The Holy Spirit brings to mind David's prophecy concerning the defection of Judas (Acts 1:16; Psa 69:25; 109:8), and the community's need to complete the apostolic circle. While the choice of Matthias as the twelfth apostle "by lots" (Acts 1:26) is strange to our 21st Century context, nonetheless, for Luke and his readers, God is directly involved in this choice, "Lord, you know everyone's heart. Show us which of these two you have chosen to take over this ministry and apostleship" (1:24-25). There is something wrong with only eleven apostles. It is important for Luke that the apostolic circle of twelve[507] is restored; thus, this "new Israel" joyfully awaits the promised baptism in the Spirit, since incompleteness is now replaced by completeness.[508]

Human determination and qualifications for apostleship (notably a witness of Jesus' resurrection[509] Acts 1:21-22) and the selection of two candidates (Acts 1:23) unite with supernatural revelation, all bathed in an atmosphere of concerted prayer (Acts 1:24), already noted in Acts 1:14.[510]

The joyful and inclusive Feast of Pentecost (Acts 2:1). Inclusive joy characterizes the very day of Pentecost (Acts 2:1). The second great feast of the religious calendar is labeled as "the Harvest Feast" ("feast of the first fruits of the harvest": ἑορτὴν θερισμοῦ πρωτογεννημάτων Ex. 23:16), "the Feast of Weeks," and "the Beginning of the Wheat Harvest" (ἑορτὴν ἑβδομάδων ... ἀρχὴν θερισμοῦ πυροῦ Ex. 34:22; Num. 28:26). Although Leviticus provides the most detail concerning the feast (Lev. 23:15-21), Deuteronomy highlights two features of this feast:

- an atmosphere of joy—("*you shall rejoice* before the Lord your God" (εὐφρανθήσῃ ἐναντίον Κυρίου τοῦ θεοῦ σου Deut 16:11).
- a concern for inclusion.

Pervo notes, "On Pentecost, the first fruits of the ecumenical harvest are taken in. The wind that erupts on this day will not abate until its storm gusts have propelled Paul to Rome."[511] The original feast was a farmers' feast for those who lived a settled life.[512] In Acts 2, the baptism in the Spirit was also "an occasion for joy and that joy was to be shared."[513] Isaiah 9:3 underscores the joyous nature of the feast, "You have enlarged the nation and increased their joy (εὐφροσύνη); they will rejoice (ευφρανθήσεται) before you as people rejoice (εὐφραινόμενοι) at the harvest, as men rejoice (εὐφραινόμενοι) when dividing the spoil."

Scripture presents such joy as inclusive, progressing from son, to daughter, male-servant, female maid-servant, Levite, resident-alien,

orphan and widow (Deut 16:11).[514] Freewill offerings provided a
celebratory joy designed to be shared with all classes of people. Luke's list
of nations in Acts 2:9-11 is certainly inclusive and is reiterated in Peter's
sermon, "this promise is to you and your children and all who are far
off" (2:39). This festival of a contagious and inclusive joy is certainly an
appropriate context for the gift of the Spirit. "The fact that it coincides
with a Jewish feast shows that the old system of worship has passed
away, and that the promises which that system foreshadowed are now
fulfilled."[515] Joyous inclusion will be voiced though charismatic tongues
when they "cross cultural barriers."[516]

Over the course of time, the farmers' feast "was eventually related
to the history of salvation, but this connection was made at a later
date and was linked with the Covenant at Sinai, in the reading of
Exodus 19."[517] Many scholars draw attention to four passages in Philo,
a contemporary of Luke, suggesting links between the giving of
the Law and Luke's understanding of the gift of the Spirit in Acts
2:[518] Regardless of Luke's nuances or allusions, the atmosphere of an
inclusive joy, surrounding this day is significant. This feast was the
most crowded of the three prescribed annual feasts to the sanctuary
and the most festive celebration that originated in a successful farmer's
harvest.[519]

The joyful miracles on the Day of Pentecost (Acts 2:1-47). The narrative
of the Day of Pentecost[520] coheres with Luke's meta-narrative of the
progression of events and themes; it cannot be understood in isolation
from the entire complex of associations. The narrative itself reveals a
simple broad structure:

- A miraculous event draws a crowd (Acts 2:1-4).
- The crowd responds in various ways (Acts 2:5-13).
- Peter replies to the crowd's response, interpreting the
  miraculous event (Acts 2:14-36) in the language of Amos'
  prophecy.
- The crowd's converts (Acts 2:37-41).
- Luke concludes this portion with a narrative-summary
  (Acts 4:42-47).

As a whole, the narrative emphasizes Luke's consistent theme that miraculous events are occasions of joy leading to effective witness.

Luke draws attention to the miraculous nature of the event in narratives of the fulfilled baptism in the Spirit (2:1-4) and the crowd's response (2:5-13). He presents two similes that highlight the miraculous:

- A sudden[521] noise from above, *like* the roar of a strong rushing wind (ἄφνω ἐκ τοῦ οὐρανοῦ *ὥσπερ* φερομένης πνοῆς βιαίας), which filled the entire house (Acts 2:2).
- Tongues *like* fire[522] separated and came to rest upon them all (διαμεριζόμεναι γλῶσσαι *ὡσεὶ* πυρός καὶ ἐκάθισεν ἐφ᾽ ἕνα ἕκαστον αὐτῶν Acts 2:4).

This numinous event can only be understood through comparative language—not literal language. Through inter-textuality, allusions may link the story to the Sinai theophany, with similar language of wind, fire and noise (Exod. 19:16-1).[523] Just as the entire house *was filled* (ἐπλήρωσεν Acts 2:2), so the people in the house *were filled* or *overwhelmed* (ἐπλήσθησαν) with the Holy Spirit (2:4).[524] In his gospel, Luke noted that both Elizabeth (Luke 1:41) and Zechariah (Luke 1:67) were filled (πίμπληι)[525] with the Holy Spirit, which led to joyful prophecy in both cases. Haya-Prats notes, "Evidently this fullness that manifests itself in wisdom, in boldness and in joy, in solemn moments and in the ordinary life of the community, must also have a confirming effect on the community, similar to that of glossolalia."[526]

For Luke, this miraculous event is the fulfillment of the Baptist's prophecy (Luke 3:16) and the promised Holy Spirit from the Father, already underscored in Luke 11:13; 24:49; Acts 1: 4, 5, 8. Luke stresses the physicality of this event, just as Jesus' baptism in Luke 3:22 emphasized the physical descent of the Holy Spirit upon Jesus, "in bodily form as a dove" (σωματικῷ εἴδει ὡς περιστερὰν).[527] The verb, "appeared" (ὤφθησαν) suggests a tangible experience. It was an event within history, not a "communal vision,"[528] since the category of vision is largely subjective and personal. The "sensation of overflowing fullness"[529] leads to the expression in tongues.

Joyous tongues (Acts 2:4-13). Luke then highlights the immediate result
of the Holy Spirit's filling, their speaking in other tongues, "they began
to speak in tongues just as the Spirit was inspiring them to speak out
loudly" (ἤρξαντο λαλεῖν ἑτέραις γλώσσαις καθὼς το πνεῦμα
ἐδίδου ἀποφθέγγεσθαι αὐτοῖς 2:5). Luke pairs the verb, "I speak out,
declare boldly or loudly" (ἀποφθέγγομαι) with speaking in tongues.
Later he also pairs that verb with Peter's bold and inspired speech,
interpreting the event to the many witnesses (2:14). Later, Luke will use
this same verb for Paul's defense before Agrippa as to the truth and
sanity of his inspired declaration (26:25).[530]

What is the exact nature of speaking in other tongues? Within the
text of Acts 2, it appears that Luke combines the tradition of glossolalia
(unintelligible ecstatic speech) and the tradition of xenoglossia (foreign
languages).[531] Luke regards this speaking to be ecstatic, since it is occasioned
by the fullness of the Spirit (Acts 2:4), speaking forth the mighty acts of
God (2:11) and the subsequent response of the mocking detractors, who
conclude that the disciples are in a drunk condition ("they are drunk with
wine"[532] γλεύκους μεμεστωμένοι εἰσίν Acts 2:13)[533]

Concurrently, the immediate focus of this ecstatic speech is on the
intelligibility of the tongues to the audience. The audience first *hears the
sound*[534] (γενομένης δὲ τῆς φωνῆς ταύτης Acts 2:6), followed by a three-
fold declaration of hearing the tongues "in their *own native language*"[535]:

- 2:6 "each one heard them speaking *in his own native
  language*" ἤκουον εἷς ἕκαστος τῇ ἰδίᾳ διαλέκτῳ
  λαλούντων αὐτῶν,
- 2:8 "we hear them in *our own native language* in which
  we were born" ἡμεῖς ἀκούομεν ἕκαστος τῇ ἰδίᾳ
  διαλέκτῳ ἡμῶν ἐν ᾗ ἐγεννήθημεν,
- 2:11 "we hear them speaking *in our own tongues the
  mighty acts of God*" ἀκούομεν λαλούντων αὐτῶν ταῖς
  ἡμετέραις γλώσσαις τὰ μεγαλεῖα τοῦ θεου.

Later, Peter states that what they *see and hear* (ὑμεῖς καὶ βλέπετε καὶ
ἀκούετε) is the immediate effect of Jesus' pouring forth of the promise

of the Holy Spirit (Acts 2:33). Luke establishes that such tongues-speaking originated in the fullness of the Spirit (2:4), was ecstatic and joyous in nature, and consisted in praise to God for his "mighty acts."[536] As Haya-Prats argues, "This joyful prayer is always fruit of a supernatural manifestation ... In the Book of Acts, we find the term μεγαλύνω preferred for expressing this ecstatic prayer of praise to God ... a prayer of rejoicing. The term ἀποφθέγγεσθαι (2:4) also expresses the sense of rejoicing."[537] These joyous tongues were understood by people in a number of foreign languages, thus preparing the way for Peter's Pentecostal message and the believing response from his audience. Even though the people understood the tongues, they also were very aware of the miraculous nature of this speaking.

The ambiguities of the text, including the mention of "hearing" (4 times), leads Pervo to the negative assessment that "the situation is anomalous and that the simplest explanation of the anomaly is to attribute it to the author, who has concocted a story that does not fit into the categories of religious experience."[538] In light of that, however, it's important to note that the effect on the crowd is mixed, hampering the effort to separate the inter-woven strands:

- 2:6 "a crowd came together and *was confused*" συνῆλθεν τὸ πλῆθος καὶ *συνεχύθη*,
- 2:7 "they *were amazed* and *were marveling*" *ἐξίσταντο* δὲ καὶ *ἐθαύμαζον*,
- 2:12 "all *were amazed*" *ἐξίσταντο* δὲ πάντες,
- 2:12 "they *were perplexed*" *διηπόρουν*,
- 2:12 "*What does this mean?*"; Positive Question: τί θέλει τοῦτο εἶναι,
- 2:13 "Others *were mocking* them and said; Negative Accusation: 'They have drunken too much wine'" *ἕτεροι* δὲ *διαχλευάζοντες* ἔλεγον ὅτι Γλεύκος μεμεστωμένοι εἰσίν.

Similar to the effects of appearances (angels, Jesus) in Luke 24, the response of the crowd is filled with drama, with similar or identical language ("I am amazed" (ἐξίστημι in Acts 2:7, 11; Luke 24:22; "I marvel" (θαυμάζω in Acts 2:7; Luke 24:12, 41).[540] Just as Luke 24 expressed a progression towards genuine trust and joyful marvel, readers see the crowd moved by the events of Acts 2 towards a positive response of trust, repentance, baptism and the reception of the Spirit; these people are also "in process." Others become detractors or "hecklers"[541] (2:18), and thus, Luke notes a recurring division in Acts.

Speaking in tongues is crucial in Acts 2 as the means by which people know of Jesus' exaltation (Acts 2:33). In terms of Luke's overall progression, people saw the crucifixion, but no one saw the actual resurrection. Numerous people witnessed the resurrected Jesus, some witnessed the ascension, and no one saw the exaltation of Jesus to the Father's right hand. However, for Luke, the tangible nature of tongues-speaking is proof of Jesus' exaltation, reception of the Spirit and subsequent pouring forth of the Holy Spirit. The audience both sees and hears this charismatic event. As Behm notes, "this philological miracle, which is no mere miracle of hearing, is the unique feature in this outpouring of the Spirit as recorded in Acts."[542]

Joyous fulfillment of Joel's prophecy (Acts 2:17-21). In response to the crowd's positive question, "What do these things mean?" (2:12), Peter responds, "This is that which had been spoken through the prophet Joel" (2:16). Peter's sermon begins with the affirmation that this charismatic event of tongues-speaking is an eschatological event, a sensory sign of the last days (2:17), and a proof that Jesus, the Messiah has completed his task, is exalted to God's right hand, receives the Spirit, and is thus able to pour forth his charismatic gifts. Joel's prophecy affirms the joyful blessings of the messianic age, inaugurated by Jesus' exaltation, which are now realized in the nascent community. Joy is the natural consequence of the messianic blessings, prophesied by Joel, now initially fulfilled on the day of Pentecost.[543]

As Johnson notes, "As a result, he has made the text foretell the working of 'wonders and signs' (*terata kai sēmeia*), which he uses to identify the prophetic figures of his story."[544] In the sermon, Peter assumes that his audience knows ("just as you yourselves know" καθὼς αὐτοὶ οἴδατε 2:22) of Jesus, who was attested by "miracles, wonders and signs" (δυνάμεσι καὶ τέρασι καὶ σημείοις). He draws upon the audience's shared tradition. Luke notes that "many wonders and signs" (πολλά τε τέρατα καὶ σημεῖα) were accomplished by the apostles (2:43).

Peter links ecstatic tongues-speaking[545] with prophesying (twice), and also with seeing visions and dreaming dreams (Acts 2:17). Luke affirms that the pouring forth of the Holy Spirit has numerous effects; the Spirit's presence is not to be reduced to tongues-speaking alone.

Baptism in the Spirit will mean the power (empowerment) to both speak and act for God. Joel's prophecy of visions and dreams will play a substantive role in the Book of Acts.[546] Such charismatic experiences and expressions are the direct result of God's "pouring out" (ἐκχέω) of his Spirit, stated three times in Peter's Pentecostal address; two of the occurrences are found in Joel's text:

- "*I will pour out my Spirit*" (ἐκχεῶ ἀπὸ τοῦ πνεύματός *μου* Acts 2:17),
- "*I will pour out my Spirit*" (ἐκχεῶ ἀπὸ τοῦ πνεύματός *μου* Acts 2:18),
- "He has he has received from the Father the promised *Holy Spirit* and *has poured out* what you now see and hear" (τῇ δεξιᾷ οὖν τοῦ θεοῦ ὑψωθεὶς τήν τε ἐπαγγελίαν τοῦ πνεύματος τοῦ ἁγίου λαβὼν παρὰ τοῦ πατρὸς ἐξέχεεν τοῦτο ὃ ὑμεῖς καὶ βλέπετε καὶ ἀκούετε Acts 2:33

Joel's prophecy is also inclusive in nature, "I will pour out my Spirit on *all flesh*" (Acts 2:17, which incorporates both genders (twice) and different age groups. It also advances the list of language groups of Acts 2:9-11. Mention of "all flesh" corresponds to the Baptist's words, *"All flesh* shall see the salvation of our God" (Luke 3:6 taken from Isa. 40:5).[547] In the Book of Acts, Luke notes the inclusive nature of God's Spirit when the good news advances from the Jewish Jerusalem into the Gentile world, including the African Ethiopian eunuch and the Gentile Cornelius (Acts 10-11).

Joel's prophecy also mentions certain cosmic phenomena (blood, fire, columns of smoke, darkening of sun, turning of the moon into blood) that will take place before the great and terrible day of the Lord (Acts 2:19b-20).[548] Jesus' eschatological discourse (Luke 21:5-36) pointed to

similar cosmic events (signs in the sun, moon and stars. On the earth
... heavenly bodies will be shaken, see Luke 21:25) that will serve as
precursors of the Parousia of the Son of Man (Luke 21:27). For Luke,
now is the time for witness in word and miraculous power. Through
the baptism in the Holy Spirit, the community now shares in this
eschatological event, the new era with the blessings and untold joy that
drives effective and powerful witness.

> Joel's prophecy refers to the joyful aspect of the gift of the Spirit
> ... in order to allow unselfish praise to God. If this gifting of the
> Spirit serves as a guarantee of the messianic age, it is not given
> as an arbitrarily established but as the exterior exuberance of
> the messianic blessings already received ... It would not be too
> bold to say that the dynamic effects are applications of the
> eschatological gift to historical circumstances.[549]

Later, Luke's readers will again encounter joyful expressions from
those who receive the promise and gift of the Spirit. The first fruits
anticipate the full harvest associated with the feast of Pentecost. Thus,
experiences with the Spirit as described in Acts can be understood as
a foretaste of the celestial fullness. The emotional joy of the messianic
blessings experienced in this age, will give way to the untold joy of the
consummation. While the baptism in the Spirit associates with tongues
in Acts 2:4, Joel's prophecy includes other charismatic expressions and
experiences that will unfold in the book of Acts.

David's joyous prophecy of the resurrection (Acts 2:25-28). In Peter's sermon,
Luke also forges a link between the powerful event of the resurrection and
an experience of joy, with three expressions, celebrated by David[550]:

- Therefore my heart *is glad* (διὰ τοῦτο ηὐφράνθη ἡ
  καρδία μου)
- and my tongue *rejoices* (ἠγαλλιάσατο ἡ γλῶσσά μου
  Acts 2:26a).
- You will fill me with *gladness* in your presence (πληρώσεις
  με εὐφροσύνης μετὰ τοῦ προσώπου σου Acts 2:28b).

The three joyous expressions emerge within affirmations of the resurrection, "paths of life" (ὁδοὺς ζωῆς) and "in your presence" (μετὰ τοῦ προσώπου σου Acts 2:28b). Joyous declarations anticipate the resurrection without corruption, which David expected (Acts 2:27).[551] A later *midrash* on Psalm 16:9 declares, "my glory rejoices over the Lord Messiah, who will rise from me."[552] Luke affirms David's prophetic role in pointing to the Messiah and his resurrection, "being a prophet ... foreseeing, he spoke concerning the resurrection of the Messiah" (προφήτης οὖν ὑπάρχων ... προϊδὼν ἐλάλησεν περὶ τῆς ἀναστάσεως τοῦ Χριστοῦ Acts 2:30-31). Since Jesus is the Messiah, prophesied by David, he could not be restrained by death. Thus, there are three affirmations of joy from David linked to his prophetic role concerning the resurrection of the Messiah.[553]

Joyous witness. Within the joyous atmosphere, the power of the Holy Spirit compels a vibrant witness expressed throughout the narrative[554]:

- "you shall be *my witnesses*" ἔσεσθέ μου μάρτυρες (Acts 1:8). "to be *a witness* with us of the resurrection" μάρτυρα τῆς ἀναστάσεως αὐτοῦ σὺν ἡμῖν γενέσθαι (1:22).
- 2:32 "we are all *witnesses* of the fact" οὐ πάντες ἡμεῖς ἐσμεν μάρτυρες.
- "he addressed them" ἀπεφθέγξατο αὐτοῖς (2:32, which employs the same verb used of the inspired utterance of tongues in 2:14).
- "With many other words he was *bearing witness* and *pleading* with them" ἑτέροις τε λόγοις πλείοσιν διεμαρτύρατο καὶ παρεκάλει αὐτούς (in 2:40).

Witness is certainly a stated purpose of the disciples' empowerment (Acts 1:8), which also includes first-hand testimony of the resurrection through the post-resurrection stories (1:22, 32). Such witness is uttered through the inspired miracle of tongues (2:4), with the declaration of the mighty acts of God (2:11), through Peter's inspired sermon (2:14), with Joel's fulfilled prophecy, and Peter's subsequent witness and pleading with the crowd (2:40).

However, this witness is borne through a joyous and effusive outgrowth of the experienced baptism in the Holy Spirit. Further, Luke's narrative summary accentuates the success of witness with the statement of about 3,000 new believers (2:41), the positive witness of the community's life-together,[555] and the daily and divine addition of people who were being saved (2:47). While the original participants and onlookers were Jewish (Acts 1-2), the scope of witness will widen to include a broader mission to the Gentiles.

A Joyous Sequel to the Pentecost Story
(Acts 3-4)

Luke pairs Acts 1-2 and Acts 3-4, both in structure and with important themes. The narrative progresses from Jesus' ministry to the pouring forth of the Holy Spirit enabling believers to speak and act for God. These themes are positioned within the joyous context of the Old Testament. Miracles are brushes on the broad canvas of the charismatic and complex nature of Jesus' ministry; they cannot be understood alone. Luke devotes two chapters to the healing of the crippled beggar, coupled with human responses and other references to miraculous power. Emotional joy permeates the narrative that moves toward joyous life-together in Luke's narrative summary.

Luke could hardly narrate the joyous experience and expression of the healed crippled beggar more graphically. Readers discover a series of verbs and participles (Acts 3:8-11) progressing from the beggar's crippled condition to standing, walking, leaping, praising God (one reference to standing, four references to walking, two references to leaping, two references to praising God). Through repetition, Luke visualizes the joyous event in a way that elicits joy from his readers. Surely they can feel the joy of this man, crippled from birth (3:2), who is now more than forty years old (4:22). He had always been dependent. Now he can independently walk and leap for joy at all the possibilities open to him. Luke intends his readers to focus also on the spontaneous praise of God, "praising God" (αἰνῶν τὸ θεόν 3:8; αἰνοῦντα τὸν θεόν 3:10), expressed by the man's physical holding on to the apostles (3:11).

The descriptive narrative uses numerous expressions of joy, both explicit and implicit. The "healing/salvation" of the beggar is a "sign" of eschatological and joyous "salvation." Luke also uses other terms to convey this eschatological period of joy: *"times of refreshment"* (καιροὶ ἀναψύξεως Acts 3:20), *"eschatological blessing"* ("in your seed all the families of the earth *will be blessed"* ἐν τῷ σπέρματι σου ἐνευλογηθήσονται πᾶσαι αἱ πατριαὶ τῆς γῆς 3:25[556]; *"blessing you* in turning of each one of you from your sins" εὐλογοῦντα ὑμᾶς ἐν τῷ ἀποστρέφειν ἕκαστον ἀπὸ τῶν πονηριῶν ὑμῶν 3:26). Thus, refreshment and blessing are gifts belonging to all receptive participants in the events of Acts 1-4.[557] Through Jesus' miraculous resurrection and exaltation, people experience great eschatological blessing and joy as they are touched by the Spirit.

Luke intends that his readership appreciate and experience the miraculous, thus continuing Jesus' ministry and fulfilling an Old Testament promise. The sequel (Acts 3-4) to the initial Pentecost story (Acts 1-2) affirms the continuation of Pentecostal power, now played out by others—including the experience, atmosphere, and emotional expressions of joy—all leading to acts of praising God.

Even when he doesn't use the explicit "witness" word family, Luke clearly argues that this wellspring of joy overflows into spontaneous and empowered witness:

- "we are *witnesses*" (ἡμεῖς μάρτυρές ἐσμεν 3:15);
- "and with great power the apostles were *bearing witness* to the resurrection of Jesus" (καὶ δυνάμει μεγάλη ἀπεδίδουν τὸ μαρτύριον οἱ ἀπόστολοι τῆς ἀναστάσεως τοῦ κυρίου Ἰησοῦ 4:33);
- Peter's inspired witness to the people in 3:12-26, "because they were *teaching* and *preaching* the resurrection from the dead in Jesus" (διὰ τὸ διδάσκειν αὐτοὺς τὸ λαὸν καταγγέλλειν ἐν τῷ Ἰησοῦ τὴν ἀνάστασιν τὴν ἐκ νεκρῶν 4:2);
- Peter's inspired witness to the religious leaders in which he is filled with the Holy Spirit and thereby *speaks* (τό

τε Πέτρος πλησθεὶς πνεύματος ἁγίου εἶπεν πρὸς
αὐτούς 4:8).

The combined witness of the miracle, joy, and inspired preaching is
powerful to the extent that more people believed than on the Day of
Pentecost. As a unit, Acts 3-4 serves as a fitting and joyful sequel to the
story of the initial Pentecost in Jerusalem.[558] Luke provides numerous
links for his readership in terms of a series of events.[559]

Luke also supplies a similar progression of themes that were noted in
Acts 1-2, which serve as the necessary background for charismatic events
and the human responses of joy and praise. There are four mentions of
the crucifixion,[560] seven references to the resurrection,[561] one note of the
ascension,[562] two explicit references to the Holy Spirit,[563] five mentions of
witness,[564] numerous terms signifying the miraculous,[565] eight mentions of
prophecy/prophets,[566] joy from the healed cripple,[567] numerous references
to the human responses of amazement, marvel from the people,[568] leading
to reception/trust,[569] joy and praise,[570] and the joyous celebration of life
together.[571]

Why does Luke reiterate the similar progression of numinous events
found in Acts 1-2, particularly in Peter's sermon? Luke invites his readers
to experience the broader tapestry of events and themes, intertwining
threads of the numinous with expressions of joy. This yields praise and
joyful witness, because the emotions are inherently connected to the
events. Thus, for example, the healing of the crippled beggar in Acts 3 is
not an isolated event that stands independently from the background of
the Jesus-story. Rather, it belongs to the entire drama in a dynamic way.

Two elements in Acts 3-4 represent advances over Acts 1-2:

1. the extensive use of the "name" (ὄνομα)[572];
2. the joy-less hostility and aggressive behavior of the reli-
    gious critics (Acts 4:1-22).

A miraculous healing draws followers and joyous new converts (Acts
3:9-11; 4:4, 21) and elicits hostile responses from the religious authorities
(4:1-3, 13-18). Luke records Peter's explanation of the miraculous event to

both groups (3:12-26—to the people; 4:8-12—to the religious authorities). The narrative summary at the end of chapter 4 (4:32-37) seems similar to the end of chapter 2 (2:41-47). Acts 2 records a miraculous event, followed by Peter's explanation of this event. However, a more careful reading of the text reveals other important threads of the tapestry.

Peter's miraculous gaze (Acts 3:4). Luke prepares for the beggar's healing (3:1-3) by providing various details: the place (outside the Temple 3:1), the time ("at the ninth hour" 3:1), biographical detail (Peter and John 3:1; the crippled beggar 3:2), the lifelong nature of the crippled beggar's condition ("from birth" 3:2), the habitual activity of the beggar ("to solicit charity" 3:2), and the beggar's expectation for charity from Peter and John (3:3).

Luke occasions the actual healing by Peter's miraculous "gaze into him" (ἀτενίσας ... εἰς αὐτὸν Acts 3:4) and his subsequent command, "look at us" (Βλέψον εἰς ἡμᾶς 3:4). The verb, "I gaze, stare" (ἀτενίζω) suggests a miraculous insight into the man. In his probing article, "Strange Stares: Atenizein in Acts," Rick Strelan draws attention to the ten cases of "staring" in Acts,[573] which can be compared with Jewish, Greco-Roman and early Christian writings. He argues that this "gaze into" suggests a divinely-inspired or prophetic insight into the man's heart.[574] He states, those who stare [ἀτενίζω] are at prayer, in ecstasy, or experiencing transported vision (7:55; 10:4; 11:16); they are "full of the Holy Spirit" and inspired with intuition or penetrative insight which gives them the ability to see "into people" (3:4; 13:9; 14:9; 23:1); [or] they have a vision which breaks into the heavenly world (1:10; 7:55). Such dynamic sight makes them, in turn, the object of reverent awe-inspired stares (3:12; 6:15).[575]

He makes similar comments on the disciples' "seeing and gazing" in the vision accorded to them in the ascension narrative (Acts 1:9-11), "while seeing ... their eyes ... gazing ... behold" (βλεπόντων ... ὀφθαλμῶν ... ἀτενίζοντες ... ἰδοὺ Acts 1:9-10).[576]

In the narrative of Acts 3, the verb "I gaze" is used of Peter and of the people who "marvel" and "gaze" upon the two apostles, "Why do you marvel at this or why do you gaze upon ('into') us as if by our own power or piety we had made this man walk?" (τί θαυμάζετε ἐπὶ τούτῳ, ἢ ἡμῖν τί ἀτενίζετε ὡς ἰδίᾳ δυνάμει ἢ εὐσεβείᾳ πεποιηκόσιν τοῦ περιπατεῖν αὐτόν; Acts 3:12). Strelan correctly concludes, "But this is no ordinary staring but a gazing at an epiphany of divine power. The crowd is in a mood of wonder and awe which gives them the intuition that Peter and John are holy even 'divine' men."[577] This "gaze into," insight, or "second-sight" is the springboard for the miraculous and joyous healing of the crippled beggar. Prophetic insight leads to action, expressed by the dual means by which the crippled beggar is healed.

First, Peter pronounces that the "name" (ὄνομα) of Jesus Christ of Nazareth is the means by which the man is healed (Acts 3:6); thereby Luke introduces the leit-motif of "the name" of Jesus Christ (person and authority), which dominates the narrative and dialogue of Acts 3-4. As Haenchen observes, "The name is no chance attribute of the person, but expresses his very essence. Hence the power of the person named, be he human or divine, is itself present in the ὄνομα."[578] Peter does not pray to the exalted Christ but simply releases the power when he speaks the name; the name itself is power, e.g. "By what power or what name did you do this?" Ἐν ποίᾳ δυνάμει ἢ ἐν ποίῳ ὀνόματι ἐποιήσατε τοῦτο ὑμεῖς;—expressed by the religious authorities (Acts 4:7).[579] Charismatic power resides in "the name."

Second, the "name" joins with Peter's command, "Rise up and walk" (Acts 3:7) and his physical touch, "seizing him by the right hand, he helped him up" (3:7). The adverb, "immediately" (παραχῆμα), stresses the instantaneous nature of the healing.[580] Of special note, Jesus' healing of the paralytic is also immediate (Luke 5:25).

Luke accentuates the miraculous healing in three ways:

1. the plethora of verbal forms in his telling of the story.
2. the frequent references to the man's healed condition throughout Acts 3-4.
3. the visible nature of the man's healed condition.

Let's examine these literary emphases more closely.
1) Luke slows the narrative with extraordinary verbal forms, which Pervo states are "overloaded"[581]:

- "the man's feet and ankles *were strengthened*"
  (ἐστερώθησαν Acts 3:7)
- "*leaping*" (ἐξαλλόμενος 3:8).
- "*he stood*" (ἔστη 3:8).
- "*he began to walk*"[582] (περιεπάτει 3:8).
- "*he entered* with them into the Temple" (εἰσῆλθεν 3:8).
- "*walking*" (περιπατῶν 3:8).
- "*leaping*" (ἁλλόμενος 3:8).
- "*praising* God (αἰνῶν 3:8).
- "*walking* (περιπατοῦντα 3:9).
- "*praising* God" (αἰνοῦντα 3:9).
- *holding on* to Peter and John" (κρατοῦντος δὲ Πέτρον καὶ τὸν Ἰωάννην 3:11).

In light of all of these references, Luke's readers certainly feel the sensory nature of the healing and joyous emotion.

With these verbal and cognate forms, Luke underscores the miraculous and joyous nature of the man's healing. Luke brings the full picture of the crippled beggar's condition, healing, and response before the readers' eyes—to visualize the entire event.[583] Luke also provides several contrasts. He juxtaposes the expectation of charity with an unexpected healing. He describes the disciples' lack of silver and gold, but also shows the tremendous resource inherent in the Jesus' powerful name. He contrasts the beggar's "blemished" condition" with wholeness. He paints a picture of a man "begging for charity," and then shows him praising God. He records a change in environment, from outside the Temple to inside the Temple.

Luke also intends that his readers associate this graphic imagery with the text and context of Isaiah 35:6, "then shall the *crippled one leap* as a deer" (τότε ἁλεῖται ὡς ἔλαφρος ὁ χωλός LXX)[584]; Isa 35 is rich in joy-vocabulary:

Words related to joy:

- "*Be glad* you thirsty desert" (εὐφράνθητι ἔρημος διψῶσα Isa 35:1).

- "Let the wilderness *exult*" (ἀγαλλιάσθω ἔρημος Isa 35:1).
- "*Encourage* one another you faint-hearted"
  (παρακαλέσατε οἱ ὀλιγόψυχοι τῇ διανοίᾳ Isa 35:4).
- "there shall be the *joy* of birds" (ἐκεῖ εὐφροσύνη ὀρνέων
  Isa 35:7).
- "they shall return to Zion with *gladness*" (ἥξουσιν εἰς
  Σιὼν μετ᾿ εὐφροσύης Isa 35:10).
- "*everlasting gladness* shall be upon their head" (εὐφροσύνη
  αἰώνιος ὑπὲρ κεφαλῆς αὐτῶν Isa 35:10).
- "for on their heard shall be *praise* and *gladness*" (ἐπὶ γὰρ
  τῆς κεφαλῆς αὐτῶν αἴνεσις καὶ ἀγαλλίαμα Isa
  35:10).
- "*gladness* shall take possession of them" (εὐφροσύνη
  καταλήψεται αὐτοὺς Isa 35:10).

Words related to salvation:

- "he himself will come and *save* us" (αὐτὸς ἥξει καὶ
  σώσει ἡμας Isa 35:4)[585]

Words related to praise and gladness:

- "for on their heard shall be *praise* and *gladness*" (ἐπὶ
  γὰρ τῆς κεφαλῆς αὐτῶν αἴνεσις καὶ ἀγαλλίαμα
  Isa.35:10)

The *gloomy* ethos of Isaiah 34 is replaced in Isaiah 35 with the *joy* and *exultation* of the travelers who return to Zion—in a joyous procession and the prophet "has in mind the actual healing of human ailments in the time of salvation."[586] An eternal joy characterizes the actual places (desert, Jordan, Lebanon, Carmel, Zion), nature (birds), the ethos ("with joy"), the experience of eternal joy ("return to Zion with everlasting joy), and the expressions of joy and salvation (praise) that replaces the "sorrow and groaning" (Isa 35:10) of Isaiah 34. Isaiah joins the joyous liberation of the exiles, and their glad procession back to Jerusalem, with the aspect of "bodily restoration."[587] Such feelings characterize the healed beggar and his audience.

Dennis Hamm alludes to the Targum of Isaiah 35:6, "Then when they see the exiles of Israel gathered together and going up to their land, even as swift harts which cannot be restrained, their tongue which was dumb shall ring with praises."[588] He also draws attention to the double-meaning that the lame man sought "monetary *alms*" (ἐλεημοσύνη Acts 3:2) but found another kind of alms, i.e., "*mercy*" (ἐλεημοσύνη)."[589]

For Luke, holistic healing had been a vital part of Jesus' agenda, expressed in Luke 4:18-19 (Isa 61:1-3; 58:6) and summarized in Luke 7:21-22 (Isa 35:5-6), with another fulfillment in Acts 3:1-10 (Isa 35:5-6). Thus, Luke's narrative reveals the healing of the crippled beggar is a continuation of Jesus' compassionate ministry. However, it also fulfills the promise of Isa 35:5-6, and it serves as a "sign" or acted parable of eschatological salvation that brings untold joy. Luke invites his readers to share the same joyous emotions expressed inherently in his writing, but also experienced by Isaiah, and by the receptive participants in this narrative of healing.

2) Luke boosts the man's healed condition with seven explicit references.[590] He is consistently present outside the temple, inside the temple, in full view of the crowd initially present who witness the miraculous healing (Acts 3:9-10), a second crowd who comes based on the report of the first crowd (3:11), and the religious authorities (4:1-3, 5-22).

3) Luke reinforces the actual healing with clear stress upon the visible nature of the healing with eleven references, including public witnesses. Luke piles on such expressions: "they were recognizing" (3:10), "all the crowd was running to them (3:11), "you see and know" (3:16), "before all of you" (3:16), "you did this" (4:7), "he stands before you whole (4:10), "seeing the healed man standing, nothing to say" (4:14), "this sign has become known" (4:16), "is visible ...we are not able to deny" (4:16), "we are not able to speak what we have seen and heard" (4:20), "at the event which had occurred" (4:21), "upon whom this event of healing which had occurred" (4:22).

The references include important prepositions and adjectives: "*before all of you*" (ἀπέναντι Acts 3:16), "*in your presence*" (ἐνώπιον Acts 4:10), *"known"* (γνωστόν Acts 4:16), *"visible"* (φανερόν Acts 4:16). As for the religious authorities, the visible nature of the once-crippled beggar causes them to "throw up their hands" and give up any attempt to deny the miracle: "they had nothing to say" (οὐδὲν εἶχον ἀντειεῖν 4:14), "What shall we do with these men?" (Τί ποιήσωμεν τοῖς ἀνθρώποις τούτοις; 4:16), "we are unable to deny" (οὐ δυνάμεθα ἀρνεῖσθαι 4:16).

Why does Luke reinforce the actual healing and the widely observable nature of the man's healing? Luke intends that his readers see the apostles' healing ministry as a continuation of Jesus' ministry, thus the actual events cannot be denied, even by the joy-less critics. Further, Luke wants his readers to see that the *"saved/healed"* (σέσωται Acts 4:9[591]) condition of the man serves as a "sign" of *"salvation"* (σωτηρία 4:12). The healing was accomplished through Jesus' name, which also is the name through which people *"must be saved"* (δεῖ σωθῆναι ἡμᾶς 4:12).[592] Luke's readers would note the dual significance of the verb, "I save/heal" (σῷζω) and the noun, "salvation" (σωτηρία) in 4:9, 12 with respect to the "healed" cripple:

- "this one has been healed/saved" (οὗτος σέσωται 4:9)
- "salvation ... in which it is necessary to be saved" (σωτηρία ... ἐν ᾧ δεῖ σωθῆναι 4:12).

Through Luke's word-play on the "save" word-family, he intimates that the man's physical healing is a sign of eschatological salvation[593]; as such, it is a prolepetic anticipation of the *eschaton*.

The impressive story extends what Jesus began through his earthly ministry. Now he continues that same focus through Spirit-empowered people (1:1), so that Luke notes "the many wonders and signs that were occurring through the apostles" (2:43). As for the religious authorities, as much as they try to avoid, deny, suppress or put a "gag order"[594] on this "sign," their silence-charge does not work, since the healed beggar is visibly before them. Pervo likens their approach to "locking the barn doors after the horse has fled."[595] Thus, for Luke, religious opposition flies straight in the face of an undeniable and miraculous healing of the crippled beggar. Since they cannot be convinced by the clear evidence before them, Luke intends that his readers probe their unmistakable meanness; their impotent obstruction is used as a counter-point to the accentuated joy.

Fulfilled prophecy (Acts 3-4). Luke also accentuates the fulfillment of the charismatic gift of prophecy in these two chapters in a similar way to the prophesied baptism in the Spirit (Luke 24:49; Acts 1:4-8) and its fulfillment (Acts 2:1-4), noted by six explicit references to prophets or prophecy and five references to the Old Testament.[596] In addition, Samuel is mentioned (Acts 4:24) along with Moses, Abraham, and David. The content of the prophetic utterances from the Old Testament deals with the fulfillment in:

- The theophany granted to Moses (Exod 3:6, 15) and relational link between Israel's fathers and God's "glorifying his servant" through the miracle performed in Jesus' name (Acts 3:13); in the affirmation, *God glorified his servant* (ἐδόξασεν τὸν παῖδια αὐτοῦ Ἰησοῦ), there is also an allusion to Isaiah's Servant Song, *my servant will be glorified* (ὁ παῖς μου δοξασθήσεται Isa 52:13 LXX).
- Jesus' suffering (Acts 3:18).
- The restoration of all things (Acts 3:21); "a restoration of the original order of creation."[597]
- The double entendre of a prophet who will follow Moses, whom "God will raise up," which Luke uses to refer to Jesus' resurrection (Acts 3:22; Deut 18:15-16).
- A threat of being "cut-off" if people do not respond to the risen Jesus (Acts 3:23; Deut 18:19; Lev 23:29).
- These days (Acts 3:24).
- Joyful blessing (mentioned twice: *shall be blessed* [ἐν] εὐλογηθήσοναι; *blessing you* [εὐλογοῦντα ὑμᾶς] for Abraham's posterity, joined with the resurrection and the gift of repentance (Acts 3:26; Gen 22:3, 18; 26:4).
- Victory of the stone over people who reject the arch-stone (Acts 4:11; Psa 118:22), now equated with the religious authorities.[598]

- The futility of raging and conspiring[599] vain things against
  the Lord and his anointed (Acts 4:25-26; Psa. 2:1-2).

Luke's text clearly highlights the fulfillment of charismatic prophecy.
For example, the verbal form, *they were gathered together* (συνήχθησαν)
reflects an Old Testament reference to the hostile nations in David's
Royal Psalm (Psa 2:1-2; Acts 4:26). This was fulfilled in Jesus' Passion,
as rulers and people *were gathered together* (συνήχθησαν Acts 4:27) in
their conspiracy to put Jesus to death. The expression, "all the prophets,"
need not be pressed with literal detail. Instead Luke points to the
comprehensive and unified witness of the Old Testament, as fulfilled
in Jesus' person, words and works. That now infuses the ministry of
the Early Church. Luke stresses continuity between the continued Old
Testament witness that now includes Jesus and the community's witness
to him, indicating that fulfilled prophecy also occasions joy.

Luke also includes the immediate fulfillment of concerted prayer to
speak the word with boldness and its immediate answer:

- *Prayer:* "and give to your servants *the boldness to speak your
  word*" (καὶ δὸς τοῖς δουλοῖς σου μετὰ παρρησίας
  πάσης λαλεῖν τὸν λόγον σου Acts 4:29),
- *Answered prayer:* In addition to the shaking of the place,
  "they were all with the Holy Spirit and *were speaking the
  word of God with boldness* (καὶ ἐλάλουν τὸν λόγον τοῦ
  θεοῦ μετὰ παρρησίας (4:34).

Luke is a careful writer. He intentionally points his readers to these cues.
Other references to the miraculous. Luke uses numerous terms to
highlight the miraculous activity of the apostles with three references
to "sign" (σημεῖον),[600] two of which refer to the "sign" of the healed
crippled-beggar, while the third reference (Acts 4:30) is part of the
prayer of the gathered community for God to increase "signs." Twice,
Luke refers to "healing" (ἴασις),[601] and the verb, "I heal" (θεραπεύω
4:14), which similarly refer to the healing of the beggar and the prayer
of the gathered community for "healings." There is one mention of

"wonder" (τέρας), which is also part of the community's prayer for "wonders." Finally, Luke mentions "power" (δύναμις) three times.[602] The first two occurrences relate to the healing of the beggar. In Peter's response to the public in 3:12, he clarifies that the "power" does not reside within him or John, but rather it flows through them.[603] The third mention of "power" opens up more general expressions of miraculous power that witness to the resurrection of Jesus in the narrative-summary (4:32-37).

The community's concerted prayer asking God to extend healings, signs and wonders (Acts 4:30) yields the answered physical shaking of the place where they were gathered (4:31). Luke confirms this in his narrative summary (4:33). His abundant references to the beggar's healing and its visibility provide a springboard for more charismatic expressions of power. Clearly, Luke intends that subsequent communities would likewise carry on their task of witness with miraculous power and joyous emotion.

The Holy Spirit. Luke also wants his readers to appreciate the Holy Spirit's dynamic role. His text in Acts 3-4 includes three explicit references to the Holy Spirit, two of which are in the context of "being filled with the Holy Spirit,"[604] leading to inspired *speaking*,[605] with boldness (παρρησία).[606] The first reference accentuates Peter's special inspiration, whereby he responds to the religious hostility encapsulated in this question: "By what *power* or in what name did you do this?" (4:7) In response, Peter is filled with the Spirit and is thereby empowered to preach an inspired sermon (4:8). Peter's inspiration is also accentuated by the religious authorities' awareness that something unique was occurring in the speech of Peter and John, "When they saw the boldness of Peter and John that they were unschooled and ordinary men, they were marveling and they were recognizing that these men had been with Jesus" (4:13). Such awareness by the religious authorities is also found in their gag-order, which includes the verb, "to speak in an inspired manner" (φθέγγομαι), "they commanded them not *to speak* (φθέγγεσθαι) or teach at all in the name of Jesus" (4:18). Luke's careful readers might note that the compound verb (ἀποφθέγγομαι) of the same verb ties to the inspired utterance in other tongues (2:4) and Peter's sermon in which he is inspired to explain (2:14) the previous question. The third reference identifies the Holy Spirit as the means by which "God spoke through the mouth of David your servant" (4:25).

Although Luke does not mention the Holy Spirit in the conversion of about five thousand (Acts 4:4), we can safely conclude that the same gift of the Holy Spirit (2:38-39) was also promised to this group. Acts 4:4 notes the numerical growth of believers in a very hurried hiatus[607] set within the context of religious hostility, before (4:1-3) and after (4:5-22). The last explicit reference to the Holy Spirit is in the context of the community's concerted prayer, which yielded the following result: "all were filled with the Holy Spirit and were speaking the word of God with boldness" (Acts 4:31).

The crowd. The crowd is "in-process" in responding to the healing. De Long is a bit pejorative in her analysis of the crowd's response when she notes that their response is a misdirected gaze.[608] She looks to their response in 4:32, "they were glorifying God" as a response they should have immediately made, following the healing and she scarcely mentions the reference to five-thousand (+) new believers in 4:4, which is sandwiched between two sections of religious hostility. The mixed nature of the crowd's response is similar to the disciples in the post-resurrection stories of Luke 24, and to the crowd's varied reactions to the miracle of other tongues in Luke 2. For Luke, this is not a problem but a graphic narrative of people who encounter the numinous. The people progressively discover the nature and meaning of this miraculous healing. What are their responses?

- *"they were recognizing"* (ἐπεγίνωσκεν) the identity of the crippled beggar (Acts 3:10).
- *"they were filled with wonder and amazement/ecstasy* at the event which had occurred with him" (ἐπλήσθησαν θάμβους καὶ ἐκστάσεως ἐπὶ τῷ συμβεβηκότι αὐτῷ 3:10).
- "all the people *ran*[609] to them ... *amazed*" (συνέδραμεν πᾶς ὁ λαὸς πρὸς αὐτοὺς ... ἔκθαμβοι 3:11).

- Peter's speech contains the rhetorical questions, "Why do you *marvel* at this or why do you *stare* ...?" (τί θαυμάζετε ἢ τί ἀτενίζετε ...; 3:12).
- In response to Peter's sermon, which includes the commands, *"repent and turn* so that your sins might be covered over"* (μετανοήσατε ... καὶ ἐπιστρέψατε εἰς τὸ ἐξαλειφθῆναι ὑμῶν τὰς ἁμαρτίας 3:19), Luke notes the positive response of the crowd: "many of those who heard to the word *trusted*" (πολλοὶ δὲ ἀκουσάντων τὸν λόγον ἐπίστευσαν 4:4). Further, the number of converts, *five thousand men* (4:4), is larger than "about three thousand persons" of 2:41. Luke's mention of five thousand "men" opens the door to women who also believed. The actual numbers are less significant than Luke's point of dynamic growth in the number of believers.
- "Because *all were glorifying God* at the event" (ὅτι πάντες ἐδόξαζον τὸν θεὸν ἐπὶ τῷ γεγονότι 4:21), the rulers were unable to punish Peter and John; the leaders can only threaten the pair.

Yes, the people didn't initially understand the significance of the event they witnessed, but neither did the disciples truly comprehend what was happening when they first encountered the post-resurrected Jesus (Luke 24), nor did the people who initially responded to the miracle of other tongues (Acts 2). The same verbs and nouns that express the human responses of Luke 24 and Acts 2 appear in the narrative of Acts 3-4. Certainly, the people need re-direction (Acts 3:12-13) from the apostles' power or piety, and to God, who has glorified his Servant Jesus (Acts 3:13). That fact does not nullify the positive nature of their emotional response to the numinous.[610]

As Haenchen notes, "they are overcome with θάμβος, the awe felt in the presence of divine activity ... and ἔκστασις: man is lifted out of his habitual life and thought by encountering the power of God. Thus, not merely the healing itself, but also the human reaction to it—in both the man healed and the spectators—belong to the realm of such accounts."[611] They are moved not only by the miraculous healing but the physical movement and vocal praise of God by the man "walking, leaping, praising God," a man, who is now no longer a crippled beggar but an extremely whole and joyous man who does not hesitate to display his emotion in public. Peter's reference to God, who *glorified* (ἐδόξασεν) his Servant Jesus (Acts 3:13) relates directly to the healing of the paralytic. Later, the same witnesses answer Peter's affirmation, *they were glorifying* (ἐδόξαζον) God" (4:21). Surely, their believing response in 4:4 to the miracle and Peter's sermon, contains the element of glorifying God as well.

The joy-less critics. Luke uses the joy-less religious authorities to accentuate the joyful atmosphere, experience, and expressions of joy inherent in the healing experience. Acts 1-2 does not include any discordant critique by religious authorities,[612] but here, Luke voices the religious critique and explains why they are both annoyed and aggressive. First, the apostles are teaching the people, but teaching should belong to the authorities alone. Second, they were proclaiming in Jesus, the resurrection of the dead (διαπονούμενοι διὰ τὸ διδάσκειν αὐτοὺς τὸν λαὸν καὶ καταγγέλλειν ἐν τῷ Ἰησοῦ τὴν ἀνάστασιν τὴν ἐκ νεκρῶν). In response, the religious authorities seize the apostles and put them in prison (καὶ ἐπέβαλον αὐτοῖς τὰς χεῖρας καὶ ἔθεντο εἰς τήρησιν Acts 4:3),

Following the apostles' imprisonment, the rulers aggressively stand the apostles in the middle of their assembly and insistently question the source of their power or name (Acts 4:7); Luke accentuates the number of people and groups engaging in the inquisition (4:5-6). Luke also highlights the senselessness of their "trial" of the apostles, "Is a healing a reason for arraigning the healer?"[613]

In response to the apostles' powerful testimony, they marvel at the boldness, source and clarity of their powerful witness. The authorities know of the apostles' charismatic relationship with Jesus (θεωροῦντες δὲ τὴν τοῦ Πέτρου παρρησίαν καὶ καταλαβόμενοι ὅτι ἄνθρποι ἀγράμματοί εἰσιν καὶ ἰδιῶται, ἐθαύμαζον ἐπεγίνωσκόν τε αὐτοὺς ὅτι σὺν τῷ Ἰησοῦ ἦσαν 4:13).

This awareness pushes them to abandon their inquisition of the apostles as they begin questioning each other regarding their response to the two apostles. Clearly, they are confused (Acts 4:15-16). Their impotence, "we are unable to deny [the miracle]" (οὐ δυνάμεθα ἀρνεῖσθαι 4:16) blends with their motivating fear, "But to stop this thing from further spreading among the people" (4:17).

In view of their impotence and fear, their only envisioned course of action is to silence the two apostles (Acts 4:17). Their deliberation and course of action inside the court yields another interrogation of the two apostles with their requirement that the apostles must cease their inspired preaching or teaching in Jesus' name (παρήγγειλαν τὸ καθόλου μὴ φθέγγεσθαι μηδὲ διδάσκειν ἐπὶ τῷ ὀνόματι τοῦ Ἰησοῦ Acts 4:18). The apostles immediately and flatly reject this gag-order (4:19-20).

In view of the crowd's praise of God, the authorities' only recourse is to threaten the apostles, which amounts to an idle threat (Acts 4:21). Their hostile intent is frustrated by their recognition that they "don't have a case" against the apostles (μηδὲν εὑρίσκοντες τὸ πῶς κολάσωνται αὐτούς 4:21). They also fear the joyful crowd, with their praise at what had occurred (διὰ τὸν λαόν, ὅτι πάντες ἐδόξαζον τὸν θεὸν ἐπὶ τῷ γεγονότι 4:21).

Luke connects the joy-less and hostile response of the religious authorities with their anger, aggression, insecurity, frustration, impotence, fear, charges, and threats. Luke contrasts all of this insecure negativity with the apostles' Holy-Spirit-inspired boldness (παρρησία), noted three times in Acts 4:13, 29, 31.[614] As a whole, joy is not only explicit and implicit in the narrative, but is also contrasted by its antithesis in the hostile but impotent aggression of religious authorities.

For Luke, sadly enough, Spirit-empowered miracles and witness do not always bring joyous conversion. Observers and participants certainly can reject the offer of a joyous new life. Luke demonstrates this through the pure meanness of the joy-less religious authorities, who are poorly motivated. Acts 4 paves the way for further Jewish hostility to the pneumatic community and their witness; Luke's readers should draw strength and encouragement in that they belong to good company, with Jesus, the apostles and the Spirit-empowered community—the various

Lucan communities are not alone in their experience of persecution and suffering.

Luke wants his readers to appreciate and experience the miraculous, which is a continuation of the ministry of Jesus and a fulfillment of Old Testament promise. The sequel (Acts 3-4) to the initial Pentecost story (Acts 1-2) affirms the continuation of Pentecostal power, now played out by others. Luke is careful to highlight the emotional experiences, atmosphere and expressions of joy—all leading to praise for God. Luke argues that empowered witness flows from this wellspring of joy, regardless of whether the explicit "witness" word-family is used in the narrative. The combined witness of the miracle, emotional joy and inspired preaching is powerful to the extent that more people believed than on the actual Day of Pentecost.

Joyous Appointments
(Acts 8:1-9:43)

Luke orchestrates narratives about key figures (Philip, Peter and John, Saul, Peter) to highlight joyous appointments when people encounter the Holy Spirit's power. The stories are knit together and are well-arranged. For Luke, the initial story of Philip's ministry in Samaria and the following account of his ministry to a black Ethiopian eunuch represents the fulfillment of the program that the risen Jesus delineates in Acts 1:8, "Jerusalem, Judea, Samaria and to the ends of the earth." Philip, Peter, and John are key players in the Samaritan experience of receiving the Holy Spirit. Saul's dramatic encounter with the risen Jesus and reception of the Holy Spirit (Acts 9:1-19) immediately leads to public proclamation and the happy outcome in the church (9:31). That account is followed by two Peter-stories, in which Jesus heals a long-standing cripple, Aeneas (9:32-35) and raises Tabitha from the dead (9:36-43). As a result, many people turn to the Lord Jesus. Once again, Luke highlights the pairing of charismatic activity with the atmosphere, experience and expression of joy, noting "there was much joy in that city" (Acts 8:5-8).[615] He also notes that the eunuch "went on his way rejoicing" (Acts 8:39). Luke narrates numerous charismatic events that he infuses with joyous emotion.

Much Joy in Samaria
(Acts 8:4-25).

The witness in Samaria is preceded by the dispersion of all, except the apostles due to persecution in Jerusalem, "all were dispersed throughout Judea and Samaria" (8:1), followed by "the ones who were dispersed" (8:4)—specifically the Hellenists. Some preliminary observations are in order.

- Mention of Samaria in Acts 8:1 and 8:5, "that city" in 8:8.616
- The apostles who stay in Jerusalem (Acts 8:1), two of whom (Peter and John) are later sent from Jerusalem to Samaria (Acts 8:14-15).
- The persecution is both general, "a great persecution" (Acts 8:1) and particular with the mention of Saul's aggression (Acts 8:1, 3).
- Luke uses inclusion in which he bookends the Samaritan story with the general preaching activity before and after this episode.

Although the language is awkward, Luke highlights the joy-eliciting good news: "therefore, on the one hand, the ones who were preaching the good news ... word (εὐαγγελιζομενοι τὸν λόγον Acts 8:4); "therefore, those who had witnessed and proclaimed the word of the Lord ... were preaching the good news" (οἱ μὲν οὖν διαμαρυτάμενοι καὶ λαλήσαντες τὸν λόγον τοῦ κυρίου ... εὐηγγελίζοντο Acts 8:25).

Further, the explicit mention of much joy in Acts 8:8 parallels the later joyful response of a receptive Ethiopian eunuch (8:39), to Philip's preaching of the good news ("he preached the good news of Jesus" εὐηγγελίσατο τὸν Ἰησοῦν 8:35).

Luke does not provide the kerygmatic progression that is provided in his earlier sermons; however, this is only natural since he reports scenes only in the third person.[617] He couples verbal declarations of the kerygma with miraculous power. The following expressions are coordinated:

- "preaching the word (good news)" (εὐαγγελιζόμενοι τὸν λόγον Acts 8:4)—by those dispersed.
- "preaching[618] the Messiah" (ἐκήρυσσεν τὸν Χριστόν Acts 8:5)—by Philip.
- "to the things being preached" (τοῖς λεγομένοις Acts 8:5)—by Philip.
- "preaching the good news concerning the kingdom of God and the name of Jesus Christ" (εὐαγγελιζομένῳ περὶ τῆς βασιλείας τοῦ θεοῦ καὶ τοῦ ὀνόματος Ἰησοῦ Χριστοῦ Acts 8:12)—by Philip.
- "the word of God" (τὸ λόγον τοῦ θεοῦ Acts 8:14)—by Philip.
- "in the name of the Lord Jesus" (εἰς τὸ ὄνομα τοῦ κυρίου Ἰησοῦ Acts 8:16)—by Philip.
- "witnessing and proclaiming the word of the Lord" (διαμαρτυράμενοι καὶ λαλήσαντες τὸν λόγον τοῦ κυρίου Acts 8:25)—by those leaving Samaria.
- "they were preaching the good news" (εὐηγγελίζοντο Acts 8:25)—by those leaving Samaria.

Thus, we find three references to "preaching the good news" (εὐαγγελίζομαι Acts 8:4, 12, 25), three notations of the "word" (λόγος 8:4, 14, 24), two uses of the all-powerful, "name" (ὄνομα 8:12, 16), one mention of the Messiah (Χριστός 8:5), and one reference to "the kingdom of God" (ἡ βασιλεία τοῦ θεοῦ 8:12). [619] We also find three other verbs related to preaching: "I preach" κηρύσσω 8:5), "I witness" (διαμαρτύρομαι 8:25), and "I speak" (λαλέω 8:25). While the various verbs and coordinated nouns refer to the same reality of the Jesus story, they provide various aspects of the kerygma, i.e. ways that the kerygma can be understood, experienced or expressed, all couched in affective language of joy.

This declaration is succinctly expressed by "the word," which may remind Luke's readers of the community's prayer to "speak the word with boldness" (Acts 4:29). This prayer brought immediate fulfillment (4:31). Luke recorded Peter's boldness before religious authorities (Acts 4-5) and in the declaration to the Samaritans (Acts 8:4, 14, 24). The theme of "witness," important in earlier chapters of Acts (1:8; 2:32; Acts 2:40-διαμαρτύρομαι), is likewise expressed by those who leave Samaria in 8:25.

In noting the essential congruity of the apostles and Philip in proclaiming the same good news, Luke intends his readers to understand that they are allies.[620] Due to the fact that the apostles, Peter and John, later come to Samaria and notice a lack of the gift of the Holy Spirit, several scholars argue that Philip's message and the Samaritan response are defective. For example, Dunn argues that Philip had preached the *Taheb* ("restorer"), based upon Deuteronomy 18:15ff., whom the Samaritans anticipated.[621] He also appeals to the gnostic origin of Simon the magician[622] in Acts 8 and the fact that Luke states that the Samaritans believed in Philip (ἐπίστευσαν τῷ Φιλίππῳ Acts 8:12) and not the "good news." However, as Barrett notes, "the first step towards faith in a full theological sense is to recognize, 'What this preacher says is true.'"[623]

Luke provides no suggestion that Philip's message and the joyous Samaritan reception were defective.[624] Luke affirms that Philip preached the Messiah (Acts 8:5), the kingdom of God and the name of Jesus Christ (Acts 8:12). Further, Luke does not state that the apostles were informed of any defective message and reception, which then leads them to "inspect"[625] and "correct."[626] Luke provides no motive for why the two apostles journeyed to Samaria. When the apostles arrive, they make no mention of Philip's defective message and they do not correct him. Dunn argues that the Samaritans cannot really be Christians because "the Holy Spirit not fallen upon them and that they had only been baptized in the name of the Lord Jesus" (Acts 8:16).

Clearly, Dunn interprets the Samaritan episode through the Pauline lens that it is the Spirit alone that makes one a Christian ("if anyone does not have the Spirit of Christ, this one is not of him [Christ]" Romans 8:9). In so doing, Dunn makes no allowance for the possibility that both Luke and Paul possess and articulate different insights about "the falling of the Spirit" (Acts 8:16).[627] For Luke, the "falling of the Holy Spirit" (8:16) or "receiving the Spirit" (8:19) or the "gift of God" (8:20) all refer to the charismatic manifestations that elicit joy and enable people to boldly speak and act for God. In Luke-Acts, Luke does not associate the baptism in the Holy Spirit with initial conversion and sanctification in the way Paul does (e.g. I Thess. 4:1-8); for Luke, the baptism or gift of the Spirit is sensorial and can be observed (e.g. Acts 2:4-6; 8:17-18).

Numinous elements in Acts 8:4-25. Luke's three-fold use of the verb, "I preach the good news" (εὐαγγελίζομαι Acts 8:4, 12, 25) implies a joyful response, and it often connects with miracles in Luke's writings, as a prelude to the Early Church's declarations and actions in terms of healing and exorcism.

Luke further specifies Philip's miraculous activity, which the Samaritans are able to "hear and see" (ἀκούειν αὐτοὺς καὶ βλέπειν Acts 8:6). The Samaritans don't just hear Philip's message, but they also hear the "loud shrieks" (βοῶντα φωνῇ μεγάλῃ 8:7)[628] from the unclean spirits which exit the possessed people. They also see both the new-found freedom of those who have been bound by unclean spirits and the healed condition of crippled persons (8:7). Thus, Acts demonstrates a movement from the particular healing of one crippled beggar in Acts 3-4 to the more general healing of many in a similar crippled condition in 8:7. Luke calls these exorcisms and healings "signs which he was doing" (τὰ σημεῖα ἃ ἐποίει 8:6).[629] Later, Luke narrates that Simon was attaching himself to Philip because of the "signs and great miracles" (σημεῖα καὶ δυνάμεις μεγάλας 8:13). In a natural manner, Luke informs his readers that miraculous signs not only accompany the apostles, but are also performed by Philip, one of the appointed deacons (6:5).[630] The community's earlier prayer for "healings, signs and wonders" (4:30) is also fulfilled by Philip, who was not included among the original twelve.

Acts 8 begins a story (Acts 8:4-8), then interrupts with a "flashback" (8:9-11), and then offers the sequel (8:12-13). Luke follows this with another sequel of the Samaritan reception of the Holy Spirit (8:14-17). The "flashback" concerning Simon sets the stage for Philip's triumph over him and his magic. Barrett reminds us that "Simon was already there and in possession of the playing field."[631] While the people were amazed and gave attention to Simon (past), now they trust (present) in Philip who preaches the joy-producing good news, concerning the kingdom of God and the name of Jesus Christ" (ὅτε δὲ ἐπίστευσαν τῷ Φιλίππῳ εὐαγγελιζομένῳ περὶ τῆς βασιλείας τοῦ θεοῦ καὶ τοῦ ὀνόματος᾽ Ἰησοῦ Χριστοῦ 8:12).

Due to the "flashback," the ordering of the text may appear to narrate the later Samaritan belief/trust after an experience of joy over signs. This causes scholars such as Dunn to remark, "the mention of 'much joy' (8:8) *precedes* the account of the Samaritan's actual conversion."[632] However, Luke emphasizes Philip's triumph over Simon with the believing Samaritans and a believing Simon, all of whom are baptized (8:12-13); Luke cannot do so without providing the necessary context for trust and baptism (Samaritans & Simon). Thus, Luke highlights the atmosphere and experience of joy, which are linked to the message, to the signs, and to the believing response with a subsequent submission to baptism. Dunn wants to limit the Samaritan response of joy only to what they heard and what they saw.[633]

Luke contrasts Philip's message, signs, and great miracles with Simon's magical prowess through Philip's triumph over Simon.[634] In a "flash-back" scene (Acts 8:9), Luke narrates Simon's activity and self-proclamation through three participles:

- "practicing magic" (μαγεύων).
- "amazing the people of Samaria" (ἐξιστάνων τὸ ἔθνος τῆς Σαμαρείας).
- "boasting that he was someone great" (λέγων εἶναι τινα ἑαυτὸν μεγάλου (8:9).

Luke then recounts the positive Samaritan estimation of Simon's magical activity and self-proclamation:

- "to whom [Simon] all the people both small and great gave their attention,"
- "saying, 'This is the power of God, the one being called Great'" (8:10)[635]
- "giving their attention to him because he had amazed them for a long time with his magic" (8:11).

Several items are noteworthy:

- The people's positive response to Simon matches his magical practice and self-promotion.
- Simon promotes Simon whereas Philip promotes the Messiah, accompanied by signs and, exorcism and, healing (8:5-7), the kingdom of God, and the name of Jesus Christ (8:12).[636]
- In the previous narrative, the Samaritans "were giving their attention" (8:6) to Philip when they hear and see Philip's signs (8:7). In the flashback scene, Luke repeats the verb, "they were giving attention" (προσεῖχον 8:10-11), in this case "to Simon" for his magical activity.
- Luke repeats the verb "I am amazed" (ἐξίστημι), twice from the Samarians to Simon (8:9, 11). After the Samaritans and Simon believe and are baptized, Simon "is amazed" (ἐξίστατο 8:13). Thus, the one who had amazed others is amazed by Philip.
- While Philip's full-orbed "good news" produces joy and trust, Simon's magic produced only amazed attention to himself.
- Simon makes no attempt to compete with Philip for the attention of the people.[637]
- Simon promotes himself as "*great*" (μέγαν 8:9) and the people say that he is "the *power* of God" (ἡ δύναμις τοῦ θεοῦ 8:10) and "the one being called '*Great*'" (ἡ καλουμένη Μεγάλη 8:10); however, he is overwhelmed by Philip's "*great miracles*" (δυνάμεις μεγάλας 8:13).[638]

Reception of the Holy Spirit. The gift of the Holy Spirit is certainly a climactic and charismatic event in Acts 8:4-25. Peter and John travel from Jerusalem to Samaria and discover something is missing in the Samaritan experience. Upon their arrival they discover a deficiency:

- "the Holy Spirit had not fallen[639] upon them" (οὐδέπω γὰρ ἦν ἐπ᾽ οὐδενὶ αὐτῶν ἐπιπεπτωκός).
- "they had only been baptized in the name of the Lord Jesus" (μόνον δὲ βεβαπτισμένοι ὑπῆρχον εἰς τὸ ὄνομα τοῦ κυρίου᾽ Ἰησοῦ 8:16).[640]

As a result of this lack, the apostles pray for them to receive the Holy Spirit (Acts 8:16), lay their hands upon them (8:17) and the effect is simply stated, "they were receiving the Holy Spirit" (ἐλάμβανον πνεῦμα ἅγιον 8:17).

Why did the apostles perceive the lack of the Holy Spirit among the Samaritan believers? What did they expect to see or hear? Was it the gift of other tongues that were received on the Day of Pentecost?[641] Was it inspired or prophetic speech? Was it ecstatic joy? Was there some other manifestation?[642] Apparently, Luke doesn't care to inform his readers of the specific nature of the Holy Spirit's manifestation in Acts 8. Still, it is clear that the reception of the gift of the Holy Spirit was sensorial and observable, to the extent that the apostles noticed the absence and Simon perceived the presence of the Holy Spirit that could be transmitted by others.

Whatever its nature, the reception of the Holy Spirit is different from the signs and great miracles that Philip performed since Simon doesn't ask for the authority to exorcise and heal, signs and great miracles, but the ability to confer the Holy Spirit that he had just witnessed (Acts 8:18-19). Clearly the reception of the Holy Spirit must have been impressive. Pervo states, "it must be quite fabulous if Simon simply had to have it."[643] Beyond this, the text is silent in terms of what was perceived in the Samaritan reception of the Holy Spirit.

Samaritan joy and trust. The story in Samaria is introduced by the explicit message of joy. Luke notes that the witnesses of the miraculous are "in-process" as they encounter the miraculous. During the first Samaritan episode, the Samaritans "were giving attention" (προσεῖχον) to Philip's message; they also heard and saw the signs Philip was doing (exorcisms & healings). Luke provides here the awkward adverb, "with one accord" (ὁμοθυμαδόν Acts 8:6), which links this event to the communal response of the Jerusalem community in 1:14; 2:1, 46; 4:24; 5:12. Generally, the adverb is used as an expression of unity in prayer. Barrett similarly notes, "They began to be united with one another as they accepted the Christian message."[644] Thus, the adverb is combined with the verb, "they gave attention," for they express a positive and unified interest in response to Philip's message and miraculous signs.

Perhaps Luke links the healing of the "many paralytics and crippled" (πολλοὶ δὲ παραλελυμένοι καὶ χωλοὶ Acts 8:7) to the healing of the crippled beggar (χωλός) of Acts 3-4. Careful readers would recall numerous statements of joy, e.g. "walking and leaping and praising God" (3:8) and the Old Testament background of Isaiah 35, a chapter that is replete with the joy-vocabulary. One man's experience (Acts 3-4) now becomes the shared joy of many in a similar crippled condition (8:7). Further, the experience of one crippled-beggar, healed (σέσωται 4:10) by the name of Jesus, is parabolic of salvation in the name of Jesus (Acts 4:12). No doubt for Luke, the same idea carries into the healing of many in Acts 8:7 with an attendant joy.

Luke then notes the effect of Philip's preaching and miraculous signs of exorcism and healing, "there was much joy in that city" (ἐγένετο δὲ πολλὴ χαρὰ ἐν τῇ πόλει ἐκείνῃ Acts 8:8). Luke notes the climax of this initial episode, marked by the atmosphere and experience of joy in response to Philip's "joy-producing good news"—expressed in both word and deed.

The report that reached the apostles in Jerusalem is clear, "Samaria has received[645] the word of God" (δέδεκται ἡ Σαμάρεια τὸν λόγον τοῦ θεοῦ Acts 8:14). The trust and subsequent baptism of the people is paralleled by Simon's trust and subsequent baptism:

People: "When they believed in Philip ... both men and women were being baptized."

(ὅτε δὲ ἐπίστευσαν τῷ Φιλίππῳ . . ἐβαπτίζοντο ἄνδρες τε καὶ γυναῖκες) 8:12,

Simon: "Now even Simon himself believed and having been baptized"(ὁ δὲ Σίμων καὶ αὐτὸς ἐπίστευσεν καὶ βαπτισθεὶς) 8:13.

Luke informs his readers that Simon *was attached* (ἦν προσκαρτερῶν), i.e. "followed" Philip, since he could see the signs and great miracles (8:13). Simon does not immediately discard his past life as a magician, for he is fascinated by Philip's great miracles. Later he expresses a desire to purchase the gift of imparting the Spirit, for all the wrong reasons.

The Samaritans not only respond with attention, trust, joy and submission of themselves to baptism but they submit themselves to the laying on of hands[646] for the impartation of the Holy Spirit, which "they were receiving" (ἐλάμβανον Acts 8:17).[647] Acts 8:20 identifies the Holy Spirit as the "gift of God" (τὴν δωρεὰν τοῦ θεοῦ).[648] Pervo argues, "The patent fact is that the Spirit comes at the opportune moment. Behind this literary device is a theological conviction: the wind blows where it wills. No institution or person can manipulate the Spirit of God, a point doubly made in this passage."[649]

The Samaritans experience their own Pentecost, uniting them with the Jerusalem community ("of one accord" ὁμοθυμαδόν). As for the apostles, "The only miracle they were in fact performing—though of course, in Christian eyes, the most miraculous of all—was the bestowing of the Spirit,"[650] which is expressed as inspired speech, heightened joy, or some other charismatic expression. For Luke, the Spirit is a gift which can be imparted to others but not fully possessed. In the joy-filled environment, the (ecstatic) Spirit is imparted, which is observable and experienced by all. Clearly, Luke is not interested in one paradigm of Spirit-reception; in the various stories of the baptism in the Spirit, "it may be more fruitful to view them as illustrations-of the variety of Christian experience."[651]

Another subtle reference to the numinous occurs with Peter's "interior insight" into Simon's heart, "*I see that you are* (ὁρῶ σε ὄντα) causing bitter judgment for yourself 'as befits a person who is held fast by sin'"[652] (8:23). Luke is quite consistent with the connection between prophecy and "interior insight,"[653] for such second sight enables Peter to see the hypocrisy of Ananias and Sapphira in 5:1-11. In Simon's case, Peter sees the wrong condition of Simon's heart, his evil, and his wicked intent (8:21-23). He understands Simon's desire to purchase "the gift of God" so that he also might be able to confer the Holy Spirit to others by laying his hands on them (8:19). Simon seems to crave another "trick" to further his fame as a magician and provide him with additional revenue. In any case, Luke contrasts God's gift with a purchase; one cannot buy "a gift."

Just as Philip's activity triumphs over Simon and his magic (Acts 8:12-13), so Peter overcomes Simon and his magical intent, "To hell with you and your money, because you thought you would obtain the gift of God with money" (8:20).[654] Peter commands that Simon repent and *pray to the Lord* (δεήθητι τοῦ κυρίου) for his evil intent (8:22), leading to Simon's petition, that Peter and John *pray to the Lord* (Δεήθητε ... πρὸς τὸν κύριον) on his behalf (8:24). He is fearful that Peter's prophesied judgment will fall upon him (8:24).[655] As Pervo states, Simon is "overwhelmed by Philip and demolished by Peter."[656] Luke establishes that Christian leaders are gifted with charismatic power, evident in effective proclamation, signs, exorcisms, healing, great miracles, and the authority to confer the gift of the Holy Spirit in a way that produces joy and trust. But they are not interested in money: "I do not have silver and gold" (3:6), now exposing Simon's motives (8:20). Pervo notes again, "Miracle, magic and money are elements of power. The episode is thus a lesson in the proper use of power."[657] Twelftree summarizes the lesson, "magic is associated with a ministry that is not Spirit-empowered but self-centered and self-aggrandizing and that seeks financial gain."[658]

Luke leaves the text open, without narrating Simon's immediate response, future activity or career. In terms of the whole of 8:4-25, Philip, Peter, and John triumph over self-aggrandizing magic with their effective proclamation in word and deed, climaxed by the gift of the Holy Spirit to the Samaritans.

Luke concludes the Samaritan episode with the continuation of the powerful and joy-producing "good news," by the apostles in Samaritan villages en route to Jerusalem. Since Philip reappears in the next episode, Luke's readers are unsure whether Philip joined them in their journey. Luke establishes that Philip's mission in Samaria was continued by the leaders of the Jerusalem community and was fully endorsed and supplemented by the "gift of the Spirit" in the several villages. All are allies.

"On his way rejoicing"
(Acts 8:26-40)

Luke provides another joyous appointment in his story of Philip and an Ethiopian eunuch,[659] who travels from Jerusalem to his homeland Ethiopia (Nubia), which is modern Sudan. Numerous approaches are offered for this episode,[660] which do not directly bear upon this joyous encounter. Similar to the *great joy* of the Samaritans in 8:8, the Ethiopian traveler goes on his way *rejoicing* after his encounter with Philip in 8:39. Also, Philip's joy-producing good news concerning "the Messiah" (8:5) in Samaria parallels the declaration, "preaching Jesus" to the eunuch (8:35). In both stories there is a movement from Jewish boundaries of particularism, for Luke advances the story-line from the half-caste Samaritans to a man, who could not belong to the older people of God. Keener notes that "God wanted this foreigner to hear this gospel; he will be not only the forerunner of the African mission, but as the first Gentile convert, the forerunner of the Gentile mission in general."[661] Also, both stories begin with, "therefore, on the one hand" (μὲν οὖν), each of which marks the start of a new section (8:4, 26).

There are also some notable differences between the two stories:

- the city of Samaria (Acts 8:5, 8) versus a road to Gaza, noted as a desert (8:26),
- public conversions of many (8:12) versus a private conversion with one person (8:36-38),
- Philip's extensive miracles (8:6-8, 13) versus no overt miracles,
- Philip is driven to Samaria by persecution (8:1, 3-5) versus divine direction (angel, Spirit) leading him to the eunuch (8:26, 29),
- interaction with Jerusalem apostles in Samaria versus no interaction between the eunuch and Jerusalem.

Luke provides several descriptors of the man. He is a eunuch, a black[662] Ethiopian, high court official, and a chief finance-minister of an Ethiopian queen. He is also returning to Ethiopia,[663] from worshipping in Jerusalem, and he is reading the Bible. As Barrett remarks, "he was certainly a rare bird."[664] Gaventa remarks that his worship in Jerusalem "indicates the receptivity of this particular individual."[665] According to Deuteronomy 23:1, "No one who has been emasculated by crushing or whose penis has been cut off may enter the assembly of the Lord." As such, the man is unable to become a full proselyte under Jewish law. Thus he is in a lesser condition than the Gentile Cornelius, whom Luke positively describes as a generous, prayerful, and "pious God-fearer" (εὐσεβὴς καὶ φοβούμενος τὸν θεὸν Acts 10:2). Cornelius could have become a proselyte while the eunuch is barred from this status.[666]

Luke reveals several charismatic events directing his readers to God's superintending guidance for this outcast. The narrative begins with a reference to "an angel of the Lord" (ἄγγελος θεοῦ Acts 8:26) who utters two crisp commands, "Get up and go" (8:26). Philip's prompt obedience is expressed by the same two verbs, "he got up and went" (8:27).[667] Similar to Peter's angelic deliverance from prison (5:19), an angel now arranges the encounter between Philip and the eunuch. Angels also surface later in Acts, with a particular role of guidance.[668] In contrast to Ananias' hesitation when told to meet Saul (9:13-14), or Peter's strong negation of a divine command ("No way!" Μηδαμῶς 10:14), Philip responds without reserve.

Luke also records further direction, this time by the Spirit, who spoke to Philip, again by two short commands, "Go and attach yourself" to this chariot (Acts 8:29). A similar combination of an "angel" and the "Spirit" is found in two opening lines of the Cornelius-story.[669] At the conclusion of the story, "the Spirit of the Lord" seizes Philip (8:39) and miraculously[670] transports him to Azotus (8:40).

Luke arranges the paragraph in such a way that the numinous is expressed through a series of miraculous "coincidences," which may well be expressed by current idiom, *It just so happened that … :*

- *The angel sent Philip to the right place at the right time* in which he encounters the eunuch, combined with unlikely elements with respect to a journey at noon[671] in a remote area, "to Gaza, this is a desert" (8:26), with no explanation.

- *Philip encounters the right person*, "and behold" (καὶ ἰδου)[672] there was a man, an Ethiopian eunuch (8:27). Luke not only identifies the man but provides information about his powerful position, the purpose of his journey to and from Jerusalem, "to worship" (προσκυνήσων).[673]
- *The eunuch was reading the prophet Isaiah*. Luke prepares for the important imperfect indicative ("he was reading") with two participles: "returning" and "sitting on his chariot" (Acts 8:28). Luke intends that his readers focus upon *what* the eunuch was reading—Isaiah.[674]
- "he was reading *the prophet Isaiah*" (8:28)
- "reading *Isaiah the prophet*" (8:30),
- "Do you understand *what* you are reading?" (a clear word-play, γινώσκεις ἃ ἀναγινώσκεις 8:30)
- "*this* was *the passage* he was reading," followed by the *actual text of Isaiah 53:7-8 LXX*.
- "concerning whom does *the prophet* speak?" (8:34),
- "beginning from *this Scripture*" (8:35).

The center-piece of the story revolves around the specific Isaiah-text.

- *The Spirit commands Philip to attach himself to the Ethiopian's chariot* (8:29). Similar to Philip's immediate and exact obedience to the angel's initial commands (8:26-27), Philip promptly obeys, "When Philip *caught up* with him" (8:30), "*to sit* with him" (8:31). Even at this point, Philip is not told what he's to do.[675]
- *The Ethiopian is eager to have Philip serve as a guide* into the text he was reading (8:31); he needs an interpreter: "How could I possibly understand without someone to guide me?"[676] He is more than ready to receive the explanation and identification of the subject of Isaiah's Fourth Servant Song.
- *At the very moment of Philip's approach, the eunuch is reading the specific text from Isaiah's Fourth Servant Song*

(Isa. 53:7-8; Acts 8:32). As Pervot notes, "The passage
(Isa. 53:7-8a LXX) is a narrative aside that could not have
been more suitable had Luke himself selected. Isa. 53:4-6,
8b, which immediately precede and follow the selection,
are highly suitable, when applied to Jesus, as an interpretation of his death as a saving event."[677] As a whole,
Isaiah's subject is passive and silent[678] in his humiliation
(ταπείνωσις), but the subject will also be exalted[679] with
countless believers.[680] As a disabled and ostracized man,
he could certainly sympathize with the servant's humiliation. He will become one of the "countless believers." As
elsewhere in Luke, the exaltation motif is more central
than the idea of the vicarious atonement.[681]

- *The Ethiopian asks the most important question about the
  identity of the individual* in Isaiah 53:7-8b, "Please tell
  me, of whom does the prophet speak this: of himself or
  someone else?" (Acts 8:34).[682] The eunuch asks an either/
  or question as to the subject of the Fourth Servant Song.
  No other options are available. As Pervo states, "This is
  evidently an ancient way of raising the question of whether
  prophetic texts apply primarily to their own times or to
  later eras."[683] The Ethiopian understands the meaning of
  the text but not the precise identification of the servant.

- *Philip is ready with an interpretive response*: "he preached
  the good news of Jesus to him" (εὐηγγελίσατο αὐτῷ
  τὸν Ἰησοῦν Acts 8:35). Luke informs his readers that
  Philip identifies the explicit subject of the Isaiah text with
  Jesus, "beginning from *this Scripture*" (8:35).[684]

The identity of this Isaian figure is the pivot point in the narrative. In
light of Luke's special interest in the fulfillment-motif, this passage
underscores the way in which the New Testament interprets the Old
Testament. For Luke, the Old Testament is not "self-interpreting,"[685]
but must be understood in the light of the primary Jesus-event,
including his person, words, and works. The participle, "beginning"[686]

(ἀρξάμενος) suggests that Philip used other Old Testament texts that pointed to the fulfillment in the Jesus-story. Although, the explicit content of Philip's message is very brief—that Jesus is the fulfillment of the Isaian text—it surely would include the elements noted in Philip's preaching in Samaria (8:4-13), e.g. the kingdom of God and the name of Jesus (8:12). Perhaps the message included something like Peter's directives in 2:38, "Repent and let each one of you be baptized in the name of Jesus Christ for the forgiveness of sins and you shall receive the gift of the Holy Spirit."

Luke is not systematic in his narratives. It is reasonable to assume that Philip was on the scene in Samaria when the apostles laid hands on the new believers for receiving the Holy Spirit (Acts 8:17). Likewise it is logical that he also spoke about the Holy Spirit to the Ethiopian. If Philip had just witnessed the Samaritan reception of the Holy Spirit, why would he not include this in his message? The Western text includes v. 37[687]; it is reasonable that a later scribe felt it was important to include a faith response. However, Luke is not interested in a consistent "order of salvation" (*ord salutis*), in his stories. Keener makes a solid case for Spirit-reception here.[688] Other *coincidences* occur:

- *"They came upon water ... 'Behold water'"* (᾽Ιδοὺ ὕδωρ Acts 8:36) for baptism of the eunuch (water is mentioned four times (8:36-twice, 38, 39). Luke notes the "just-then" nature of the appearance of water for baptizing the eunuch,[689] made explicit by the expression, "Behold water" (᾽Ιδοὺ ὕδωρ 8:36). Clearly God is superintending this amazing encounter.
- *Philip baptizes the eunuch* (Acts 8:38). Before the actual baptism, the eunuch raises the rhetorical question, "What is to prevent me from being baptized?" (8:36). Instead of a verbal response, "Nothing should stand in the way," Luke makes the answer clear through Philip's action when he baptizes the eunuch. As Spencer comments, the verb, "I prevent/exclude" (κωλύω) "confirms and illuminates the boundary-breaking nature of the eunuch's baptism."

Support is found in other Lucan texts where the verb emerges in texts of inclusion and exclusion.[690] Philip's response is immediate, for he baptizes the eunuch. In light of the eunuch's worship in Jerusalem and reading of Scripture, Gaventa suggests that the Ethiopian experienced an alternation, not a pendulum-like conversion or transformation.[691]

"The Holy Spirit snatched Philip and transported him to Azotus" (Acts 8:39-40).[692] As Marshall notes, "this is an abrupt ending to the story, and it is considerably eased by a longer form of the text,"[693] found in the longer ending of the Western text, which states that when Philip and the eunuch came up out of the water, "the Holy Spirit fell upon the eunuch. An angel of the Lord transported Philip" (πνεῦμα ἅγιον ἐπέπεσεν ἐπὶ τὸν εὐνοῦχον. ἄγγελος δὲ κυρίου ἥρπασεν τὸν Φίλιππὸν 8:39). Due to the fact that the adjective "Holy" follows "Spirit," it can be argued that the whole phrase "might have dropped out by accident."[694] The natural flow of the text would have linked coming out of the water (ἀνέβησαν ἐκ τοῦ ὕδατος 8:39) with the descent of the Spirit upon the eunuch.[695] Other scholars, such as Pervo[696] and Metzger[697] argue for the shorter and more difficult reading. In any case, the longer ending, with the mention of the angel corresponds with the initial appearance of the angel to Philip in 8:26 and the descent of the Holy Spirit corresponds with the gift of the Spirit to the Samaritans (8:17). Even though the longer ending may not have been original, surely the descent of the Spirit on the eunuch can be assumed, expressed by the eunuch's "joy" (8:39).

Luke intends his readers to view the charismatic dimension as including not only Philip's extensive miracles in the Samaritan episode (Acts 8:6-7, 13), but also embracing the providential ordering of the narrative, with the implied, "It just happened that ...," which is made explicit by the repeated particle, "behold" (ἰδού Acts 8:27, 36). Further, the angel/Spirit not only initially brings Philip and the eunuch together at the beginning of the episode but also separates them at the end.

Luke notes that the eunuch *"went on his way rejoicing"* (ἐπορεύτο γὰρ τὴν ὁδὸν αὐτοῦ χαίρων Acts 8:39). Accordingly, Lampe argues that this expression is "not a mere piece of 'padding' to the narrative, but to indicate that he was in fact possessed of the Spirit after his baptism."[698] He also draws a connection with 13:52, "And the disciples were filled with joy and with the Holy Spirit." Consequently, Lampe notes that for Luke, "the Spirit is essentially, as we have observed, the power guiding the missionary expansion of the Church and assisting the progress of the Gospel by signs, by prophesying, and speaking with tongues."[699] Thus, the episode links joy with charismatic encounters.[700] The very fact that the eunuch went back to Ethiopia rejoicing certainly suggests that he had received the Spirit.[701]

One other item not in the text is Philip's miraculous transport when they emerge from the water. Luke's readers can only surmise that through this, the Ethiopian experienced a confirmation of the supernatural character of the entire event. Luke uses the affective language of the Ethiopian's joy, paralleling the emotional response of the Emmaus pair, "Were not our hearts burning within us as he was speaking to us in the way, as he was opening up the Scriptures?" (Luke 24:32). In both instances, joy follows the explanation of Scripture, a supernatural transport, and a journey on the way.

Luke links providential and numinous events with joy in at least two ways. First, his terminology notes the repetition of "preaching the good news" (8:35, 40). Second, Philip's joyous and miraculous activity in Samaria will carry over into the coastal cities as Philip journeys *en route* to Caesarea (8:40). This town becomes Philip's home, the place where he is labeled "the evangelist" ("into the house of Philip the evangelist" εἰς τὸν οἶκον Φιλίππου τοῦ εὐαγγελιστοῦ 21:8)).

Joy is vital for the inclusion of the Ethiopian eunuch in the new people of God. Since the eunuch possessed and read the scroll of Isaiah, we surely might expect he was familiar with Isaiah 56:3-8. This includes an emphatic pronouncement that eunuchs and foreigners would be incorporated into God's household.[702] The Ethiopian is both a eunuch and a foreigner. The man is disadvantaged, disabled, and marginalized. His trip to Jerusalem for the purpose of worship no doubt reminded him of his exclusion from the Jewish cult. Now, he realizes there is nothing to "forbid" (κωλύω 8:36) his full inclusion among God's people, without

Jewish obligations to fulfill. Spencer concludes, "Only in the newly constituted messianic community established through Jesus Christ (whom Philip proclaims) does the Ethiopian eunuch at last find a home among the people of God."[703]

The sphere of inclusion and universalism widens through the book of Acts. Joyous inclusion will embrace Saul, the arch-enemy of the Christian community (Acts 9)[704], the Gentile Cornelius (Acts 10-11), and the broader Gentile community through the decision of the Jerusalem Council (Acts 15). Even though Haenchen sees this episode between Philip and the Ethiopian as a parallel and rival account to the story of Peter and Cornelius,[705] the conversion of the Ethiopian eunuch stands on its own as a partial fulfillment of Acts 1:8, "from Jerusalem, to Judea, to Samarian to the end of the earth." It also looks back to the Baptist's preaching, "all flesh shall see the salvation of God" (Luke 3:6).[706]

"Philip's pioneering step to the Gentiles should not be overlooked or minimized, but it must be kept in perspective. Philip blazes a trail, so to speak into Gentile territory, which Peter then follows and expands."[707] Luke intimates that this influential believer is filled with the Spirit and able to preach the good news "to the end of the earth" in his own sphere of influence.[708] As the mission enlarges, the charismatic dimension continues with joyous affection.

A Joyous and Anticipatory Appointment
(Acts 9:1-31)

Again, Luke interweaves his stories, for Saul's violent aggression that preceded the Samaritan story (Acts 8:1-3), now progresses to more extensive persecution, after the Samaritan narrative. Luke suggests this with the adverbial clause, "Saul, *still* breathing threats and murder" (9:1). Saul travels to Damascus seeking letters of extradition for men and women of "the Way,"[709] intending to bring them back to Jerusalem. Luke's offers three accounts of Saul's encounter with the risen Jesus (Acts 9; 22; 26). [710] Coupling these with allusions in Pauline letters, Luke alerts his readers to the critical importance of the event for Paul and for the expanding church. For Luke, Saul's conversion is a pivotal event and turning point[711], since the risen Jesus chooses Saul to be the major catalyst in extending the good news beyond the confines of Israel to the Gentiles. The mention of his vocation to the Gentiles (9:15) anticipates the Peter-Cornelius story (10:1-11:18), with its two climactic scenes of joy. In Acts 9, three miraculous scenes lead to their happy outcome in 9:31. The chapter resonates with dramatic and charismatic events when Saul becomes the champion of the very movement he was trying to exterminate.[712] One of the strongest arguments for the historical basis of the resurrection is found in the dramatic encounter between Paul and the risen Jesus, with the subsequent Gentile mission. No other event would lead the staunchest opponent of the Jesus-story to become the leading proponent of the good news of a resurrected and living Lord.

Luke provides three miraculous scenes with a biographical interchange that builds to a climax:

Scene I—Jesus and Saul on the road to Damascus (9:3-9)
Scene II—Jesus and Ananias in Damascus (9:10-16)
Scene III—Saul and Ananias in Damascus (9:17-19)

The third scene climaxes the previous two, as the risen Jesus brings together two people in a complementary manner. Both Saul and Ananias are overcome by the risen Jesus. The result of Saul's transformation leads to public proclamation in both Damascus and Jerusalem, and the happy contentment, growth, and encouragement in the church, in Judea, Galilee, and Samaria (9:31).

Scene 1—Jesus and Saul on the road to Damascus (9:1-9)
A comparison of the three accounts (22:1-16; 26:9-18) reveals similarities and some variance; perhaps the differences are due to the different audiences, whom are addressed. The points of agreement are:

- Paul is thrown to the ground on the way to Damascus,
- A heavenly light appears,
- Paul hears the words, "Saul, Saul, why do you persecute me?"
- The answer, "I am Jesus whom you are persecuting,"
- Paul's fellow travelers are affected by the event, even though details are different.[713]

The fact that Paul's companions (in two accounts) hear a sound/voice (φωνή) establishes that this was *not a subjective,* but *an objective appearance* of the risen Jesus. The purpose of the parallel accounts with the differences in detail may "on the one hand establish Paul's companions as witnesses, but on the other hand reserve the appearance to Paul alone."[714]

The light causes Paul to fall to the ground; the effect upon Paul is described as "being dazed" or "dazzled," joined with his loss of sight. Haenchen notes, "it seems to follow that Saul saw Jesus only as he beheld this tremendous blaze of light. As the persecutor, Paul experiences the same 'light/glory' that the persecuted Stephen saw in a vision, immediately prior to his death (7:55-56). Perhaps Luke imagined the occurrence that Saul's companions saw only a formless glare where he himself saw in it the figure of Jesus."[715]

Luke makes the case for a theology of personal encounter in which the risen Jesus speaks in very direct ways to his people. Prior, Saul was committed to the written Torah and ancestral tradition in an objective and rational manner. Now the personal Lord directly addresses him, asks questions, provides concrete direction for his personal and vocational life, heals him, and empowers him with the Holy Spirit. This is no Lord who only can be viewed through the lens of Scripture and tradition alone. This is a living Lord who directly encounters and engages him in dialogue. The witnesses who hear the voice affirm the reality of the occurrence. As a whole, the narrative reflects the genre of the prophetic call.[716]

Jesus' address contains a solemn repetition of his name, "Saul, Saul," a feature that is often found in theophanies (Gen. 22:11; 46:2; Ex. 3:4; I Sam. 3:10).[717] The text of Acts 9:5 establishes that Paul does not immediately recognize the one who now confronts him, but asks the question, "Who are you Sir (κύριε)?"[718]

In his answer, Jesus fully identifies himself with his persecuted followers: "Why do you persecute me?" In Luke's narrative, this inaugural experience of the exalted Jesus leads to the awareness of the close association of Jesus and his people.[719]

The pathos in Jesus' words (9:4-5) sharply contrasts with Saul's hostile demeanor and behavior (9:1-2). The risen Jesus shatters Saul's former estimation of him and his followers (9:1). Saul had been persecuting Christians as misguided adherents of a false Messiah. In his view, God had publicly cursed Jesus: "cursed/accursed [by God] is everyone who hangs upon a tree" (Deut 21:23). The fact of crucifixion was the clearest proof to Saul that Jesus had been a deceiver. But now, God allows Paul to see with his own eyes that the accursed one is the exalted Jesus, the Lord of glory, the very proof of the new creation.

Paul's later understanding of grace finds root in this event. Though he had abused Jesus by abusing God's people, the risen Jesus does not confront Saul with judgment, but with grace. It is impressive how quickly the Lord turns from Saul's great wrong, "persecuting me." Jesus approaches with grace alone. He simply identifies himself as "Jesus," followed by a striking contrast, "but" (ἀλλά) in v. 6 as if to say, "What you have been doing is over and past and is no more; get up and enter the city and it shall be spoken...." Luke's account includes no enumeration of sins, no detailed list of violations of God's laws or punitive remarks about the sanctity of human lives. It is as though his new life has already begun. "Luke constantly drives home the idea that *Christ himself* brought about this change of front. Paul did not dream of becoming a Christian or a missionary. The idea that Luke wanted to suggest a psychological explanation such as modern psychology would offer is completely wrong; on the contrary, Luke wishes to show that *no* human evolution is responsible for the change, but an act of God—and that alone!"[720]

Luke juxtaposes Saul's powerful aggression (9:1-2) with Saul's dependent and passive condition (9:8), as a blinded Saul now must be led by the hand. The blindness is not punitive, but purposeful, pointing to Saul's present helplessness and the power of the risen Jesus to overpower him, and then to heal his blindness and fill him with the Holy Spirit. Saul only learns what he must immediately do—go to the city, led by others. Even the divine passive in 9:6, "it shall be spoken" (λαληθήσεται) surely implies that Saul will follow through with obedience to the word of God.

The temporal designation may be significant for Luke, "And he was three days without sight, and neither ate nor drank" (9:9). Haenchen notes, "It would be wrong to construe it as punishment: it is simply the natural consequence of his beholding the heavenly light."[721] Rackham suggests a possible allusion to Jesus' own burial, "He is crucified with Christ, and the three days of darkness are like the three days in the tomb. But on the third day with Christ, he rises from the dead in baptism; after this he is filled with the Holy Ghost—his Pentecost."[722] Perhaps, the motif of fasting suggests, "holding oneself in disciplined readiness for further revelation (e.g. Ex. 34:28; Dan. 10:2-3)."[723]

Scene II—Jesus and Ananias in Damascus (9:10-16).

The new scene narrates the dialogue between the risen Jesus and Ananias, described as a "disciple" (μαθητής). Later Paul identifies him as a devout Hebrew (22:12-14). Since Ananias had not fled from threats of persecution, he may well represent a conservative Christian Jew, who believed it was possible to be a pious Jew and a Christian. Ananias' expression, "Here am I, Lord" (ἰδού ἐγω κύριε), suggests a readiness and attentiveness to the word of the Lord.[724] In addition to the miraculous encounter, Luke's readers would see divine guidance in that he is given Saul's exact address, a particular home on "the street called 'Straight'" (9:11).

Ananias' response reflects his initial fear, since he is well aware of Saul's aggressive and murderous behavior (9:13-14). His fear is countered by the Lord's words (9:15-16) as Jesus informs Ananias that Saul has prayed and has received revelation in a vision (ἐν ὁράματι 9:12) that Ananias will come, bringing healing power for his blindness. With amazing candor, the risen Jesus informs Ananias that Saul is a "vessel of choice" to bear Jesus' name to Gentiles, their kings, and the children of Israel and a person who must suffer for Jesus' name.

> "But the Lord said unto him,
> 'Go your way:
> For he is a chosen vessel [vessel of election][725] unto me,
> to bear my name[726] before the Gentiles,
> and their kings, and the children of Israel
> and how much he must suffer for my *name's sake*'" (9:15-16)

Martin notes, "Paul felt responsibility as the key eschatological apostle sent by God in the final time (Col. 1:24-29; Eph. 3:1-13). Thus, it may be argued that Paul's commission was certainly a part of his entrance into new life as a Christian, but it cannot be the sum-total of it."[727]

For Luke, Paul will appear before three groups in the course of his missionary endeavors:

- Jews (13:5, 14; 14:1; 1613; 17:1-4, 10, 17; 19:8)
- Gentiles (17:22; 18:6-11; 19:10)
- A king (26:1-29)

Jesus also speaks of Saul's vocation of suffering, later expressed by Luke:

- suspicion by Paul's companions (9:21, 26,)
- attempts on his life (9:24, 29)
- abuse by Jews of the *Diaspora* (13:45ff.; 14:2ff, 19; 17:5ff.; 19:23ff.)
- fractured relationships with fellow workers (15:37ff.)
- scorn and persecution by Gentiles (16:19ff.; 17:32f.; 19:23ff.)

Scene III—Saul and Ananias in Damascus (9:17-19).

Ananias greets Saul as "brother Saul" (Σαοὺλ ἀδελφέ), quite possibly "simply hailing his fellow Jew with the word of racial kinship ... putting Paul at ease—telling him that his past was not held against him, something which may well have worried Paul ... ."[728] The expression also implies the full sense of Christian brotherhood (9:17). The term, "brother[hood]," expresses the unique bond among Christians, anticipated by Jesus (Luke 8:19-21—"my brothers and mothers are the ones who hear the word of God and practice it"). Thus, the new sense of the community bond, "brotherhood [sisterhood]" that Jesus had anticipated is realized here in Ananias' greeting.

Ananias then follows Jesus' instructions. As he lays his hands upon Saul, Saul's sight is restored, and he is filled with the Holy Spirit (9:17), is baptized, and then strengthened with food. By virtue of receiving the Spirit, everything else follows. Receiving the Spirit is mentioned prior to and independent of baptism; that is why Ananias has been sent: "you might regain sight and be filled with the Holy Spirit." Although Luke does not mention "tongues," the experience may certainly be implicit.[729] Luke's expression, "filled with the Holy Spirit," echoes the same language of the first Pentecost, "and all were filled with the Holy Spirit" (2:4). It is noteworthy that Paul's filling with the Spirit is mediated through Ananias, who is not one of the apostles. It appears that Paul's experience was a three-day event, encompassing the time from the Damascus Road to his baptism.

Although Luke makes no explicit mention of joy in Saul's Pentecostal experience, he certainly would assume that his readers would imagine such joyous affection accompanying Saul's vibrant experience. Readers, then and now, should not press Luke for a systematic order for each Pentecostal experience. Luke does not apply one solitary recipe for Spirit-reception. Similarly, affective language that characterizes other passages of Spirit-reception would naturally be expected here, and "spill-over" with Saul's transformation, his healing, his experience of grace, his new vocation, his experience of the Spirit and his baptism. Why would it not? Luke's notifies his readers that this is the Pauline Pentecost, so by virtue of his reception of the Spirit, Saul stands equally with the twelve.

Immediate effects of Saul's dramatic encounter (Acts 9:19b-31). When Saul is then baptized, Luke sounds the keynote of the new convert's "preaching" (κηρύγμα)—Jesus is both the Son of God (9:20) and the Messiah (9:22). His immediate (εὐθέως) proclamation leads to the "utter amazement" (ἐξίσταντο) of the people in Damascus and their fearful response, given their knowledge of Saul's vita. Saul, who had been strengthened (ἐνίσχυσεν 9:19) by food, is further empowered (ἐνεδυναμοῦτο (9:22) as he "confounds/throws into consternation" the Jews with his declaration. A death threat leads to Saul's escape from Damascus.

His arrival at Jerusalem is met with similar suspicion from believers. Barnabas intervenes, allaying their skepticism. Evidently, Saul had some conversation with Barnabas about his dramatic encounter with the risen

Jesus. For the Jews, Barnabas verifies Saul's legitimacy as a bona-fide *disciple* through his report of Saul's encounter. Initially Saul had tried to attach himself to the disciples (9:26), but now he develops a ministry with the Hellenists. Another death threat follows, but Saul's new-found brothers learn of the plot and escort him to Caesarea and then, to Tarsus (9:29-30).

A joyous narrative-summary (9:31). The communal relief of Saul's utter transformation (from violent aggressor to a major proponent of the Jesus-movement) leads to a sense of well-being (εἰρήνη) for the "Church" (ἐκκλησία), here used in the catholic sense, since it refers to the whole of Judea, Galilee, and Samaria. "Peace" is coupled with "reverence" (φόβος) of the Lord and "encouragement" (παράκλησις) of the Holy Spirit. These Christian affections are then modified by two participles, "being built up" (οἰκοδομουμένη), and "journeying" (πορευομένη) in the whole of these geographical areas. The Church is no longer confined to Jerusalem. As Haenchen suggests, "A new period of history is now beginning. Paul's call brings the persecution to an end."[730] The Church is also "growing externally in numbers" (ἐπληθύνετο). As a whole, the community enjoys the presence of the Holy Spirit with its accompanying benefits and affections.

Anticipatory Miracles
(Acts 9:32-43)

Peter now re-enters the narrative, after his powerful activity in Samaria. This time the setting is Lydda and then Joppa. Luke narrates two miracles (πράξει Πέτρου), which anticipate the Peter-Cornelius episode that governs the following chapters (Acts 10:1-11:18).[731] In succinct language, Luke introduces a crippled Aeneas, bedridden for eight years, whom Peter found in Lydda.[732] Upon discovering him, Peter simply states, "Aeneas, Jesus Christ heals[733] you" (Αἰνέα, ἰᾶται σε᾽ Ἰησοῦς Χριστός 9:34), with the following command, "Get up and make your bed." The healing is instantaneous (εὐθέως ἀνέστη) and leads to the climax that "all those who lived in Lydda and Sharon saw him (a walking Aeneas), and turned to the Lord" (9:35). Luke does not inform his readers that Peter prayed or laid his hands on Aeneas. Haenchen aptly comments,

"Luke, who does not readily waste time or space on incidentals and is in addition bent on attaining a climax, has dispensed with everything superfluous and recounted it entirely in his own words, to bring out (in verse 34) the point that the real performer of the miracle is Jesus."[734] Joy is expressed by action. Most certainly, Aeneas has a joyous new lease on life, and as people witness the proof of Jesus' power through a walking Aeneas, surely the widespread turning to the Lord also is infused with joy.

The second miracle story concerns Tabitha (Dorcas), a "disciple" (μαθητρία),[735] in Joppa. Luke introduces her with praise for her good works and charity (9:36). She became deathly ill, died, and then is washed, perhaps "in anticipation of the hoped-for restoration to life?"[736] Thus Peter is summoned from Lydda[737] with the expectation of help, although Luke does not inform his readers what they anticipated. Upon his arrival, the mourning widows present evidence of Tabitha's charity, coats, and undergarments; their grief is significant. Luke's readers are drawn into the emotions of the story as they anticipate something grand. At that point, Peter dismisses the women, kneels in prayer, turns to the dead body and says, "Tabitha, get up" (9:40). Tabitha responds by opening her eyes and then sits up, at which point, Peter takes her by the hand, calls for the Christians (ἅγιοι) and widows, and presents her as living (ζῶσαν) to them (9:40-41). Luke would have his readers know that the new community is miraculous in nature and in accord with prophets of the Old Testament[738] and Jesus.[739]

Similar to Lydda, the miracle of raising Tabitha moves to the dramatic climax, "many trusted in the Lord" when "this became known to all of Joppa" (γνωστὸν δὲ ἐγένετο καθ᾽ ὅλης τῆς Ἰόππης 9:42). Joy is again expressed by what people do. Luke leaves his readers to draw the connection between the deep grief of the widows at Tabitha's death and their untold joy upon seeing her fully restored to life. As for the residents, their new-found trust in the Lord Jesus is surely couched in joy as well, since they witness the power of God in raising the dead. Luke's final mention of Peter's stay in Joppa at the home of Simon, the tanner (9:43) prepares his readers for the Peter-Cornelius story.

Gentiles Magnifying God and Jews Glorifying God
(Acts 10:1-11:18)

It will be shown that Luke provides two historical progressions, each building towards a joyous climax, one in the Cornelius-Peter story and another in the response of the Jerusalem Church. Although scholars attend to the events, they have not focused on affective language which builds towards an emotional peak.[740]

Luke's readers encounter two interlocking visions (for Cornelius[741] and Peter), two people who don't know each other, two separate journeys, paraphrased repetitions, shared stories of charismatic experiences. Luke blends divine direction[742] and human decision,[743] divine purpose in the midst of human perplexity, people *in-process*, divine *coincidence* and corroborations of the Holy Spirit. Luke invites his readers to join the atmosphere of joyous celebration as a Gentile group experiences the baptism in the Holy Spirit, coupled with a jubilant Jerusalem Church. The very length of the narrative speaks of its importance.[744]

Why does Luke tell this story? Luke emphasizes the extension of the Christian mission to the Gentiles in a public way,[745] which later occasions the official and celebratory confirmation by the Jerusalem Council in Acts 15. Luke has established that universal mission is high on God's agenda.[746] This narrative is the third of three conversion stories, involving two individuals (Philip and the Ethiopian eunuch—8:26-40; Saul and Ananias—9:1-19; Cornelius and Peter—10:1-11:18). In each case, two persons are brought together by God. [747]

Luke arranges his charismatic stories through various scenes in progression. Proper exegesis must include the emotions of the text that reach a climax in both stories. The first progression of events includes:

- An angel and Cornelius (Acts 10:1-9a)—send servants for Peter.
- Peter's vision of a menagerie of unclean animals (10: 9b-16)—go with Cornelius' servants.
- Peter and Cornelius (10:17-48)—*joyous climax* with the baptism in the Holy Spirit.

The second progression of events includes one scene in Jerusalem that incorporates:

- Accusation of Peter's behavior (table-fellowship) with Cornelius (Acts 11:1-3).
- Peter's defense, expressed through paraphrased charismatic stories (11:4-17).
- A joyous climax, "they glorified God" (ἐδόξασαν τὸν θεὸν 11:18).

Luke arranges the material to lead his readers to appreciate the joyous climax of both progressions. Yes, Luke highlights the divine will for Gentile inclusion in so many ways, and yet, he does so with affective language "as the Church tries to catch up to God's initiative."[748] Through a vision and voice, Peter learns that God shows no partiality[749] (προσωπολήμπτης) but is inclusive (Acts 10:34). When Peter meets Cornelius, he informs him of his learned lesson from the heavenly sheet with the unclean animal-menagerie—to stop regarding foods as unclean since God has cleansed them. As Marshall notes, "it would be a short step"[750] to transition into the more important principle that persons should not be regarded as common or unclean (10:28). Now, Peter is beginning to understand[751] the broader truth about God—that God plays no favorites. "Therefore, the door is open to anyone who fears God and works righteousness as Cornelius does (10:22)."[752]

The climactic gift of the Holy Spirit with the expression in tongues is part of the larger whole of charismatic experiences in Acts 10:1-11:18, which include affective language. The story features personal experiences, atmospheres and expressions of joy—a joy that surely reaches out to Luke's readers. In so many ways, people experience different dimensions of supernatural power. At the same time Luke provides no distinct "order of salvation" (*ordo salutis*), since Luke's conversion stories vary so much in sequence.[753]

Charismatic incursions dominate the narrative as "God works from two sides at the same time"[754] to achieve his purpose of including Gentiles in the new community of faith.

In his vignettes, Luke uses the interchangeable terms "vision" (ὅραμα)[755] and "trance/ecstasy" (ἔκστασις).[756] The term *vision* "signifies the act by which the recipient of the vision is granted a vision, or the state of being in which he receives his vision."[757] The word *trance/ecstasy* suggests "a state of being brought about by God, in which consciousness is wholly or partially suspended."[758] The terms describe the charismatic experience of both men and are combined in Acts 11:5. The twin terms are either paired with an angel[759] or voice (φωνή)[760] and are understood as "revelation."[761]

Luke complements Cornelius' vision of the angel and Peter's trance, in which Peter hears a voice for the expressed purpose of bringing Peter and Cornelius together. They engage in preliminary conversation[762] before the "meat of the matter," an explanation of the Jesus-event and the baptism in the Holy Spirit for Cornelius, his family, and close friends (Acts 10:44-46a). For Luke, complementary stories of charismatic encounters are told, retold, and paraphrased in the retelling.[763]

For his readers, Luke couples divine incursions with divine "coincidences."[764] Luke specifies the timing of Peter's trance with the appearance of Cornelius' three messengers. The language, "and behold" (καὶ ἰδού)[765] is repeated, specifically with respect to Cornelius' messengers upon their arrival: "and behold the men" (Acts 10:17); "behold three men" (10:19); "and behold at once three men" (Acts 11:11). The unique timing leads Peter to apply the message of the cleanness of foods to the inclusive cleanness of people. For Luke, the timing is pivotal, "It just so happened that ..." God coordinates the two events—not happenstance—framed in a similar way with the Philip-Ethiopian story.

Charismatic events in Peter's preaching. As Haenchen notes, Peter's sermon (Acts 10:34-43) to Cornelius' large gathering "amounts to a resumé of the Christian message."[766] The sermon is not propositional but recounts the charismatic story of Jesus. Peter's story incorporates the broad kerygmatic progression of events that were integral to his earlier sermons.[767] However, Luke adds an opening expression, "you know" (ὑμεῖς οἴδατε 10:37), which "suggests to the reader that the events of Jesus' life were broadly known."[768]

The *sent word* (Jesus story) is a joy-producing good news of peace, which affirms his exaltation, "he sent his word to the sons of Israel, this one is Lord of all" (Acts 10:36). Luke's language reflects the fulfillment of Old Testament prophetic texts. He alludes to Psalm 107:20 (LXX Psa. 106:20), "He sent his word and healed them and delivered them from their destruction [graves]"[769] Given that Peter's sermon includes Jesus' healings and deliverances, the Old Testament text is entirely appropriate. The language of Acts 10:36, "preaching the joy-filled news of wholeness" (εὐαγγελιζόμενος εἰρήνην διὰ ᾽Ιησοῦ Χριστοῦ), corresponds to Isaiah 52:7, "How beautiful on the mountains are the feet of those who bring good news, who proclaim peace, who bring good tidings, who proclaim salvation." The good news of great joy announced to the shepherds applies both to the Jewish people (Luke 2:10), and Gentiles (Luke 2:14), "people of divine pleasure." Pervo states, "The gentile mission forecast in both the infancy stories and in the inaugural synagogue sermon of Jesus has now become a reality."[770]

Peter's declaration, "this one is Lord of all" (Acts 10:36), reflects that Jesus' Lordship applies to both the Jewish people and successive generations of Gentiles, including Cornelius and company. Peter opens the door "to all peoples for they are invited to share with Israel in this messianic peace."[771] Once again for Luke, joy is contagious, effusive, and inclusive.

In Peter's mini-gospel, Luke highlights the source of Jesus' charismatic power through two clauses:

- "how God anointed him with the Holy Spirit and power" (ὡς ἔχρισεν αὐτὸν ὁ θεὸς πνεύματι ἁγίῳ καὶ δυνάμει Acts 10:38a).
- "because God was with him" (ὅτι ὁ θεὸς ἦν μετ᾽ αὐτοῦ Acts 10:38b).

The first clause alludes to Jesus' baptism (Luke 3:21-22), several references to the Holy Spirit and/or power (Luke 4:1—twice, 14) and Jesus' inaugural address (Luke 4:18ff, from Isa 61:1-2; 58:6). The second clause underscores the prominent Old Testament theme, "*I will be [with you]* (*ehyeh*)," most notably in Exodus 3:12-14. As in Acts 2:22, the proof that God was *with* Jesus is expressed through his miraculous activity.

As a result of Jesus' personal Pentecost, Jesus carried on his charismatic activity of "doing good and healing all who were oppressed by the devil" (εὐεργετῶν καὶ ἰώμενος πάντας τοὺς καταδυναστευομένος ὑπὸ τοῦ διαβόλου Acts 10:38).[772] As Barrett comments, "the work of Jesus constitutes God's decisive attack upon the (personally conceived) power of evil."[773] The totality of Jesus' charismatic activity is also reinforced by the clause, "all the things which he did" (πάντων ὧν ἐποίησεν 10:39). Jesus does good things for people, heals, delivers, and liberates them to gratitude and untold joy, a joy that anticipates the *eschaton*. In this sermon, Luke describes Jesus' career more than he did in earlier sermons. Since he's addressing a Gentile audience, Peter even traces it back to the Baptist's preaching (10:37).

Although the crucifixion, "hanging upon a tree" (κρεμάσαντες ἐπὶ ξύλου Acts 10:39)[774], was *the* tragic human decision, Jesus' numinous resurrection expressed a divine decision vindicating Jesus' ministry and his death. Luke highlights the resurrection with two clauses: "God raised up this one on the third day" (10:40); "after his resurrection from the dead" (10:41).

The powerful resurrection is followed by charismatic post-resurrection experiences; the event of "[God] caused him to be seen" (Acts 10:40), which is fortified by the physicality of eating and drinking with the risen Jesus, "we ate and drank with him" (10:41).[775] Luke advances the theme of witness[776] as "the proclaimer [Jesus] becomes the proclaimed,"[777] leading to the Lordship of Jesus over all.

The baptism in the Holy Spirit is front and center, which leads to the climactic response of joy, both in the narrative of Cornelius-Peter (Acts 10:44-48) and the story of the church's happy response in Jerusalem (11:15-18). In preparation for that event, the Holy Spirit is active in speaking and directing Peter.

- "While Peter was struggling to make sense of the vision, *the Spirit* informs him of the presence of the three men and directs him to go with them *without hesitation* (10:19b-20).

- "*The Spirit* said to me to go with them *without hesitation*" (11:12).

The Holy Spirit, along with an angel and/or voice[778]—all work collectively to bring Peter and Cornelius and company together. This sets the stage for the climactic event.

Peter hardly finishes his sermon about the Jesus-event before the Holy Spirit falls upon all—"while Peter was still speaking these things, the Holy Spirit fell upon all who were hearing the message" (Ἔτι λαλοῦντος τοῦ Πέτρου τὰ ῥήματα ταῦτα ἐπέπεσεν τὸ πνεῦμα τὸ ἅγιον ἐπὶ πάντας τοὺς ἀκούοντας τὸν λόγον Acts 10:44). As Dunn notes, "there is the emphasis on the visible impact of the Spirit. The Spirit 'fell upon' them (as in 8:16); something 'hit' them; there was a visible impact of invisible power."[779] The interruption of the Holy Spirit is a literary "device he [Luke] uses again later, and although in his own summary of the events, Peter will say, "I had just started speaking" (11:15), it is obvious that Luke has had him say everything needful."[780] Perhaps, with Kilgallen, "Peter had progressed some of the way, but not all of the way, in his discourse to Cornelius—when the Spirit came."[781]

This is the fifth recorded baptism in the Spirit (Acts 2:1-4; 4:3; 8:17; 9:17-18), although it may also be implicit in the story of Philip and the Ethiopian (8:38-39, esp. in the Western text). The baptism in the Spirit of Cornelius and company is expressed with different terms in both the narrative and Peter's report in Jerusalem:

- "the Holy Spirit *fell* upon all who were hearing the word" (ἐπέσεν τὸ πνεῦμα τὸ ἅγιον ἐπὶ πάντας τοὺς ἀκούοντας τὸν λόγον 10:44a),
- "that even upon the Gentiles *the gift of the Holy Spirit was poured out*" (καὶ ἐπὶ τὰ ἔθνη ἡ δωρεὰ τοῦ ἁγίου πνεύματος ἐκκέχυται 10:44b),
- "*speaking in tongues* and *magnifying God*" (λαλούντων γλώσσαις καὶ μεγαλυόντων τὸν θεόν 10:46),
- "such ones who *received* the Holy Spirit" (οἵτινες τὸ πνεῦμα τὸ ἅγιον ἔλαβον 10:47),

- "the Holy Spirit *fell* upon them" (ἐπέσεν τὸ πνεῦμα τὸ ἅγιον ἐπ᾽ αὐτοὺς 11:15),
- "but you *will be baptized* in the Holy Spirit" (ὑμεῖς δὲ βαπτισθήσεσθε ἐν πνεύματι 11:16),
- "Therefore, if God *gave* the same *gift* to them" (εἰ οὖν τὴν ἴσην δωρεὰν ἔδωκεν αὐτοῖς ὁ θεὸς 11:17).

Luke records that the Holy Spirit fell[782] (twice), is a gift (twice), which God gave (once), poured out (once), is a baptism in the Holy Spirit (once), something that is received (once) and is expressed in the ecstatic behavior of speaking in tongues and magnifying God (once). The nouns and verbs look at the same incursion of the Holy Spirit from different perspectives. In Acts 2, tongues-speaking was paired with the intelligibility of the tongues (Acts 2:6-11). Here in Acts 10, the listeners of the tongues understand that they are magnifying God.

For Luke's readers, the effusion of the Holy Spirit is spontaneous, dynamic, joyous, effusive, contagious, and not occasioned by human activity. Peter does not pray and lay his hands upon Cornelius and company to receive the Holy Spirit (Acts 8:14-17—in Samaria). The Holy Spirit both interrupts and erupts. For Cornelius and company, the observable and sensorial experience is expressed by an ecstatic and joyful speaking in tongues and magnifying God (10:46). For Luke, everything in the preceding narrative and dialogue builds towards this climax of Acts 10, which is expressed through affective language.

Luke parallels the joyous nature of this Gentile event with the experience of 120 Jewish believers on the Day of Pentecost (Acts 2).[783] Luke makes the comparison explicit: "*as even we*" (ὡς καὶ ἡμεῖς 10:47); *just as* even he did upon us in the beginning" (ὥσπερ καὶ ἐφ᾽ ἡμᾶς ἐν ἀρχῇ 11:15); "the *same* gift" (τὴν ἴσην δωρεὰν 11:17); "*as* even to us" (ὡς καὶ ἡμῖν 11:17). Earl Richard concludes, "These graphic terms function as a semantic field in establishing the paradigmatic character of this Pentecost episode ... a thematic continuity and suggests a unitive function for the original Pentecost story."[784]

Luke could hardly make the comparison sharper.[785] The upshot? Since the Gentile believers have experienced their Pentecost, the door is wide open for their inclusion without restriction.[786] While Max Turner labels this gift as "the Spirit of prophecy,"[787] the expression, "the charismatic power (empowerment) to speak and act for God," is more appropriate, since "prophecy" can be more narrowly limited to verbal proclamation alone. In this baptism in the Spirit, Luke does not include anything about personal faith or repentance. Later, in Acts 10:43, Luke mentions forgiveness and the believing response, followed by the statement that repentance is a gift given to Cornelius' household (11:18).

As a seal of their Spirit-baptism, nothing should stand in the way of their Christian baptism (Acts 10:47-48); it is a baptism in the name of Jesus Christ, used elsewhere in the context of salvation.[788] The real emphasis in the text is Spirit-baptism—not water-baptism, which is not noted in Acts 11.[789] While Luke highlights the sensorial nature of their baptism in the Spirit, their experience is part of the larger context of numinous experiences in 10:1-11:18 in which divine incursions are linked with dialogue of individuals and groups.

Further, the gift of the Spirit is a vital part of the Christian resumé, expressed in the progression of events in the Jesus-story, climaxed by Jesus' Lordship and pouring forth of the Holy Spirit in charismatic experience and expression. The same anointing that Jesus received with power to do good things and heal (Acts 10:38) is now available to Gentile communities. Not only does their story parallel the initial Pentecost, but it is similar to Jesus' own anointing with the Spirit for the purpose of life-giving ministry.

People are "in-process" as they are "converted." Through the narratives, Luke knits together individuals and groups—all experience types of "conversion" when they are drawn into the Gentile reception of the Holy Spirit and the subsequent report to the Jerusalem Church (Cornelius, his three messengers, Peter, his six companions, the Jerusalem Church). As in Luke 24, people successively discover the significance of a miraculous event. All are led to a climactic experience and expression of joy. Luke arranges the material with suspense to allow his readers to discover the progression of people in their understanding, attitudes, and experiences.

Cornelius. Instead of providing all the Cornelius-descriptors at the beginning, Luke provides additional material concerning Cornelius the

Centurion as the story progresses: Cornelius' position as a Centurion from the Italian cohort and character, "pious and fearing God with all his house"[790]; "giving alms liberally to the people, praying constantly to God" Acts 10:1-2); "your prayers and alms have ascended as a memorial into the presence of God" (10:9) [791]; "a righteous man and fearing God and a great reputation among the Jews" (10:22); "your prayer has been heard and your alms have been remembered before God" (10:31); and Cornelius' vision of the angel, while he was praying (10:31).

Pervo notes that "Cornelius has gone as far as possible on his 'spiritual journey' toward membership in the people of God ... at the 'dead end' of God-fearing piety, unable to take the final step of full conversion, which would presumably require abandonment of his office."[792] He represents the very best of Gentile spirituality.[793]

How does Cornelius respond to the numinous? Luke expresses his initial reaction to the angel with two participial expressions, "but he having stared" (ὁ δὲ ἀτενίσας)[794] "becoming terrified" (ἔμφοβος γενόμενος Acts 10:3). The adjective, "terrified" (ἔμφοβος) echoes similar responses in Luke 24: women's reaction to the appearance of two angels (Luke 24:5) and the early community in response to the risen Jesus (Luke 24:37). When Cornelius' terror is quelled through angelic reassurance (10:4), he responds with instant obedience to the angel's two commands ("send" and "summons" Peter). He calls two servants and one devout soldier, tells them the story[795] of his angelophany and sends them on their way to bring Peter from Joppa to Caesarea (10:7).[796] In contrast to Peter's initial refusal to two commands ("No way" Μηδαμῶς 10:4; 11:8), Cornelius instantly obeys the angel's two commands.[797]

Luke does not initially inform his readers as to why Cornelius is to summon Peter. In Acts 10:22, Luke's readers discover that Cornelius is to "hear a message from you [Peter]" (ἀκοῦσαι ῥήματα παρὰ σοῦ). Later, readers learn from Cornelius that he had been told that Peter would disclose "all things that had been commanded by the Lord" (10:33). Luke highlights that God has "called for the meeting." Still later, Luke informs his readers that the substance of Peter's instructions would be "a message, through which you and your household will be saved" (ὃς λαλήσει ῥήματα πρὸς σὲ ἐν οἷς σωθήσῃ καὶ πᾶς ὁ οἶκός σου (11:14). Thus, just as Cornelius is "in process," so Luke's readers grow as they grapple with the significance of this narrative as Luke guides them through his story.

Cornelius' understanding deepens as he shares his story with Peter and the others (his messengers, extended family, close friends, and Peter's six companions, "from the circumcision").[798] Luke draws others into the story line through paraphrased repetitions. As Tannehill notes, "The sharing of what has happened with additional persons is sufficiently important that it is highlighted with repeated direct discourse ... It is through this process that the recipients of the initial vision discover the purpose of their visions."[799]

Prior to Peter's arrival, Cornelius is an a state of eager expectation (ἦν προσδοκῶν[800] Acts 10:24). His response to the numinous is expressed by what he does when he first meets Peter, "falling down to his knees in homage"[801] (10:25).[802] Although Peter deflects this gesture, "Get up, for I also am a mortal" (Acts 10:26), his physical posture nonetheless expresses his sense of the supernatural at work in the recent events. After narrating his angelophany, Cornelius expresses gratitude to Peter for his journey to Caesarea, "you were kind enough to come" (Acts 10:33). For Luke, receptivity is all-important.[803]

Luke also highlights Cornelius' seriousness about what they will hear. All now anticipate, *in God's presence* (ἐνώπιον τοῦ θεοῦ Acts 10:33), what Peter has been commanded to say. They all sense the magnitude of the message they await. Their attitude could be no more expectant or promising.

Cornelius' three messengers (two servants and one devout soldier[804]). The three men similarly discover the significance of their journey in a progressive manner. They obey, make their journey and summon Peter. They praise Cornelius' character, summarize Cornelius' revelatory encounter with the angel, and inform Peter of the purpose of their journey. Their task is to summon Peter so as to hear his message (Acts 10:22). They share everything they know.

The three Gentiles stay for the night, experiencing Peter's hospitality, and then journey with Peter and his six companions to Cornelius' home. Luke's readers would conclude that the three were part of the "many who were gathered together"[805] as they learn more of the two visions, hear Peter's address, and experience the baptism in the Spirit.

Peter. For Luke, Peter is likewise in a discovery-mode, which Dunn labels as "the conversion of Peter."[806] The three initial references to "food/hunger" (Acts 10:10) prepare the reader for the angel's command, "slaughter and eat" (10:13) from the unclean menagerie in the sheet (10:11-12). Peter rejects the commands, "No way Lord" (Μηδαμῶς κύριε), "never" (οὐδέποτε). He goes on to explain why he refuses the command: "I have never eaten anything common or unclean" (ὅτι οὐδέποτε ἔφαγον πᾶν κοινὸν καὶ ἀκάθαρτον 10:14).[807] Bruce adds the implication, "and I am not going to begin now."[808] His rejection is met with the voice's stern command, "That which God has cleansed, stop regarding as common" (Ἃ ὁ θεὸς ἐκαθάρισεν, σὺ μὴ κοίνου 10:15).[809] As Barrett notes, "If God decides to treat a thing as clean, it is clean."[810] The divine verdict stands firm, trumping Peter's refusal.

For Peter and the Jews, the command to slaughter and eat indiscriminately from the menagerie including reptiles was no minor issue. It challenged their Jewish identity. In Israel's history, various heroes and heroines refused unclean food under pressure, even under the prospect of death (see Dan 1:1-8 and 1 Macc 1:61-63[811], as well as Tobit 1:10-13).

Peter moves from refusal to confusion as he transitions from vision to reality. Luke twice informs his readers about Peter's perplexity: "As Peter *was at a loss in his own mind* as to what this vision might mean" (Acts 10:17), "While Peter *was reflecting*[812] concerning the vision" (10:19). In Peter's haze, the Spirit informs him that three men are looking for him. The Spirit also directs him to accompany them, because they have been divinely sent (10:21). Luke's readers will note the different means of divine communication. A *voice* in the vision speaks to Peter (10:13, 15), but an *angel* speaks to Cornelius (10:3-6), While Peter struggles to understand the vision, the *Spirit* now speaks (10:19), telling Peter to go with Cornelius' messengers.

The three messengers summarize Cornelius' vision with his order to summon Peter. Peter welcomes them into Simon the Tanner's home (a Gentile), exercises hospitality [813] in hosting the Gentile messengers, learns of their order from Cornelius, and no doubt shares food with them, before departing the next day with them to Cornelius' home.

The divine "coincidence" pairs Peter's dream and his puzzlement with the timing of the messengers' arrival, "It just so happened that." What thoughts flit through Peter's mind that night and on the morrow's journey? How does this dream about indiscriminate eating relate to the arrival of the Gentile messengers? The messengers tell Peter he is to say something to Cornelius (Acts 10:22), but what message does God want Peter to convey? Just as it was important for Cornelius to obey the angel's commands, so now Peter must obey the Spirit's voice, going to Cornelius' home, even without fully understanding the journey's purpose. Obedience is the necessary response, while understanding will follow later. Twice Luke states that Peter went "without hesitation" (μηδὲν διακρινόμενος 10:20; μηδὲν διακρίναντα 11:12; also "without objection" ἀναντιρρήτως 10:29).

Through the arrival and conversation, Peter experiences his own unique "conversion" through a contrast between his past attitude ("how it is unlawful[814] for a Jew to associate with or to visit any other foreigner"[815] Acts 10:28a) and his current stance. Luke relates this in Peter's explanation, "God showed me that I should not call any man common or unclean" (10:28). Shared table-fellowship is another lesson Peter must learn, a lesson questioned by religious objectors in 11:3.

Peter's brief summary of his own vision is recounted to the Jerusalem Church (Acts 11:5-10), and later summarized in 15:7-9. Shared stories are vital in disclosing God's purpose. However, Peter doesn't yet know what he is to say to Cornelius and company. Just as Cornelius' messengers *inquired* (ἐπυνθάνοντο 10:18) for Peter's exact location, now Peter *inquires* (πυνθάνομαι) as to the reason he was sent (10:29). Peter still has much to learn and much to share.

Something must have occurred in the transition from Peter's inquiry about what he is to say and his bold[816] and obedient[817] resumé of the Jesus-event. Was it directly due to Cornelius' rehearsal of his vision? Or did the Holy Spirit reveal the content of Peter's message? Readers are not told, yet the transition is noteworthy.

Peter's opening affirmation of God's *impartiality* (προσωπολήμπτης Acts 10:34)[818] is something Peter *is just beginning to understand* (καταλαμβάνομαι 10:34). Thus, Luke reveals Peter's movement from impartiality of food, to impartiality of people, to an impartial God who is *accepting* (δέκτος) of people, without any sort of ritual requirement (circumcision or food).

Peter then witnesses the powerful descent of the Holy Spirit that "hit" Cornelius and company, "upon all who were hearing the message" (Acts 10:44). Surely, this pouring out of the Spirit surprised and astonished him, as it also amazed "those believers of the circumcision," who shared Peter's earlier view. He had nothing to do with this powerful descent of the Spirit, since he did not pray or lay hands on them. No doubt, Peter shares in the joy of this occasion as the Gentiles begin speaking in tongues and magnifying God (10:46). This joy then spills over into Peter's awareness that their experience matched his on the Day of Pentecost (10:47). This convincing sign prompts Peter to instruct that all should be baptized (10:48).[819] Luke also notes that Peter and his six companions are hosted in a Gentile home (10:48) for several days.

Peter's six companions. Peter's six companions (described as "certain of the brothers" in 10:23, "believers from the circumcision" in 10:44, "six men" in 11:12) develop in their own "conversion." Like Peter, they had been prejudiced against Gentiles. However, when they witness the baptism in the Spirit of the Gentile believers, they respond with joyous and "ecstatic astonishment" (ἐξέστησαν 10:45-46).[820] Their response parallels the response of the Jerusalem crowd with the joyful healing of the crippled beggar in 3:9-10. With a causal clause ("because" ὅτι), Luke explains why his six companions were astonished, "because the gift of the Holy Spirit was being poured out *even* upon the Gentiles" (10:45). Further, the reason ("for" γάρ) they know the gift of the Holy Spirit was poured out is their witnessing the ecstatic behavior of the Gentiles, "for they were hearing they speaking in tongues and magnifying God" (ἤκουον γὰρ λαλούντων γλώσσαις καὶ μεγαλυνόντων τὸν θεόν 10:46). De Long notes, "The amazement of witnesses offers another link between this conversion and healings earlier in the narrative, a connection strengthened by Peter's reference to Jesus' acts of healing in his speech to Cornelius."[821]

Like Peter, they are overcome by charismatic encounter and recognize the divine will and activity in the gift of the Holy Spirit. They heard Peter's sermon, knew of the paired-visions, traveled to Caesarea, shared in mutual hospitality and table-fellowship and saw the powerful baptism in the Spirit and registered no complaint. As Johnson notes, "they would deny their own experience if they were to controvert it."[822]

Peter's six men "of the circumcision" implicitly stand as silent but important witnesses to "those of the circumcision" in Jerusalem, who take issue with Peter's behavior (Acts 11:2).[823] It is important to note that the accusation is not made by the apostles, but "those of the circumcision" in Jerusalem.[824] Luke does not provide his readers with any conversation between Peter's six men and the believers "of the circumcision." Nonetheless, the six companions are present with Peter in this confrontation with "those of the circumcision" in Jerusalem. Did the six add their voice to Peter's narrative? Did they nod their heads in approval? Luke doesn't inform his readers.

The Jerusalem Church. When Peter returns to the Jerusalem Church, "those of the circumcision" criticize him, taking issue/dispute[825] with his mutual hospitality and table-fellowship with uncircumcised Gentiles. It is striking that the complaint is not that Gentiles "received the word" (Acts 11:1) or had been baptized (10:48). The issue is mutual hospitality and table-fellowship: "you entered [a home] of uncircumcised men and you ate with them" (11:3). Readers should not find fault here with the Jerusalem Church, since their stance towards Gentiles mirrored Peter's prior position. As a whole, the church also needs to be convinced of the divine purpose and will. In essence, the Church needs its own "conversion." As De Long notes, "The objection thus introduces an important question into the narrative; will the restored community in Jerusalem accept this new and surprising direction in the divine visitation?"[826]

Through Peter's report, Luke leads readers toward Peter's next learning stage concerning table-fellowship and hospitality. God removes obstacles of foods and Gentile uncleanness; since God is inclusive, he is also currently at work in the removal of social obstacles hindering social relationships between Jew and Gentile. Peter had lived in a Gentile home, had been hospitable to Gentile messengers, and had visited another Gentile household. Now the issue of social relationships between Jew and Gentile is major.

Peter defends his actions and boldly proclaims God's activity in the human interaction with the divine. Luke highlights Peter's initial statements, "Peter began and explained[827] everything to them, precisely in order as events occurred" (Acts 11:4). Peter does not begin with a propositional argument. Rather, he shares the story of his vision, followed by the "coincidental" arrival of Cornelius' messengers, the direction by the Spirit, Cornelius' angelophany, and the dynamic baptism in the Spirit of the Gentiles. Peter's shared story wields convincing power.

In Acts 10:5-12, Luke describes the progression of Peter's transition through a series of sequential and verbal expressions that brought him to Cornelius:

- "I was praying"
- "I saw"
- "staring"
- "I was contemplating"
- "I saw"
- "I heard"
- "I said [in objection]"
- [implied objection overcome—three fold repetition of voice]
- "I came"
- "we entered"

The key "take-away" from Peter's vision is the divine command, "Stop regarding as unclean that [people] which God has already cleansed" (11:9; 10:15). "Peter's speech redirects the objection to the Gentiles as ἀκροβυστίαν to a focus upon them as people who by believing have received from God the same gift as have Jews within the restored community."[828]

Peter briefly summarizes Cornelius' vision, recounts his journey to Cornelius, and testifies to the Spirit's powerful and spontaneous descent upon the gathered community (Acts 11:12-15). Peter invites his Jerusalem audience to match the experience of Cornelius and company with their own encounter with the Holy Spirit, "just as upon *us* in the beginning" (11:15). The Jewish audience is also faced with Jesus' fulfilled prophecy, "On the one hand, John baptized in water but you will be baptized in the Holy Spirit" (1:5).[829] The prophetic promise, given to a small group of Jewish believers, now opens up to the Gentile community (11:16). Peter's experience in seeing and hearing the Gentiles' joyous speaking in tongues and magnifying God opened his understanding that Jesus' previous promise in 1:5 is wide-open. Johnson notes, "This is an example of how later experience forces the *recollection* of a saying of Jesus, as well as its extension in application."[830]

This experience leads to the rhetorical question, "Could I hinder God's activity?" (Acts 11:17), with the obvious answer, "No." The implication for the Jerusalem Church is also clear, "Could they also hinder God's activity?" They must transition with "the confirmation of the community."[831] Turner remarks, "The Jerusalem Christians acknowledge that if God has given Cornelius' household the same prestigious gift of the Spirit of prophecy as Jewish Christians received at Pentecost, then he must have allowed these Gentiles the same 'repentance' previously only known to the Israel of fulfillment (5:31-32), and set them on the same path leading to life."[832]

The climax of the second narrative in Jerusalem supervenes when the Jerusalem Church glorifies God, "After hearing these things [Peter's narrative], their opposition ceased[833] and they glorified God" (ἀκούσαντες δὲ ταῦτα ἡσύχασαν καὶ ἐδόξασαν τὸν θεὸν Acts 11:18a). Pervo translates the clauses, "These words stilled their objections and brought forth praise."[834] The entire community expresses the awe, weightiness, impressiveness that belongs to the "glorify" (δοξάζω) word-family. They voice joyous awe to God for what he has done in the lives of these Gentiles. Thus, we see notable transformation from "*hearing* ... that the Gentiles received the word of God" (ἤκουσαν ... ὅτι καὶ ἔθνη ἐδέξαντο τὸν λόγον τοῦ θεοῦ 11:1) and some taking issue with Peter (11:2) to "*hearing* (ἀκούσαντες) these things, i.e. the story, and then, ceasing their objection and *glorifying* God" (11:18).

The charismatic reality of the Cornelius event advances to God's glory, finding explanation, "Look at this, God gave the conversion to new life, *even*[835] to the Gentiles" ("Αρα καὶ τοῖς ἔθνεσιν ὁ θεὸς τὴν μετάνοιαν εἰς ζωὴν ἔδωκεν Acts 11:18). Here, the baptism in the Spirit is not the same as "repentance to new life," since earlier in Peter's first sermon, repentance is a precursor to receiving the gift (2:38). Repentance may well mean a positive turn to the new activity of God; here it is a gift given to Gentiles. Yes, faith, repentance, salvation are all part of the mix of the Pentecostal experience and gifts. However, Luke fails to provide a consistent pattern of an "order of salvation" and should not be read through Pauline eyes. Luke intends that his readers feel the emotional joy of the baptism in the Spirit for Cornelius and the joyous thanks the Jerusalem Church renders to God for what he has done. He wants his readers to know that miraculous events of a walking Aeneas, resuscitated Dorcas and the baptism in the Spirit for Cornelius' household are all the direct result of the ascended and glorified Jesus, who pours forth the Holy Spirit that enables people to act and speak for God.

Peter's shared stories possess convincing power. The only appropriate response to these charismatic events is joyous praise. Here, repentance/conversion (μετάνοια) is God's gift, and it should be expressed in changed attitudes and behavior reflecting God's inclusive desire and will. That includes mutual hospitality (receiving Gentiles and entering Gentiles' homes), the very issue raised in Acts 11:2. God abolishes religious and social obstacles (circumcision, food-laws, people, table-fellowship and social interaction). Consequently, his people "catch up" to God's activity, responding with joyous praise for this radical event.

Luke immediately follows this story with a narrative regarding the foundation of a Gentile Christian community in Antioch (Acts 11:19-26). The implications for participants of 10:1-11:18 will be addressed in an official way by the Jerusalem Council (Acts 15).[836] However, Luke clearly wants his readers to pause and celebrate in the joyous transformation of Peter, his six companions, Cornelius and company, Cornelius' messengers, the Jerusalem Church, including "those of the circumcision." All are in the process of "conversion" to a new and joyous way of life.

Luke invites his readers to celebrate in the two joyous climaxes (Acts 10:44-46; 11:18); he wants his readers to feel the same astonishment as they experience joy and glorify God for the way God interacts with people to bring about conversion and the empowerment of the Spirit. Such transformation and empowerment will result in new attitudes, shared stories, inclusive behavior and release from prejudice. It will introduce a unified people with a unified mission, mutual table-fellowship and hospitality, obedience to divine direction. This will all happen in the context of joyful experiences, joyful atmospheres, and joyous expressions; such joy also anticipates the *eschaton*. Thus, "the scene of Cornelius' belief is not only revelatory to the Gentiles but also to the new community, which must come to see that the extension of the visitation to the Gentiles will demand a transformation of their own context."[837] Even though God initially sent his word to the "sons of Israel" (Acts 10:36), God obliterates ethnocentricity[838] and purposes a universal mission that includes all, without social barriers.

A Powerful Mission with Attendant Joy
(Acts 11:19-30; 13:1-14:28)

Luke follows the climactic and joyous response of the Jerusalem Church for the inclusion of Gentiles (Acts 11:18) with a narrative. The joy-producing "good news" advances in both geographical and demographical settings. Affective language courses through Luke's stories, as the Gentile mission "officially" begins and is expressed in charismatic dimensions. Luke provides vignettes of:

1. Joyous Life-together in Syrian Antioch (11:19-30).
2. Mission from Antioch (13:1-14:20).
3. Return Journey to Antioch (14:21-25).
4. Report Back to Antioch (14:26-29). 839

Luke includes demographic terms that characterize his audience when Barnabas and Paul present the good news: Jews in Jewish synagogues, synagogue officials, Greeks, God-fearers, a Roman senator with an attendant magician[840] and numerous Gentiles from pagan settings. The "good news" runs its course, even in contexts of rejection or persecution.[841]

Let's examine those narratives in more careful detail.

1. Joyous Life-Together in Syrian Antioch (Acts 11:19-30). Luke links Stephen's death and the subsequent persecution of the Church (8:1-4) to the scattering of believers from Jerusalem. This moves him to his focal point in Syrian Antioch (11:19). Believers "are preaching the word" (λαλοῦντες τὸν λόγον 11:19) to Jews only, complemented by other unnamed persons (from Cyprus and Cyrene), who are "speaking to the Greeks[842] by preaching the good news about the Lord Jesus to the Greeks" (ἐλάλουν καὶ πρὸς τοὺς Ἑλληνιστάς, εὐαγγελιζόμενοι τὸν κύριον Ἰησοῦν 11:20). Curiously, these other evangelists also work miracles. Proclamation of the good news of Jesus' lordship in word and miracle would find more fertile ground with the Greeks than the proclamation of Jesus' Messiahship.

Luke coalesces the joyous proclamation with the detail, "the hand of the Lord was with them" (ἦν χεὶρ κυρίου μετ' αὐτῶν Acts 1:21).[843] The presence of charismatic power validates the message and is joined with Spirit-inspired "boldness of speech" (παρρησία),[844] even in hostile settings. Dunn notes, "Luke can vary the imagery he uses to describe divinely enabled success (e.g. 2:47; 9:31; 11:23; 12:24)." [845] Luke records the powerful response of both Jews and Greeks, "a great *number* of people turned[846] to the Lord" (11:21).

When news of the Antioch success reaches Jerusalem, Barnabas[847] is dispatched from Jerusalem to Antioch.[848] His arrival suggests the union between the mother church and Antioch. Luke highlights Barnabas' response with a word play through a cause-effect relationship, between Barnabas "seeing the *grace*[849] of God" (ἰδὼν τὴν χάριν [τὴν] τοῦ θεοῦ) and his emotional reaction, "*he rejoiced*" (ἐχάρη Acts 11:23).[850] As elsewhere in Luke-Acts, grace denotes divine favor.[851] In this context, it signifies the powerful and joyful grace in the conversion[852] of Jews and Gentiles.

Luke confirms Barnabas' joyful reaction with the reason for his joyful response, "because (ὅτι) he was a good man and *full of the Holy Spirit* and faith" (11:24). Luke corroborates that the Antioch community enjoyed the same joyful messianic blessings experienced by the Jerusalem Church. As a man of the Spirit, Barnabas perceives God's powerful activity in the positive response of Antioch to the full-orbed good news, including verbal proclamation, miraculous activity and experienced joy. Thus, he rejoices.

His joy naturally leads him to act in an elated manner. Through another word play, Luke notes that Barnabas, "the son of *encouragement*" (υἱὸς παρακλήσεως Acts 4:36),[853] "*encourages* all to remain[854] loyal to the Lord with all their hearts" (παρεκάλει πάντας τῇ προθέσει τῆς καρδίας[855] προσμένειν τῷ κυρίῳ 11:23). Haenchen notes, "Luke has a reason for this commendation: it shows that Barnabas' assent to the Antiochene mission was more than a human decision; it was prompted by the Holy Spirit."[856] For Luke, Barnabas' approval of the Gentile mission is critical.[857]

Luke's penchant for numbers[858] accentuates Barnabas' effectiveness, "a substantial crowd" "was added[859] to the Lord" (Acts 11:24, 26). In between the two statements of a substantial crowd, Luke states that Barnabas sends for Saul in Tarsus to join him in Antioch; thus, Saul comes and the two men co-teach the church (ἐκκλησία)[860] for an entire year (11:25-26).[861] Their collaborative efforts yield converts, first named as "Christians," or "Messianists."

Within this joyous community of encouragement and teaching, Luke notes the arrival of charismatic prophets[862] from Jerusalem with a specific focus on Agabus (Acts 11:27-28).[863] Upon his arrival, the Western text includes the statement, "there was much rejoicing" (ἦν δὲ πολλὴ ἀγαλλίασις).[864] "Through the Spirit" (διὰ τοῦ πνεύματος), Agabus predicts[865] an imminent and widespread famine. [866] Luke emphasizes two things:

1. Agabas' prophecy is fulfilled, "which occurred" (ἥτις ἐγένετο 11:28) under Claudius' reign.[867]

2. The prophecy led to financial help[868] or "service" (διακονία 11:29) for needy people in Jerusalem, to be delivered to the "elders"[869] by the apostolic pair, Barnabas and Saul (11:29-30).[870] This collection solidifies the gracious relationship between Jerusalem and Antioch.

Luke highlights the joyous life-together of the "Christians" in Antioch, the base of operation. He pairs Antioch's atmosphere, experience and expressions of joy with expressions of the supernatural. This all yields a burgeoning Christian movement. He also matches joy with grace and encouragement, and he links the Holy Spirit with character, charismatic prophecy, and generosity. Luke intends that his readers draw near to this vibrant community in their internal life-together and external witness, as he prepares his readers for the pair's Holy-Spirit directed missionary enterprise (Acts 13:2).

2. *Mission from Antioch (Acts 13:1-14:25).* In a Spirit-directed commissioning scene, Luke identifies specific prophets[871] and teachers[872] within the Antiochene community[873] (13:1-3). These charismatic persons, outside of Jerusalem offer a balanced approach to Christian ministry. The prophets are noted for Spirit-inspired revelation to the community, and teachers represent fidelity to the Christian message. Luke lists Barnabas first and Saul last, suggesting the relative importance of the pair, preparing for their Spirit-directed appointment (13:2).[874] Luke establishes that "the vigour of Paul's mission to the Gentiles grew immediately out of the spiritual vitality of the Antioch church."[875]

Within the context of worship and fasting, the Holy Spirit speaks. Luke accentuates the Holy Spirit's direction (indicative) in the midst of five participles:

- "while worshipping the Lord" (λειτουργούντων[876] δὲ τῷ κυρίῳ 13:2)

- "fasting" (νηστευόντων 13:2)
- *"the Holy Spirit spoke" (εἶπεν τὸ πνεῦμα τὸ ἅγιον* Acts 13:2)
- "then after fasting" (τότε νηστεύσαντες 13:3)
- "having prayed" (προσευξάμενοι Acts13:3)
- "after laying their hands on them" (ἐπιθέντες τὰς χεῖρας αὐτοῖς Acts 13:3).

The specific voice of the Holy Spirit is heard in the context of worship. Presumably the message comes through a prophecy of one of the five persons. Fasting, worship, and prayer provide the atmosphere for the Spirit-ordered selection and subsequent laying on of hands for commissioning. This describes a community seeking to know God's will in a disciplined manner. It reflects Acts 6:6, "hands are laid on the office-bearer to equip him with divine power."[877]

Ernest Best distinguishes between previous evangelism that was not intentional, e.g. as a result of persecution, and a planned mission: "the church at Antioch is shown as taking a decisive new step in deliberately setting aside men who are to travel into old and new areas ... We are here concerned with a more or less fully organized mission for which a plan was made beforehand."[878] He also suggests, "The spread of the Gospel can no longer take place haphazardly but is to be a planned activity of the Church, carried out by certain people on behalf of the whole Church ... representatives of the whole group ... their extended selves."[879]

For Luke, the Spirit's voice is crucial for the unfolding mission from the Antiochene Church ("the Holy Spirit spoke" as noted in Acts 13:2;"being sent by the Holy Spirit" in 13:4; "Paul, after being filled with the Holy Spirit" in 13:9; "the disciples were being filled with joy and the Holy Spirit" in 13:52).

The Spirit-directive is emphatic, noted by the particle "now, then, therefore" (δή), used with commands "to give them greater urgency"[880]: "*Therefore separate* for me Barnabas and Saul" (Acts 13:2).

The Spirit then expresses the purpose for the pair's separation, "for the work for which I have called them" (13:2). Aune labels this prophecy as a "prescriptive oracle, a type of prophetic speech in which the supernatural speaker enjoins a particular type of action or behavior."[881] Luke uses the term *work* (ἔργον) with inclusion, since the *work* is used in both the commissioning scene and the report-back after the mission, "for the *work* which they now had completed" (εἰς τὸ ἔργον ὃ ἐπλήρωσαν 14:26).[882] Clearly the work is grounded in the call "to a special task,"[883] expressed through the perfect tense, "I have called" (προσκέκλημαι).

Luke combines the divine will, expressed through prophecy, with the human response to the divine word, including the laying on of hands and releasing the pair for specific work. Barnabas and Saul have been enmeshed in the life-together of the Antioch church. They taught for a year, participated in financial contribution, worshiped, fasted and prayed, and now they are released for their Spirit-directed mission. Johnson notes, "The point clearly, is to demonstrate the social character of the apostolic mission."[884] In addition, the pattern of sending out emissaries in pairs corresponds to the earlier mission of the disciples (Luke 10:1); it accentuates "team-leadership."[885]

The Spirit trumps magic and leads to a joyous conversion (Acts 13:4-12). Luke reiterates that Barnabas and Saul were "sent by the Spirit" (13:4), referring to their Spirit-appointment in 13:2. Thus, the pair arrive in Cyprus. They proclaim God's word in Salamis in Jewish synagogues (13:5), but Luke makes no mention of any Jewish response. Perhaps Luke hurries over this stage of their journey to get to the main event in Paphos—the Spirit's triumph over magic and the joyful conversion of a Roman proconsul (senator). Luke records the narrative of a power-encounter with a magician who "was with"[886] Sergius Paulus. This narrative is followed by the climax of a joyous and trusting response by the senator. Luke lays out the story through several contrasts and alternations between four characters:

Bar-Jesus	Barnabas & Saul/Paul	Sergius Paulus
Identity: A certain Jewish magician, a false prophet named Bar-Jesus who was an attendant of the proconsul Sergius Paulus (13:6-7); Elymas the Magician, for that is what his name means (13:8)	*Identity*: "Baranabas and Saul" (13:7) "Saul, who is also called Paul" (13:9)	*Identity*: The proconsul Sergius Paulus (13:7)
Character and Action: "False prophet" who "opposes" [887] the apostolic pair, seeking to "turn away" (διαστρέφω) the proconsul from "the faith" (13:8) and "pervert" (διαστρέφω) the "straight ways of the Lord" (13:10)	*Character and Action*: In response,[888] "Paul, being filled with the Holy Spirit" (13:9) "stared into him" (Elymas 13:9); prophetic curse that impugns Bar-Jesus/ Elymas' identity, character, hostile action and its immediate consequence: "You are the son of the devil and an enemy of everything that is right; You are full of all kinds of deceit and trickery. Must you always pervert the straight ways of the Lord?"	*Character and Action*: "an intelligent man" (13:7) "summoned for Baranabas and Saul; he wanted to hear the word of the Lord" (13:7) *Climactic Response*: "When the proconsul saw what had happened, he believed, being astonished at the teaching of the Lord" (19:12)
Result of the prophetic curse: "Immediately a mist and darkness fell upon him and he groped about, seeking someone to lead him by the hand" (13:11)	*Prophetic consequence*: "Now, behold, the hand of the Lord is against you. For a time you will be blind and unable to see the light of day" (13:11).	

Luke arranges the material to note the movement from Jew to Gentile: preaching in Jewish synagogues (13:5) on Cyprus' eastern side to an encounter with an important Roman official on the western side (13:7). This official is more important in rank than Cornelius (Acts 10-11).[889] Luke contrasts Bar-Jesus/Elymas[890] with the wise and understanding Sergius Paulus, and with Paul, who is filled with the Holy Spirit. In Paul's interchange with Bar-Jesus (i.e. "Son of Joshua or Son of Jesus") Paul calls him "Son of the devil." Luke juxtaposes "straight ways" with "crooked ways" and contrasts Elymas, who is "filled with deceit and trickery" and Paul who is "filled with the Holy Spirit."

Thus, the real clash happens between the Holy Spirit and the devil. Luke differentiates Elymas as a false prophet with Paul as a genuine prophet, exercising prophecy in his supernatural "stare into" Elymas.[891] Through the repetition of the verb, "I turn away/pervert" (διαστρέφω), Luke uses Elymas' opposition as a foil to highlight Sergius Paulus, introduced as an "intelligent man." Luke leads his readers through Sergius Paulus' positive movement from "wanting[892] to hear the word of the Lord" to his trusting and astonished response (13:12). Luke highlights the Holy Spirit's role through repetition (two statements about Saul and Barnabas being sent by the Holy Spirit in 13:2, 4, and one account of Paul, being filled with the Spirit in 13:9, which occasions his prophetic insight.[893] Luke also reveals his emphasis on fulfilled prophecy, with the immediate (παραχρῆμα 13:11) fulfillment of Paul's curse of temporary blindness.[894]

Luke reveals some similarities between Saul's encounter on the Damascus Road and this confrontation with Elymas: temporary blindness and the need to be led by the hand (9:8; 13:11b); Saul as a staunch opponent of "the Way" and the magician's attempt to pervert "the ways of the Lord" (9:2; 13:10).[895] The language of "making straight ways" is thoroughly Jewish, for it reflects prophetic announcements (Hos 14:10; Isa 40:3-4 cited by Luke 3:4-6). Peter possessed similar insight into Simon Magus, "your heart is not straight before God" (Acts 8:21). As Johnson notes, "The phrase wonderfully sums up a path of opposition to God's work."[896] In Antioch, Luke used the term, "the hand of the Lord" to describe the miracles of unnamed Greeks (11:20).Now Luke uses the "hand of the Lord" in the context of a punitive miracle in Paphos.

The narrative builds to the climax of the senator's believing response to the fulfilled curse, "Then when the proconsul saw what happened, he believed," followed by Luke's explanation for why the senator believed, "for he was astonished by the teaching about the Lord." The astonishment "can mean any strong emotional response."[897] Here, "the teaching about the Lord" is paired with the fulfilled prophecy of Elymas' miraculous punitive blindness.

Surely, Luke accentuates the senator's progression from wisdom and good sense, to his openness, positive movement and desire, along with his observation of the fulfilled punitive miracle, to his trust. Luke wants his readers to notice his explanation for the senator's trust—astonishment. The verb, "I am astonished" (ἐκπλήσσω) is paired with the preposition "by" (ἐπί), which often occurs "after verbs which express feelings, emotions or opinions."[898] As with previous stories, Luke builds the narratives of people who are in the process of discovery, leading to the climax of a joyous experience. In this case, his narrative focuses on the conversion of a high-ranking Roman official. Yes, the account includes the triumph of a Spirit-filled Paul's prevailing over magic. But more importantly, Paul's punitive miracle brings the closing climax of Sergius Paulus' faith coupled with joyous astonishment at Paul's teaching (word and miracle). Emotional language flows through this story.

Luke then narrates a joyous mission in Antioch of Pisidia. He provides extensive references linking the numinous with the joyous responses of Gentiles (Acts 13:48) and the Pauline company (13:52). Paul emerges as the central figure ("those around Paul" 13:13), already intimated in the previous encounter with Bar-Jesus and Sergius Paulus. In a synagogue, after the reading of Torah and the prophets, the synagogue officials ask the group if there is "a word of encouragement, i.e. sermon (τίς ... λόγος παρακλήσεως 13:15)[899] to be shared with the gathered people; Paul is ready to respond with an extended sermon.[900]

Paul's sermon addresses two groups in the synagogue, "Men of Israel" and "You Gentiles who fear God" (13:16). Later in the same sermon, Paul addresses the same group as, "Brothers" and "You, in your midst who fear God" (13:26). The "word of exhortation/encouragement" (13:15) becomes "the word of this salvation that was sent" (13:26).

Similar to Peter's speeches (Acts 2:25; 3:13-26) and Stephen's speech (6:2-53),[901] Paul's sermon rehearses Israel's history, now with a special focus on David, and is noted by a progression of events (verbs) in which God is the active subject.[902] David's kingship is the source, leading to the point, "God *brought* to Israel the Savior Jesus" (13:23).[903] Through the rehearsal, Luke reminds the readership of Israel's illustrious history, which now reaches beyond to include Gentiles as well. The kerygmatic progression[904] emphasizes the incorruptible resurrection (13:25-32).

Fulfilled prophecy is high on Luke's agenda,[905] for the prophets include Old Testament and New Testament prophets. Luke reveals specific ways that prophecies are fulfilled in the Jesus-event and in the narrative. Typologically, Habbakuk's warning, "that which is written in the prophets," serves as judgment ("marvel and perish" θαυμάσατε καὶ ἀφανίσθητε Acts 13:41) for the scoffers who reject the divine word (13:40-41; Hab 1:5). Speaking for God, both Habbakuk and Paul describe a work, expressed by a repetition of a noun and the related verb: "*a work, which I am working* in your days, *a work*, which you would never believe even if someone explained it to you" (ἔργον ἐργάζομαι ἐγὼ ἐν ταῖς ἡμέραις ὑμῶν, ἔργον ὃ οὐ μὴ πιστεύσητε ἐάν τις ἐκδιηγῆται ὑμῖν 13:41).

The very prophecy of warning and judgment is fulfilled when the jealous and joy-less Jews talk abusively against Paul's message (13:45); later they incite the leading women and men, stir up a persecution against the pair, and eject them from their region (13:50).

Since the term *work* (ἔργον) begins this narrative (Acts 13:2) and "caps off" the report-back (14:26), it is striking to find a repetition of *work* (ἔργον), coupled with the verb, *I work* (ἐργάζομαι) in the middle of their mission in Antioch in Pisidia.

The same prophecy of warning and judgment leads to a Spirit-inspired boldness of speech (παρρησιασάμενοι 13:46), as the apostolic pair vents the consequences of the Jews' behavior. "Since you have rejected it [the word of God, i.e. the Jesus-event] and you judge yourselves uworthy of eternal life," (ἐπειδὴ ἀπωθεῖσθε αὐτὸν καὶ ἀξίους κρίνετε

ἑαυτοὺς τῆς αἰωνίου ζωῆς), behold we are turning to the Gentiles"
(13:46). The Jews who *judge* Jesus as *worthy* of *death* (13:27), now *judge*
themselves as *unworthy* of *eternal life* (13:46). Again, joyless critics are
jealous of Gentile inclusion.

Although Paul remains committed to the temporal priority of the Jews,
God's new work includes receptive Gentiles. "The mission is universal,
but it must follow a prescribed order. The Jews must be addressed first. If
they reject the gospel, the missionaries are free to begin the second phase
of their mission."⁹⁰⁶

Fulfilled prophecy resurfaces when Paul supports his Gentile
ministry with the fulfilled commission from Isaiah's Servant Song, "I
have appointed you to be a light for the Gentiles, that you might be
[bring] salvation to the ends of the earth" (Acts 13:47; Isa 49:6).⁹⁰⁷ Luke's
purpose statement for Paul's Gentile ministry, "to the ends of the earth"
is also a prophetic fulfillment of Jesus' promise in Acts 1:8, "to the ends
of the earth." Paul is now summoned to fulfill Israel's mission; this text
is a "programmatic prophecy."⁹⁰⁸ Luke can hardly highlight the charism
of prophecy more emphatically than he has done through the sermon
and its aftermath.

As a counter-point to joy-less rejection, Luke emphasizes the joyful
reception of others. When the pair leaves the synagogue, the response
is positive, for the people invite the apostles to speak again about these
matters on the next Sabbath. However, "many Jews and devout proselytes"
just cannot wait for the next Sabbath (Acts 13:43). The language reflects
joyous excitement. The apostolic pair urges them "to remain in the grace
of God" (προσμένειν τῇ χάριτι τοῦ θεοῦ 13:43). On the next Sabbath,
Luke expresses the large number with hyperbole, "Nearly all the city was
gathered to hear the word of the Lord" (13:44).

Luke records the Gentiles' joyous response upon learning of the pair's
turn to them (Acts 13:46) and discovering Paul's appointment to be a light
to the Gentiles. Luke recounts their emotional and climactic response of
joy, "they were rejoicing and were glorifying the word of the Lord and
they believed, all who were appointed for eternal life" (ἔχαιρον καὶ
ἐδόξαζον τὸν λόγον τοῦ κυρίου καὶ ἐπίστευσαν ὅσοι ἦσαν
τεταγμένοι εἰς ζωὴν αἰώνιον 13:48). The two imperfect tenses

suggest their ongoing rejoicing and glorifying, which accompany their moment of trust (aorist).

Joy is the fitting climax, embracing their positive acceptance of the "word of encouragement" (Acts 13:15), "the word of this salvation" (13:26), reception of the kerygmatic progression of events (13:28-33), "the good news of the promise" (13:32), fulfilled prophecy throughout the sermon, "these things" (13:42), and "the word of the Lord" (13:44, 48). Luke then narrates that, after their joyous and trusting response, "the word of the Lord" was continuing to spread through the whole region" (13:49). Luke accentuates Gentile-joy, for they also belong to the people of God and experience salvation. Johnson notes, "The response of 'joy' signals acceptance of God's visitation ... The code words used here by Luke indicate that this foundation is an authentic realization of the Church; it is filled with joy ... and of the Holy Spirit."[909]

Jewish jealousy leads to their contradiction of the pair's message, including abuse[910] heaped upon the apostolic pair (Acts 13:45), followed by persecution and their physical coercion and ejection of Paul and Barnabas from their region (13:50).

Subsequent to their expulsion, Paul and Barnabas shake the dust off their feet and travel to Iconium (Acts 13:52).[911] However, Luke again underscores the joy of the believers in Antioch with the fullness of the Holy Spirit, "And the disciples were being filled with joy and the Holy Spirit" (οἵ τε μαθηταὶ ἐπληροῦντο χαρᾶς καὶ πνεύματος ἁγίου 13:52). Again, the imperfect tense, "they were being filled' (ἐπληροῦντο) expresses their ongoing experience[912] of joy and the Holy Spirit. Luke alternates between the verb, "I fill" (πληρόω), the adjective, "full" (πλήρης), and another verb "I fill" (πίμπλημι)—all of which connect joy with, "being filled with the Holy Spirit" and some miraculous manifestation.[913] While the Jews "were filled with jealousy" (13:45), the new disciples "were being filled with joy and the Holy Spirit" (13:52). Surely, Luke opens his readers to charismatic joy of the Holy Spirit and miracles.

In Iconium, Luke's readers learn of a powerful but divisive mission (Acts 14:1-7). Luke reveals the familiar pattern of preaching in synagogues, Jewish opposition, and a turn to the Gentiles. Luke contrasts the pair's powerful mission in Iconium and the joy-less reaction, most notably from the Jews. A great number of Jews and Greeks trust in the pair's message (14:1), followed by Jewish refusal and poisoning of minds (14:2).⁹¹⁴ The missionary pair remains in Iconium for an extended time, continuing to perform miracles, "being bold in speech in the Lord who confirms the word of his grace by enabling them to do miraculous signs and wonders through their hands" (παρρησιαζόμενοι ἐπὶ τῷ κυρίῳ τῷ μαρτυροῦντι τῷ λόγῳ τῆς χάριτος αὐτοῦ, διδόντι σημεῖα καὶ τέρατα γινέσθαι διὰ τῶν χειρῶν αὐτῶν Acts 14:3).⁹¹⁵

Subsequently the multitude divides, followed by an attempt by some Gentiles and Jews with their leaders to abuse and stone the apostles (14:4-5). When the apostles learn of the murderous attempt, they escape and finally arrive in Derbe, "and there they were preaching the good news" (κἀκεῖ εὐαγγελιζόμενοι ἦσαν Acts 14: 6-7).⁹¹⁶ Luke presents the charismatic and joyous mission of the missionary pair woven into hostile and murderous settings.

Charismatic power is expressed in: a) the great number of Jews and Greeks who put their trust in the message, b) Spirit-empowered boldness of speech in the context of hostility, c) the signs and wonders, which confirm the word of his grace. Luke intends to make Paul equal to Peter with the mention of "signs and wonders." Haenchen observes that the miracles "are not an isolated event, an exceptional case, but a link in a long chain."⁹¹⁷

Joy is implicit in the expression, "in the word of his grace" (14:3), which Luke has already paired with "joy" (χαρά 11:23). A further intimation of joy is found in the periphrastic construction in 14:7, "they were preaching the good news" (εὐαγγελιζόμενοι ἦσαν), which emphasizes their continued preaching in word and charismatic power.

Luke then recounts a joyful healing, human responses, and murderous aggression (Acts 14:8-20). Paul effects a healing of a crippled beggar, similar to Peter's healing of a crippled beggar in Jerusalem (3:1-9),⁹¹⁸ with numerous parallels:

- the long-term and hopeless condition of the paralytic, which accentuates the miraculous healing (3:2; 14:8).
- the verb, "I sit" (κάθημαι 3:10; 14:8).

- attention given to the apostles, "seeing Peter and John" (3:3), "he listened to Paul as he was speaking" (14:9).
- the "supernatural stare into him" (ἀτενίζω) of the healer (3:4; 14:9).
- the participle, "seeing" (3:3; 14:9).
- a command, "Rise and walk" (3:6), "Stand up straight on your feet" (14:10).
- verbs that describe the effects, "leaping ... and was walking ... walking and leaping ... walking" (3:8), "he leaped and was walking" (14:10).
- the effect upon onlookers and a following sermon.

The Jewish context for healing in Acts 3 juxtaposes with the Gentile setting in Acts 14. Luke accentuates Paul's loud cry of command, "he [Paul] said "with a loud voice" (εἶπεν μεγάλῃ φωνῇ 14:10), which Haenchen associates as one "driven by the Spirit or demon."[919]

One particular point of contrast lies in the beggars' faith-conditions. The crippled beggar in Acts 3 gives no evidence of faith; he merely hopes for financial charity. In 14:9, Paul perceives that the cripple "has faith to be healed" (ἔχει πίστιν τοῦ **σωθῆναι**).[920] Luke's readers would no doubt remember the double-entendre of the verb, "I save/heal" (σῴζω) and the noun, "salvation" (σωτηρία) in 4:9, 12 with respect to the "healed" cripple. The healing is an acted parable of salvation. Since the stories are parallel, Luke would assume that his readers imagine a similar joy of the healed/saved beggar and onlookers.

Since Paul's audience is Gentile, the crowd and their priest sense the numinous nature of the event and interpret the source of his healing as the descent of their pagan deities in the persons of the pair, "the gods have descended unto us in human form" (Acts 14:11). They see Barnabas as Zeus and identify Paul as Hermes (14:12).[921] Their excited announcement spills over to their offer of wreaths and their intent to sacrifice bulls for the pair.

Even after Paul's mini-sermon in 14:15-17, the apostles could scarcely keep the crowd from sacrificing to them (14:18). Yes, the crowd's excited response is misdirected, but they recognize the miraculous power and are receptive to God's visitation. Marshall aptly suggests, "If the local people had failed to honor the gods as gods on their previous visit, they were anxious not to repeat this error."[922]

In violent fashion, the apostles react to their deification, "tearing their clothes, rushing out to the crowd, crying out and saying, 'Men, why are you doing these things? We also are only men, humans like you'" (14:14-15). Just as Peter rejected personal power or piety as the source of healing (3:12) and disallows Cornelius' worship (10:25-26), so the apostles reject personal worship in a passionate manner. The expression is meant to "state the shared human condition and deflect divine honor."[923]

Luke narrates Paul's mini-sermon to the Gentiles, with the participle, "preaching the good news" (εὐαγγελιζόμενοι). The good news directs the excited people to turn from worthless things to the living God (Acts 14:15). Since God is one, the conclusion is firm: "abandon Gentile polytheism." Luke uses the verb "I turn" (ἐπιστρέφω) extensively in Acts for describing conversion;[924] it involves a turning *from* and turning *to*.[925] In his sermon, Paul points to God's creation and his beneficent care, described as "doing good" (ἀγαθουργῶν 14:17). Both creation and ongoing providence are miraculous, including rain and agricultural fertility, and the joy that it produces for people, "filling you with food and joyful hearts" (14:17). While the sermon is a Gentile-apologetic, Paul argues as a Hebrew, for all of creation and providence is a miracle. God is involved in creation, beneficent activity, and gifts of joy for humans.[926] Keener notes, "'filling you with joy' here might implicitly point to the higher filling with joy that is available in full submission to God's purposes (Acts 13:52)."[927] Luke grounds the Jesus-event from the foundation of God's beneficent creation and providential care that elicits joy from humans.

Following the sermon, the apostles depart from Antioch and Iconium, dogged again by hostile Jews. The thwarted plot to stone Paul (Acts 14:4-5) now progresses to an actual stoning,[928] followed by dragging Paul outside the city and supposing him to be dead. Somehow, Paul gets up, surrounded by disciples, and returns to the very city that had just stoned him (14:19-20). Luke does not inform his readers how Paul could stand up after being stoned and left for dead. Pervo states, "Theologically, 'the decisive point is that this messenger of God is not discouraged, but resumes his task."⁹²⁹ Luke concludes these events in Lystra with the apostles' departure to Derbe (14:20).

3. *Return journey to Antioch (Acts 14:21-25).* During the pair's return journey to Antioch, they continued to "preach the good news to that city" [Derbe] (εὐαγγελισάμενοί τε τὴν πόλιν ἐκείνην 14:20-21)⁹³⁰ and "made a large number of disciples" (μαθητεύσαντες ἱκανούς). Retracing their previous steps, they travel through Lystra and Iconium and arriving at Antioch [of Pisidia]. Luke notes that in this city, which previously expelled them, the pair continues their life-giving activity, "strengthening the hearts of the disciples and encouraging them to remain in the faith" (ἐπιστηρίζοντες τὰς ψυχὰς τῶν μαθητῶν παρακαλοῦντες ἐμμένειν τῇ πίστει (14:22).⁹³¹ With the revisits to various towns, Luke emphasizes the pair's pastoral concern. Coupled with their encouraging and joyful words, they also communicate the hard reality that "through many persecutions it is necessary for us to enter the kingdom of God." The apostles no doubt reflect upon their frequent and violent persecutions on this journey. The believers in Antioch of Pisidia could vividly remember how the pair had previously suffered in their city.

Luke records another development, the first appointment of elders in each church, coupled with the manner of appointment, "with praying and fasting, they entrusted them to the Lord, in whom they had put their trust" (Acts 14:23). Fasting and prayer in the context of a formal appointment⁹³² serves as an inclusion with 13:1-3, when Saul and Barnabas were set apart. This paragraph concludes with geographical movement from Pisidia, leading to the pair's arrival in Syrian Antioch, coupled with the preaching of "the word," which is consistently linked with another expression, "the word of the Lord."

4. *Report back to Antioch (Acts 14:26-28).* Luke comes full circle with his mention of "Antioch from which they had been commended" (14:26). The geographical reference was the point of origin, "from which" (ὅθεν) they had been sent apart and commissioned for their missionary journey (13:1-3). The periphrastic perfect participle, "they had been commended," emphasizes their enduring state, characterizing their entire ministry.

Luke also notes the object of their commendation is "to the grace of God for the work which they had fulfilled" (14:26). Their entire ministry reveals a divinely commissioned "work," which they had fulfilled (Hab 1:5; Acts 13:41).

In Acts 14:27, Luke summarizes the report-back to the gathered church with two statements:

- "all the things that God had done through them" (ὅσα ἐποίησεν μετ᾽ αὐτῶν).
- "how God had opened the door of faith[933] to the Gentiles" (ἤνοιξεν τοῖς ἔθνεσιν θύραν πίστεως).
-

The correlative, "all the things/everything" (ὅσα) is used of quantity and number,[934] and refers to the totality of God's activity through them in preaching, bringing good news, miracles, and the varied responses to their full-orbed ministry, including joy, the Holy Spirit, encouragement, grace, and praise for God. The second statement reflects the over-riding extension of the good news to Gentiles, whether they be God-fearers or pagans. While the narrative maintains the temporal priority of the Jew, this commitment is not exclusive, but inclusive and well-established in the entire Antioch-narrative.

Luke recounts the shared story of a vibrant church in Antioch and the mission emanating from this community. The narrative's over-riding thrust establishes that the mission stands in continuity with Israel and is inclusive, for the "good news" is preached to the Gentiles. Luke also establishes a close interplay with human efforts to "preach the good news" and God, who works with the Barnabas, Saul and the Antiochene community. Human decisions and actions link with divine activity.

Luke also couples the mission with miraculous events and attendant joy. The full narrative frequently refers to the atmosphere, experience, and expression of joy, woven into the fabric of the story-line, reflecting Luke's joy-vocabulary:

- five uses of the joy-eliciting verb, "I preach the good news" (11:20; 13:32; 14:7, 15, 21).

- three references to the verb, "I encourage" (11:23; 13:42; 14:22).
- three explicit mentions of "joy" (11:23; 13:48, 52)—other similar responses are implicit.
- "gladness of heart" (14:17).
- four references to "grace" (11:23; 13:43; 14:3, 26).
- an excited but misdirected fear of the numinous (14:11-14, 18).

Several stories build to the climax of joy and praise. The positive and joyous responses are also viewed against the meanness of the joy-less critics, who are motivated by envy, insecurity, and fear (Bar-Jesus in Acts 14:8-10; the Jews in 13:45, 50; the Jews with their leaders, the prominent women and men in 14:5; the Jews again in 14:19). Their rejection of the apostles and the message leads them to abuse the apostles, casting them from their region. Luke records an attempted and actual stoning.

Luke wants his readers to embrace the charismatic and joyous dimensions of the Christian life. The Holy Spirit is real, personal, and powerful and bequeaths joyous gifts leading to wholeness of life and joy, and to bold proclamation, even amidst hostility. Luke's shared stories possess convincing power. Initial conversion, charismatic experience, and subsequent growth yield sheer delight. Luke's stories reveal a joyful God who wills life and joy for his people, both now and in the coming *eschaton*.

A Joyous Salvation
(Acts 16:11-40)

Luke's Philippian narrative offers several charismatic scenes building towards a joyous climax. In addition to the apostolic pair, the narrative includes three stories: a) a woman named Lydia; b) a demon-possessed slave girl; c) a jailer and his family. Luke follows these stories with a sequel, reflecting the cultural tension of shame and honor when Paul and Silas leave Philippi. Commentaries concentrate on the jailer's conversion but fail to notice the affective language of joy.

Luke uses inclusion to book-end this important narrative,[935] for Lydia and her home open and conclude the Philippian story (Acts 16:11-15, 40).

Luke informs his readers that God opened her heart to Paul's message. He notes her baptism, along with her household. Then, "she exhorted" (παρεκάλησεν) the Pauline company to stay in her home (11:15); she extended the sacred rite of hospitality.[936] After the miraculous events in 16:11-39, the apostolic pair returned to Lydia's home and "encouraged" (παρεκάλησεν 16:40) the people gathered there. Lydia serves as a contrast with the demon-possessed slave girl (16:16). She is well-to-do, free, described as a "God-fearer" (σεβομένη 16:14), is genuinely open to the Christian message. Her conversion is quietly described. The slave-girl, on the other hand, is not well-to-do. She is controlled both by "a spirit" (πνεύματι 16:18) and by human masters, but she is freed in a spectacular manner.

Luke prepares his readers for the slave-girl's exorcism by highlighting her identity, what she does, and what she says. In terms of identity, she is possessed by Python, i.e. "the serpent or dragon that guarded the Delphi oracle,"[937] associated with a spirit of divination, then ventriloquism, with a spirit dwelling within her belly; she also utters ecstatic prophecies (μαντευομένη 16:16). Keener defines spirit-possession, *"any altered state of consciousness indigenously interpreted in terms of the influence of an alien spirit."*[938] In short, she feeds the religious libido of people who seek her prophetic guidance. Luke notes that she made *substantial profit* (16:16) for her male masters. He reiterates this in 16:19, "her masters saw that the hope of *their profit* was gone." Her actions in the narrative are significant. She "follows," i.e. she dogs the pair for several days (16:17-18). She cries out[939] the identity of the pair and their offer of salvation, "These men are the slaves of the Most-High God, who announce to you, the way of salvation" (16:17). Possessed by an evil numinous power, she recognizes the numinous nature of the apostolic pair and their salvation-offer. She is a slave of the serpent, while they are slaves of the Most-High God. Her identification of the "Most-High"[940] serves as a "convenient common denominator" for both Jews and Gentiles for "the supreme being."[941] Similarly, "salvation" (σωτηρία) was a common goal for both Jews and Gentiles. Her salvation from the "spirit of divination," corresponds to the jailer's plea (16:30).

This story is similar to Luke's narratives of Jesus' exorcisms in which demons recognize Jesus' identity and are expelled by Jesus (Luke 4:34; 8:28),[942] followed by a plea to leave the area (Luke 8:37; Acts 16:38).

Luke states that Paul's "annoyance" (διαπονηθεὶς Acts 16:18)—not compassion)— occasioned the exorcism. In contemporary language, she was dogging the pair. Yes, this woman repeatedly advertised the pair, but this is the wrong kind of publicity. Her promotion is unwelcome, so Paul silences the confession. Why? A genuine faith response of faith can never issue from demonic forces, nor should their confession be allowed to compel human confession. Genuine response can only come from free agents. It must be spontaneous rather than forced. Both Jesus and Paul elicit a trust response, but they will not force faith upon the beholders.

Jesus cast out demons by his own authority, but Paul exorcises the slave-girl by "the name of Jesus" (Acts 16:18). Paul's brief command, "I command you *to go out* (ἐξελθεῖν), leads to the succinct effect, "*it went out* (ἐξῆλθεν) at that very moment" (16:18). Genuine freedom now comes to this slave-girl. Dunn demeans her as "a dim-witted slave girl"[943]; however, she is a victim of a controlling spirit and greedy owners who used her and her condition to fill their bank account. Now, she is a person in her own right, delivered from demonic and human control.

Her masters see only one thing—the loss of profit, for her fortune-telling days are over "the hope of their profit *went out*" (ἐξῆλθεν Acts 16:19). The verb *went out* corresponds to the demon's exit from the slave-girl in 16:18. The joy-less men cannot see that something grand has happened in her life. They resort to violence, seize the apostolic pair, and drag them to the city's rulers, then magistrates, with a trumped-up anti-Semitic charge that these men are upsetting the city and are overturning common customs. Luke juxtaposes "being Jews" with "us Romans" (16:20-21). Ironically, the owners, who accuse the two apostles of agitation are themselves agitators. They falsify their accusation, since an individual exorcism would not hold up in a secular court. Luke intimates the irony of "us Romans" with the reality that the apostolic pair are Roman citizens (16:37-38). Paul's trump-card is suspended, but he plays it later in the story's sequel.

Other joy-less critics enter, aligning with the magistrates—the crowd, then the policemen (*lictors*), who disrobe the pair and repeatedly beat them with sticks (Acts 16:22-23).[944] Finally the jailer imprisons them in the innermost cell with their feet in wooden stocks (16:23-24). There is no trial—only a mob-scene, leaving the pair in great pain, in a cramped position, and in maximum security. Paul and Silas, who had shattered the bonds of a slave-girl, are now confined in shackles.[945]

Luke prefaces the earthquake with mention of Paul and Silas' joyous activity, "praying and singing hymns to God" (Acts 16:25), and the attentive listening of the other prisoners. Luke consistently reveals that both Jesus and the early community prayed in decisive or critical moments. The prison's atmosphere doesn't resound with groaning, cursing, or defending—it resonates prayer, hymns, and attentive listening. As Tertullian noted, "The legs feel nothing in the stocks when the heart is in heaven."[946]

Luke describes the earthquake as "sudden" and "great," followed by the immediate result (ὥστε) of shaken foundations of the prison. For his readers, Luke intimates that the great earthquake is in response to the joyful praise and prayer of the imprisoned pair (Acts 16:25-26).[947] Two other miracles occur, accentuated by the adjective *all*: "*all* the doors [of the prisoners' cells] were opened," "*all* the shackles [of the prisoners] were released" (16:26). Luke highlights the pair's miraculous deliverance, for they had been imprisoned in the innermost prison with feet in stocks (16:24). Pervo states, "The ancient narrator expected the audience to recognize a miracle."[948] An implicit miracle also occurs, for none of the released prisoners seize the opportunity for escape. Luke does not inform his audience as to how or why this happened, but certainly this is remarkable.

The earthquake awakens the sleeping jailor, who believes the worst— all of the inmates have escaped. The jailor, making a snap-decision to preserve his honor by killing himself, reaches for a sword. Emotional language fills the story as the jailor progresses from death to life.[949] Somehow, Paul knows his suicidal intent and calls out with a loud voice, "Don't harm yourself," followed by the explanation for why the jailor should not follow-through with his suicide, "for (γάρ) we are all here."

Luke doesn't inform his readers as to how Paul knew this. His description of the jailor's quick actions and reactions are highly emotive: "he calls for a light in the dark prison, rushes in, is trembling with fear, falls before Paul and Silas and leads them outside of the prison" (Acts 16:29-30a).

Once outside, the jailor asks the all-important question, "Sirs, what must I do to be saved?" (Acts 16:30b).[950] What did the jailor know at this point? At the least, he surely has heard the joyous singing. He also experienced the violent earthquake, and he heard Paul's knowledge of a full headcount of prisoners. The jailor is emotionally shaken, perhaps even stunned that the pair are divine men have been supernaturally vindicated. Pervo states, "The prison-keeper perceives that no one but a god or a beneficiary could know these things."[951]

Paul quickly answers the jailor's question with a command and promise, "Believe on the Lord Jesus Christ and you will be saved, you and your household" (Acts 16:31). He follows with further instruction, "the word of the Lord" (16:32). Luke provides a word-play with the term "sir/Lord" (κύριος): the jailor addresses the missionary pair as "Sirs" (κύριοι 16:30), and Paul directs him to trust "the Lord (κύριον) Jesus Christ" (Acts 16:31), followed by instruction. Thus, worship deflects from "divine men" to the real Lord. The jailor seeks salvation from the apostolic pair. But Jesus is the real source of true salvation, already proclaimed by the slave-girl (16:17), and now extended to the jailor and his gathered household.[952]

The jailor then bathes their wounded backs and submits himself and his household to baptism (Acts 16:33). Chrysostom notes, "He washed and he was washed; he washed them from their stripes, and was himself washed from his sins."[953] He then leads the pair to his home and extends middle-eastern hospitality with a meal, labeled as "risky hospitality" by Keener.[954]

Luke's climax expresses shared joy and trust, embracing the jailor and his household, "the household rejoiced with exuberance because all had come to trust God" (ἠγαλλιάσατο πανοικεὶ πεπιστευκὼς τῷ θεῷ Acts 16:34b). Although Luke does not mention the Holy Spirit, it is surely implicit in the strong verb, "I exult"[955] (ἀγαλλιάομαι)—an exuberant joy filled all. Exultant joy and trust replace the previous "trembling" (ἔυτρομος 16:29), leading to a shared meal, even at midnight. Certainly, this is a celebration of joyous salvation.⁹⁵⁶

The story's sequel occurs at daybreak when the mob-mentality has died down. The magistrates decide to release the two prisoners; perhaps they believe that the pair has learned their lesson. They dispatch the police to the jail to release the pair (Acts 16:35), and the jailer quickly informs the pair that they are free to depart.

An interchange transpires between Paul, the jailer, and the magistrates, concerning a cover-up plan. The previous day's violence was public and shamed the pair. Paul now plays the trump-card of the apostolic pair's Roman citizenship. As Roman citizens, their rights had been violated. They had no trial with inquiry—only seizure, beating, and imprisonment. With humor, Luke contrasts the *public* events and a *secret* sending: "being *publicly* beaten without a public trial" and "now they want to cast us out *secretly*" (Acts 16:37). Paul requires a public release. Once the magistrates learn of their Roman citizenship, they hastily honor the Paul's request, providing a formal escort. Thus, the city officials, police and jailer, who had shamed Paul and Silas in a public way, are themselves publicly embarrassed. In the episode, Paul and Silas do not escape when the earthquake provides a chance, nor secretly "escape" when the jailor informs them of their release from prison.

Paul and Silas return to Lydia's home and "encouraged" (παρεκάλεσαν) the people in her household (Acts 16:40) before departing. Philippian generosity extended to the pair progresses with repeated gifts to Paul during his subsequent travels and imprisonment (Phil 4:10-16). Paul also references the persecution of believers in Philippi (Phil 1:27-30).

Paul and Silas, like Jesus recognize the reality of the numinous spirit-world and are victorious over this demonic sphere. Luke highlights God's rescuing power with Lydia and her household and with a slave-girl. He also describes an earthquake, opened prison doors, loosened chains, and Paul's knowledge of the non-escaping prisoners and the jailor's suicidal action. All of this leads to the joyous and climactic salvation of a jailor and his household, with an intimation of the Holy Spirit. For Luke's readers, the story encourages in the midst of suffering. It underscores the reality that suffering is not in vain, for believers belong to the good company of others who have suffered and prevailed in a joyous manner. Like Paul and Silas, Luke's community draws strength by praying and singing praises in the midst of suffering.

Charismatic Power and Joy in Ephesus
(Acts 18:24-19:20)

It is unfortunate to discover a new chapter division in Acts 19:1, for Luke joins five paragraphs beginning in 18:24, all recounting events occurring in Ephesus.[957] Further, there is inclusion with respect to Paul and his travel plans on either side of the five paragraphs ("set sail from Ephesus" in 18:21; Paul leaves Ephesus with the eventual goal of reaching Rome in 19:21[958]).

Paragraph 1 (Acts 18:24-29):	Paragraph 2 (19:1-7):	Paragraph 3 (19:8-12):	Paragraph 4 (19:13-16):	Paragraph 5 (Acts 19:17-20):
Apollos	Paul and the Ephesian disciples	Paul's charismatic ministry in Ephesus	The seven sons of Sceva	Christian triumph over magic

Luke intends his readers to link paragraphs one and two:

- both paragraphs mention Ephesus, where Apollos and Paul arrive (18:24; 19:1).
- both narratives are situated in a Jewish context (Old Testament Scripture in 18:24, 28; 19:3, as well as linking the Ephesian disciples' baptism with John's baptism in 19:3).
- the Spirit is central in both paragraphs (18:25; 19:6).
- Apollos surfaces in both paragraphs (18:24:19:1).
- Luke mentions a deficiency in belief/experience connected with "the baptism of John" (18:25; 19:3).
- the deficiencies of Apollos and the Ephesian disciples are remedied (18:26; 19:5-7).

Paragraph three: Paul's charismatic ministry in Ephesus, causes the effects in paragraphs four and five. Luke notes the progression from Paul's powerful ministry inside the synagogue for three months (Acts 19:8) to Jewish hostility (19:9), to a teaching ministry in Tyrannus' "Lecture Hall" for two years (19:9-10). Luke advances the narrative when God performs extraordinary miracles through Paul, even to the extent that articles of cloth (i.e. relics) are successfully used in both healings and exorcisms. The result clause, "with the result that ... evil spirits departed" (ὥστε ... τά τε πνεύματα τὰ πονηρὰ ἐκπορεύεσθαι Acts 19:12), causes the seven sons of Sceva to mimic Paul's exorcisms in paragraph four.

Paragraph four: The comic and failed attempt of Sceva's seven sons to exorcise demons in causes the awe-filled and joyous response of Jews and Greeks, with the resulting denunciation of magic in paragraph five. The people witness the dramatic contrast between Paul's successful exorcisms and the comical and failed attempt of wandering Jewish exorcists, who flee from the powerful demon in a naked and wounded state (Acts 19:16). Luke highlights the cause-effect nature of this contrast:

- Cause—"when this became known (τοῦτο δὲ γνωστὸν) to all the Jews and Greeks who lived in Ephesus" (19:17a).
- Effect—"awe fell upon all of them and they magnified the name of the Lord Jesus" (ἐπέπεσον φόβος ἐπὶ πάντας αὐτοὺς καὶ ἐμεγαλύνετο τὸ ὄνομα τοῦ κυρίου Ἰησοῦ 19:17b).

This joyous reaction climaxes the preceding narratives. Further, Luke notes the trust-response when "many of those who believed" (πολλοί τε τῶν πεπιστευκότων 19:18), which results in a public confession of magical practices and a costly bonfire of secret books of magic and spells (19:18-19).

Luke rounds out the Ephesian-narrative with a resultant summary statement that expresses the charismatic power of "the word of the Lord," embracing the preached message and the charismatic power seen through the entire Ephesian narrative. Luke states, "In such manner, the word of the Lord was growing in a mighty way 'from strength to strength'"[959]

(Οὕτως κατὰ κράτος τοῦ κυρίου ὁ λόγος ηὔξανεν καὶ ἴσχυεν Acts 19:20). Luke combines the prepositional clause, lit., "according to *power*" (κατὰ κράτος) with the verb, "it was growing *in might*" (ἴσχυεν) to emphasize the dynamic power of the Christian message. Luke applies the same verb for the powerful demon who "overpowered" (ἴσχυσεν) the would-be exorcists (19:16). Now the verb highlights the mighty advance (ἴσχυεν) of the Christian message in word and charismatic power. The two imperfect tenses, "it was growing" (ηὔξανεν) and "it was growing in might" (ἴσχυεν), suggest the ongoing charismatic power of "the word of the Lord." This very charismatic power is the means by which Paul decides on his travel plans, culminating in Rome, "Paul decided *in/by the Spirit* (ἐν τῷ πνεύματι 19:21).

In the five paragraphs, Luke multiplies terms that link the core message to charismatic power:

- "the way of the Lord" (Acts 18:25).
- "the things concerning Jesus" (18:25).
- "the way of God" (18:26).
- "Jesus is the Messiah" (18:28).
- "Jesus" (19:4).
- "the name of the Lord Jesus" (19:5)combined with baptism, the coming of the Holy Spirit, paired with speaking in tongues and prophecy" (19:6).
- "the things concerning the kingdom of God"[960] (19:8).
- "the way" (19:9).
- "the word of the Lord" (19:10).
- "the name of the Lord Jesus" (19:13), characterized by charismatic power, "the name of the Lord Jesus" (19:17).
- "the word of the Lord" (19:20).

The first two paragraphs are Jewish in nature, and paragraph three begins in the synagogue, before the transition to the "Lecture Hall" and other undisclosed locations. This is the last time that Luke records Paul's activity in Jewish synagogues. Thus, the Ephesian-stay is transitional for Paul's journey to Rome. Luke repeats hyperbolic language, "*all* the Jews and Greeks," underscoring Paul's powerful impact in the lecture-hall: "to hear the word of the Lord" in 19:10; those who witnessed and learned of the Paul's powerful exorcism over the would-be Jewish exorcists in 19:17.

Key individuals, groups, and audiences develop when they discover and experience God's power. Commentators frequently denigrate the persons with pejorative labels such as "eccentric," "fringe groups,"[961] "degenerate"—and fail to appreciate that they belong to many others, who flourish when they discover and experience the power of the risen Jesus, through the Holy Spirit.[962] Luke shares a much kinder view of persons than commentators, when he unpacks the effects of the Christian message and the role of the Holy Spirit in the Jesus-movement.

Apollos. In his introduction to the Apollos story, Luke portrays the charismatic nature of Apollos' ministry with five statements: "an eloquent/ learned man," "powerful in the Scriptures," "instructed in the way[963] of the Lord,"[964] "possession by the Spirit of God, i.e. "aglow with the Spirit," "speaking and teaching accurately the things concerning Jesus"[965] (Acts 18:24-25b). The participial clause, "aglow with the Spirit" (ζέων τῷ πνεύματι 18:25) can refer to his spiritual passion. However, the link with the Holy Spirit is natural, for the clause is followed by three verbs of verbal proclamation with Apollos as subject, "he was speaking," "he was teaching," "he began to boldly speak" (18:25-26). Thus the Holy Spirit fuels Apollos'bold teaching in the synagogue. Elsewhere in Luke, the word family, "I speak boldly" (παρρησιάζομαι) frequently refers to the Holy Spirit and links with the filling of the Holy Spirit (4:31). Similarly, Paul uses the verb, "I boil, seethe" (ζέω) in connection with the Spirit, "being aglow with the [Holy] Spirit" (τῷ πνεύματι ζέοντες Rom. 12:11). As Barrett states, "Words should be given their plain sense."[966]

Amidst such praiseworthy comments, Luke notes a deficiency in Apollos' message, "understanding only the baptism of John" (18:25). When Apollos begins to speak, Priscilla and Aquila discern a need to supplement his message. They take him aside, presumably to their home,[967] to fill in this lack. Luke does not record a public confrontation— only a pastoral and private discussion. Bruce notes the presence of many strands in primitive Christianity.[968] Two expression stand out. Apollos had been instructed in "the way of the Lord" and was *accurately* (ἀκριβῶς) teaching the things concerning Jesus" (18:25). Luke qualifies his statements when the pair explain "the way of God" (τὴν ὁδὸν [τοῦ θεοῦ]) *more accurately* (ἀκριβέστερον) to him (18:26).

What did the pair recognize? There is a deficiency but not false teaching. Was it Christian baptism that Apollos didn't preach or perform? Did Apollos not urge personal faith in Jesus? Due to the context of the following paragraph, it appears that Apollos needed empowerment from the Holy Spirit. This moves front and center when Paul converses with the Ephesian twelve. Haenchen comments, "Scholars think mostly of the Christian baptism in the Spirit."[969] Did Apollos not urge baptism in the Holy Spirit? Although Luke does not specify the exact lack or how the apostolic pair supplemented the need, the paired stories of Apollos and the Ephesian twelve suggest the baptism in the Spirit. Keener notes, "Knowing *only* John's baptism may also mean that he was unaware that the greater Spirit-baptism that John announced was now made available … Apollos may have had the Spirit (18:25, if this is the meaning) without the clear articulation of it."[970] John's baptism emphasized the more important Spirit-baptism (Luke 3:16). Although Apollos only knows "the baptism of John," there is no reference to Apollos being re-baptized.

Luke accentuates the powerful effect of what the pair conveyed to Apollos—his greater effectiveness. The author emphasizes that, after Apollos is encouraged to go to Corinth, armed with a letter of recommendation to the Corinthian disciples, his ministry is even more successful. Luke piles up expressions that bolster Apollos' helpful and powerful ministry in Corinth: "he was of great help to the believers," "he powerfully refuted to the Jews," "in a public manner," "demonstrating through the Scriptures that Jesus is the Messiah" (Acts 18:27b-28), "through grace" (διὰ τῆς χάριτος 18:27). "Grace" may refer to Corinthian believers, "those who had come to believe *through grace*." It also may refer to Apollos' activity of helping the Corinthians, "he gave great help to believers *through (divine) grace*" (18:27). Haenchen translates the clause, "he greatly helped those who had become believers *by his (particular gift of) grace*."[971] Since Acts includes numerous expressions related to Apollos' fuller ministry, it is more natural to conclude that "grace" refers specifically to Apollos' effective ministry of "great help."

Even though Paul emerges as the central figure in the next Ephesian paragraphs, Luke affirms the important work of others as bearers of the Spirit, including Priscilla, Aquila, and Apollos.[972] While ties with the Jerusalem Church remain strong, Luke points to the widening role of others engaged in the Jesus-movement, with no direct ties to Jerusalem.[973]

The Ephesian twelve. The paired story of the Ephesian twelve begins with Apollos' stay in Corinth and Paul's departure for Ephesus. Upon Paul's arrival, he chances upon "certain disciples" (τινας μαθητὰς Acts 19:1), noted in 19:7 as twelve in number. He asks them a probing question, "Did you receive the Holy Spirit when you believed?" (Εἰ πνεῦμα ἅγιον ἐλάβετε πιστεύσαντες; 19:2).[974]

Four points need to be affirmed:

- The term "disciples" is always used in Acts to refer to believers. [975]
- Paul assumes that they are believers (πιστεύσαντες).
- Luke does not state that the twelve disciples were disciples of the Baptist, only that they had been baptized with John's baptism.[976]
- The narrative is paired with the Apollos story through noting and then filling a deficiency.

What does Paul notice causing his probing question? Does he perceive an absence of charismatic expression and accompanying joy? Again, Luke's references to the Spirit are not primarily soteriological,[977] but charismatic, with his emphasis on empowerment through which people speak and act for God. Haya-Prats states, "Acts does not attribute to the Holy Spirit the origin of the Christian life nor the religious-moral behavior of the community, but that it does, in an incidental way (implicit but sufficiently clear), attribute to him an extraordinary empowerment of the Christian life."[978] Yes, Paul's writings indicate there is no "Spirit-less Christian" (Rom. 8:9). However, Luke's concern is not in defining who is "in" and who is "out." Such classifications represent Western proclivities. Luke presents Apollos and the Ephesian twelve as people in progress, needing to be filled and empowered with the Holy Spirit.[979] Correspondingly,

Luke intends that his readers grow in their certainty, understanding, and experience of the Jesus-event and the charismatic dimension of the Spirit.

In answer to Paul's question about their reception of the Holy Spirit, the Ephesian disciples respond, "We have not even heard that there is a Holy Spirit" (Ἀλλ' οὐδ' εἰ πνεῦμα ἅγιον ἔστιν ἠκούσαμεν Acts 19:2b). This can hardly mean that John, who was steeped in the Old Testament, never spoke to his followers about the Holy Spirit. Given Luke's understanding of the Spirit, their response might well mean that they had not heard of the charismatic gift of the Holy Spirit. Pervo suggests, "One popular resolution involves construing the verb 'is' (now) present."[980] That is, they do not know of the powerful and personal baptism in the Spirit that is vital in the various Pentecosts, which had also been a vital part of Saul's transformation (9:17-18).[981] Keener notes, "Such disciples, already exercising faith in what they know, appear to respond readily to the more complete gospel."[982] Keener also affirms, "they have not followed John's testimony to its conclusion (Luke 3:16)."[983]

When Paul learns they had only experienced John's baptism,[984] he states that John's baptism was a repentance baptism but was also preparatory "for trust in the one coming after him, that is in Jesus" (εἰς τὸν ἐρχόμενον μετ αὐτὸν ἵνα πιστεύσωσιν, τοῦτ᾽ ἔστιν εἰς τὸν Ἰησοῦν Acts 19:4), and the baptism in the Spirit. Luke suggests that the twelve should refocus their trust, submitting to baptism in the name of the Lord Jesus. This is the fifth time that Acts draws a contrast between John the Baptist and Jesus (1:5; 11:46; 13:25; 18:25; 19:3-4).[985] Most significantly, in Acts 1:5, Jesus takes over the words of the Baptist, "the promise which you heard *from me*, to refer to both the initial and subsequent Pentecosts in Acts, "you shall be baptized in the Holy Spirit in a few days."[986]

After baptizing the Ephesian twelve,[987] Paul lays his hands on them and "the Holy Spirit came upon them, and they were speaking in tongues and were prophesying" (ἦλθε τὸ πνεῦμα τὸ ἅγιον ἐπ᾽ αὐτούς, ἐλάλουν τε γλώσσαις καὶ ἐπροφήτευον Acts 19:6).[988] As in Samaria, the gift of the Holy Spirit and accompanying charismata accompany the laying on of hands (8:17) and not baptism.[989] The fact that the Ephesian twelve "were prophesying" reminds Luke's readers of Peter's affirmation, taken from Joel, "they shall prophesy" (twice in 2:17-18).

Luke associates proper doctrine, personal experience, baptism, and Spirit-baptism. Implicitly, this text belongs to other vibrant Spirit-reception passages that refer to rejoicing (χαίρω), glorifying (δοξάζω), praising (αἰνέω), blessing (εὐλογέω), confessing (ἐξομολογέω), magnifying (μεγαλύνω), and speaking with inspiration (ἀποφθέγγομαι). These activities all occur in inspired and ecstatic contexts. Certainly, the joyous reception of the Spirit by the Ephesian twelve is expressed through tongues and prophecy.

This Pentecost-story recalls the first, when believers "were declaring the mighty acts of God" (Acts 2:11) in a day marked by inclusive joy. Similar to the Cornelius episode, "the ecstatic utterances give physical energy of the transforming spiritual energy (see 10:46)."[990] The fact that Luke mentions *twelve* Ephesian disciples may reflect another Lukan concern—a reconstituted Israel, now alive with the charismatic Spirit.[991] Luke underscores the reception of the Holy Spirit with accompanying joy, demonstrating that emotions accompany discipleship within the widening Jesus-movement.

Paul stands with other leaders in the Christian community as key instruments in bestowing the Spirit. Priscilla, Aquila, and Paul are channels for the needed Spirit. It is pointless to be overly precise as to the actual deficiencies or exactly how a deficiency is overcome; that is not Luke's point. Luke intends that his readers see how Christian leaders discern needs and seek to supplement them through teaching and empowerment. Does Luke ask his readers to probe their own charismatic power to speak and act for God?

Paul's charismatic ministry in Ephesus. Initially, Paul's ministry begins with three months of powerful preaching in the Ephesian synagogue, noted by the verbal expressions, "he was boldly speaking" (ἐπαρρησιάζετο), "reasoning" (διαλεγόμενος), and "convincing (πείθων) [the audience] about the things concerning the kingdom of God" (Acts 19:8). In comparison with other short synagogue ministries (e.g. Thessalonica 17:1-9), it is remarkable that he could maintain a teaching presence in a synagogue for this length.

The resulting Jewish aggression is expressed by three verbal expressions: certain ones "became obstinate" (ἐσκληρύνοντο); "they were refusing to believe" (ἀπείθουν); "maligning (κακολογοῦντες) the way" (Acts 19:9). Luke's readers discover another word-play—Paul was *convincing* (πείθων 19:8) while the Jews were *refusing to believe* (ἀπείθουν 19:9). This aggression leads Paul to move his disciples to Tyrannus' lecture hall, where he continues his "reasoning" (διαλεγόμενος) for two years (19:9-10). With hyperbole, Luke notes the powerful outcome, "with the result that (ὥστε) *all* the Jews and Greeks who lived in the province of Asia, heard the word of the Lord" (19:10).

Luke communicates the enhancement of Paul's powerful ministry "with extraordinary miracles (δυνάμεις τε οὐ τὰς τυχούσας)[992] that God was doing through Paul's hands" (Acts 19:11). Luke follows with a result clause, "with the result that" (ὥστε), which joins three infinitive clauses of an extraordinary sort: "handkerchiefs and [work] cloths/aprons *were removed* (ἀποφέρεσθαι) from his skin and taken to the sick, people *were released* (ἀπαλλάσεσθαι) from their sicknesses, the evil spirits *left* (ἐκπορεύεσθαι) them [the affected persons]" (19:12). Thus Luke pairs Paul's powerful preaching in the synagogue with the miracles effected through Paul's hands. He follows that by describing miracles of healing and exorcism occurring as people bring mere cloths that Paul had touched to sick and possessed persons. Rationalists have great difficulty with passages such as these.

Luke features Paul's charismatic power, similar to healings/exorcisms through Peter's shadow (Acts 5:12-16). [993] In straightforward language, "without embarrassment,"[994] Luke associates Paul's ministry of preaching "the word of the Lord" (19:10) with powerful healings and exorcisms even through cloths. Keener suggests, "What is clearest is that Luke emphasizes that Paul, apostle to the Gentiles, worked miracles no less spectacular than those by the group of Jerusalem apostles."[995]

The seven sons of Sceva. Implicitly, Paul's exorcisms cause wandering Jewish exorcists, including the seven sons[996] of Sceva[997], to mimic Paul's exorcisms of unclean spirits, "using the name of the Lord Jesus/by Jesus whom Paul preaches" (Acts 19:13). The demoniac's response, "Paul I know" (19:15), makes the connection explicit. Luke pairs the term "exorcists" (ἐξορκισταί) with the related verb, "I charge/bind/

adjure" (ὁρκίζω) to connect their exorcist-vocation (19:13),[998] followed by one specific attempted exorcism (19:15).

From the numinous perspective, the unclean spirit "knows and understands"[999] the identities of both Jesus and Paul, but he refuses to respect the identity and activity of the seven sons. Implicitly, the demon would submit to the authority of either Jesus or Paul and leave. The would-be exorcists count on a third-hand source for their authority, thus leading to the demon's question, "But who are you?" (Acts 19:15).[1000] Garrett makes a cogent remark, "what is important is not whether the exorcist 'knows' the name of Jesus, but whether the demons 'know' the exorcist as one who has truly been invested with authority to call upon that name."[1001] Earlier, Luke stated that the possessed slave girl knows the identity of Paul and Barnabas, "slaves of the Most High God" and the salvation-content of their proclamation (16:16-17).

Not only does the possessed man disrespect the authority of these seven exorcists, but he leaps upon them, overpowering them so that they flee, naked and wounded (Acts 19:16).[1002] Twelftree rightly comments about the verb, "I overpower" (ἰσχύω), "in contrast to Jesus' saying that Satan as the 'strong man' is defeated by his exorcisms (ὁ ἰσχυρός, Luke 11:21), here it is the sons of Sceva who are ἴσχυσεν or mastered by the evil spirit."[1003] The story is filled with humor, e.g. "magic names can boomerang."[1004] Normally demons flee from the exorcist(s), but in this case, the would-be exorcists flee from the man with the strong-armed demon who both overpowers and humiliates them (19:16).

Thus, Luke suggests that "the name of Jesus" can only be used by someone whom Jesus legitimately authorizes. "In Acts 19:15-16, when the spirit 'masters' and 'overpowers' the seven sons, the spirit's violent non-compliance demonstrates with equal but opposite force that the seven sons have no such authority."[1005] The response from the unclean demon exposes that these seven sons are not true pneumatics. God's Spirit cannot be manipulated. Pervo notes, "When the conclusion is taken into account, it appears that 19:13-17 is a parody of a particular exorcism (Luke 8:26-39)."[1006] The focus of the narrative is not the relief of the possessed man, but the utter frustration of the opposition in the failed attempt.

Acts juxtaposes this failure with Paul's successful exorcisms, accomplished even through cloths that he has touched.

Christian triumph over magic. The charismatic power of the narrative profoundly touches the populace, "*all* the Jews and Greeks," when "this became known" (τοῦτο δὲ ἐγένετο γνωστὸν Acts 19:17),[1007] i.e. the triumph of a true exorcist (Paul) over false Jewish exorcists, graphically portrayed in the flight of nude and wounded brothers.

Charismatic power ignites a very expensive bonfire when many (πόλλοι) Christians[1008] came, confessing [their sin/magical practices], making their practices known,[1009] with a number of them (ἱκανοί) renouncing their magical practices, bringing forth their books [of spells], and burning them in a public manner (Acts 19:18-19).[1010] Clearly these Christians admit to being wrong. To emphasize the powerful effect, Luke states the collective monetary amount,[1011] originally spent for all these magical books—50,000 pieces of silver—an impressive fortune. These Christians were not coerced, but voluntarily offered their expensive magical books to the bonfire. Appropriately, Garrett notes, "Luke's purpose in composing these two verses was not to give a precise tally of who confessed what, but to emphasize the sweeping victory of the Lord over the powers of darkness, even in Ephesus, noted center of the magical arts."[1012] As with other confrontations with magic in Acts (Simon, the slave-girl), both money and magic stand condemned.

Luke builds a progression of miracles that builds towards the climax in two coordinated affirmations:

"awe fell upon all of them" (ἐπέπεσεν φόβος ἐπι' πάντας αὐτοὺς)

"and"

"the name of the Lord Jesus was magnified" (ἐμεγαλύνετο τὸ ὄνομα τοῦ κυρίου Ἰησοῦ). (Acts 19:18)

In Ephesus, this joyous climax follows Apollos' empowerment, the baptism in the Spirit of the Ephesian twelve, Paul's three-month ministry in the Jewish synagogue and two-year ministry in the lecture hall, when "all the Jews and Greeks heard the word of the Lord" (19:10, 17),[1013] and the "extraordinary miracles" that God was doing through Paul's hands" and cloths that had contacted Paul's skin.

Luke has previously linked "fear" (φόβος) or "religious dread" with the joy-vocabulary ("I magnify" μεγαλύνω) in concert with charismatic power (Luke 1:11-14; 2:9-10; 24:36-41; Acts 2:43-47; 5:12-16). He presents the verb, "I magnify" (μεγαλύνω) in other charismatic contexts: angelic encounter (Luke 1:46, 58); in response to the apostles' miracles including healings and exorcisms through Peter's shadow (Acts 5:13-16); in concert with tongues-speaking (10:46). He also uses the related substantive, "great/mighty deeds" (μεγαλεῖοι) in charismatic contexts: Mary's song of praise in response to the numinous (Luke 1:49); the content of tongues-speaking (Acts 2:11). Luke's vocabulary places Paul's joy-filled and charismatic ministry in Ephesus in continuity with earlier accounts in Jerusalem, Judea, and Samaria. In addition, the linked verbs of "awe" and "magnify" are used in contexts of additional believers (9:31; 10:46).

The Ephesians' joyous response materializes in the bonfire of magical books, expressed as public acts of repentance by those who had become believers (Acts 19:18). Luke frequently portrays repentance in a positive manner, expressed in physical and attitudinal ways (Luke 3:10-14), noted in Acts 11:17, as "the gift of repentance," accompanying the baptism in the Holy Spirit for Cornelius and his household.

Repentance means far more than simple sorrow for one's sins. For Luke, it often means a positive and joyous turn to the new and joyous activity of God. Fittingly, Tannehill remarks, "But the primary and basic message is not 'You must repent' but the good news: the time of fulfillment of the promises, the time of salvation has come. God is powerfully at work in the world, changing things, and this provides a special opportunity in which you, too, can change."[1014] Repentance involves a "joyful discovery that one is included in God's salvation, making possible a transformed life."[1015] For the Ephesian Christians, their joyful discovery of God's charismatic power leads them to act out of transformation. Their old ways of magical practices must be renounced in a public manner as they adhere to God's new and joyous activity.

Giving thanks to God he was encouraged

(Acts 28:11-31)[1016]

Following the shipwreck and rescue, Luke contrasts the Maltese natives' positive welcome and hospitality (Acts 28:1-10) with the Roman Jews who do not "listen"[1017] to Paul (Acts 28:24-25). He then juxtaposes these Jews with Gentiles "who will listen" (28:28). Paul, who had been "honored with many honors" by the natives (28:10), should have been "honored" by the Jews in Rome. Instead, he was tragically rejected. For Luke, joyful receptivity to God's emissaries means everything. What importance does this final episode have for this study, since it carries no explicit mention of miraculous events such as healings?

The text intimates a link between numinous events and joy. Luke highlights prophecy and fulfillment, "The Holy Spirit spoke to your forefathers," followed by a quote from the LXX of Isaiah 6:9-10 (Acts 28:26-27).[1018] Just as Isaiah was sent to speak to Judah, so Paul is divinely sent to speak to the Roman Jews—with the same tragic result. The language of Isaiah's text highlights an unnatural and illogical situation, for the organs of the ears, eyes, and hearts usually hear, see, and understand. However, in this case, the very organs of discernment don't work. When Paul introduces Isaiah's text, Luke's readers notice the pronoun, "your (ὑμῶν) forefathers" (28:25), which distances Paul from his joy-less critics. Previously Paul stated his own loyalty to the Jewish people and their customs (28:17). Thus, Isaiah's prophecy is also fulfilled in Paul's day, and the Holy Spirit is the source and means of prophetic inspiration and fulfillment. Luke has already established the link between the Holy Spirit and fulfillment of Old Testament texts.[1019] In Paul's message, he also implicitly refers to satisfaction of the Law of Moses and the Prophets, now fulfilled "concerning Jesus" (Acts 28:23).

When Paul preaches to the Roman Jews, Luke summarizes Paul's message through a variety of intertwined and interdependent terms:

- "the hope of Israel" (Acts 28:20),
- "the kingdom of God" (twice 28:23, 31),
- "concerning Jesus" (28:23)

- "the things concerning the Lord Jesus Christ" (28:31)
- "this salvation of God" (28:28).

These expressions embrace events, content, receptivity, and Christian affections. The "*hope of Israel*" includes Paul's "hope of the resurrection of the dead" (23:6; 24:15), as well as "hope in what God has promised our fathers" (twelve tribes 26:6-7). As an emotion, hope fueled the disciples' question about restoring the kingdom to Israel (1:6). This desire was initially fulfilled in the promised gift of the Holy Spirit (1:8; 2:1-4), for this was because Israel's hope as well.

The twice-mentioned, "*kingdom of God*" (Acts 28:23, 31), serves as inclusion with Jesus' instruction in 1:3 about "the things concerning the kingdom of God."[1020] From the outset of Jesus' ministry (Luke 4:43) to the conclusion of Paul's ministry in Rome, God's kingdom is central. From Luke's perspective, Jesus and the Christian community both proclaim and "do" God's kingdom with empowered activity and attendant joy—all of which anticipate the *eschaton*.

"The things concerning Jesus" (Acts 28:23, 31) certainly refer to Jesus as the fulfillment of the Law of Moses and the Prophets (28:23), but there is more. From Luke's perspective, "the things concerning Jesus," refer to the entirety of the Jesus-event: his miraculous birth, powerful ministry, crucifixion, resurrection, exaltation, reception of the Spirit, and subsequent pouring forth of the gift of the Holy Spirit. The vast majority of commentators stop short with the resurrection. For example, Conzelmann states that the expression "includes the whole ministry (including the death and resurrection),"[1021] but he fails to see that Jesus' exaltation and pouring forth of the Holy Spirit are all a vital part of the Jesus story as well (2:33). Johnson comments, "within the Jerusalem messianic community, there was a realization of a restored and authentic Israel, living out the true blessings of Abraham which were brought to realization by the gift of the Holy Spirit."[1022] Even as a prisoner in Acts 28 (also Acts 26:6-7), Paul argues that the "hope of Israel" is bound up with the full-orbed kingdom of God (word and power) and the things concerning the *whole* of the Jesus-event.

Healing rises at the conclusion of Isaiah's text, "and I shall heal them" (Isa. 6:10; Acts 28:27). In the original setting, Isaiah's text links "healing" with reference to a restored relationship with God.[1023] In Luke-Acts, healing is consistently paired with the presence and power of God's kingdom, proclaimed and experienced in miraculous ways,[1024] expressed earlier through the double-entendre of the crippled beggar (4:10-12).

The expression, "This salvation of God" (Acts 28:28), reminds Luke's readers of the aged Simeon's joyful utterance, "my eyes have seen *your salvation*" (τὸ σωτήριόν σου Luke 2:30) and the Baptist's promise, "all flesh shall see the *salvation of God* (τὸ σωτήριον τοῦ θεοῦ Luke 3:6; Isa. 40:5).[1025] Simeon's prophecy about "light for the revelation of the Gentiles" (Luke 2:32) is fulfilled, now in Rome, "they themselves [the Gentiles] will listen" (Acts 28:28); however, at this point in Rome, Simeon's prophecy about "the glory of your people Israel" (Luke 3:22) is as yet, unfilled; "the salvation of God" is inclusive. Tragically, here, in Rome, numerous Jews reject Israel's hope, God's kingdom, Jesus, healing, and salvation.

Paul's teaching, "with all *boldness* unhindered" (μετὰ πάσης παρρησίας ἀκωλύτως Acts 28:31), also intimates the Holy Spirit's power, for Luke has frequently paired the Spirit with the verb, "I preach with boldness" (παρρησιάζομαι) or noun, "boldness/confidence of speech" (παρρησία).[1026] Paul's confident declaration in Rome over the course of his two-year house-arrest was inspired from without—from a supernatural source. Fittingly, Haenchen remarks, "Imprisonment does not compel Paul to passivity, but must rather serve to show his activity in the brightest light."[1027]

Other implicit references to joy emerge. Twice, Luke mentions *brothers* (Acts 28:14-15), who are warm and receptive Christian brothers and are contrasted with the joy-less Jewish brothers who reject Paul (28:17, 21). Receptive brothers "receive the honorable mention, which is its due."[1028]

Luke states that Paul and company ("we"), "*were encouraged* (παρεκλήθημεν) to remain/stay with them for seven days" (Acts 28:14) and experience hospitality. Subsequently, another Christian group arrives. When Paul sees them, Luke says that Paul, "*having given thanks to*

God" (εὐχαριστήσας τῷ θεῷ), received *encouragement* (θάρος 28:15).
The same expression, "giving thanks," echoes Paul's joyous behavior and
cheer in the impending shipwreck (27:35-36). Now, Paul gives thanks,
even in the face of his impending fate in Rome. Luke notes that Paul
received "encouragement" by the presence of these Christian brothers.
The word *encouragement* (θάρσος), can mean "courage," and is also
cognate with the verb, "I am cheerful, take courage" (θαρσέω).[1029]

Christian affections, including joy and hope, precede and permeate
Paul's ministry to Roman Jews and Gentiles. Paul's joyous message
includes charismatic dimensions of Israel's hope, God's kingdom, Jesus'
entire story, and acts of healing, all in the context of a Spirit-empowered
boldness. With Luke's final word, "unhindered" (ἀκωλύτως), he
leaves the book open-ended in a positive manner. Pervo states, "For the
unphilosophical and nontheological, it puts in one sharp word what
the Pastor required seventeen (Greek) words to place in the mouth of
Paul: '[T]hat is my gospel, for which I suffer hardship, even to the
point of being chained like a criminal. But the word of God is not
chained.'"[1030] During the two-year house-arrest Paul continues to receive
"all who were coming to him" (Acts 28:31), which refers to Gentiles and
Jews, who "were being persuaded" (ἐπείθοντο) by Paul's "persuading"
(πείθων 28:23-24) activity.[1031]

Now, Luke's audience reads of no further Jewish resistance during his
two-year mission. He was "unhindered." Luke's final words about Paul's
ministry correspond to Jesus' promise of a Holy-Spirit empowered
witness "to the ends of the earth" (Acts 1:8). Now with a limitless
mission, with the ringing promise "they will hear" (i.e. take it to heart
and joyfully respond), Paul's witness is a clear and unambiguous answer
to the hanging question of the disciples in 1:6, "Is it at this time that
you are about to restore the kingdom to Israel?" The presence and power
of the kingdom of God will be proclaimed in word and miraculous
activity. The ending of Acts reflects "an opening to the continuing life of
the messianic people,"[1032] for the community is empowered to continue
"what Jesus began to do and teach" (1:1). God in his faithfulness provides
the "hope of Israel," thus the door is open as to how that hope would
fully be realized and enjoyed. The messianic community, with deep

Jewish roots, continues its outreach to both Jew and Gentile *in the power and joy of the Holy Spirit*. Joyful and inclusive receptivity to God's power fuels this transformation.

NOTES

453   Acts includes other Pentecostal stories. For instance, Peter compares the experience of Cornelius, "just as even with us" (Acts 15:8; 17), with the experience of the community in Acts 2.

454   Numerous points of comparison: 1) Post-resurrection appearances of the risen Jesus (Luke 24:33-34, 36; Acts 1:3); 2) Proof of Jesus' post-resurrection physicality (Luke 24:36-43; Acts 1:3); 3) The promise of the Father (Luke 24:49; Acts 1:4); 4) The centripetal missionary movement from Jerusalem (Luke 24:47-48; Acts 1:8b); 5) the role of witness (Luke 24:48; Acts 1:8b); 6) An emphasis upon staying in Jerusalem (Luke 24:47, 49; Acts 1:4, 8); 7) The parting of Jesus and return of the apostles to Jerusalem (Luke 24:51-52; Acts 1:9, 12); 8) Mention of two angels with bright garments (Luke 24:4, 23; Acts 1:10). Charles H. Talbert, *Literary Patterns, Theological Themes and the Genre of Luke-Acts* (Missoula, Montana: Scholars Press, 1975), 58-61. See also Richard I. Pervo, *Acts: A Commentary* (Minneapolis: Fortress Press, 2009), 32.

455   Three accounts: Paul's encounter with the risen Jesus (Acts 9, 22, 26); the Cornelius story (Acts 10, 11, 15); versions of the Jerusalem Council letter (Acts 15:20, 28-29; Acts 21:25). See Ernst Haenchen for similar remarks, "each answering the needs of the moment." Ernst Haenchen, *The Acts of the Apostles* (Bernard Noble and Gerald Shinn, transl.; Philadelphia: The Westminster Press, 1971), 146.

456   Acts 1:3; 2:23, 36.

457   1:3, 22; 2:24, 31, 32.

458   1:3a, 3b, 6-8, 9-11.

459   1:10

460   1:2, 9a, 9b, 19, 11, 22.

461   2:25, 30, 33, 36.

462   1:2, 4, 5, 8, 16; 2:4a, 4b, 17, 18, 33, 38, 39-variously expressed.

463   2:2, 3, 4, 6a, 6b, 8, 11, 17 (three references), 18, 19, 22a, 22b, 29-31, 33, 43.

464   1:8, 22, 32; 2:14, 32, 40.

465   2:6, 7, 12a, 12b, 13.

466   2:37, 38, 41, 44, 47.

467   Luke uses the adjective "all" (πᾶς) fourteen times (1:8, 14, 19; 2:5, 7, 12, 17, 21, 32, 36, 39, 43, 44, 45); the adjective "each" (ἕκαστος) four times (2:3, 6, 8, 38). Luke interrupts the narrative with an extensive list of nationalities "from every nation under heaven," who were present on the Day of Pentecost (2:9-11) to draw attention to inclusion, also expressed through Joel's prophecy

that confronts sexism and ageism (2:17-18) and women in the expectant and prayerful community (1:14).

468 1:14 "all were attaching themselves together in prayer *with one accord*" (ὁμοθυμαδόν); 2:46, italics added.

   1:15 *"at the same place\together"* ἐπὶ τὸ αὐτὸ; 2:1, 47.

469 1:4; 2:42, 46 (twice).

470 An expression suggested by Haya-Prats, 30.

471 Contra Haenchen, that the selection of the twelve apostles was mediated through the Holy Spirit., 139.

472 A similar statement in the prologue of Luke's Gospel, "in order that you might know ... the certainty" (ἵνα ἐπιγνῷς . . . τὴν ἀσφαλείαν Luke 1:4).

473 The verb συναλίζω can mean both "bring together, assemble" or "eat (salt) with." Since Peter later refers to eating and drinking with the resurrected Jesus (Acts 10:41), Acts 1:4 would refer to table-fellowship. BDAG, 781-782. See Craig S. Keener for his argument for a "metonymy for sharing a meal," Craig S. Keener, *Acts: An Exegetical* Commentary, Vol. I, (Grand Rapids: Baker Academic, 2012), 675. See Henry J. Cadbury, "Lexical Notes on Luke-Acts," *JBL*, 45 (1926), 305-322. He provides extensive research and concludes that the verb means, "to spend the night with." 310-317.

474 A deponent verb. See Pervo, 31.

475 Haenchen, 141.

476 The "promise" (ἐπαγγελία) of the Holy Spirit (2:33, 39) is epexegetical, i.e. the promise is the Holy Spirit.

477 Three baptisms surface in Acts 1-2: 1) John's baptism (1:5); 2) Baptism in the Spirit (Acts 1:5); 3) Baptism in Jesus' name (Acts 2:38, 41). Baptism in the Spirit means the pouring forth of the Pentecostal Spirit with power.

478 E.g. the connection between Luke 3:16; Acts 1:5; Cornelius in 11:16; the experience in Ephesus described in Acts 19:1-7.

479 Robert C. Tannehill, *The Narrative Unity of Luke-Acts*, Vol. 2 (Minneapolis: Fortress Press, 1994), 12.

480 Tannehill, Vol. 2, 13. The "baptism in the Spirit/promise/gift" is far more than Conzelmann's "substitute in the meantime for the possession of ultimate salvation." Hans Conzelmann, *The Theology of St. Luke* (Geoffrey Buswell, transl.; New York: Harper & Row Publishers, 1953), 95.

481 In Acts 2:38-39, Luke pairs, "gift" (δωρεά) and "promise" (ἐπαγγελία) to refer to the baptism in the Holy Spirit: "You will receive the *gift of the Holy Spirit* ... For *the promise* is to you ...)."

482 Haya-Prats, 68.

483 Haya-Prats, 68.

484 Haenchen notes "the first mention of the problem of the Gentile mission, which will make itself felt again and again in Acts, right up to 28:28." 143.

485 See Luke 24:47-49.

486   Witness of the resurrection is also necessary for an apostolic successor to Judas (Acts 1:22). See Haya-Prats for a helpful chart on the "witness"-vocabulary. 101-103.

487   Haya-Prats, 65.

488   E.g. the guiding role of the Spirit of Jesus in Acts 16:6-7 when Paul is need of direction, subsequent to two failed attempts.

489   See the power that will overshadow Mary in Luke 1:35; Jesus' power subsequent to his victory over temptation in Luke 4:1, 14; power over unclean spirits in Luke 4:36; almost a fluid substance in Luke 5:17; a physical drain that Jesus feels in Luke 8:46; power given to the twelve and seventy-two in Luke 9:1; 10:9, 13, 17-19; power understood as Jesus' miracles in Luke 10:13 and Luke 19:37.

490   Pervo, 42.

491   "Power" (δύναμις) is used eight other times in Acts (Acts 3:12; 4:7, 33; 6:8; 8:10, 13; 10:38; 19:11) and fifteen times in Luke's gospel.

492   Pervo, 42-43.

493   Keener, Vol. I, 681.

494   Haya-Prats, 47.

495   The association "times and seasons" (χρόνοι Acts 1:6; χρόνοι, καίροι Acts 1:7) with "restoration" (ἀποκαθιστάνω Acts 1:7) is similarly expressed in Acts 3:21-22, "times of refreshing" (καίροι ἀναψύξεως Acts 3:21) and "until the seasons of restoration" (ἄχρι χρόνων ἀποκαταστάσεως).

496   Johnson alludes to Moses (Exod 19:16) and Elijah (1 Kgs 18:44) with reference to the two "men," *The Acts of the Apostles* (Collegeville, MN: The Liturgical Press, 1992), 31. Pervo similarly argues. 45-46.

497   Pervo, 46.

498   Paul Elbert, "An Observation on Luke's Composition and Narrative Style of Questions," *The Catholic Biblical Quarterly* 66 (2003), 98-109.

499   Elbert, 102.

500   Elbert, 104.

501   See Keener, vol. I, 731.

502   Thus, there are various sequences for Spirit-reception in Acts. See Graham H. Twelftree, *People of the Spirit: Exploring Luke's View of the Church* (Grand Rapids, MI: Baker Academic, 2009), 97 for a helpful chart on the items and order of various Pentecosts in Acts. Similarly, Keener comments, "Luke allows for a diversity of pneumatic experience (8:12-17; 10:44-48; 19:5-6) and presumably invites his audience to show the same courtesy." Keener, vol. I, 681.

503   Johnson, *The Acts ...* , 28.

504   The verb, προσκαρτερέω is also found in Acts 2:42, 46; 6:4; 8:13; 10:7. Thus, we find six occurrences in Acts with only four references elsewhere in the New Testament.

505   We find eleven occurrences "of one accord" (ὁμοθυμαδόν) in Acts, compared to just one occurrence in the rest of the New Testament.

506   Keener, vol. I, 781.

507   Luke uses the numeral "eleven" (ἕνδεκα) four times to emphasize the incomplete number of apostles (Luke 24:9, 33; Acts 1:26; 2:14). Luke devotes eleven verses to this decision, which reintegrates the community.

508   Johnson notes that Judas' betrayal was not simply an individual failure, but "it splintered the numerical and symbolical integrity of the group." Johnson, *The Acts ...* , 39. Jesus stresses the twelve in Luke 22:30.

509   This qualification relates to the "eyewitnesses from the beginning" (οἱ ἀπ' ἀρχῆς αὐτόπται) in Luke's prologue to his Gospel (Luke 1:2).

510   Pervo labels the prayer as "unison speech," that "manifests the marvelous unity of the community." 55.

511   Pervo, 71.

512   Roland de Vaux, *Ancient Israel: Vol. 2: Religious Institutions* (New York: McGraw-Hill Book Company, 1965), 494.

513   J. H. E. Hull, *The Holy Spirit in the Acts of the Apostles* (New York: The World Publishing Company, 1967), 52.

514   Lev 23:23 also mentions the "poor" and the "stranger."

515   de Vaux, 495. In the period of the exile, Tobit weeps over the loss of joy and shared celebration, which should envelop the feast (2:1-8). "Your feasts shall be turned into mourning and all your joy (πᾶσαι αἱ εὐφροσύναι) shall be turned into lamentation" (Tobit 2:6).

516   Keener, Vol. I, 823.

517   de Vaux, 494.

518   Notably Hull, 54: Decalogue 9:33-Acts 2:2, 3, 7; Decalogue 11-Acts 2:3; Special Laws 31 (189)-Acts 2:9; 1:8; 2:11). J.C. Rylaarsdam, "Weeks, Feast of," *The Interpreter's Dictionary of the Bible*, Vol. 4 (Nashville: Abingdon Press, 1962), 828. See also Hull, 53. However, there is no clear evidence for a link prior to 200 C.E.

519   See de Vaux for an extensive description of the feast. 495.

520   Luke surely connects, "When the promised day of Pentecost had come" (ἐν τῷ συμπληροῦσθαι τὴν ἡμέραν τῆς πεντηκοστῆς Acts 2:1) with a nearly identical expression in Luke 9:51, "When the time up to his (Jesus') exaltation had run its course" (ἐν τῷ συμπληροῦσθαι τὰς ἡμέρας τῆς ἀναλήμψεως αὐτοῦ). The translation is given by E. Lohse, *TDNT*, Vol. VI, 50

521   The word "sudden" suggests "wondrous, awesome . . . Luke's intention to describe a supernatural event." C. K. Barrett, *The Acts of the Apostles* (Edinburgh: T & T Clark, 1994), 71.

522   "something shaped like a tongue," Barrett, *The Acts ...* , 114. See John's statement, "he shall baptize you with the Holy Spirit and fire" (Luke 3:16).

523 See similar language above in Philo's Decalogue. Also in other theophanies (1 Kgs 19:12; Exod 3:2; 13:21ff.).

524 Keener notes multiple fillings later in Acts that follows initial experience. Keener, Vol. I, 806.

525 Elsewhere in Acts, filling with the Holy Spirit is associated with boldness of speech (Acts 4:8) in the context of a physical shaking of a place (Acts 4:31), a healing (Acts 4:17), perception of an exorcist's motivation (Acts 13:9). See Haya-Prats for a helpful chart of the verbs in the Spirit passages in Acts, 55-56 with specific emphasis upon the aorist tenses.

526 Haya-Prats, 117.

527 In a helpful manner, Twelftree draws significant parallels between Jesus' own Pentecost (Luke 3:21-22) and the initial Day of Pentecost. 75.

528 Contra Twelftree, 72.

529 Haya-Prats, 116.

530 On the note of ecstasy, see G. Behm, "αποφθέγγομαι," Vol. I, *TDNT,* 447.

531 See Keener, vol. I, 814, for numerous parallels and contrasts between Luke and Paul on speaking in tongues.

532 A periphrastic construction, emphasizing the enduring state, i.e. of drunkenness.

533 This accusation is similar to Paul's warning against public tongues-speaking without an interpreter. There are many parallels between Acts 2:1-4, 13 and I Cor. 14:23, "So if the whole church comes together *at the same place* (ἐπὶ τὸ αὐτὸ) and *all speak in tongues* (πάντες λαλῶσιν γλώσσαις) and uninitiated or unbelievers enter, will they not say *you are crazy* (μαίνεσθε)?" It is outside the purview of this study to delve into Paul's argument concerning glossolalia in I Cor. 12-14.

534 Although the text holds initial ambiguity of the "sound" (ἦχος Acts 2:2), Luke draws attention to the sound of tongues-speaking (2:6b).

535 Keener notes that the charismatic tongues cause "cross-cultural barriers with their prophetically inspired message." Vol. I, 823

536 The expression, "the mighty acts of God" (τὰ μεγαλεῖα του θεου Acts 2:11) parallels the account of Peter and Cornelius in Acts 10:46, where tongues is linked with the praise of God, "hearing them in tongues and magnifying God" (αὐτῶν λαλούντων γλώσσαις καὶ μεγαλυνόντων τὸν θεόν).

537 Haya-Prats, 174.

538 Pervo, 64-65.

539 See Haya-Prats for a treatment of the various verbs, 123-124.

540 An important verb for Luke as a joyous response to miraculous events.

541 Keener, Vol. I, 851.

542 G. Behm, "γλῶσσα," *TDNT*, Vol. I, 725.

543 Luke makes four changes to Joel's prophecy: 1) "after these things" (Joel 2:28) as compared to "in the last days" (Acts 2:17); 2) repetition of "they shall prophesy" (Acts 2:17-18); 3) addition of the pronoun, "my" that affirms that

both genders are God's servants (2:17-18); 4) localizing wonders and signs both "above" and "below" (2:19).

544   Johnson, *The Acts...* 48.

545   Different expressions are used, "in other tongues" (ἑτέραις γλώσσαις Acts 2:4); "in their own language" (τῇ ἰδίᾳ διαλέκτῳ ... αὐτῶν 2:6); "in our own native language in which we were born" (τῇ ἰδίᾳ διαλέκτῳ ἡμῶν ἐν ᾗ ἐγεννήθημεν 2:8); "in our own languages" (ταῖς ἡμετέραις γλώσσαις 2:11). The longer ending of Mark contains the term "in new tongues" (γλώσσαις ... καιναῖς), which is also described as one of the "signs" (σημεῖα Mark 16:17)

546   Moses in Acts 7:31; Stephen in 7:55-56; Paul and Ananias in 9:3-10, 12; Peter in 10:3, 17, 19 and 11; Paul in 16:9-10, 18:9 and 27:23. The term "vision" (ὅραμα) does not emerge in all these references, but can certainly be implied; further, some visions are put into the context of the night, thus dreams.

547   This last affirmation of Isa 40:5 is not found in the parallel accounts of Mark 1:3 or Matt 3:3.

548   Some scholars, such as F.F. Bruce, see links between the cosmic dimensions of the crucifixion and the cosmic events noted by Joel and Luke; however, links with Jesus' eschatological discourse are more solid. F. F. Bruce, *The Book of Acts* (Grand Rapids: William B. Eerdmans Publishing Co., 1988), 62.

549   Haya-Prats, 68-69

550   Psa 16:8-11.

551   In building the case for Jesus' resurrection, not David's resurrection, he repeats Psa 16:10 in Acts 2:27 and 31. He then quotes from Psa 110:1.

552   *Midrash Tehillim* on Psa 16:9.

553   Keener also notes, "The theme of joy here (and in Acts 2:28) is probably deliberate." Vol. I, 948.

554   Witness also figures into the ascension account of Luke 24:47-48, which joins with power, "repentance and the forgiveness of sins will be preached in his name to all nations, beginning in Jerusalem. You are witnesses (ὑμεῖς μάρτυρες) of these things . . . until you have been clothed with power (δύναμιν) from on high."

555   "experiencing/finding" favor with all the people" (Acts 2:47).

556   Abrahamic promise in Gen 12:3; 22:18; 26:4.

557   See Luke 24:50-51 for two references to Jesus' blessing the gathered community.

558   Contra Barrett who states that there is "no evident connection," 174.

559   See also Keener, vol. 2, 1040 for other parallels.

	Acts 2	Acts 3-4
Mention of Temple	2:46 "daily devoting themselves to the Temple"	3:1 "Peter and John were going up to the Temple"
Prayer(s)	2:42 "devotion to prayers"	4:1 "at the time of prayer"
An initial miracle that draws a crowd	2:4-6 "speaking in tongues," leading to a "multitude"	3:7-8 healing of the cripple, which "all the people saw" (3:9), followed by the running of all the people to them" (4:11)
Initial responses of amazement from the crowd	2:6-13 "confusion, amazement, marveling, perplexed"	3:10-12 "awe, amazement, marvel"
A sermon that follows initial responses	Acts 2:14-36 Pentecost sermon	Acts 3:12-26—Peter's sermon to the crowd; 4:8-12 Peter's sermon to the religious authorities
Repentance motif	2:38 "Repent"	3:19 "Repent and turn"; 3:26 "in the turning of each one of you from your sins"
Response of believing	2:41 "the ones who received his word" 2:44 "All that believed"	3:16 "through faith in his name"; 3:16 "faith which is through him" 4:4 "which heard the word believed"; 4:32 "of them that believed"
Numerical note of conversions	2:41 "about three thousand"	4:4 "about five thousand men"
Many signs and wonders	2:43 "many signs and wonders occurred through the apostles"	3:1-10 a particular sign of healing a cripple; sign in 4:16, 22, 30; wonders in 4:30
Mention of possessions	2:45 "selling of goods and possessions" for the needy	3:6 "Silver and gold I do not have"; 4:34-35, 37—extensive description of selling and giving
Concluding narrative-summary	Acts 2:41-47	Acts 4:32-37

560   Acts 3:13, 14-15, 18; 4:10, 33.

561   Acts 3:13, 15, 22, 26; 4:10, 33.

562   Acts 3:21.

563   Acts 4:8, 31.

564   Acts 3:15; 12-36; 4:2, 8, 33.

565   *Sign* (σημεῖον) in 4:16, 22, 30; *Healing* (ἴασις) in 4:22, 30; *I heal* (θεραπεύω) in 4:14; *Wonder* (τέρας) in 4:30; *Power* (δύναμις) in 3:12; 4:7, 33; miraculous shaking of the place of the gathered community in 4:31.

566   Acts 3:18, 21, 22, 23, 24, 25; 4:25, 26-27.

567   Acts 3:8, 9, 11.

568   Acts 3:10 (twice), 11, 12.

569   Acts 4:4, 21, 32.

570   Acts 4:21, 24, 32, 33 (twice).

571   Acts 4:24, 32, 33 (twice); sharing of goods and property in 4:34-37.

572   The "name," in Joel's prophecy (Acts 2:21 = Joel 2:32) and Peter's invitation to be baptized in the name of Jesus Christ (Acts 2:38). Nine occurrences of "the name" in Acts 3-4: 3:6, 16 (twice); 4:7, 10, 12, 17, 18, 30.

573   Rick Strelan, "Strange Stares: Atenizein in Acts," *Novum Testamentum* Vol. XLI, 3 (1999), 234-255.

574   Similarly, Haenchen notes the gaze "is meant to establish the inner contact necessary for the miracle." 199.

575   Strelan, 255. A similar argument in a later article. Rick Strelan, "Recognizing the Gods (Acts 14:8-10)" *New Testament Studies,* 46 (2000), 488-503. See also Anitra Bingham Kolenkow, "Relationships between Miracle and Prophecy in the Greco-Roman World and Early Christianity," *ANRW* 2.23.2 (1980), 1470-1506. Keener, vol. 2, 1063 suggests that the man has the faith to be healed. However, Luke does not make this explicit as he does in Acts 14:9.

576   Strelan, 250. Haenchen wrongly concludes that this "inner contact" is identical with pagan miracle stories, 202.

577   Strelan, 252. See J. Lyle Story, "If this man were a prophet, he would have known," *Journal of Biblical and Pneumatological Research* Vol. 5 (2013).

578   Haenchen, 200.

579   A similar question, posed to Jesus about his "authority" (ἐξουσία) to forgive sins in the healing of the paralytic (Luke 5:24).

580   Frequently used by Luke in miracle-stories (Luke 1:64; 4:39; 5:25; 8:44, 47, 55; 13:13; 18:43; Acts 5:10; 12:23; 13:11).

581   Pervo, 100.

582   An inceptive imperfect.

583   Greek use of *ekphrasis.* Haenchen suggests, "the process unrolling before our eyes", 198.

584   Isa 35:3 also contains the promise that God will "strengthen the weak hands and make firm the feeble knees."

585   In a general way, De Long notes the transition of the verb "I save" (σώζω), used in Luke's gospel for "healing" to the shift in Acts referring to "salvation" or "conversion." 205

586   Otto Kaiser, *Isaiah 13-39* (R.A. Wilson, transl; Philadelphia: The Westminster Press, 1974), 362.

587   Kaiser, 362.

588   Dennis Hamm, "Acts 3,1-10:The Healing of the Temple Beggar as Lucan Theology," *Biblica* 67 (1986), 312. On the verb, "to leap," he alludes to Joel 2:5; Hab 1:8; Isa 55:12, Nah 3:17; Mic 2:13.

589   Hamm, 316. Other Isaian texts link the pilgrimage of the returning exiles with the experience, atmosphere and expressions of joy and praise (Isa 42:16; 43:16, 19; 45:13; 49:11; 51:10; 57:14; 62:10), noted by De Long, 206.

590   Acts 3:7; 12, 16; 4:9 (twice), 10.

591   The perfect passive participle (τὸν τεθεραπευμένον) emphasizes the man's healed condition, *the man who had been healed.*

592   Three references to "sign" (σημεῖον) in Acts 4:16, 22, 30.

593   The "save word-family" is critical for Luke, which is accentuated in Acts through repetition: "salvation" (σωτηρία), used six times (see Acts 4:12; 7:25; 13:26, 47; 16:7; 27:34); "I save" (σώζω), used thirteen times (see Acts 2:21, 40, 47; 4:9, 12, 11:14; 14:9; 15:1, 11; 16:30, 31; 27:20, 31); "salvation" (σωτήριον), used once.

594   Pervo, 118.

595   Pervo, 119.

596   Acts 3:13 (Exod 3:6, 15); Acts 3:22 (Deut 18:15-16); Acts 3:25 (Gen 22:18; 26:4; 12:3); Acts 4:11 (Psa 118:22); Acts 4:25 (Psa 2:2).

597   Haenchen, 209.

598   See the use of Psa 118:22 at the conclusion of Jesus' Parable of the Wicked Tenants (Luke 20:17).

599   μελετάω, BDAG, 500.

600   Acts 4:16, 22, 30.

601   Acts 4:22, 30.

602   Acts 3:12; 4:7, 33.

603   Barrett, 188.

604   The expression, "being filled with the Holy Spirit" refers to a momentary and special inspiration, in addition to the fullness of the Spirit in Acts 2:4, which then leads to *speaking* with tongues.

605   Acts 4:8 Πέτρος πλησθεὶς πνεύματος ἁγίου εἶπεν πρὸς αὐτούς; Acts 4:31 καὶ ἐπλήσθησαν ἅπαντες τοῦ ἁγίου πνεύματος καὶ ἐλάλουν τὸν λόγον τοῦ θεοῦ μετὰ παρρησίας.

606   See Keener, Vol. 2, 1144-5 on this consistent theme.

607   It is sandwiched between two temporal indicators, "it was evening" (Acts 4:3) and "the next day" (Acts 4:5).

608   De Long, 197.

609   Johnson translates the verb as "surged." *The Acts of the Apostles,* 66.

610 Dunn suggests that the word ἔκστασις "implies the numinous," 41. Contra De Long, who makes pejorative comments about the crowd's responses, 195.

611 Haenchen, 200-201.

612 The crowd's only critique is the sarcastic comment by some that the tongues-speakers were drunk (Acts 2:13)

613 Haenchen, 217.

614 A clear link with Jesus' earlier promises of inspiration and boldness by the Holy Spirit in the context of religious or secular trials: "the Holy Spirit will teach you what to say in the same hour" (Luke 12:11-12); "a mouth and witness which none of your adversaries will be able to withstand or contradict" (Luke 21:14-15).

615 The commentaries reveal a great deal of attention to sources (Philip, Peter, or Simon), the geographical location of the city of Samaria and the towns of Samaria, possible links between Simon and what is said elsewhere about him in Jewish (Josephus) or Christian post-apostolic fathers, and his possible links with Gnosticism. These issues lie outside of our sphere of concern. Our attention is devoted to what Luke intends to say to his readers in the narrative.

616 Charles Scobie argues for a Stephen-Philip group "as representative of some type of Palestinian sectarian Judaism ("Northern"? Galilean?), with little use for the Jerusalem cult." Charles H. H. Scobie, "Development of Samaritan Christianity," *New Testament Studies*, 19 (year?), 399.

617 With the exception of the verbal interchange in the second person between Simon and Peter (Acts 8:18-24).

618 The imperfect tense refers to Philip's ongoing preaching when the various miracles occurred.

619 E.g. the name which healed the crippled beggar in Acts 3:6; 4:7, which is also an acted parable of salvation, "Salvation is found in no one else, for there is no other name under heaven given to people, by which we must be saved" (Acts 4:12). Pervo states, "In short, 'the name' makes 'the kingdom' present and effective." 210.

620 Barrett, 399.

621 James D. G. Dunn, *Baptism in the Holy Spirit* (Naperville, IL: Alec R. Allenson Inc., 1970), 63. Similarly in his later commentary, J. G. Dunn, *The Acts of the Apostles*, 109. See the use in John 4:25, "the one who would restore all things."

622 Wayne Meeks provides a broad survey of research that broadsides Haenchen's argument that links Simon and pre-Christian Gnosticism, e.g., "The Acts account stands apart from all the later sources, for there is nothing gnostic about it." Wayne A. Meeks, "Simon Magus in Recent Research," *Religious Studies Review* Volume 3 (1977), 138.

623 Barrett, 408. For the verb, "I believe" (πιστεύω) with the dative, see Acts 16:34; 18:8.

624 *Contra* Dunn, *Baptism in the Holy Spirit*, 63. Keener, Vol. 2, 1517, argues that Samaritan faith was not defective.

625 Barrett, 399. Bruce argues for "supervise the expansion of the faith," 220.

626   *Contra* Pervo who argues that the apostles were sent "to regularize the activity," 203, or "to show that all legitimate missionary activity received approval from the Jerusalem apostles." 204.

627   For similar argument see Stronstad, 63-65; Haya-Prats, 130-134; Keener, Vol. 2, 1522, states "a 'bias' read into Luke from an inflexible application of Pauline theology."

628   Similarly in Luke 4:33; 9:39.

629   Stephen was also a deacon, not an apostle, who was performing signs (Acts 6:8).

630   Philip is later found in Caesarea (Acts 8:40; 21:8) where he is identified as an evangelist. From Acts 21:8, in the "we" passage, Luke indicates some indication of his own contact with Philip.

631   Barrett, 406.

632   Dunn, *The Acts of the Apostles*, 108.

633   Dunn, *The Acts of the Apostles*, 108.

634   Research concerning Simon is voluminous, but the concern is with Luke's message. For extensive treatment of magic, see David Aune, "Magic in Early Christianity," *ANRW*, Vol: 2.23.2 (1980), 1507-1557. Also, Susan R. Garrett, *The Demise of the Devil: Magic and the Demonic in Luke's Writings* (Minneapolis: Fortress Press, 1989).

635   K. Haacker suggests that it means "an expression of deity." "Samaritan," *NIDNTT*, Vol. 3, 457.

636   In a compelling chapter, Graham H. Twelftree argues that Luke's key indictment of Simon is that he is a "false prophet," and he builds his case by comparing the other "magicians" in Acts (Elymas in Acts 13:4-12; the slave girl in 16:16-24; the seven sons of Sceva in 19:13-17). Graham H. Twelftree, "Jesus and Magic in Luke-Acts," *Global Perspectives in Honor of James D. G. Dunn for His 70th Birthday* (New York: T & T Clark), 46-48.

637   Twelftree notes the connection with Theudas in Acts 5:36, "declaring himself to be somebody" (λέγων εἶναι τινα ἑαυτόν), "Jesus and Magic in Luke-Acts," 48. At the same time, the argument for competition between Philip and Simon is not stressed, as Twelftree states; the text highlights Philip's victory.

638   See Pervo for several points of contrast between Philip and Simon, 204.

639   The verb "I fall upon" (ἐπιπίπτω) is a Lucan verb, used in Acts 10:44; 11:15 for the "falling of the Spirit upon Cornelius and company.

640   The two periphrastic perfect participles emphasize the enduring state.

641   So Haenchen, 304.

642   Bruce notes, "the receiving of the Spirit ... was accompanied by glossolalia or comparable manifestations," 222.

643   Pervo, 214.

644   Barrett, 403.

645   Barrett correctly notes that the perfect form, "has received" (δέδεκται) is an equivalent to believing. 410. See also Acts 2:41—"those who *accepted his word* (οἱ μὲν οὖν ἀποδεξάμενοι τὸν λόγον) were baptized."

646 The imposition of hands is not to be understood as regularized throughout Acts as if this is the fixed-pattern, e.g. on the Day of Pentecost, nothing is stated about the laying on of hands in Acts 2. See Pervo for Luke's lack of regularity, regarding baptism, laying on of hands, reception of the Spirit. 213.

647 Luke does not tell his readers whether Simon received the Holy Spirit or not; however, there is no grounds for excluding him from being a recipient.

648 Similar use in Acts 2:38; 10:45; 11:17.

649 Pervo, 213.

650 Haenchen, 308.

651 Keener, Vol. 2, 1524.

652 Marshall, 169. Perhaps an allusion to the LXX of Deut 29:19; MT 29:20.

653 See my article, "If This Man Were a Prophet . . . He Would Know . . . Luke 7:39."

654 Peter's expression serves as a curse against Simon.

655 The D-Text possesses the comment that Simon wept continually as he made his request (πολλὰ κλαίων οὐ δελίμπανεν).

656 Pervo, 207.

657 Pervo, 216.

658 Twelftree, "Jesus and Magic in Luke-Acts," 55.

659 The term εὐνοῦχος should be understood literally of a physically castrated man (BDAG, 323); in this case, the Ethiopian eunuch is also described as a "court official" (δυνάστης) of the Ethiopian queen's court.

660 See Keener, Vol. 2, 1536 for parallels with Luke 24. Numerous scholars find allusions to other biblical and non-biblical texts in terms of structure and thought: Pervo sees parallels with the Emmaus story (Luke 24:13-35), conversion of King Izates of Adiabene (Josephus *Antiquities.* 20:44-46), Elijah/Elisha tradition (1 Kgs 18; 2 Kgs 2), 218-220; parallels with 2 Kings 5—Thomas Brodie, "Towards Unraveling the Rhetorical Implication of Sources in Acts: 2 Kings 5 as One Component of Acts 8, 9-40," *Biblica* 67 (1986), 41-67; chiastic structure of Acts 8:25-40—F. Scott Spencer, "The Portrait of Philip in Acts," *JSNT* 67 (1992), 132, Elijah and Elisha stories, 135-141, Emmaus narrative, 141-145; parallels with Zephaniah 2-3—William Kemp Clarke, "The Use of the LXX in Acts," in Frederick J. Foakes Jackson and Kirsopp Lake, *Prolegomena II*, 101-102. While certain parallels exist and may color the narrative, it is altogether a different matter to regard the Philip-Eunuch story as Luke's creation, borrowed from certain biblical and non-biblical texts.

661 Keener, vol. 2, 1545.

662 In a persuasive manner, Martin emphasizes the "African blackness" in his article, which is often omitted in numerous commentaries and articles. 110-116.

663 Several scholars make a persuasive case for regarding Ethiopia as "the end of the earth" (ἕως ἐσχάτου τῆς γῆς Acts 1:8) from many biblical and non-biblical sources. Spencer, 151; Tannehill, Vol. II, 107-111; Clarice J. Martin, "A Chamberlain's Journey and the Challenge of Interpretation for Liberation," *Semeia* (1989), 116-120; Pervo, "Here all of the focus falls on an individual

who symbolizes not only 'the ends of the earth,'—universalism—but also the nature of individual faith.", 227; Martin Hengel, *Acts and the History of Earliest Christianity* (Philadelphia: Westminster, 1979), 80; Gaventa, 102. Thus, for Luke, the conversion of the Ethiopian eunuch serves as an initial fulfillment of the promise in Acts 1:8. The scope will then be enlarged by conversion of Paul who will carry "my name to the Gentiles and their kings" (Acts 9:15), the conversion of the Gentile Cornelius (Acts 10-11), the decision by the Jerusalem Council (Acts 15), Paul's successive missionary travels, culminating in Rome (Acts 28). Contra Haenchen, who states that "Philip would have forestalled Peter, the legitimate founder of the Gentile-mission." 314

664 Barrett, I, 426.

665 Gaventa, 104.

666 Spencer, 160-165, makes a compelling argument that equates this eunuch with a "God-fearer." "Elsewhere in Luke-Acts, φοβέομαι and σεβέομαι are applied broadly to 'anyone who reveres God' (Acts 10:35; 18:13; Luke 1:50), 164. *Contra* Haenchen, who argues from silence that Luke did not regard the man as a Gentile. 314.

667 See the same verbs in the Saul episode (Acts 9:3-6, 11-12, 15) and Cornelius story (10:9, 10-13, 20, 22).

668 Acts 10:3, 7, 22; 11:13; 12:7-11, 23; 27:23.

669 In Acts 10:3, an angel speaks to Cornelius while in 10:19 the Spirit speaks to Peter.

670 Dunn discounts the miraculous transport. *The Acts* ... , 115.

671 The expression "at noon" (κατὰ μεσημβρίαν Acts 8:26) is preferable to the possible meaning, "towards the south," for it underscores the unusual time of the encounter. See also Beverly Roberts Gaventa, *From Darkness to Light: Aspects of Conversion in the New Testament* (Philadelphia: Fortress Press, 1986), 101-102.

672 The same expression is frequent with the Cornelius story (Acts 10:17, 19, 21, 30; 11:11).

673 A future participle indicating the purpose for his travel to Jerusalem.

674 Three references to reading: once in Acts 8:28, and twice in 8:29.

675 In the Cornelius story, the Spirit is again the decisive force (Acts 10:19-20; 11:12).

676 Pervo, 217.

677 Pervo, 225.

678 Passivity is expressed by the passive voices of the verbs, "was led" (ἤχθη), "was taken up\exalted" (ἤρθη), "was removed" (αἴρεται), the Servant's dumbness in the experience of humiliation, "dumbness" (ἄφωνος), "he did not open his mouth" (οὐκ ἀνοίγει τὸ στώμα αὐτοῦ), and the fact that another will tell (διηγήσεται) his descendants, Acts 8:32-33.

679 Pervo and Haenchen understand that the verb "I take up/away" (αἴρω Acts 8:33) should be understood as referring to the exaltation subsequent to Jesus' resurrection. Pervo, 225-226. Haenchen, 312.

680 The term γενεά in this text can refer to Jesus' "life span" or "generation" or "spiritual descendants." In the context of this paragraph, Pervo aptly understands

681   the verse, "Then the sentence means: 'The number of his disciples will grow incalculably, because he has become the Exalted.'" Pervo, 312. See also Barrett I: 431.

681   Luke 1:48, 52; 3:5-6 from Isa 40:4-5; 14:11; 18:14; See Pervo, 225; Spenser, 176-178; Dunn, *The Acts of the Apostles*, 115.

682   Edward J. Young notices that the question "is the first recorded instance of the question being asked." Edward J. Young, "Of Whom Speaketh the Prophet This?" *Westminster Theological Journal* 11 (1949), 132.

683   Pervo, 226.

684   The Western text states that in his explanation, Philip "was in the Spirit."

685   Pervo, 225.

686   See the use in a similar passage, "beginning from the baptism of John" (Acts 1:22); Jesus uses the Old Testament Scripture (Luke 24:25-27, 44-47), as does Peter in his sermons.

687   A response from Philip and a creedal affirmation by the eunuch, "Philip answered and said to him, 'If you believe with your whole heart, it is possible.' The eunuch answered and said, "I believe in Jesus Christ, that he is the Son of God.'" As Bruce Metzger notes, "There is no reason why scribes should have omitted the material, if it had originally stood in the text . . . Its insertion into the texts seems to have been due to the feeling that Philip could not have baptized the Ethiopian without securing a confession." Bruce M. Metzger, *A Textual Commentary on the Greek New Testament* (New York: United Bible Societies, 1971), 359-360.

688   Keener, Vol.2, 1595.

689   The verb "I baptize" (βαπτίζω) in the eunuch episode (Acts 8:36, 39) matches two references in the Samaritan episode (8:12-13).

690   Spencer, 183-184. Not excluding a strange exorcist in Luke 9:49; not hindering little children in Luke 18:15-17; lawyers who exclude others in Luke 11:52; not excluding Cornelius and company from baptism in Acts 10:47; "Who was I that I could hinder God?" in 11:17.

691   Gaventa, 106-107. In Acts 10:1-11:18, Cornelius is another such devout person.

692   This transport is similar to the transport of Jesus from the Emmaus home (Luke 24:31b) after Jesus' promise-fulfilment teaching to the Emmaus pair.

693   Marshall, 165.

694   Marshall, 165.

695   See also, G.W.H. Lampe, *The Seal of the Spirit* (London: Longmans, Green and Co, 1951), 65, 67.

696   Pervo, 228.

697   Metzger, 360-361.

698   Lampe, 65. Haenchen, Pervo, and Barrett say almost nothing about the eunuch's joy.

699   Lampe, 65.

700   Spenser's otherwise excellent article doesn't deal with the important topic of the Spirit and joy in this narrative.

701   Bruce, *The Book of Acts*, 178.

702   See Spenser for other texts related to exclusion and inclusion of eunuchs, 166-172.
       See Psa 67:31-32 LXX; Zeph 3:9-10 LXX.

703   Spencer, 172.

704   Paul is a "vessel of choice ... to bring my name before Gentiles" (Acts 9:15).

705   Haenchen, 315.

706   Luke is the only evangelist who contains this line from Isa 40:5.

707   Spencer, 187.

708   See Martin for thoughtful comments on "interpretation for liberation." 125.

709   The term, "the Way" (ἡ ὁδός) is used in an absolute sense (9:2; 19:9, 23; 22:4;
       24:14, 22), possibly traced to the words of Jesus, "I am the way..." (Jn. 14:6).

710   D. M. Stanley, "Paul's Conversion in Acts: Why the Three Accounts?" *The
       Catholic Biblical Quarterly*, vol. 15, 319.

711   Charles W. Hedrick, "Paul's Conversion/Call: A Comparative Analysis of the
       Three Reports in Acts," *JBL*, 100/3 (1981), 421.

712   It is beyond our scope to trace through all of the different approaches taken
       as to how and why such a transformation occurred in Paul, e.g. psychological,
       change of religions, change in self-understanding. Saul's position in the Jewish
       community, coupled with his fierce persecution of Christianity, clearly demands
       the conclusion that he went to Damascus *not in preparation for the gospel but in
       aggressive and conscious opposition to the gospel.*

713   9:7—companions hear a voice—nothing; 22:9—companions see the light—
       hear no voice; 26:14—nothing is said about seeing or hearing—they fall to the
       ground.

714   Conzelmann, 71.

715   Haenchen, 321-322. Haenchen notes a parallel with Deut 4:12, "you heard the
       voice of words, but you saw no form."

716   a. Self-revelation of God (Theophany, Christophany); b. Overwhelming effect—
       fear (R. Otto—mysterium tremendum); c. Announcement of mission (verbal);
       d. Human objections raised; e. Human objections are overcome; f. (Signs).
       Examples such as Moses, Jeremiah, Ezekiel, Amos.

717   So, "Martha, Martha" (Luke 10:41), "Simon, Simon" (Luke 22:31).

718   See the response of Cornelius to the angel in Acts 10:4.

719   Gal 1:13; 1 Cor 12:12f.; 1 Cor 8:12; Gal 2:20; Col 1:27

720   Haenchen, 328.

721   Haenchen, 323.

722   R.B. Rackham, *The Acts of the Apostles*, (London: Macmillan, 1930), 133.

723   Dunn, *The Acts of the Apostles*, 122.

724   Unlike Samuel (1 Sam 3:4-5), Ananias knows the identity of the Lord. See Keener,
       Vol. 2, 1645 for the similarity of the paired experiences.

725   The expression, "vessel" (σκεῦος) is used in a positive manner, which contrasts
       with the expression, "vessel of his wrath" from Jeremiah (50:25=27:25 LXX). On
       the term "vessel of choice/election," cf. Rom 9:21-23; 2 Cor 4:7; 2 Tim 2:20f.

726   Six references of "the name," referring to Jesus (9:14, 15, 16, 21, 27, 28).

727   Ralph P. Martin, *Reconciliation: A Study of Paul's Theology*, (Atlanta: John Knox Press, 1981.

728   Dunn, 74. Dunn notes that ἀδελφός is used 57 times in Acts—36 times equivalent to 'my fellow Christian(s)' (leaving aside 9:17 and 22:13), and 19 times in reference to the national and spiritual kinship of Jew to Jew."

729   See Keener, Vol. 2, 1662.

730   Haenchen, 333.

731   Mention of Peter's residence with Simon the tanner (9:43) anticipates the Cornelius story, where Peter's exact location is given by the angel to Cornelius (10:6).

732   Luke's penchant for mentioning the "duration of a sickness ... underlines ... the reality of the miraculous healing." Keener, Vol. 2, 1707.

733   A striking indicative—not an imperative.

734   Haenchen, 341.

735   The only feminine word for "disciple" in the NT.

736   Haenchen, 339.

737   A three hour journey.

738   1 Kgs 17:17-24; 2 Kgs 4:30-37.

739   Jairus' daughter in Luke 8:49-56.

740   For example, Ronald D. Witherup follows Haenchen's scenic structure (seven scenes), but never mentions the element of joy in the narrative of Acts 10:44-48 or Acts 11:18. Instead he argues for the climax of hospitality in both narratives. Ronald D. Witherup, "Cornelius Over and Over and Over Again: 'Functional Redundancy' in the Acts of the Apostles," *JSNT,* 49 (1993), 51-52 (45-66). He does mention angels and visions but makes no mention of tongues.

741   Pervo calls Cornelius a "successor to the centurion of Luke 7:1-10," 265.

742   Tannehill Vol. Two, calls this "divine promptings . . . which require human action or reflection.", 128

743   *Contra* Haenchen, who argues, "Luke virtually excludes all human decision ... They compellingly prove that God, not man is at work ... very nearly the twitching of puppets," 362.

744   The observations do not include source-critical work but focus upon Luke's message. Haenchen offers source-critical work. 355-363.

745   Contrasted with the private event of a Gentile African eunuch in Acts 8:26-40; he is heard of no more in Acts.

746   "a light of revelation to the Gentiles"—by Simeon (Acts 2:32); "all flesh shall see the salvation of God"—by the Baptist (Luke 3:6; Isa 40:5 LXX); Jesus' ministry to outsiders (e.g., Luke 7:1-10); "forgiveness of sins "to all nations"—by Jesus (Luke 24:47); "to the end of the earth"—by Jesus (Acts 1:8); "to all who are far off"—by Peter (Acts 2:39)

747 See Gaventa for numerous narratives of "double-visions." Beverly Roberts Gaventa, *From Darkness to Light*, (Philadelphia: Fortress Press, 1986), 109-111. Keener, Vol. 3, notes that such double-visions "reinforce their validity."

748 Johnson, *The Acts of the Apostles*, 187.

749 A Hebrew idiom, "to lift the face of someone," thus, "to show favoritism."

750 Marshall, 186.

751 The verb, "I perceive" (καταλαμβάνομαι) is an inceptive present tense.

752 Tannehill, Vol. Two, 137.

753 Gaventa sees no "order of salvation" in Acts 2:38 but "an effective conclusion to Peter's speech." 98. In the Cornelius story, baptism follows the gift of the Holy Spirit; in Acts 2:38, baptism appears as a consequence of repentance, followed by the gift of the Spirit; in Acts 8:16, the Samaritans are baptized, followed by the delayed gift of the Spirit; in 19:5, baptism is followed by the gift of the Spirit.

754 Tannehill, Vol. Two, 132.

755 Acts 10:3, 17, 19; 11:5.

756 Acts 10:10; 11:5.

757 BDAG, 577.

758 BDAG, 245. Bruce, *The Acts of the Apostles*, notes "a state in which a man stands outside of himself," 217. Further the noun is related to the verb ἐξίστημι in Acts 10:45 (elsewhere in Acts 2:7, 12; 8:9, 11, 13; 9:21; 12:16). In Acts 11:5, the term "trance" "is much stronger than in 3:10." Barrett, *Commentary on Acts*, 505.

759 In Acts 10:3, an angel, "distinctly" (φανερῶς), which adds realism to the experience; in 10:7, an angel speaking to him; in 10:22, a revelation by a holy angel; in 10:30, a man in shining clothes; in 11:13, an angel.

760 Acts 10:13, 15, 16 (implied voice, three times); 11:7, 9, 10. God's voice—not some impersonal voice.

761 The verb χρηματίζω expresses divine revelation, injunction, warning, direction, or prophecy. BDAG, 885.

762 The participle, "conversing" (συνομιλῶν Acts 10:27) precedes the two repeated visions.

763 See Witherup, "Cornelius Over . . . ," 47, for a definition of "functional redundancy," designed to ensure a full and unambiguous reception of the message." He parallels the retelling of Cornelius' story with the three-fold telling of Saul's call-narrative in Acts 9, 22, 26. 62.

764 Surely Luke's readers "smile" at the coincidence. Pervo notes the "coincidence" as a "theological pleasure." 265.

765 Same language (καὶ ἰδού) in Acts 8:27, "and behold a man" and "behold water" in Acts 8:36.

766 Haenchen, 276. See C. H. Dodd, *The Apostolic Preaching and its Developments* (London: Hodder & Stoughton, 1936), 56.

767 Acts 2:17-36; 3:12-26.

768 Gaventa, 119.

769 Psa 107:20 is later alluded to in Acts 13:26, "the word of this salvation was sent."

770   Pervo, 277.

771   Tannehill, Vol Two, 140. Keener, Vol. 3, 1800, notes, "If one Lord rules over all, then he is for all."

772   See also Acts 2:22; 7:9.

773   Barrett, *Commentary on Acts*, 525. See also Luke 11:17-20.

774   Similar language in Acts 5:30. The text alludes to the curse of Deut 21:23, "Cursed is everyone who hangs on a tree." Paul uses the same language in Gal 3:13. Max Wilcox argues for an allusion to the "wood" used in Gen 22:6a, 7b, 9, with respect to the sacrifice of Isaac. Max Wilcox, "Upon the Tree—Deut. 21:22-23 in the New Testament," *JBL* 96/1 (1977), 85-99.

775   Luke 24:36-43; Acts 1:3-4.

776   "witnesses selected by God" (Acts 10:41; "to bear witness" (10:42), "the prophets bear witness" (10:43)

777   Pervo, 277

778   Readers should not sharply distinguish the terms since the Holy Spirit, vision, trance, angel and/or voice—all are directed towards the same end of bringing Peter and Cornelius together for the climactic encounter. See Acts 8:26.

779   Dunn, *The Acts of the Apostles*, 146.

780   Johnson, *The Acts of the Apostles*, 195. On Acts 11:15, see John K. Kilgallen, "Did Peter actually Fail to Get a Word in?", *Biblica* Volume 71 (1990) 405-410. Kilgallen argues against Dibelius' view that the Holy Spirit descended before Peter had begun his speech. The verb, "I begin" (ἄρχομαι) "is a literary device of Luke meant simply to make the story more exciting or engaging for the reader ... that we can suppose that there was more that Peter wanted to say. If this is so, then, 11:15 can be understood to represent what Luke had already presented in 10:34-43", 409.

781   Kilgallen, 409

782   The same language used in Acts 8:16 of the falling down of the Holy Spirit upon the Samaritans. Other terms are used elsewhere to refer to the same reality: Acts 1:8, the verb, "I come upon" (ἐξέρχομαι); Acts 2:4 the verb, "I am filled" (πίμπλημι).

783   Vocabulary: "I am astonished/ecstatic" (ἐξίστημι) in Acts 2:7, 12 and 10:45; "I pour out" (ἐκχέω) in 2:17, 18 and 10:45); "tongues" (γλῶσσα) in 2:11 and 10:46); "baptize" (βαπτίζω) in 1:5 and 11:17 related to 10:44-46; "I receive" (λαμβάνω) in 2:38; "gift" (δωρεά) of the Holy Spirit in 2:38 and 10:45, also 8:18).

784   Earl Richard, "Pentecost as a Recurrent Theme," *New Views on Luke and Acts* (Collegeville, MN: The Liturgical Press, 1990), 143.

785   See Max Turner, *Power from on High* (Sheffield: Sheffield Academic Press, 1966), 380-381. *Contra* Bruce, *The Book of Acts*, 216, who argues that "this event was not so much a second Pentecost, standing alongside the first, as the participation of gentile believers in the experience of the first Pentecost." Dunn narrowly understands this experience to be that of conversion-initiation. *Baptism*, 70-82.

786 Pervo notes that the gift of the Spirit serves as "a fundamental justification for the gentile mission," 266.

787 Turner, 381.

788 See Acts 2:21, 40, 47.

789 Keener, Vol. 3, 1814, emphasizes the "*qal vahomer* argument; if the greater was true, then how much more should the lesser be true." Perhaps baptism is implicit with the verb, "I hinder" (κωλύω), which is found in the narrative (Acts 10:47) and Peter's report (Acts 11:17). However, Peter's word about his inability to hinder God is more general than baptism. Dunn notes, "it was the Spirit, not baptism which rendered circumcision irrelevant," Dunn, *The Acts of the Apostles*, 151.

790 In Witherup's argument, the theme of hospitality is climactic, due to the numerous references to the "house"—vocabulary (οἶκος, οἰκία, οἰκοδομέω) in the passage (Acts 10:2, 22, 30; 11:12, 13, 14). Witherup, 50.

791 The assurance of this remembrance (to the good) carries the implication that Cornelius may be sure of the aid of God now or in the future." William C. van Unnik, "The Background and Significance of Acts X 4 and 35," *Sparsa Collecta: The collected essays of W.C. van Unnik Part One* (1973), 247.

792 Pervo, 267-268.

793 "Cornelius is addressed like a Jew by the angel and portrayed as a Jew by the narrator." Tannehill, Vol. Two, 133.

794 See discussion on Acts 3:4 for the use of the verb.

795 The verb, "I narrate/tell the story" (ἐξηγέομαι) is an important Lucan word (Luke 24:35; Acts 10:8; 15:12, 14; 21:9) and only outside of Luke in John's prologue (John 1:18).

796 Philip has already been at Caesarea (Acts 8:40).

797 As a soldier, he knows both the taking and giving orders (Luke 7:8).

798 Witherup argues that the theme of hospitality is conveyed by the prefixed preposition, "with" (σύν) with several verbs in this meeting (συνέρχομαι, συγγενεῖς, συναντάω, συνομιλέω). 5. See also Gaventa, 116, 128. F. Bovon, "Tradition et rédaction en Actes 10:1-11, 18" *TZ*, Vol. 26. 1 (1970), 27 (22-45).

799 Tannehill, Vol. 2, 130.

800 A present supplementary participle.

801 Pervo, 259.

802 See Acts 14:8-18; 28:1-6 for a similar reverence for Paul.

803 Links with the "welcome" (δέχομαι) word-family: the Samaritans "welcomed" (δέδεκται Acts 8:14) the word of God; Cornelius is "welcomed" (δεκτός 10:35) by God; the Jerusalem community "heard that even the Gentiles "welcomed" (ἐδέξαντο 11:1) the word of God.

804 Johnson, *The Acts of the Apostles*, states that this soldier "shares Cornelius' values," 183. The adjective "devout" (εὐσεβής) is related to the noun, "piety" (εὐσεβεία) in Acts 3:12 and the verb, "to practice piety" (εὐσεβεῖν) in Acts 17:23; the forms are frequently found in the Pastorals.

805   "he [Peter] finds many gathered together" (εὑρίσκει συνεληλυθότας πολλούς
       Acts 11:27).

806   Dunn, *the Acts of the Apostles*, 134. Also Witherup, 49.

807   See Lev 11:1-45; 10:11. Peter's language reflects Ezekiel's attitude, "No way
       Lord (μηδαμῶς κύριε), God of Israel, surely my soul has not been defiled
       with uncleanness (ἀκαθαρσίας); nor have I eaten that which is defiled with
       uncleanness; nor have I eaten ... neither has any corrupt flesh entered into my
       mouth" (εἰς τὸ στόμα μου Ezek 4:14). The rejection is later expressed in Acts
       11:7-10 to the Jerusalem Church.

808   Bruce, *The Book of Acts*, 206.

809   There is a chiasm between Peter's rejection and the angel's command: A –
       common, B –unclean B′ –cleansed, A′ – regard common. See also the link with
       Luke 11:41, "Give for alms those things that are within and see, everything will
       be clean (πάντα καθαρά) for you."

810   Barrett, *Commentary on* Acts, 509.

811   "But many in Israel stood firm and were resolved in their hearts not to eat
       unclean food (τοῦ μὴ φαγεῖν κοινὰ I Macc 1:62).

812   Gaventa draws attention to the intensive preposition, διά with the verb, 115.

813   "therefore inviting them in, he made them guests" (εἰσκαλεσάμενος οὖν
       αὐτοὺς ἐξένισεν Acts 10:23) in a home where Peter was also "a guest"
       (ξενίζεται Acts 10:6, 18). Later Peter will be a guest in Cornelius' home for
       several days (τότε ἠρώτησαν αὐτὸν ἐπιμεῖναι ἡμέρας τινάς 10:48).
       Witherup notes that in an unclean home, "Peter's temporary residence provides
       a preview of the story about to unfold." 48.

814   The term ἀθέμιτον reflects the language of the *taboo*.

815   An original meaning of the "Philistine" in the LXX.

816   Reinforced, "And Peter opened his mouth and said" (Ἀνοίξας δὲ Πέτρος τὸ
       στόμα εἶπεν Acts 15:34).

817   "all the things that you have been commanded by the Lord" (πάντα τὰ
       προστεταγμένα σοι ὑπὸ τοῦ κυρίου Acts 10:33).

818   Jouette M. Bassler argues for different views of impartiality, "Paul thus interprets
       impartiality as the elimination of all categories, while Luke interprets it as the
       opening of one category to worthy members of another." Jouette M. Bassler,
       "Luke and Paul on 'Impartiality'," *Biblica*, Volume 66 (1985) (546-552), 552.

819   The same rhetorical use of the verb, "I hinder/forbid" (κωλύω) also occurs in
       Acts 8:36 in the context of baptism, "What is there that would *forbid* me from
       being baptized?" "Can anyone *forbid* water for baptizing such people?" in Acts
       10:47.

820   Luke frequently uses the verb, "I am astonished" (ἐξίστημι) in numinous
       encounters (Astonishment of Jesus' parents in Luke 2:47; attributed to parents
       of the dead girl in 8:56; women at the tomb in 24:22; the crowd on the Day of
       Pentecost in Acts 2:7. 12; the people of Samaria and Simon overcome by Philip

(miracles overcome magic) in Acts 8:9, 11, 13; all who heard him in 9: 21; all in Rhoda's house in 12:16.

821   De Long, 253.

822   Johnson, *The Acts of the* Apostles, 201.

823   Bruce, *The Acts of the Apostles*, labels the Jerusalem people "of the circumcision" as "sticklers for circumcision," 229.

824   Luke's readers might draw the link between these critics and the critics' accusation of Jesus for table-fellowship with the wrong sort of people, e.g. Luke 5:30; 15:1-2; 19:7.

825   There is a play on words with the verb, διακρίνω. It is stated twice that Peter journeyed to Cornelius "without hesitation" (Acts 10:20; 11:12); in Acts 11:2, the verb is used of accusation; in Acts 15:9, the verb is similarly used in terms of making no distinction between "them [Gentile believers] and us [Jewish believers]."

826   De Long, 254.

827   Luke uses the verb "I explain" (ἐκτίθημι) is a figurative sense to denote, "I set forth." BDAG, 245. The bold declaration is also paired with the adverb, "in order" (καθεξῆς), i.e. "one after the other," "point by point." The same adverb is used in Luke's earlier prologue, "it seemed good also to me to write an *orderly* account," Luke 1:3.

828   De Long, 255.

829   This goes back to John's prophecy in Luke 3:16.

830   Johnson, *The Acts of the Apostles*, 198. Turner understands the prophecy to mean the "cleansing and restoring of Israel through the executive power of the Holy Spirit which he pours out." 387.

831   Gaventa, 120.

832   Turner, 382.

833   The verb, "I am quiet, silent" (ἡσυχάζω), in this context suggests the translation, "I cease opposition," since the following clause expresses their verbal praise of God.

834   Pervo, 262.

835   Keener, vol. 3, 1828, notes the conjunction, "even" (καί), "reflects their surprise (albeit a *pleasant* surprise)."

836   Specifically, the issue of circumcision will surface in Acts 15.

837   De Long, 256.

838   On the ethnocentric perspective, see Mark A. Plunkett, "Ethnocentricity and Salvation History in the Cornelius Episode," *SBL* (1985), 465-479.

839   Pervo, 290, dismisses the account, "The account is hard to swallow." 290. Haenchen doubts that the journey actually occurred. 439. The major question concerns Luke's purpose. What is Luke's message in these stories?

840   This story is treated in Chapter 8.

841   Peter's prison escape is included in Chapter 8.

842   The term can be translated as "Hellenists," but the context argues for the translation, "Greeks."

843   The powerful divine hand is noted in 4:28-29.

844   Noted in Acts 4:29; 11:19; 13:46; 14:3.

845   James Dunn, *The Acts of the Apostles*, 155.

846   A common Lukan verb to express conversion (Luke 1:16-17; 22:32; Acts 3:19, 9:35; 14:15; 15:19; 26:18; 28:27.

847   Luke's readers would note the two previous appearances of Barnabas: 1) the gift of his property for those in need (Acts 4:36-37); 2) his affirmation of Saul, the former-persecutor to suspicious Jews (9:26-27).

848   This parallels the dispatch of Peter and John to Samaria from Jerusalem (Acts 8:14). Also, the report-back of Peter relative to the Cornelius-story (11:3). Jerusalem is still a focal point.

849   In the Antioch story, grace occurs four times (Acts 11:23; 13:43; 14:3, 26).

850   Reminiscent of Gabriel's annunciation to Mary, "Rejoice, oh favored one" (χαῖρε, κεχαριτωμένην Luke 1:28).

851   Luke 1:30; 2:40, 52; 4:22; Acts 2:47; 4:33; 7:46.

852   BDAG, 878.

853   See Joseph of Arimathea (Luke 23:50); Stephen (Acts 6:5, 8, 55).

854   Same infinitive in Acts 13:43, "to remain in the grace of God" (προσμένειν τῇ χάριτι τοῦ θεοῦ); "to remain in the faith" (ἐμμένειν τῇ πίστει 14:22), in encouraging contexts.

855   The expression designates purpose of heart or determination.

856   Haenchen, 367.

857   Keener, Vol. 2, 1846.

858   About 3000 on the Day of Pentecost (Acts 2:41), 50000 (4:4), number multiplied exceedingly (6:6); daily growing in number (16:5).

859   No doubt the divine passive, i.e. "God added." Other similar uses in Acts 2:41, 47; 5:14.

860   This is the first mention of the "church" outside of the Jerusalem community.

861   Haenchen dismisses the historicity of this extended stay. 367.

862   Prophets will be mentioned in Acts 13:1 as well as in the context of the Jerusalem Council (15:32).

863   Luke does not explain why the prophets came from Jerusalem.

864   The Western text also suggests the beginning of the "We-passages," "when *we* were gathered together."

865   The verb, "I indicate beforehand, foretell" (σημαίνω Acts 11:28) is used here to indicate "what is to happen." BDAG, 747. Agabus will later surface in Acts 21:10 in a prophetic role. Once again, Pervo, 296 discounts the story as something that Luke created.

866   The expression, "over all the inhabited earth" (ἐφ' ὅλην τὴν οἰκουμένην Acts 11:28) is no doubt hyperbolic as in Luke 2:1 with the census taken. Scholars vary in terms of Luke's hyperbolic statement of the extent of the famine.

867 Haenchen, 375, states, "The primary intention of the note 'which came about under Claudius' is not to fix a historical date but to establish the fulfilment of the prophecy."

868 Luke does not indicate how the prophecy specifically led to the contribution for the mother church in Jerusalem.

869 The first time where the term, "elders" emerges; they will surface in the Jerusalem Council (Acts 15:2-6, 22-23; 16:4).

870 See Acts 2:45; 4:32-37 in connection with Barnabas. Opinions vary as to the relationship with Gal 1-2 and the collection for the poor in Jerusalem.

871 For a description of prophets and prophecy in connection with Acts 13:1-3, see David Aune, *Prophecy in Early Christianity* (Grand Rapids: William B. Eerdmans Publishing Company, 1983), 190-192

872 The only reference in Acts to "teachers."

873 Barrett notes that Luke was "familiar with both prophets and elders and took them for granted." 559.

874 A diverse organization of leaders: twelve apostles; seven deacons (Acts 6:1-6); James and the elders (11:30; 12:17). Luke's readers already know of Paul's prior appointment as "a vessel of choice to carry my name before the Gentiles and their kings and before the people of Israel."

875 Dunn, *The Acts of the Apostles*, 172.

876 The verb, "I serve" (λειτουργέω), was a secular term, i.e. in public service, was also used in the LXX for the service of the priests, and came to denote "the various ways in which the religious man serves God." BDAG, 470.

877 E. Lohse, "χείρ," *TDNT*, Vol. IX, 433.

878 Ernest Best, "ACTS XIII. 1-3," *JTS*, 11 (1960), 345-346. He argues that the rite of laying on of hands in Acts 13:3 is based upon the Levites' custom (Numb 8:10), which included the idea of "separation" (ἀφοριεῖ Numb 8:11) and "work" ("with the result that they shall work the works of the Lord" ὥστε ἐργάζεσθαι τὰ ἔργα Κυρίου Num 8:12).

879 Best, 348.

880 BDAG, 178.

881 Aune, 265-266.

882 Two other references to a divine work taken from Habakkuk 1:5 in Paul's sermon.

883 BDAG, 715.

884 Johnson, *The Acts of the Apostles*, 226.

885 Keener, Vol. 2, 1982.

886 The expression "was with" (ἦν σὺν) indicates that "he was in the service of" the senator. See Graham Twelftree, "Jesus and Magic in Luke-Acts," *Jesus and Paul*, (ed. B. J. Oropeza, C. K. Robertson, Douglas C. Mohrmann; New York: T & T Clark, 2009), 50. Twelftree also notes examples of prophets, diviners, including Jews who serve in an advisory role for political leaders.

889 Perhaps Luke intends a certain ἀπολογία for the Jesus-movement that it is not opposed to Rome.

890 Theories abound as to the double name for the Jewish magician that include numerous etymologies. Perhaps Elymas is a nickname. It is assumed that they identify the same person.

891 Of fourteen occurrences of the verb, "I stare" (ἀτενίζω) in the New Testament, twelve references occur in Luke-Acts. For a more lengthy approach to "prophetic insight" in the book of Luke, see Lyle Story, "If This Man Were a Prophet, He Would Have Known . . . ," *Journal of Biblical and Pneumatological Research*, Volume Five (Fall, 2013), 68-93

892 The verb, "I seek/wish" (ἐπιζητέω) is followed by an infinitive of purpose, "to hear" (ἀκοῦσαι 13:7).

893 Luke frequently notes the incursion of the Holy Spirit in human affairs (Acts 4:31; 8:29, 39; 10:44; 16:6).

894 Garrett argues for a link between Paul's curse and the curse formula in Deut 28:28-29, i.e. that the Lord shall strike those who forsake him (v. 20), so that they shall grope at noonday, as the blind grope in darkness. She also draws attention to the light and darkness imagery in IQS 2:11-19 in the context of idolatry.

895 See Keener, Vol. 2, 2009 for a helpful chart.

896 Johnson, *The Acts of the Apostles*, 224.

897 Johnson, *The Acts of the Apostles*, 225.

898 Contra Pervo, who states that the senators' conversion "is just stated as though it were that of a washer-women," 327. Garrett, along with Pervo, states that the narrative of the senator "functions primarily as a foil for the confrontation between Paul and Bar Jesus." 80.

899 Haenchen summarizes some synagogue practices, 407-408.

900 Johnson, *The Acts of the Apostles*, 237, draws parallels between Jesus and Paul as they begin their ministry.

901 While Pervo argues that all of the speeches are "unhistorical," 334, he does affirm that the several speeches, "demonstrate the unity of the Christian message and messengers." 334.

902 Acts 13:17, 18, 19, 20, 21, 22.

903 See 2 Sam 7:12—instead of a monarch who arises, fulfillment comes with Jesus as "Savior" (σωτήρ).

904 A similar pattern to Peter's preaching in Acts 2:14-36.

905 Acts 13:23-41.

906 Tannehill, Vol. Two, 173.

907 In Isa 49:1, the Servant is Israel; in Isa 49:5-6,the Servant has a mission to Israel.

908 Johnson, *The Acts of the Apostles*, 244.

909 Johnson, *The Acts of the Apostles*, 242-243.

910 The expression, βλασφημοῦντες, can mean abuse or "blasphemy against Christ."

911 It was customary for Jews, re-entering Israel, to "shake off the [Gentile] dust from their feet," symbolic of present purity (see Luke 9:5; 10:11; Acts 18:6; 22:22f.).

912 See Acts 13:48 for the two imperfect tenses.

913   Acts 2:4; 4:8, 31; 6:5; 7:55; 9:17; 11:24; 13:9, 52.

914   Literally, "they made evil the souls of the Gentiles against the brothers."

915   See Acts 5:13 for the same expression.

916   A periphrastic construction in the imperfect tense, denoting continual activity.

917   Haenchen, 423.

918   The story also is similar with Jesus' healing of the paralytic in Acts 5:17-26.

919   Haenchen, 425. He also alludes to Ezek 2:1, "he sprang up and was walking" (ἥλατο καὶ περιεπάτει).

920   There is mention of "faith in his name" (ἐπὶ τῇ πίστει τοῦ ὀνόματος Acts 3:16) that has made this man whole, although the subject of faith is unclear as to whether it was the faith of Peter and John or the crippled beggar

921   Dunn, *The Acts of the Apostles*, 190, argues for an allusion to a story about Zeus and Hermes, Ovid, *Metamorphoses* 8.620-724.

922   Marshall, 237.

923   Johnson, *The Acts of the Apostles*, 249.

924   Acts 3:19; 9:35; 11:21; 15:19; 26:18, 20.

925   A similar use in 1 Thes 1:9 in a similar context.

926   The mini-sermon is similar to Paul's Aeropagus address (Acts 17:16-34).

927   Keener, Vol. 2, 2171.

928   Paul mentions stoning in II Cor. 11:25, which links with Paul's call, "how much he must suffer" (Acts 9:16).

929   Pervo, 360.

930   Alludes to the use of the verb, εὐαγγελίζομαι in Acts 14:7.

931   The use of the infinitive, "to remain" (ἐμμένειν) parallels the use in 11:23, "to remain" (προσμένειν) in the Lord; Acts 13:43, "to remain" (προσμένειν) in the grace of God.

932   The term "elders" may simply mean "Christian leaders" and not the "elders" in the Pastoral Epistles.

933   Certainly a Pauline expression (1 Cor 16:9; 2 Cor 2:12; Col 4:3).

934   BDAG 586.

935   In a previous narrative, Antioch served as inclusion (Acts 11:19-14:28).

936   See Keener, Vol. 4, 2408-2402 for the motifs of patrons, clients, reciprocity, and hospitality.

937   BDAG, 728.

938   Keener, Vol. 4, 2442.

939   The imperfect tense, "she was crying out" (ἔκραζεν), coupled with the present participle, "saying" (λέγουσα Acts 16:17), and the temporal note, "for many days" (Acts 16:18), emphasizes the continual harassment.

940   The term, ὕψιστος, is equivalent with *el elyon*, the divine designation (Gen 14:18, Num 24:16; Isa 14:14; Dan 3:26).

941   Bruce, 312-313.

942   See Acts 19:12, 15.

943   Dunn, *The Acts of the Apostles*, 221.

944   Paul alludes to this in 2 Cor 11:25 and 1 Thess 2:2, "having suffered and been abused, just as you know, in Philippi." See Keener, vol. 4, 2477-2488 for extensive discussion of the abuse and imprisonment.

945   Pervo, 406.

946   *To the Martyrs*, 2.

947   In Acts 4:31, an earthquake follows worship, prayer, suffering, and joy (5:41).

948   Pervo, 411.

949   See Keener, vol. 4, 2497-2507 for an excursus on suicide.

950   A similar question on the Day of Pentecost (Acts 2:37).

951   Pervo, 412.

952   Tannehill parallels this story and the events in Acts 2-5 in terms of "type-scenes." Tannehill, Vol. Two, 200-203.

953   John Chrysostom, *Homilies on Acts 36:2.*

954   Keener, vol. 4, 2513.

955   Elsewhere, Luke uses the verb to indicate joyous and religious responses to divine visitation (Luke 1:47; 10:21; Acts 2:26—in a Scripture quotation).

956   The book of Philippians is often characterized as Paul's epistle of joy, due to the frequency of the joy-vocabulary.

957   Lampe notes that Paul's coming to Ephesus highlights "another decisive movement in the missionary history." 365.

958   Pervo, 482, draws a parallel with Luke 9:51, "Jesus set his face like a flint to go to Jerusalem," i.e. "the city of his destiny."

959   Pervo's apt paraphrase, 474.

960   The term "kingdom of God" is also used at the beginning and ending of Acts (Acts 1:3; 28:31).

961   E.g. noted by Pervo as the winning over of sects or incorporation of fringe groups into the mainstream church, 467. Similarly Haenchen, 557, summarizes the Ephesian ministry, "Paul wins over the sects."

962   Barrett raises a number of questions that lead to "yes" or "no" answers as to the status of Apollos and the Ephesian twelve, coupled with "why" questions in trying to harmonize the accounts of Apollos and the Ephesian twelve—which may well not be on Luke's mind. C. K. Barrett, "Apollos and the Twelve Disciples of Ephesus," *The New Testament Age*, Vol. I (ed. William C. Weinrich; Macon GA: Mercer University Press, 1984), 30 (29-39).

963   Luke's frequent term to describe the Christians, the community, their manner of life, and the Christian message (Acts 9:2). The term "way" (ὁδός) is used three times in the Ephesian narrative (Acts 18:25; 26; 19:9).

964   The term, "Lord" (κύριος) in this context suggests the risen Lord Jesus.

965   The expression intimates the later explicit statement, in Acts 18:28—the power to prove that Jesus is the Messiah.

966   C. K. Barrett, "Apollos and the Twelve Disciples of Ephesus," 30.

967   Suggested rendering of προσλαμβάνω in BDAG, 717.

968   Bruce, *The Book of Acts*, 360.

969   Haenchen, 551.

970   Keener, Vol. 3, 2806.

971   Haenchen, 358.

972   See the many references to Apollos in 1 Cor 1:12; 3:4-11, 22; 4:6; 16:12.

973   This is counter to Ernst Käsemann's thesis that Paul is the most important figure so that Luke "could not allow him [Apollos] to appear as an authorized teacher of the Church until he had in some way incorporated him into the apostolic fellowship." Ernst Käsemann, *Essays on New Testament Themes* (transl. W. J. Montague; Philadelphia: Fortress Press, 1964), 167. Käsemann's common term for this thrust is expressed as *Una sancta apostolica*, or *Fr*ükatholizismus. From 1 Cor 3:6, we learn that Apollos stands on equal footing with Paul, but not as a subordinate to Paul, "I planted and Apollos watered ..." *Contra* Pervo, 461.

974   The aorist participle, πιστεύσαντες, can mean either, "when you believed" or "after you believed."

975   *Contra* Twelftree, *People of the Spirit*, 93-94—who states that "they were not true disciples or Christians," based upon the indefinite pronoun, "some/certain ones." Marshall, 306, inserts the clause, "*appeared to him* to be disciples."

976   *Contra* Käsemann, who believes that the Ephesian twelve were the Baptist's disciples. 148. Marshall makes the same link, 306.

977   *Contra* Dunn, *Baptism in the Holy Spirit,* , who argues, "The twelve Ephesians are therefore further examples of men who were not far short of Christianity, but were not yet Christians because they lacked the vital factor—the Holy Spirit."

978   Haya-Prats, 190.

979   Luke uses similar language in the prologue to his gospel: "accurately" (ἀκριβῶς) and "the things *you have been taught*" (κατηχήθης Luke 1:3-4), used in the Apollos story. Just as Theophilos needs the "certainty" (ἀσφάλεια), so Apollos needs the way of God, "more accurately" (ἀκριβέστερον) deposited in him.

980   Pervo, 468.

981   Similarly, Tannehill, Vol. 2, 233, suggests, "they have not heard that there is a new outpouring of the Spirit through Jesus."

982   Keener, Vol. 3, 2817.

983   Keener, Vol. 3, 2819.

984   *Contra* Pervo, 469. This does not suggest that the expression means an acknowledgment of the Baptist as a savior.

985   At the same time, in Peter's speech to Cornelius and his household, John the Baptist and his baptism are regarded as the beginning of the good news (Acts 10:37). This does not mean that Luke is interested in an anti-Baptist polemic that has been advocated by several scholars, who also find an anti-Baptist polemic in the fourth gospel.

986   See Luke 3:16 for the emphasis upon baptism in the Spirit.

987   The term, baptism "into the name of the Lord Jesus" is used of the Samaritan believers in Acts 8:16.

988   The imperfect tenses, "they were speaking" and "they were prophesying" suggest continuous activity.

989   There is no clearly defined sequence of events between baptism and the gift of the Spirit, e.g. with Cornelius, the gift of the Spirit occurs before baptism (Acts 10:47).

990   Johnson, *The Acts of the Apostles*, 338.

991   See earlier comments on Acts 1:12-26 with the need to replace Judas with a twelfth apostle—pointing to a Spirit-filled and reconstituted Israel.

992   The use of the negative, "not" (οὐ) with the participle, "common, ordinary" (τουχούσας) is emphatic and emphasizes the extraordinary nature of these miracles.

993   Similar to the woman with the hemorrhage (Luke 8:44). After extended discussion, Haenchen summarily rejects the historicity of these events, in his assumption that Paul can only glory in weakness. Haenchen, 563. Other scholars such as Ben Witherington III, argue that it is the "faith" of the afflicted persons that is the means of healing. Ben Witherington III, *History, Literature and Society in the Book of Acts* (Cambridge: Cambridge University Press, 1996), 578.

994   Johnson, *The Acts of the Apostles*, 340.

995   Keener, vol. 3, 2839.

996   Later in the narrative, the demon overpowers "both" (ἀμφοτέρων Acts 19:16), suggesting only two. Perhaps the term "both" refers to only two of the seven brothers or the term "both" is used in the broad Greek usage, "all."

997   It is beyond this study to probe the label, "a certain Sceva, a high priest." See Pervo, 476-477 for a full discussion. Using Josephus, B. A. Mastin argues that Sceva does not necessarily mean the Jewish high priest. B. A. Mastin, "Scaeva the Chief Priest," *Journal of Theological Studies*, 27 (2), (1976), 405-412.

998   Garrett fittingly comments, "the brothers, like the Samaritan magician, mistook the Christian wonders for feats of magic." 92.

999   The verb, "I know" (γινώσκω) and "I understand" (ἐπίσταμαι) here mean the same thing. See Acts 2:36; 9:24; 10:28; 15:7.

1000 This event is prefigured in Jesus' earlier statement about the divided-kingdom principle (Luke 11:14-23).

1001 Garrett, 93. In his gospel, Luke has already noted how demons "know" the person of Jesus (Luke 4:34, 41; 8:28).

1002 Garrett also appeals to Luke 11:21-22, with respect to the verbs, "I overpower" (κατακυριεύω), "I am mighty" (ἰσχύω), the substantive, "the strong one" (ὁ ἰσχυρος), 93. In addition, the expression, "the one who is stronger" (ὁ ἰσχυρότερος) is important. Since Jesus is the one who is stronger than the strong man and overpowers him, he is thus able to plunder the strong man's spoils (τὰ σκύλα), i.e. the persons who have been possessed by demons.

1003 Twelftree, "Jesus and Magic in Luke-Acts," 53.

1004 See Pervo, 475-476 for an extended discussion on the comical nature of the story.

1005 Garrett, 94.

1006 Pervo, 476. See also Luke 4:34-37.

1007 See a similar remark by Paul's adversary, Demetrius who claims that Paul's influence has spread in "nearly all of Asia" (Acts 19:26).

1008 Arguments related to when the Christians believed and when they renounced magic are beside Luke's point.

1009 The term, "practices" (πράξεις) is made more specific in the following clause, "of those who practiced sorcery" (τῶν τὰ περίεργα πραξάντων).

1010 Since magical power was bound up with *secrecy* of these books, the *public* divulgence, in addition to their burning renders these books impotent. Pervo, 481, also suggests that "Consignment to flames is a means of purification."

1011 The verb, συμψηφίζω means "I count up, compute the price."

1012 Garrett, 97. Similarly with Pervo, 465, "epiphanies of divine power demonstrating the defeat of rival forces."

1013 Luke's hyperbolic language, "all the Jews and Greeks," accentuates the extensive effect of charismatic power.

1014 Robert C. Tannehill, *The Shape of Luke's Story: Essays on Luke-Acts* (Eugene OR: Cascade Books, 2005), 88-89. Tannehill devotes an entire chapter to "Repentance in the Context of Lukan Soteriology," 84-101.

1015 Robert C. Tannehill, *The Shape of Luke's Story*, 94. See references in Luke 5:29-35; 15:1-32; 19:6; Acts 8:8, 39; 13:48, 52.

1016 Studies that deal with the book's ending, interaction with Roman Christians, and Paul's positive hope for Israel (Rom 9-11) lie outside the purview of this analysis. Others have pursued these questions: Barrett, *Acts*, Vol. II, 1235-1237; J. T. Sanders, *The Jews in Luke-Acts* (Philadelphia: Fortress Press, 1987); D. Slingerland, "The Jews in the Pauline Portion of Acts," *JAAR* 54, (1986), 305-321; Pervo, 685; Bruce, *The Book of Acts*, 508-509; Johnson, *Acts of the Apostles*, 475-476; Tannehill, *Narrative Unity*, vol. II, 349-350; Dunn, *The Acts of the Apostles*, 355-356. Luke portrays Paul speaking to Roman Jews—not to all Jews. The Jewish rejection in Rome reflects a pattern of Jewish rejection in Jesus' day (Gospel of Luke) and the early Christian leaders and their communities (Acts)—but this does not signify universal Jewish rejection.

1017 The word family, "hear/listen" (ἀκούω) is critical in Acts 28: the Roman Jewish leaders say, "We would like to listen (ἀκοῦσαι) what your views are" (28:22); Paul's quote from Isa 6 contains four uses: "with hearing (ἀκοῇ) you will hear and not understand,"; "they heard (ἤκουσαν) with heavy/slow ears"; "lest . . . they should hear (ἀκούσωσιν) with their ears" (28:26-27), and the negative hearing of the Jews contrasts with the Gentile's hearing, "they, themselves [the Gentiles] will hear" (ἀκούσονται 28:28).

1018 The citation from Isa. 6:9-10 corresponds with Paul's earlier citation (Isa. 49:6; Acts 13:47).

1019 "the Holy Spirit spoke through David's mouth" in Acts 1:16; "who spoke, by the Holy Spirit through David's mouth" in 4:25.

1020 Acts 8:12; 14:22; 19:8; 20:25.

1021   Conzelmann, *Acts of the Apostles*, 227.

1022   Johnson, *The Acts of the Apostles*, 474.

1023   The metaphor of "healing" is used elsewhere by the prophets for a restored relationship with God: "whenever I would *heal* Israel" (Hos. 7:1); "it was I who *healed* them [Israel]" (Hos 11:3); "*I will heal* you of your backsliding" (Jer 3:22); "he [God] will respond to their pleas and *heal* them" (Isa 19:22).

1024   Luke 5:17; 6:18-19; esp. 9:2, 6; 10:9; Acts 9:34; 10:38.

1025   The clause is unique to Luke.

1026   Acts 4:29-31.

1027   Haenchen, 730.

1028   Haenchen, 730.

1029   Acts 27:22, 25, 36.

1030   Pervo, 688.

1031   These Jews diverge from the Jews "who were disbelieving and in sharp disagreement" (Acts 28:24-25).

1032   Johnson, *The Acts of the Apostles*, 476.

CHAPTER 8

JOYOUS LIFE-TOGETHER

Unless one can understand this constant mood
of victorious, jubilant happiness, he simply will
not understand primitive Christianity.
–JOHANNES WEISS

Luke provides select narrative-summaries of joyous life-together in his Acts account. These summaries tend to be descriptive in nature, yet Luke also elicits and cultivates the kind of Spirit-filled communities that are joy-filled, attractive, and winsome to outsiders. Martin Dibelius has argued that Luke provides summaries to fill the mosaic of individual and popular stories. "Anyone combining such elements into a whole, as Luke did, was forming a mosaic and had to fill in any gaps which were left between the stones of the mosaic."[1033] For Luke, these summaries serve as a "lived-theology"—this is the joyous way life is meant to be lived in community. Keener suggests, "… these summaries invite Luke's audience to participate in the mission."[1034] Another important piece surfaces as communities seek to discern God's will and make practical decisions in a changing landscape (Acts 15). Luke encases these discussions, decisions, and implementation in contexts of great joy.

1) First Narrative Summary (Acts 2:42-47). Luke includes key elements characterizing affective experiences, atmosphere and expressions of the nascent community:

- Apostles' teaching, community's fellowship, breaking of bread, prayers (2:42).
- Wonders and signs, religious awe, unity, sharing of possessions (2:43-45).
- Attendance at the Temple, sharing food, an atmosphere of joy and praise, positive favor with the people, and effective witness (2:46-47).

Luke repeats the verb, "I hold fast to something, continue or persevere in something" (προσκαρτερέω), used for the persistent devotion of believers to several activities (2:42) and to daily attendance at the Temple (2:46). Earlier, Luke used the same verb for persistent and joyful devotion to prayer as the early community happily awaits the promised Holy Spirit (1:14). Similarly, Luke's important adverb, "of one accord" (ὁμοθυμαδόν) in 2:46, emerges in the context of concerted prayer (1:14). For Luke, the narrative-summary connects the new community to the Temple (2:46; 5:12, 42). As Conzelmann notes, "In its attitude to the Temple, we see the community taking over its inheritance of redemptive history."[1035] Indeed, the next story of the crippled beggar likewise takes place outside the Temple, where Peter and John are going to pray at the prescribed hour (3:1).

Those who had been baptized in the Spirit "entered the *koinonia*, the fellowship, established by common participation in Christ and in his heavenly gift."[1036] From the very outset, "all were filled with the Holy Spirit" (Acts 2:4), and now they are knit together. Clearly this harmony of shared possessions, shared food, and general unity grows from the freeing work of the Holy Spirit enabling Christians to "let go" of possessions. Luke intimates that the coming of the Holy Spirit on the day of Pentecost naturally flows into the story of the community's life together. A joy-filled community freely shares with others in need.

Luke establishes that the community was also marked by miracles, "many wonders and signs were occurring[1037] through the apostles" (πόλλα τε τέρατα καὶ σημεῖα διὰ τῶν ἀποστόλων ἐγίνετο Acts 2:43), and thereby he describes an atmosphere of religious awe felt by every person (πάσῃ ψυχῇ φόβος 2:43).

Luke emphasizes the joyous nature of life-together with four different expressions:

> "sharing food *with exultant joy* and *simplicity of heart*"
> (μετελάμβανεν τροφῆς ἐν ἀγαλλιάσει καὶ ἀφελότητι
> καρδίας 2:46),
> "*praising God*" (αἰνοῦντες τὸν θεὸν 2:47)
> "*experiencing favor* with all the people" (ἔχοντες χάριν πρὸς
> ὅλον τὸν λαόν 2:47).

Luke expresses these affirmations using nine imperfect verbs and six present participles. Grammatically, this demonstrates that the actions are not simply descriptors of a particular day. Rather, they represent on-going customary activity. The declarations are both horizontal (sharing food and experiencing favor) and vertical (praising God).Haya-Prats notes, "Rejoicing appears to overflow from the first moment in which the presence of the messianic gifts are perceived."[1038]

The same joy of Acts 1-2 is now expressed in shared meals in Acts 2:42-47. The author includes three specific references to eating together:

> "in the breaking of bread" (τῇ κλάσει τοῦ ἄρτου 2:42),
> "breaking of bread from house to house" (κλῶντές τε κατ'
> οἶκον ἄρτον 2:46)
> "sharing food" (μετελάμβανεν τροφῆς 2:46).[1039]

Luke sets the atmosphere for eating bread together, "with exultant joy[1040] and simplicity of heart." This does not imply that Luke was countering suspicion about their communal meals.[1041] While it is possible to envision the sharing in the Lord's Supper, the text is not explicit. Readers only need to recall the numerous instances in Luke's gospel where joy is inherent in eating-episodes, e.g. various banquets and the context and trilogy of parables in Luke 15.

In addition, Luke affirms the positive witness, "experiencing[1042] favor with all the people." The quality of their life-together creates a positive impression. Esteem is the by-product of the believing community's harmony, unity and joy. Emotional joy and praise rise naturally from the experience of receiving grace. Acts describes a group of people continually voicing exultant praise in both the Temple and individual homes.

The positive witness of the community draws enlarged numbers, "as the Lord was daily adding believers[1043]" (Acts 2:47) to the three thousand new believers. The joy and praise, experienced and expressed on Easter (Lk 24:50-53), now become more expansive in light of the Pentecost-event. "Through this depiction, Luke not only foreshadowed the glorious future but also depicted the formation of Christian community as an eschatological event, a miracle."[1044] Thus, Luke intimates that the combination of joy, miracles, and vibrancy of the community's life-together elicits additional believers. This joyful community experiences "favor" (χάριν) and attracts outsiders. Keener notes an evangelism through lifestyle.[1045] Luke makes the case that the community's joyous life-together and winsome witness originates in the Holy Spirit as its dynamic force.

2) Second Narrative Summary (Acts 4:32-37). Luke's second summary parallels the narrative-summary of Acts 2:41-47. As in the first narrative summary, miraculous power also is evident in Acts 4:

> Prayer for *speaking the word with boldness* (μετὰ παρρησίας πάσης λαλεῖν τὸν λόγον σου 4:29).
>
> Prayer for *healings, signs, and wonders* (ἴασιν καὶ σημεῖα καὶ τέρατα 4:30).
>
> Answered prayer for wonders with the *physical shaking of the place where they are gathered* (ἐσαλεύθη ὁ τόπος ἐν ᾧ ἦσαν συνηγμένοι 4:31).
>
> Answered prayer for *speaking the word with boldness* (ἐπλήσθησαν ἅπαντες τοῦ ἁγίου πνεύματος καὶ ἐλάλουν τὸν λόγον τοῦ θεοῦ μετὰ παρρησίας 4:31).
>
> A *great* and *powerful* witness to the *resurrection* (καὶ δυνάμει μεγάλη ἀπεδίδουν τὸ μαρτύριον οἱ ἀπόστολοι τῆς ἀναστάσεως τοῦ κυρίου Ἰησοῦ 4:33).

Luke emphasizes the presence and power of the Holy Spirit, who not only effects miracles but creates a joyful community, which is knit together ("one heart and one soul" ἦν καρδία καὶ ψυχὴ μία 4:32), and in which participants freely share possessions (4:34-37). Luke pairs the expression "with great power" (δυνάμει μεγάλη 4:33) with "great grace" (χάρις μεγάλη 4:33). Here, "great grace" seems to emphasize great *divine* favor, while in 2:47 the community enjoy "favor" with all the *people*. Thus, grace and joy are partnered, and miracles are linked with both grace and experienced joy.

Due to the similarity of both narrative-summaries (2:41-47; 4: 32-37), we can also conclude that the joyous praise in 2:46-47 spills over into the narrative-summary of 4:32-37, since both passages highlight the sharing of possessions. Why should 21ˢᵗ Century interpreters expect Luke to be exhaustive in his narrative-summaries? In the second narrative-summary, Luke devotes more space to the sharing of possessions and land (4:34-37), for he describes the hypocrisy of Ananias and Sapphira (5:1-11) and the fearful consequence in their instant deaths. The ideal in 4:32-37 is shattered by its antithesis in 5:1-11.

3) Third Narrative Summary (Acts 5:12-16). Luke emphasizes the charismatic dimension, from the beginning of the paragraph to the end (5:12—"Through the hands of the apostles, many signs and wonders were occurring among the people"; 5:16 "All were being healed"). Luke connects this summary with the first two by mentioning miracles ("with great power the apostles were bearing witness of the resurrection" 4:33). Clearly he describes a supernatural community.[1046] The earlier prayer of the community for "healings, signs and wonders" (Acts 4:30) is initially fulfilled in 4:33, "and with great power the disciples were bearing witness ... ," and later fulfilled in 5:12-16 as a divine response to their concerted prayers. While the second summary follows religious hostility (4:1ff), the third summary incites more aggressive behavior by the religious authorities (5:17ff. "beating" in 5: 40), and the powerful statement about the apostles' "rejoicing" (χαίροντες), because they were considered worthy to be shamed for the name (of Jesus).

Peter's miraculous activity in Acts 3 now broadens to include the apostles as miracle-workers (5:12), although Peter and his shadow are highlighted as a means of healing (5:15). Luke contrasts the believing community's joy with the hostility of joy-less religious leaders (4:1ff.; 5:17). Yet, despite threats and gag-orders by the authorities, the number of believers continues to grow as more believers *are added*[1047] (προσετίθεντο 5:14). Jesus is the head of a burgeoning movement.

From the grammatical standpoint, the text includes seven imperfect verbs,[1048] four present participles[1049] and three present infinitives.[1050] Taken together the paragraph narrates the continual miraculous activity of the community, rather than a singular event. The only aorist verb occurs in describing the supernatural effect of Peter's shadow ("in order that his shadow *might hover* (ἐπισκιάσῃ) over certain individuals" in 5:15), with the implication that sick/possessed persons were immediately healed at the moment when Peter's shadow shaded them.[1051] Barrett states, "It must be recognized that Luke believed (see explicitly v. 12) that supernatural powers accompanied the great apostles ... this power was separable from the apostles who did not possess it in their own right ...."[1052]

The divine shadow signals God's presence and power (see Psa 91:1; 139:12) and may allude to the Hebrew *Shekinah*. P. W. Van Der Horst argues from anthropology that "the shadow plays an important role. It is conceived as the soul of a person, or at least as a very vital part of himself."[1053] From 5:16, Luke believed that such incidents could occur. In this instance, "Luke uses this concept of shadow in order to extol Peter's healing power."[1054] Pervot aptly summarizes the thrust, "No more astounding piece of miracle-working is described in the NT; Peter does not need to speak, to touch, or, it seems to give any attention to the sick person. In the background is the notion that the shadow is an extension of one's person or personality."[1055]

In terms of biographical elements, Luke begins with a broad and public narrative of charismatic power, "among the people" (5:12), followed by statements about the nature of the people and crowds. The term "people" (λαός) is found twice (5:12-13) and is later replaced by two occurrences of the term, "crowd" (πλῆθος 5:14, 16). The first "crowd" of believing men and women arises from within Jerusalem (5:14), while the second "crowd" comes from villages surrounding Jerusalem (5:16).[1056] The contagious report of miracle activity draws them to Jerusalem. Thus, the healing mission expands from the confines of Jerusalem, i.e., "in Jerusalem and all Judea" (1:8). Luke mentions signs and wonders (5:12) at the beginning of this miracle-paragraph, clearly revealing his high estimation of them.[1057]

Luke carefully notes the extensive responses of both groups as they witness and participate in widespread healings and exorcisms. The signs

and wonders draw all the people "in one accord" (ὁμοθυμαδόν Acts
5:12)[1058] to Solomon's porch. Barrett notes, "The supernatural power at work
in the community was manifested not only in the gathering of believers
but in miraculous cures."[1059] In this paragraph, only one questionable
response emerges from "the others who did not dare to join them" (τῶν
δὲ λοιπῶν οὐδεὶς ἐτόλμα κολᾶσθαι αὐτῶν 5:13). Who are "the others"
(οἱ λοιποί)? While Pervo makes the comment, "In short, exegetes must
attempt to say what they think Luke meant." He follows Haenchen in
his suggestion that these are non-believers who "kept their distance—
not ... out of enmity ... but in reverent awe."[1060] Perhaps the numinous
aspect of the Ananias-Sapphira story, with instantaneous deaths (5:1-11)
and subsequent fear,[1061] combined with the many signs and wonders (5:12),
led some to feel religious dread. This small group is contrasted[1062] with
the people's exaltation of the apostles (5:13). Johnson aptly suggests, "The
apostles appear as numinous figures and like the *mysterim tremendum et
fascinosum*, they both repel and attract."[1063] Thus, an aura or atmosphere
of holy awe radiates from the leading figures of the new community,
especially Peter.

Luke highlights the numerical growth of new believers, "And so grew
the great number of those believing in the Lord, multitudes of men and
women" (5:14). Luke then notes the result of such large numbers of
people, "so that they actually" (ὥστε καὶ)[1064] brought the sick into the
streets on cots and pallets, hoping that when Peter passed by, even his
shadow might fall on any of them" (5:15)—with the implied wholeness
of their restoration.The numerical growth expands to surrounding towns,
drawing a crowd which again "carries the sick" (φέροντες ἀσθενεῖς)
and those "tormented by evil spirits" (ὀχλουμένους ὑπὸ πνευμάτων
ἀκαθάρτων 5:16). Luke highlights an encompassing statement, "And all
were healed" (οἵτινες ἐθεραπεύοντο ἅπαντες 5:16)—both the sick and
those tormented by evil spirits. Just as the Holy Spirit was victorious over
Satan's inspired lie (5:3, 9), so the Spirit is active in exorcisms. Similarly,
just as the healing of the crippled beggar evoked religious hostility (4:1ff.),
so the massive healings of 5:12-16 provoke outrage/envy from religious
authorities, "they were filled with envy" (ἐπλήσθησαν ζήλου 5:17). The
people respond with joyous praise, "the people glorified them [the apostles]"
(ἐμεγάλυνεν αὐτοὺς ὁ λαός 5:13). The verb, "glorify" (μεγαλύνω) is

translated, "exalt, praise, extol,"[1065] and is aptly translated by Haenchen, "to sing their praises."[1066] Luke regards the various healings as signs of God's in-breaking love that brings wholeness of life, including trust and affective responses of joy.[1067]

Joyous contagion surfaces in the people's response, as they make every effort to bring sick friends or relatives on pallets in a rapid-fire manner, to the extent that more and more people come needing healing and deliverance. Luke intends that his readers visualize the implicit atmosphere of joyous contagion, expectation and fulfillment as friends and relatives are healed and exorcised. How could joy not be a vital part of peoples' experiences and expressions of joy and praise? Luke concludes this miracle-filled and joy-filled narrative summary with the words, "and all were healed" (Acts 5:16). As Barrett notes, this reference "could not end more impressively."[1068]

Thus, this narrative-summary serves as an interlude that:

- Highlights the numerical and spontaneous growth of the community.
- Emphasizes the supernatural power to heal "all," including those tormented by unclean spirits.
- Reiterates the unity of the community.
- Highlights the joyous response of the masses.
- Prepares the reader for the more formal persecution of the apostles by the joy-less critics.

4) Fourth Narrative Summary (Acts 5:41-42). Luke introduces his fourth summary, "And they [the apostles] were going forth from the Sanhedrin, *rejoicing (χαίροντες)* because they had been considered worthy to suffer abuse for the sake of the name" (5:40). The context sheds light on the mini-narrative-summary. The miraculous signs/wonders/healings by all the apostles (highlighted in 5:12-16) attract a jealous response from religious authorities ("they turned green with envy"[1069] 5:17). These envious leaders seize and imprison the apostles in a public jail (5:18).[1070] Through angelic deliverance, the apostles once again stand teaching in the Temple, and they are returned to the authorities. After their angelic deliverance, they are not "seized" but "led" to the council with a "minimum of force"[1071] (οὐ μετὰ βίας 5:26). The explanation for minimal force is fear of the people, with a possible stoning in view (5:26).[1072]

The whipping and abuse of the apostles parallels the punishment Pilate meted out to Jesus, "I [Pilate] will have him punished and then I will release (ἀπολύσω) him" (Luke 23:22b). As the apostles are drawn into the Jesus-kerygma, they experience joy in identifying with Jesus' suffering. Their abuse is for Jesus' "name," which embodies Jesus' person, words and works, and the good news that "Jesus" is the promised "Messiah" (Acts 5:42b).

Luke highlights an oxymoron, linking shameful abuse with honor, or suggesting that public shame actually is a source of rightful pride ("they were considered worthy ... of suffering disgrace" (κατηξιώθησαν . . . ἀτιμασθῆναι Acts 5:41b). Luke's paradoxical inversion of values, shame = honor, is fundamental to his gospel (e.g. Luke 6:22-23; 14:11; 18:9-14). Marshall notes, "Not only did the punishment not deter the Christians. It also filled them with joy."[1073] This is what Thompson labels as a "joy notwithstanding."[1074] Luke explains why the apostles were filled with joyous affection: ("because" ὅτι) they suffered abuse for the name. Sorrow, hurt, and avoidance are normal human responses to suffering. Instead, the apostles respond with joyous enthusiasm. How is this joyful response related to the numinous? What clues does Luke provide?

From the grammatical standpoint, we find two imperfect tense verbs followed by present participles, which emphasize continued activity with "no end to mark"[1075] or "no end in sight":

Imperfect Tense	*Participle*
"they were going forth" (ἐπορεύοντο) "they were not ceasing" (οὐκ ἐπαύοντο) and "proclaiming the good news" (εὐαγγελιζόμενοι 5:42).	"rejoicing" (χαίροντες Acts 5:41) "teaching" (διδάσκοντες)

The use of the imperfect tenses coupled with present participles mirrors the language of the previous narrative summary (Acts 5:12-16), which accentuated the apostles' ongoing miraculous activity, and punctuated by "daily" (5:42).

Luke leads his readers to notice that warnings, commands, and aggression[1076] are countered by Holy-Spirit empowered defiance in the bold proclamation of the joy-eliciting good news (5:42). These believers cannot be bullied by gag-orders and beatings.[1077]

Thus, for the apostles, nothing changes. They are still in the Temple precincts (Acts 5:42; see 5:20)[1078] and in scattered homes (5:42; 2:46), preaching the good news through inspired words and supernatural activity, with the emotional effects of joy felt by all. For Luke, such bold proclamation is clear evidence of the Spirit's power and inspiration.

With this short summary Luke closes the first portion of Acts, wherein his readers learn of the faith-filled, Spirit-empowered, and joy-infused community that witnesses to the kerygmatic progression of events. The community of believers grows in number, performs miracles, lives out charity, practices prayer, experiences joy and favor, thrives under persecution, is emboldened by the Spirit and experiences divine protection.

Through repetition, Luke provides several vignettes of apostolic witness in the context of joyous life-together. As Tannehill notes, "Repetition is a means of emphasis. Selective emphasis enables narrators to convey the view they regard as most important for correct interpretation of the narrated events."[1079] This is what Luke has composed. The apostolic proclamation through word and miracles is fused with narratives of joyous life-together. For Luke, the witness emerges in a contagious manner from the well-spring of joy as people encounter the numinous in so many ways. The Holy Spirit inspires the proclamation, the miracles, the enthusiastic atmosphere, experiences and expressions of a spontaneous and infectious joy. In subsequent narratives, that manifold, joyous and courageous witness will extend beyond the confines of Jerusalem and Judea (1:8).

5) Making decisions together-celebrating God's inclusionary purpose (Acts 15:1-16:5). How does a joy-filled community go about making decisions? For Luke, the Jerusalem Council represents a grand moment in Salvation-History. In the search for Gentile identity, the Jewish community rediscovers and redefines its own identity.[1080] Luke provides a case of a "lived-theology," which is encased within joyous bookends. Luke invites his readers to experience various points of tension, to see how the conflict was managed and how it even advanced the Christian cause and message, all in an atmosphere of joy. Clearly the community seeks God's will in changing circumstances, locations, ethnic groups, pressing issues, and conflicts—all in settings of joy. [1081]

Various elements of conflict surface[1082]: issues of exclusion and inclusion; terms of admission for Gentile salvation; circumcision[1083]; adherence to the Law of Moses (Acts 15:1, 5); table-fellowship (15:20, 29; 21:25). The story may reveal other implicit problems: the potential divide between two geographical centers (mother-church in Jerusalem and daughter-church in Antioch), and a possible separation between apostolic leaders. Luke describes situations that threaten the unity, peace, joy, and future of the Church.

This important narrative begins within an atmosphere, experience, and expression of joy: "in narrating the conversion of the Gentiles, they [Paul & Barnabas] were causing *great joy* for the brothers" (ἐκδιηγούμενοι τὴν ἐπιστροφὴν τῶν ἐθνῶν, καὶ ἐποίουν *χαρὰν μεγάλην* πᾶσιν τοῖς ἀδελφοῖς Acts 15:3). It concludes with a happy response, "upon reading [the official letter], they [Antiochene Church] *rejoiced* in its *encouraging message*" (ἀναγαγόντες δὲ ἐχάρησαν ἐπὶ τῇ *παρακλήσει* 15:31). Even in describing a painful separation between Paul and Barnabas (15:1-2, 5), the text highlights joy before, during, and after the community's decision (15:37-39). The joy-eliciting good news runs its course (16:5). Luke intends to cultivate joy in his readers as they reflect on both the council's process and decision.

Luke interweaves the various threads of miraculous events and accompanying joy as the community works its way through a conflict-resolution that actually leads to a celebratory advance of the Christian mission and message. These elements belong to the introduction to the Jerusalem Council (Acts 15:1-5), as well as the deliberations, decision and implementation of the Jerusalem Council (15:6-29), and the joyful response to the Council's decision (15:30-35). Luke follows this with the anti-climax of Paul and Barnabas' separation (15:36-41), and Paul's ministry in Lystra, Derbe and other cities where the Council's decision was communicated (16:1-5).

Luke combines charismatic power, the divine initiative, and joyous experiences with Gentile-inclusion[1084] noted through many verbal forms:

- "everything God *had done*" (ὅσα ὁ θεὸς ἐποίησεν Acts 15:4).[1085] The pronoun, "all that" (ὅσα) includes both their verbal proclamation and miraculous activity of what God did (ἐποίησεν).
- "God *made a choice*" (ἐξελέξατο ὁ θεὸς 15:7). Peter's initial statement refers to God's choice of him as the means by which the Gentiles would both hear (ἀκοῦσαι) the good news, and they would trust (πιστεῦσαι),[1086] clearly referring to the climactic experience of Cornelius and company (10:1-11:18).
- "God ... *witnessed*" (ὁ ... θεὸς ἐμαρτύρησεν Acts 15:8).[1087]
- "[God] *by giving* the Holy Spirit" (δοὺς τὸ πνεῦμα 15.8) to Cornelius and company in a powerful, spontaneous, and joyous manner (10:44-45).
- "*He made no distinction* between us and them"[1088] (οὐθὲν διέκρινεν μεταξὺ ἡμῶν τε καὶ αὐτῶν Acts 15.9), in terms of the Pentecostal experience given to those on the initial Day of Pentecost and Cornelius and company.[1089]
- "[God] *cleansing* their hearts by faith" (τῇ πίστει καθαρίσας τὰς καρδίας αὐτῶν 15:9). Mention of divine cleansing of Gentiles also answers to the Cornelius-story, when Peter strongly objected to the command to kill and eat unclean food.
- "the miraculous signs and wonders *God had done*" (ὅσα ἐποίησεν ὁ θεὸς σημεῖα καὶ τέρατα ἐν ἔθνεσιν 15:12), recounted by Barnabas.[1090]
- "God ... *showed his concern to take*" (ὁ θεὸς ἐπεσκέψατο λαβεῖν[1091] 15:14). The verb, "I show concern, I visit"

(ἐπισκέπτομαι) can mean: a) "select carefully," b) "visit with friendly intent," c) "take care of" or "show concern."[1092] The verb expresses God's affection and feeling-involvement with his people.[1093]

- The quote from Amos (Acts 15:16-17; Amos 9:11-12) uses three verbs in four expressions in the first person singular, where God is the speaker: "I will return" (ἀναστρέψω); "I will rebuild" (ἀνοικοδομήσω) twice; "I will restore" (ἀνορθώσω) 15:16. Further, the last line also affirms the divine initiative, "says the Lord who does these things" (λέγει κύριος ποιῶν ταῦτα) 15:17.

Thus, Luke provides a total of 13 expressions affirming the divine initiative and activity in Gentile-inclusion. Human figures acknowledge God's prior initiative and action in numinous events. In highlighting God's activity, Luke suggests that the nascent community, in joyous celebration, catches up with God's purposeful activity in joyous celebration. Luke seeks to cultivate these joyous emotions and behaviors among his readers.

Luke also reinforces the crucial role of the Holy Spirit in the deliberations:

- "by giving the Holy Spirit to them [Cornelius & company] *just as he did to us*" (δοὺς τὸ πνεῦμα τὸ ἅγιον *καθὼς καὶ ἡμῖν*) in 15:8.
- "the Holy Spirit came on all [Cornelius & company] who heard the message" (ἐπέσεν τὸ πνεῦμα τὸ ἅγιον ἐπὶ πάντας τοὺς ἀκούοντας τὸ λόγον) in 10:44.
- "that the gift of the Holy Spirit had been poured out had been poured out even on the Gentiles" (ὅτι καὶ ἐπὶ τὰ ἔθνη ἡ δωρεὰ τοῦ ἁγίου πνεύματος ἐκκέχυται) in 10:45.
- "They have received the Holy Spirit *just as we have*" (οἵτινες τὸ πνεῦμα τὸ ἅγιον ἔλαβον *ὡς καὶ ἡμεῖς*) in 10:47.

- "the Holy Spirit came on them *just as he had come on as at the beginning*" (ἐπέσεν τὸ πνεῦμα τὸ πνεῦμα τὸ ἅγιον ἐπ᾽ αὐτοὺς ὥσπερ καὶ ἐφ᾽ ἡμᾶς ἐν ἀρχῇ) in 11:15.

- "God gave them *the same gift as he gave us*" (τὴν ἴσην δωρεὰν ἔδωκεν αὐτοῖς ὁ θεὸς ὡς καὶ ἡμῖν) in 11:17.

Four of the six references compare experiences, through conjunctions "just as" (καθὼς, ὡς, ὥσπερ), the adjective "same" (ἴσος), and the temporal reference "in the beginning" (ἐν ἀρχῇ).[1094] Luke's readers understand that brief references in Acts 15 to the coming of the Spirit upon Cornelius and friends (Acts 10-11) links them with those receiving the Spirit in 2:1-4. This certainly invited joyous celebration for Luke's audience.

Paul Elbert links Pauline expressions concerning Spirit-reception and Luke's stories, "Luke provides the narrative-rhetorically expected examples and precedents."[1095] Dunn also notes, "As elsewhere in Acts, the Spirit is the central feature in the process of conversion-initiation,"[1096] understood by Dibelius as a "regularizing tradition 'of a good while ago.'"[1097] As a result of the Spirit's activity, the apostles and brothers had concluded that God was now granting life to the Gentiles on the basis of faith. This marks a joyous climax for both Cornelius and company (10:44-46) and the leaders in Jerusalem (11:18).

Luke also forges a link between the Holy Spirit and "signs and wonders" (σημεῖα καὶ τέρατα 15:12).[1098] This favorite Lukan expression refers to the tangible means by which God witnesses to the Jesus-event, found in Luke's summaries.[1099] In Acts 15, one of the "signs and wonders" certainly refers to the coming of the Spirit upon Cornelius and friends. For Luke, God's manifest presence is itself a form of preaching, since "signs and wonders" elicit conversion (2.37-42). Joy surrounds all of these events.

Just as verbalized preaching elicits complex responses, the same can be said about the preaching value of signs and wonders. They both attract and repel people who are either predisposed to reception or rejection of the Jesus-event. For Luke, the reception of the Spirit is manifest and is recognized by others providing assurance of new life and empowerment for witness, all rising from a well-spring of joy. Luke intends his readers to be people of the Spirit, whose lives are marked by joy, faith, signs and wonders, even as they wrestle with particular conflicts in their communities.

Luke also underscores the Holy Spirit's activity in the decision-making process (15:28), "it seemed best (ἔδοξεν) to the Holy Spirit and to us."[1100] The people and their leadership sensed the Spirit's activity, both in the decision itself and the resolve to send the letter through several emissaries. Keener calls the decision, "a charismatic decree."[1101] Conzelmann states, "This verse contains the Lukan concept of church and Spirit."[1102] The text suggests the close engagement of the human and the divine in tandem. Since the Spirit was active among Gentiles (notably In Cornelius) even before an apostle arrived, and since the Spirit was at work in Gentile conversion (Acts 13-14), then the Spirit also must be at work in helping the Jerusalem Church and its leaders enlarge their ways of thinking, feeling and discerning, "so they can participate in the world of God's reign—the world of the Spirit's power—a world, not limited by a particular set of social, ethnic or religious prescriptions."[1103] The world of the Spirit is not to be isolated from human thinking, emotions, decisions, and implementation, especially when there is a commitment to be Christians *together*; joyous inclusion reigns supreme.

Luke also substantiates the decision through James' argument of fulfilled Scripture. The text declares that Scripture agrees (συμφωνοῦσιν) with the experience of Gentile inclusion (15:15). As Johnson notes, "He does not say, 'This agrees with the prophets,' but 'The words of the prophets agree with this."[1104] Thus, the text reveals a startling reversal, similar to the way in which the Gentiles' experience of salvation is the gauge by which Jews are measured (15:11). Current experience finds support in the sacred text of fulfilled prophecy. Thereupon, James appeals to the LXX of Amos 9.11-12 to support the new experience.[1105] On Luke's use of Amos 9.11-12, Robert Wall suggests, "Gentile conversion does not annul God's promise of a restored and redeemed Israel, but rather expands it; nor does faith (rather than Torah observance) as the condition of Gentile conversion contradict God's plan of salvation, but rather confirms it. The second half of

Acts provides a narrative that supports and explains this theological consensus reached at Jerusalem."[1106]

James' conclusion begins with the logical result, "therefore" (διό) to be drawn from the preceding discussion and is followed by his statement, "It is my opinion/judgment" (ἐγὼ κρίνω 15:19). Their shared experience is finally what matters most. Both groups must give and take, creating a consensus that will mean a "win-win" decision for both groups; the voice of each group has been heard and respected. Consensus is highlighted in 15:25, "So we all agreed ..." The final decision does not come by advice or suggestion; the decision stands good since it is authorized by the Jerusalem Council (leaders and church). The decision rises from the Jewish perspective as to: a) how Jews are to celebrate Gentile inclusion based on divine grace and Gentile faith, b) how Jews are not to harass Gentiles (3rd person in 15:19) and how the Jews are not to burden "you" [Gentiles] (2nd person in 15:28—Gentiles in Antioch) with anything more than some essentials. Gentiles are to be sensitive to Jewish sensibilities. Since there are at least three versions[1107] of the decision, discussions abound as to the exact minimal restrictions that the Gentiles must concede concerning their nature, ritual, moral, or a combination of both:

Acts 15:20 (discussion)	Acts 15:29 (letter)	Acts 21:25 (later narrative)
Pollution of idols	Idols	Idols
Sexual immorality	Blood	Blood
Strangling of animals	Strangling of animals	Strangling of animals
Blood	Sexual immorality	Sexual immorality

Charles Savelle, along with others,[1108] provides extended discussion for each of these terms,[1109] which lie outside the focus of this essay. Luke would not have concerned himself with minute distinctions between ritual and moral stipulations. The items on the list constitute practices that would have been abhorrent to Jewish Christians, meat that had been offered to idols (pagan worship), sexual immorality (obvious) and the eating of meat of animals that had been strangled, since the blood was still in the meat. Since blood was associated with life, it was reserved for God alone (Lev 17:10-12). This concession represents the Spirit's will, and these stipulations are not overly burdensome for Gentiles (15:28). Even though the restrictions are labeled as "essentials," they are not "essential for the salvation of the Gentiles" (15:11). Rather, they are "essential" for table-fellowship between Christian Jews and Christian Gentiles. Dunn calls them "minimum terms for mutual recognition and association ... rules of association."[1110]

The Spirit animates the reinterpretation of the Amos text. "Once again, we cannot fail to be impressed by the extent of his sources and his ability to make effective use of his scriptural material."[1111] As Thomas states, "It appears that the experience of the Spirit in the community helped the church make its way through the hermeneutical maze."[1112] Thus James' appeal to an Old Testament precedent clearly trumps the Jewish-Christian precedent.

Luke also narrates the presence and activity of two "prophets," Judas and Silas, who were present during the Council's deliberation-process and decision. They also accompanied Paul and Barnabas in their report-back to the Antiochene church. The text describes them as selfless "men who have risked their lives for the name of our Lord Jesus Christ" (15:25-27). They are described as "prophets" who "encouraged" (παρεκά λεσαν) the community with many words (15:32).

Joy permeates the narrative from the beginning to end of the council's decision and implementation and is also expressed by the "joy-filled greetings" (χαίρειν) at the beginning of the actual letter. Subsequently, the foursome (Paul, Barnabas, Judas, Silas) deliver and read the letter, and provide further confirmation to the awaiting church in Antioch. The response? "They rejoiced in the encouraging message" (ἐχάρησαν ἐπὶ τῇ παρακλήσει Acts 15:31). Thus, Luke encases the Jerusalem Council's narrative within an atmosphere, experience and expression of joy and encouragement.

Other important words from the joy-vocabulary appear: the link between "joy" (χαρά) and "grace" (χάρις) in Acts 15:11, "through the grace of the Lord we believe" (διὰ τῆς χάριτος τοῦ κυρίου πιστεύομεν); 15:40—"being commended to the grace of the Lord" (παραδοθεὶς τῇ χάριτι τοῦ κυρίου); "Peace" (εἰρήνη) describes the send-off of Judas and Silas with the blessing of peace (15:33) back to the Jerusalem Church. Further, two other words appear of the verb, "I preach the joy-eliciting good news": 15:7—Peter notes how he had been singled out to preach "the word of the good news" (τὸν λόγον τοῦ εὐαγγελίου); 15:35—after the joyful acceptance of the official letter, Paul, Barnabas, and many others remain in Antioch, "teaching and preaching the good news ... the word of the Lord" (διδάσκοντες καὶ εὐαγγελιζόμενοι ... τὸν λόγον τοῦ κυρίου). Again, joy is the correlative of the "good news."

Taken together, the numerous dynamics lead to an emotive reception and happy advance of the gospel, noted in Acts 15:30-35 and 16:1-5, also highlighted in another Lukan summary (16:5). Doubtlessly, the community is relieved that their identity and practice are confirmed both by the letter and its emissaries. Gentiles are glad to accommodate Jewish Christians, so they might live together without tension. Barnabas and Mark go to Cyprus, while Paul and Silas travel to Syria and Cilicia, 'strengthening' (ἐπιστηρίζων 15:41; cf. 15:32 of Judas and Silas) the churches (15:41). Paul then retraces his steps on his first missionary journey—in Derbe and Lystra (16:1-5), and selects Timothy as a companion (16:1-3), before the more extensive journeys unfold into Europe. Talbert notes, "Nothing can stop the gospel, not even divisions among missionaries."[1113] In 16:4, Paul delivers the decisions from the Jerusalem Council, "they delivered the decisions reached by the apostles and elders in Jerusalem for the people to obey" (16:4). Originally, the extent of the Council's decision involved Antioch, Syria and Celicia (15:23), but now the decision extends beyond these places.

The happy advance of God's word is a result of the Jerusalem Council's decision, "So the churches were strengthened in the faith and grew daily in numbers" (16:5). The imperfect verbs "they continued to be strengthened" (ἐστερούντο) and "they continued to grow" (ἐπερίσσευον) affirm the ongoing growth in the community's inner life and numerical growth (16:5).

The theological narrative of Acts 15 reveals much about the joyful and joint involvement of the divine and the human, as the community of faith seeks to discern God's will in changing circumstances. The author intertwines charismatic elements with joyous human decisions, showing also the resulting responses of joy. These dynamics are important considerations as the Spirit-filled Church makes its witness in an ever-changing landscape. Luke would wish that his readers cultivate this "lived-theology" in their own faith-communities, through joyous participation.

Notes

1033   Martin Dibelius, *Studies in the Acts of the Apostles* (London: SCM PRESS LTD,1973), 127.

1034   Keener, Vol. 1, 992.

1035   Hans Conzelmann, *The Theology of St. Luke* (Geoffrey Buswell, transl.; New York: Harper & Row Publishers, 1953), 147.

1036   G. B. Caird, *The Apostolic Age* (London: Gerald Duckworth & Co. LTD, 1955), 66.

1037   The imperfect, "were occurring" (ἐγίνετο) suggests numerous miracles over a period of time.

1038   Haya-Prats, 169.

1039   See "eating together" in Acts 1:4.

1040   The verb, "I exult" (ἀγαλλιάω) of David's joy in Psa 16:9, is fulfilled in the resurrection-joy in Acts 2:26.

1041   *Contra* Haenchen, 193.

1042   A natural nuance of the verb, "I have" (ἔχω), BDAG, 332-333.

1043   "those who were being saved" (τοὺς σῳζομένους Acts 2:47).

1044   Pervo, 95. For a discussion on this narrative-summary, see DE LONG, 246-247.

1045   Keener, Vol. 1, 1003.

1046   Even though the paragraph contains awkward transitions (Acts 5:13a coupled with 5:12, 13b, 14), "miracle working is the theme." C. K. Barrett, *Acts* (ICC), Vol. I (Edinburgh: T & T Clark, 1994), 273.

1047   The verb (προστίθημι), used of numerical growth in Acts 2:41, 47; 11:24, seems to merge into believers. *Pace* Barrett, 274, "virtually equivalent to becoming a Christian." Also Hans Conzelmann, *The Theology of St. Luke* (Geoffrey Buswell transl.; New York: Harper & Row Publishers, 1953), 215.

1048   Acts 5:12, "many signs and wonders *were occurring* (ἐγίνετο) among the people"; 5:12 "They *were* (ἦσαν) all together in one accord"; 5:13 "no one *was daring* (ἐτόλμα) to join them"; 5:13 "the people *were magnifying* (ἐμεγάλυνεν); them"; 5:14 "believers *were being added*" (προσετίθεντο); 5:16 "All the crowd *would come* together" (συνήρχετο); 5:16 "all *were being healed*" (ἐθεραπεύοντο).

1049 Acts 5:14 "*ones believing* in the Lord" (πιστεύοντες τῷ κυρίῳ); 5:15 "whenever Peter *would come*" (ἐρχομένου Πέτρου)-a genitive absolute; Acts 5:16 "*carrying* (φέροντες) the sick and *the ones being demon possessed*" (ὀχλουμένους) by unclean spirits."

1050 Acts 5:14, "*to join* them" (κολλᾶσθαι); 5:14 "*to carry* (ἐκφέρειν) the sick"; 5:15 "to place" (τιθέναι).

1051 Roughly similar to the effect of Paul's handkerchiefs and aprons (Acts 19:12).

1052 Barrett, 277.

1053 P. W. Van Der Horst, "Peter's Shadow," *New Testament Studies* 23, 205; he argues for an allusion to Luke 1:35.

1054 Van Der Horst, 210.

1055 Pervo, 136.

1056 The expression, "of the surrounding cities of Jerusalem" probably means towns or villages. Haenchen, 243.

1057 Acts 2:43 for the concerted prayer for "healings, signs and wonders" (Acts 4:30), also fulfilled in Acts 5:12.

1058 Luke uses the term "of one accord" (ὁμοθυμαδόν) ten of eleven occurrences in the NT.

1059 Barrett, 276.

1060 Haenchen, 242. He notes that Luke replaces Mark's "the outsiders" (οἱ ἔξω Mk. 4:11) with "the others" (οἱ λοιποί Luke 8:10). Also supported by F. F. Bruce, *The Acts of the Apostles: The Greek Text with Introduction and Commentary* (Grand Rapids: Wm. B. Eerdmans Publishing Company), 137.

1061 The expression, "And great fear seized all who were hearing these things" is repeated in Acts 5:5, 11.

1062 Note the strong adversative, "but" (ἀλλά) in Acts 5:13.

1063 Johnson, *Acts*, 95.

1064 Bruce, 138.

1065 BDAG, 497.

1066 Haenchen, 242.

1067 See earlier comments on Isa. 35 with the crippled beggar (Acts 3:1-10).

1068 Barrett, 278.

1069 Pervo, 138.

1070 See the previous arrest in Acts 4:3 of only Peter and John.

1071 Pervo, 138.

1072 See above for the two occurrences of "people" and "multitude" in Acts 5:12-16.

1073 Marshall, 131.

1074 Thompson, 20.

1075 C. K. Barrett, Vol. 1, 300.

1076 Acts 4:17, 19, 21, 29; 5:50.

1077 Acts 4:20, 28, 29, 31; 5:12-16, 21, 28, 29, 42.

1078 Dunn notes the movement away from the Temple in subsequent chapters, "another locus of Christianity is emerging," 74.

1079 Tannehill, Vol. 2, 75.

1080 See Michaeil Enyinwa Okoronkwo, *The Jewish Compromise as a Conflict-Resolution Model (A Rhetoric-Communicative Analysis of Acts 15 in the Light of Modern Linguistics* (Bonn: Borengäser, 2001), 279.

1081 This study cannot reconstruct the relationship between Acts 15 and Gal. 2, but to probe the transformative value of the story, and its appropriation by various faith communities. See Keener, Vol. 4, 2195-2206 for extensive discussion, including I Corinthians.

1082 Luke uses numerous nouns and verbs to accentuate the conflict: "dissension" (στάσις) and "sharp debate" (ζητήσις οὐκ ὀλιγή—litotes 15:2; 14:27) in Antioch, "controversial matter" (ζήτημα) in Jerusalem (15:3), "this matter" (ὁ λόγος οὗτος 15:6); "much dispute" (πολλή ζητήσις 15:7). Luke expresses the demand as a "yoke" (ζυγός 15.10), a "burden" (βάρος 15:28), which amounts to challenging God (τί πειράζετε τὸν θεόν; 15:10), a form of harassment (παρενοχλεῖν 15:19) in which "they disturbed" (ἐτάραξαν) you and were "troubling" (ἀνασκευάζοντες) your minds by what they said" (15:24). The verb, "to become silent" (σιγᾶν 15:12-13), contrasts with the previous heated discussion.

1083 See Keener, Vol. 4, 2215-2222 for an excursus on circumcision.

1084 God's purposeful activity in Acts 13:47 (Isa 49:6), "I have made you a light for the Gentiles, that you may bring salvation to the ends of the earth."

1085 Nearly identical with Acts 14:27.

1086 Two infinitives of purpose.

1087 The theme of witness is also accentuated in other texts (Acts 14:3; 10:43; 23:11).

1088 The verbal form, "he made no distinction" (οὐθὲν διέκρινεν) expresses divine determination of the divine/human story of the former vision (10.9-16, 20; 11.2-17). Through his visionary-lesson, Peter interprets God's decision.

1089 Luke provides a word play with "I make no distinction" (διακρίνω): "without hesitating" (Acts 10:20; 11:12); "took issue" (11:2). Thus Peter learns that "there is no partiality (προσωπλήμπτης) with God" (Acts 10:35). Peter, discovers the truth is directed to "catch up" with God's nature and policy of non-discrimination.

1090 Luke points to the pair's previous ministry in which "the hand of the Lord was upon them" (ἦν χεὶρ κυρίου μετ᾽ αὐτῶν 11:21), numerical growth (13:4-12); "the Lord confirming the word of his grace, 'giving signs and wonders' (14:3); healing of a crippled beggar (14:8-10); divine activity through Barnabas and Paul 14:27.

1091 An infinitive of purpose, reinforcing the divine initiative and action.

1092 BDAG, 298.

1093 The verb is important for Luke and joins with joy (Luke 1:68, 78; 7:16; Acts 7:23; 15:36).

1094 See the discussion on Acts 10:1-11:18.

1095 Paul Elbert, "Possible Literary Links Between Luke-Acts and Pauline Letters Regarding Spirit-Language," Ed. Thomas L. Brodie, Dennis R. MacDonald and Stanley E. Porter, *The Intertextuality of the Epistles* (Sheffield: Phoenix, 2006), 241.

1096 Dunn, *Acts*, 201.

1097 Martin Dibelius, *The Book of Acts* (ed. K. C. Hanson; Minneapolis: Fortress, 2004), 145.

1098 The word "power" (δύναμις) is also linked with "signs and wonders," often in the same context (Acts 2:22; 3:12; 4:7; 4:33; 6:8; 8:13; 10:38; 19:11; "powerful" [δύνατος] in 7.22).

1099 Stephen's reference to "signs and wonders" finds support in Moses (7.36—Exod 3:12; 4:1-17).

1100 See Acts 15:22, 25 for the use of the verb, "it seems best" (δοκέω).

1101 Keener, Vol. 4, 2291.

1102 Conzelmann, 120.

1103 Lois Malcolm, "Conversion, Conversation and Acts 15," *Crux*, vol. 22, Number 3 (Summer, 2002), 252.

1104 Johnson, *Decision-Making in the Church*, 84.

1105 Perhaps the opening expression is drawn from Jer 12.15-16 and the closing phrase from Isa 45.21-23. See Keener, vol. 4, 2243-2258 for extensive discussion of James' use of the Amos-text.

1106 Robert Wall, "Israel and the Gentile Mission in Acts and Paul," *Witness to the Gospel: The Theology of Acts* (ed. I. Howard Marshall and David Peterson; Grand Rapids: Wm. B. Eerdmans, 1994), 449-450.

1107 Textual traditions offer varied forms of this four-fold list. The Western text ethicizes the items (idolatry, sexual immorality, bloodshed and the negative form of the Golden Rule, "and not to do to others whatever they do not wish to be done to themselves"), while the uncials B and ℵ combine both the ritual and ethical (food sacrificed to idols, sexual immorality, meat of strangled animals, eating blood—no mention of the Golden Rule).

1108 See Keener, Vol. 4, 2258-2279 for extensive discussion on the prohibitions, especially, "Samples of Jewish Rules Expected of Gentiles," 2266.

1109 Charles H. Savelle, "A Reexamination of the Prohibitions in Acts 15," *Bibliotheca Sacra* 161 (October-December 2004), 449-68. Marcel Simon, "The Apostolic Decree and its Setting in the Ancient Church," *BJRL*, no. 52 (1969), 437-460.

1110 Dunn, 204.

1111 Anthony Tyrell Hanson, *The Living Utterances of God: The New Testament Exegesis of the Old* (London: Darton, Longman and Todd, 1983), 87.

1112 Thomas, 118.

1113 Talbert, 145.

CHAPTER 9

JOYOUS DELIVERANCE FROM THREATS

When she recognized Peter's voice, she was so overjoyed,
she ran back without opening the door.
–ACTS 12:14

Luke's narrative in the book of Acts offers a record of the apostles'
deliverance from prison and shipwreck. The author frames these events
in joyous contexts.

"Rejoicing . . . because they were considered worthy to be insulted for
the name" (Acts 5:41). Luke's narrative-summary of joyous "life-together"
(5:12-16) flows into the apostles' imprisonment in a public jail, followed
by an angelic deliverance (5:17-42).[1114] God releases the twelve from jail
through an angel[1115] who opens the door, leads them out of prison, and
instructs them to go and stand in the Temple to speak to the people "all
the words of this life" (5:19-20).[1116] The apostles obey the angel and teach
in the Temple precincts at sun-up (5:21).

Luke's readers smile as religious powers are clueless about the
miraculous deliverance. The leaders issue a summons to bring the
apostles to the hearing, only to discover the prisoners have escaped
(5:23). Luke and his readers know where they are and what they are
doing.[1117] A second person makes a subsequent report that the freed
apostles are teaching without restraint in the Temple (5:25). The first
report regarding the empty cell brings confusion, "they couldn't figure
what was going on"[1118] (5:24). Luke's readers know the apostles "are

doing precisely what they were told to do"[1119] by the angel. The second report of the apostles' return to the Temple yields a charge to "lead" the apostles to the council (5:26). Curiously enough, the authorities fail to ask the apostles how they escaped from a locked and guarded prison.

Through their deliverance from prison, Luke confirms that God is on the apostles' side. The religious *powers* are *powerless*. In fact, their confusion makes them look ridiculous, and then Luke shows them humiliated and cowed by their fear of the people and the apostles. From Luke's perspective, expressed through Gamaliel's reasoning,[1120] the religious authorities could be "fighting against God" (Acts 5:39). Surely, the apostles' rejoicing in 5:41 directly relates to their confidence in God's supernatural power, evidenced in their angelic deliverance. As Barrett notes, "the angel increases the confidence of the apostles and the wrath of their opponents."[1121] Surely, the joy-less critics are shamed by the escape, the popular response, and their own impotence.

Luke provides Peter's "mini-sermon," embracing the previously preached kerygmatic progression of events that builds to a joyful and powerful witness and highlights the vital role of the Holy Spirit (Acts 5:30-32).

The numerous miracles (Acts 5:12-16) reflect Jesus' exaltation and subsequent pouring forth of the Holy Spirit, which empowers the community to speak and act for God. Luke intends for his readers to see that the kerygma, beginning with Jesus' crucifixion, leads to empowered and joyful witness. Pervo notes, "As proof of 'these matters,' the apostles add to their own testimony, the manifestation of the Spirit, not Scripture here, but a present gift, one example is their eloquent speech, delivered in concert (cf. Luke 12:11-12)."[1122] The key point is that the Holy Spirit joins with the joyful "witness"[1123] of God's saving activity through what the apostles do and say.[1124] Gamaliels' wise counsel (Acts 5:34-39a) counters the murderous intent of infuriated and jealous Jewish leaders (Acts 5:33). The joy-less critics heed Gamaliel's advice (5:39b), opting only to beat the apostles and issue another gag-order (5:40), which the apostles disobey. The apostles "do not stop teaching and preaching the good news about

Christ Jesus" (ἐπαύοντο διδάσκοντες καὶ εὐαγγελιζόμενοι τὸν Χριστόν, ᾽Ιησοῦν 5:42). They continue their activities in the context of a well-spring of joy, "they were rejoicing ... because they were considered worthy to be insulted for the name" (χαίροντες ... ὅτι κατηξιώθησαν ὑπὲρ τοῦ ὀνόματος ἀτιμασθῆναι 5:41). A powerful climax of joy!

Peter delivered from prison (Acts 12:1-25). Luke provides another joyous occasion, with the nascent community's ecstatic celebration of Peter's miraculous deliverance from prison. The first deliverance (Acts 5) is described with a minimum of words. The religious authorities express no explicit interest in how the apostles were delivered. They simply accuse the apostles of disobeying the gag order (5:27-28). In contrast, Luke's 'record of this second prison escape highlights its miraculous nature. In another incident recorded in Acts 16:19-40, an earthquake releases prison's doors, but no one escapes, including Paul and Silas.

Suggestions abound as to allusions with other arrest, trial and deliverance scenes. [1125] For the purpose of this review, the key question remains, *What does Luke want his readers to learn?* Some preliminary observations are in order:

Use of inclusion. Luke encases this story within the overall narrative in an artful manner, using numerous "bookends":

- *Food shortage.* Luke contrasts generous gifts by the disciples to benefit Jerusalem's needy people (11:27-30) with the quarrel the people of Tyre and Sidon had with Herod, related to a food supply (12:20). [1126] The opening expression, "In that time" (12:1) links Peter's prison-escape with the relief fund, noted in 11:27-30.
- *Saul and Barnabas.* The pair is entrusted with the monetary gift for people in Judea (11:30). They later finish their gracious "service" in Jerusalem (12:25).
- *Two morbid deaths.* James is beheaded at the beginning of the narrative (12:2) and Herod Agrippa I dies a gruesome death, "eaten by worms" (12:23). [1127]

- *Spread of the word of God.* The brief summary statement in Acts 12:24 of the spread of God's word is consistent with other condensed summaries before and after Acts 12 (6:7; 9:31; 19:20). All of these are positioned within charismatic settings. The context of persecution encases three of the mini-summaries.
- *John Mark.* Luke introduces John Mark and his mother Mary (12:12). This young man will later accompany Saul and Barnabas in their "service" to Jerusalem (12:25) and will be a companion to the apostolic company (13:5; 15:39).
- *Angelic kicking.* An angel kicks (πατάσσω) a sleeping Peter, leading him to freedom. Later, an angel strikes (πατάσσω) Herod with a hideous death (12:23).
- *Voice.* Luke contrasts Rhoda's recognition of *Peter's voice* (τὴν φωνὴν τοῦ Πέτρου 12:14) with the people's recognition of Herod's *voice of God* (Θεου φωνὴ 12:22).
- *James.* Luke introduces Jesus' brother James into the narrative in Peter's directive, "Go and tell James" [about Peter's miraculous deliverance] (12:17). James will emerge as the leader of the Jerusalem church (15:13; 21:18), one of the three church "pillars" (στύλοι Gal. 2:9), who also witnessed the resurrected Jesus (I Cor. 15:7).[1128]

Pervo similarly notes "the unit is, broadly speaking, chiastic."[1129] Such indicators, included before and after the story, frame the events of Acts 12 and reflect authorial activity.

Acts 12 sets angelic deliverance in the context of Herod's gruesome aggression against the apostles, and the people's compliance in the time of the Passover.[1130] The previous aggression by religious leaders now progresses to an attack by Herod, a political figure.[1131] The general purpose statement, "to harm some of the church" (12:1), is followed by the particular brutality of beheading John's brother James "with a sword" (μαχαίρῃ 12:2).[1132] Since the beheading "was pleasing to the Jews" (12:3),[1133] Herod sees opportunity to increase his popularity by turning his sight on another victim, Peter, the leading apostle. "Herod does not make empty threats. The king is attacking the church from the top down."[1134] Thus, he proceeds to arrest Peter (12:3) and put him into prison, intending to bring Peter before the people [for execution[1135]]. However, since the Passover is at hand, public execution will have to wait.

In this story, Luke reveals his commitment to effective prayer (although God's answer is not immediately believed) and real miracles, including the tangible and sensorial nature of God's miraculous power intersecting human affairs. Luke's record embraces historical events, affecting what is seen, what is heard, and what is touched. Luke piles up terms reinforcing the maximum security established for the prisoner Peter:

- *Four squadrons of four soldiers* guard him (12:4) and keep him in custody (12:5-6), with an implied fate similar to James.
- *Four* of the sixteen soldiers in their watch take turns—two guards are chained to the sleeping Peter, while two serve as sentries at the door. In that context, Luke's readers will wonder how Peter could possibly escape.
- *The first gate, the second gate, and the iron gate* (12:10) heighten the impenetrable nature of these barriers.

Luke's detailed description of security measures highlights the wonder of the prison-escape. Miraculous power overwhelms human power, expressed through numerous terms:

a) "Behold" (ἰδού 12:7). Luke uses the particle "behold" to introduce the numinous nature of the impending angelophany.[1136]

b) "An angel of the Lord appeared" (12:7).[1137] Luke uses the verb, "I stand by, near, approach, appear" (ἐφίστημι) often with the connotation of suddenness,[1138] which he also uses elsewhere with the sudden appearance of angels (Lk 2:7; 24:4).

c) "A light shone in the prison" (Acts 12:7). The shining light here conveys the divine presence[1139]—it is supernatural in nature but it doesn't disturb either the sleeping Peter or the four guards.

d) "[the angel] kicked Peter in the side, raised him up ... the chains fell off his hands." The angel follows this with five crisp commands: Get up quickly, belt up your robe, put on your sandals, put on your cloak, follow me (12:7-8). The verb "I kick/strike" (πατάσσω) is strong, jolting a sleeping Peter to freedom. The four guards remain unaware of the loosened chains or the supernatural light. Peter obeys the commands, "he did thus" (12:8) and "was following" (12:9).

e) "[the iron gate] was opened to them on its own accord" (12:10). Luke's readers know that the expression, "swung *on its own accord*" (αὐτομάτη) was supernaturally caused, "without visible cause,"[1140] allowing the two to pass to the city street.[1141]

In the combined details, Luke's readers recognize this was no subjective vision, but a real event. As Pervo notes, "Getting the chains off is no problem. Getting Peter dressed is."[1142]

Even though Peter physically moves, he "imagined that he was seeing a vision" (ἐδόκει δὲ ὅραμα βλέπειν Acts 12:9). Readers recall Peter's previous experience was a personal vision (10:10) of an animal menagerie coupled with the "voice" (10:13). Thus, awakening from sleep, Peter might easily conclude this is another vision. On the street outside of the prison, the angel suddenly leaves, and Peter becomes fully aware that this was a real angelophany with a real deliverance: "Now I truly know (i.e. without a doubt) that the Lord sent his angel and delivered me from Herod's hand and all the expectations of the Jewish people" (12:11). Luke transitions from the adjective "real" ("not real" οὐκ . . . ἀληθές), which Peter didn't believe (12:9), to the adverb "truly/really" (ἀληθῶς 12:11), which Peter now believes. Luke reinforces Peter's transition with the participle, "when this had dawned upon him" (συνιδών τε 12:12).[1143] He grows in his awareness as he moves from sleep, to a hazy awareness, to the joyously sober realization, "Now I truly know" (Νῦν οἶδα ἀληθῶς) (12:11). Luke underscores Peter's physical deliverance in the disciple's report to the gathered community at Mary's home, "how the Lord led him out of prison" (12:17).

Left alone in the street, Peter makes his way to the familiar home of Mary the mother of John Mark.[1144] Peter must share his joyful deliverance with fellow believers. A slave girl, named Rhoda, entrusted with the responsibility of opening the gate to guests,[1145] recognizes Peter's voice at the external gate, but (δέ "on the contrary"[1146]) doesn't open the internal door (12:14). Thus, Peter continues standing out in the cold, so to speak, with an unopened gate and door. Luke's irony is vibrant. An angel opens prison doors and a massive iron gate for Peter, but now he stands before another gate and door. This time the door and the gate remain closed. Luke explains that Rhoda succumbs to joyous excitement. Luke uses the expression, "from joy" (ἀπὸ τῆς χαρᾶς) in a similar way to the disciples' reaction to Jesus in a post-resurrection appearance, "still disbelieving from joy (ἀπὸ τῆς χαρᾶς) and marveling," i.e. "too good to be true" (Lk 24:41). Thus overwhelmed with joy, Rhoda, is unable to do the logical thing—open both the gate and door to let Peter in. Leaving Peter knocking at the gate, she makes a "bee-line" to the people inside announcing that Peter is at the gate. Luke creates playful humor or "comic relief"[1147] to describe the joyous comedy of excitement.

However, Rhoda's joyous announcement brings a demeaning and chauvinistic retort from those inside Mary's home. In Luke 24:11, the women's announcement of an angelic encounter and announcement of a resurrected Jesus brought a demeaning male response, that their report was "nonsense" (λῆρος). If the response to the women in Luke 24 was intended to shame the women, then how much more striking is the community's belittling response to a "slave-girl?" They first say, "You're crazy" (Μαίνη Acts 12:15).[1148] When Rhoda continues to insist[1149] that her report is true, the community infers that she had misread the person at the door and they conclude that she is hallucinating, "it must be Peter's angel"[1150] (24:15)—but not Peter himself.[1151] Although Luke twice notes the community's constant engagement in prayer for Peter, he intimates that the pray-ers didn't really believe in an immediate and miraculous answer to their fervent prayer. All of this occurs while Peter is still knocking at the door "until someone comes up with a brilliant idea: let's see who is at the door."[1152] Finally, the gate and door open and they see a real Peter.

The community, which is in transition, responds in a climactic manner, "they were ecstatic" (ἐξέστησαν Acts 12:16). Frequently, Luke uses the verb "I am astonished/ecstatic" (ἐξίστημι or ἐξιστάνω) to express the joyous emotions felt by people who encounter miraculous events (8:9, 11, 13). The verb "reflects the powerful religious experience of the early Church."[1153] Although Dunn sees this as a "comic sequel,"[1154] it is more apropos to embrace the climactic emotions of the gathered community. No doubt, the community now shares Rhoda's joy in their answered prayer, recognizes the presence of a real Peter, and celebrates Peter's miraculous deliverance. Since Peter must silence the gathering (Acts 12:17), readers may reasonably infer a joyful commotion accompanied by a million simultaneous questions.

Thus, Luke highlights both the miraculous dimensions of this prison-rescue story and the climactic and joyous responses of Rhoda and the community gathered in Mary's home. God answers prayer, even when the community is slow to believe in tangible answers.

In the larger context, this story is encased within the Herod-story. Acts 12 also outlines the political leader's demise, moving from brutal aggression (Acts 12:1-3) to his impotence (not finding Peter in prison 12:19), to his gruesome death (12:23). His downfall is the direct result of his aggression against the apostles, and his megalomania—his approval of the popular response that he speaks with the voice of God—not men (12:22). Luke explains Herod's immediate death in the clause, "because he did not give glory to God" (ἀνθ᾽ ὧν ἔδωκεν τὴν δόξαν 12:23). Luke juxtaposes this failure to glorify God with the prayerful community, who earlier glorified (ἐδόξασαν) God for the gift of repentance given to the Gentiles (11:18).[1155]

God's miraculous power is at work in the reversals.[1156] The narrative that starts out with Herod's brutality in taking life (Acts 12:2) ends with Herod's life taken from him (12:23).[1157] Similarly, the people's compliance with Herod's cruelty (12:3) and their "evil-expectation" (12:11) lead nowhere, since Peter is delivered, not just from prison, but also from immediate death. In addition, veneration of Herod dissolves with his gruesome death. In contrast, the gathered community begins in a weakened, threatened, and vulnerable position. One of the apostles is executed, and the leading spokesman appears to be next on the chopping block. God's power, displayed through a plethora of means, delivers Peter from Herod, and also causes the Christian proclamation and movement to grow and multiply (12:24).[1158] Luke also introduces his readers to John Mark, who accompanies Barnabas and Saul (12:25) as their helper (13:5).

In the midst of these reversals, Luke highlights the atmosphere and experience of a prayerful community, even though it is slow to believe in an immediate answer. Within this setting, Luke reiterates how joy and ecstasy are direct responses to charismatic activity. Further, even though the "bookends" of the story are morbid deaths (James and Herod), nonetheless, there is not only room for joy but also room for humor, comedy or theological pleasure, as Luke's readers smile when Rhoda leaves Peter out in the cold, still knocking—a slave-girl is so overcome with joy that she doesn't think to open the outer gate.

Cheer up (Acts 27:1-28:10). In Paul's final voyage, this time to Rome, Luke provides an adventure story that pairs miracles and joy, strangely enough in a typhoon, shipwreck, rescue, and snakebite. These events vindicate Paul and his mission. Emotional language pervades the stories. Scholars certainly differ in their approaches to this adventure story.[1159] Our main interest is Luke's purpose in devoting so much literary space to this sea voyage. What *take-away* does he intend for his readers, and how does he use emotional language in this narrative? A few initial observations are in order:

Luke uses inclusion with the "kindly and friendly" (φιλανθρώπος) approach to Paul at the beginning and end of the story, contributing to the warm emotional atmosphere:

- Julius the Centurion "treats Paul in a *kindly and friendly manner*" (φιλανθρώπως ... χρησάμενος Acts 27:3) at narrative's beginning.
- The Maltese natives[1160] "showed *exceptional*[1161] kindness to us" (παρεῖχον οὐ τὴν τυχοῦσαν φιλανθρωπίαν ἡμῖν 28:2),
- Publius (the Chief of Malta) "welcomed and showed hospitality for us for three days in a *kindly fashion*"[1162] (ἀναδεξάμενος ἡμᾶς τρεῖς ἡμέρας φιλοφρόνως ἐξένισεν 28:7) at the story's end.

- Luke highlights this warm relationship between Paul and Julius up-front, since the centurion is a key player in the story. Although he, with others, initially rejects Paul's prophetic warning (Acts 27:11), he later follows Paul's advice about escaping sailors (27:30-32) and thwarts the soldier's plan to kill all prisoners (27:42-44) prior to the shipwreck. He wants to spare Paul's life.

- The driving force in the adventure story is Paul's prophetic word (Acts 27:10, 21-26), which intervenes in the midst of crises. Luke affirms Paul's charismatic power at sea, in the midst of a shipwreck, in the natives' response that Paul must be "a god" (28:6), and also in Paul's extensive healing ministry in Malta (28:8-10).

- Numerous persons in the narrative are in-process as they discover more about God's purpose (Paul, Julius, sailors, soldiers, natives, Publius, and Malta's population).

The story can be sketched with six paragraphs focusing on Luke's purpose, without specific attention to geographic and nautical details. Luke involves his readers with the emotions of the text, with his vocabulary of joy related to charismatic events surfacing at various points, even in this story of disaster. Paul and Luke summon their respective communities to joy, seemingly undiminished in the midst of real adversities.

Paragraph 1: A foreboding start (Acts 27:1-8). The initial journey to Rome begins with a warm atmosphere, for Julius extends kindness to Paul by freeing him to go to his friends for needed provisions (27:3). Luke then counters that warm opening with four explicit premonitions of lurking danger in the journey to a place called "Good Harbor" (27:8), an ironic name since it is not really safe for a ship's winter stay (27:4, 7-twice, 8). Luke heightens the tension, intimating the dangers that lie ahead in the voyage to Rome. His wording prepares the reader for Paul's first prophecy.

Paragraph 2: Paul's first prophecy (Acts 27:9-12). Luke's forewarning continues, "Much time had been lost and sailing had already become dangerous, because it was after the Fast" (27:9). Most scholars assign the Fast to October 5; thus Luke informs his readers of dangerous sailing conditions before winter's onset. Paul urges the Centurion and sailors, "Men, I perceive that our voyage is about to be disastrous and bring much loss, not only of the cargo and ship but even our own lives" (27:10).

Luke's mention, "with *disaster* and much *loss*" is reiterated in the following paragraph with Paul's second prophecy, "this *disaster* and *loss*" (Acts 27:1). Some interpreters conclude that Paul gives human advice as an experienced traveler, which is then contradicted by his later prophecy that "not a life would be lost" (27:22).[1163] Paul has been shipwrecked three times (2 Cor 11:25), but this does not make him a nautical authority.

Luke portrays Paul as a prophet, warning of disaster including loss of cargo and life. This first prophecy is then qualified by his second prophecy, when he assures the sailors that no lives will be lost. As Marshall notes, "the fact that Paul speaks with certainty of disaster rather than merely of the possibility may support the supposition of divine guidance behind his statement."[1164] Paul is a charismatic prophet, whose words are fulfilled when he exhorts, warns, strengthens, encourages, and summons the sailors to joy, even in the midst of chaos and an impending shipwreck. Even Haenchen, who dismisses the historicity of the narrative, says, "Paul was against the voyage; not as a meteorologist ... not as a traveler ... but from prophetic alliance with God. The ship will sink with all hands."[1165]

Paul's first prophecy goes unheeded by the ship's authorities, for "the majority" take the calculated risk to sail the forty-mile route to Phoenix, which offers a safer harbor to winter the ship (Acts 27:12). Pervo states, "The professionals had reason for disagreeing with him."[1166] Luke's readers regard Paul's initial prophecy as inspired and foreboding, given the four previous references to the difficulties already encountered and the time that had already been lost (27:9). Luke prepares his readers for the worst when the professionals agree on the gamble.

Paragraph 3: The storm (Acts 27:13-20). The start of the voyage to Phoenix deteriorates to a violent "Northeaster" of hurricane force (27:14). The ship's crew makes major efforts to regain control in the midst of protracted darkness—all to no avail (27:16-20), since darkness eliminates ability to plot a nautical course. Crashing into the shoals of North Africa spells sure death for all.

The downward spiral climaxes in the statement in Acts 27:10b, "finally, all hope of our being saved was gradually being abandoned" (λοιπὸν περιῃρεῖτο ἐλπὶς πᾶσα τοῦ σῴζεσθαι ἡμᾶς). This is emotionally charged language. The imperfect tense of περιαιρέω, "was gradually being abandoned," leads to the implication of hope's demise.

Luke introduces the important motif of the "save" vocabulary: "I save" (σῴζω); the compound, "I save/rescue" (διασῴζω); the noun, "salvation/deliverance" (σωτηρία) (Acts 27:20, 31, 34, 43, 44; 28:1, 4). The same idea joins with "loss" (27:22, 34). Thus, the initial abandonment of hope of "salvation" (27:20) will contrast with Paul's compelling prophecies of salvation as they unfold and find fulfillment within the narrative.[1167]

Paragraph 4: Paul's second prophecy (Acts 27:21-26). *"Since almost nobody wanted to eat* because of anxiety or seasickness,"[1168] Paul intervenes with a reminder of his first prophecy of "disaster and loss" (27:10, 21) in language that resembles "I told you so" (27:21). Once again he "urges" (παραινέω 27:9, 22) another course of action.

Instead of a warning in the midst of their emotional despair, Paul urges them "to cheer up" (εὐθυμεῖν), followed by an explanation (γάρ) for why they should be cheered, "for not one person of you will be lost" (Acts 27:22)[1169]; only the ship will be destroyed. How does Paul know this? He explains his certainty through an oracle of reassurance[1170] from an angel.

Narrative Setting:	"For (γάρ) last night, an angel of the God, whose I am and whom I serve, stood beside me, saying,
Admonition:	'Stop fearing,
Address:	Paul.
Reason:	It is necessary for you to stand trial before Caesar;
	and
	behold, God has graciously given to you the lives of all who are sailing with you.'" (27:23-24).

Paul's initial prophecy needed to be heeded. Now this second prophecy rises to another level, for it is based upon an angelic appearance with words of reassurance and explanation (reason).[1171] A couple of observations are important.

- Luke highlights Paul's intense commitment and personal piety; Paul belongs to this God whom he actively serves.
- Luke uses the impersonal verb, "it is necessary" (δεῖ), thirty-seven times in Luke-Acts, to express divine will.[1172] In this paragraph, Luke includes it three times (27:21, 24, 26). Paul reiterates the divine "must" that drives the narrative, expressed through prophetic language.
- The assurance includes a "behold" (ἰδού) statement that shifts from Paul's divine "must" to stand trial before Caesar, now to reassure all of his travelers that God has given them to Paul, "Behold, God has graciously given (κεχάρισται) to you [Paul] all the ones sailing with you" (27:24). Following Paul's word to "cheer up," Luke provides another word from his joy-vocabulary (χαρίζομαι), used in the perfect tense, to emphasize their enduring condition, "all have been graciously given [by God] to Paul." There will be no "salvation" that doesn't include "all."[1173] Joyous emotions rise in the midst of disaster.
- God does not still the typhoon. Once the decision is made to take the calculated risk, nature takes over. Paul is "*not* portrayed as a *theios aner* ("divine man") whose will can bend the forces of nature to his own."[1174]

After his second prophecy, Paul tells the sailors again, "Therefore, cheer up men" (διὸ εὐθυμεῖτε, ἄνδρες Acts 27:25). He also provides another explanation, "for (γάρ) I believe in God that it will happen in the same manner as has been spoken to me" (27:25). The perfect tense, "has been spoken" (λελάληται) again underscores Luke's theme of prophecy-fulfillment. Paul summons the sailors to find their "cheer" in Paul's sure belief ("for I believe") of prophetic fulfillment.[1175] He trusts something they can bank on, "for they do believe that Paul speaks divine truth."[1176] In the midst of his call to cheer, he includes one caveat, "it is necessary (δεῖ) for us to run aground ('crash'[1177]) on some island" (27:26), which reiterates Paul's earlier statement (27:22). Luke emphasizes Paul's prophetic voice in predicting the destructive outcome, but also encouraging and summoning cheer in chaos.

Paragraph 5: Shipwreck (Acts 27:24-44). When Luke narrates the ill-fated voyage, he wants his readers to notice three more interventions, each containing the theme of "salvation":

- Paul's intervention with the sailor's escape (27:3-32).
- Paul's intervention with food (27:34).
- The Centurion's intervention in the soldiers' plan to kill escaped prisoners (27:42-44), with the result that "everyone was saved," whether by swimming or floating on the ship's debris (27:44).

Two times Paul "encourages" (παρακαλέω Acts 27:33-34) those on the ship with him "to take food" (27:33-34), with the explanation, "for this food is for your salvation." With hyperbole, he reassures them once again, "Not one of you will lose a single hair from his head."

Luke then records how Paul, in Jewish fashion, "took some bread and gave thanks[1178] to God in front of them all. Then he broke it and began to eat" (Acts 27:35). For Luke, it is important that Paul does this "in the presence of all of them"—it serves as a public witness. Seeing and hearing this, "all became cheerful" (εὔθυμοι δὲ γενόμενοι πάντες), and "all partook of food" and "ate enough" (27:37), before lightening the ship (27:38).[1179]

What is Luke's purpose? In the midst of an impending shipwreck, a destroyed ship, and lost cargo (but no loss of human life), Paul's prophecies come true. But his repeated and encouraging call "to cheer up" (εὐθυμεῖν—Acts 27:22, 25) also is realized when "all became cheered up" (εὔθυμοι δὲ γενόμενοι πάντες 27:36). Why the emotional alteration from depression and hopelessness to "cheer?"

Yes, taking food expresses hope that the men want to live and are thereby nourished for the next arduous task of making it to shore. Yet there is more. The men draw strength and cheer from Paul, his prophetic role, the angelic message, Paul's trust in God, his constant pastoral reassurances. Now he also offers a public example, "before them all." The men imitate Paul's joyful example, "taking bread, giving thanks to God, breaking the bread and eating". It will mean their "salvation" (Acts 27:34) in the midst of a shipwreck. Paul's public witness, charismatic power and joy, along with his trust in the unseen God, combine with physical nourishment—all cause the men to become buoyant.

While there may be a Eucharistic allusion, it is certainly not primary for Luke. His interest rests in the driving force of Paul's prophecies and their fulfillment (Acts 27:10, 21, 24-25, 34, 44), coupled with the summons to cheer, joy, and thanksgiving. Not only does Paul receive assurance from the angel, but he shares that assurance with the depressed sailors (27:24-37), effectively summoning them to experience the joy for themselves.

The Centurion intervenes because of his friendship with Paul; that is central. The Centurion wants to spare Paul's life, thus he keeps his soldiers from executing any prisoners. Julius' intervention fulfills Paul's prophecy, "God has graciously given to you [Paul] those sailing with you" (Acts 27:24). All are spared because of God's commitment to Paul's journey to Rome. Luke cogently states the fulfillment of all of Paul's prophecies and assurances, "and thus it happened that all were saved on the land" (27:44).

Paragraph 6: Paul on the Island of Malta (Acts 28:1-10). The story begins with reiteration, "all were saved" (27:44), now expressed through the participle, "after we were saved" (28:1). Subsequently, the shipwrecked party discovers they landed on the Island of Malta. Several items emerge:

- Luke highlights the exceptional kindness[1180] of the Maltese natives, through their welcome and hospitality, "they gathered all of us [around the fire]" (Acts 28:2). Perhaps the ship's members are apprehensive about the local natives. However, the locals participate in the rescue by taking care of the physical needs of all. Because of inclement weather, they light a fire and warm up the wet and cold shipwrecked victims (28:2).

- Luke highlights the native's quick reversal in their attitude towards Paul. When Paul gathers brushwood to fuel the native's fire, a viper hidden in the brush clings to Paul's hand. He shakes the snake into the fire. The natives quickly conclude that Paul "surely[1181] must be a *murderer*, since justice has caught up with him, "for though he was saved from the sea, Justice[1182] has not allowed him to live" (28:4). They wait, expecting Paul to bloat up or fall dead from a poisonous bite. When their expectations are not met, they quickly conclude that Paul is *a god* (Acts 27:6). These kind natives understand that a numinous power delivered Paul from a poisonous snakebite, "if someone can withstand deadly serpents, then some divine *dynamis* must be at work in him." In this case, Paul does not deflect the native's misconception that he "must be a god," as he had done with the Lycaonians (Acts 14:8-13).[1183] While there is no overt verbal evangelism, it is enough for Luke that the messengers welcome the company with hospitality, reflecting an attitude of receptivity to God's gracious visitation.
- Publius, the island's "Chief," likewise expresses hospitality for Paul and company. Luke highlights this with three expressions: "welcomed us as guests," "for three days in a *kindly manner*," "he entertained [us] as guests" (Acts 28:7). Emotions of kindness, warmth, and hospitality characterize both the islanders and their "Chief."
- Publius' father becomes sick with fevers and dysentery, which leads Paul to approach him, pray, lay his hands upon him, leading to the man's miraculous healing, "he healed him" (Acts 28:8). Now, Paul becomes Publius' benefactor.
- That healing prompts a verbal report, drawing the rest of the island's sick to Paul, resulting in extensive healings

(Acts 28:9). Luke uses two imperfect verbs to convey their ongoing activity, "they were coming" and "they were being healed." Paul then becomes the benefactor of the entire island during a full three-month stay. Thus, the healing and beneficent ministry of Jesus continues through his witnesses.

- The final response of the natives is joyful. "They honored us with many honors and they put on board the things we needed" (Acts 24:10). Although the noun, "honor" (τιμή) can refer to "honor" and "payment/price/honorarium,"[1184] the translation, "honor" is more suitable for the dative ("*with* many *honors*" πολλαῖς τιμαῖς) and is cognate with the related verb, "they *honored*" (ἐτίμησαν). The next clause adds further detail, for the natives provide the Pauline company with needed items for the final leg of their journey to Rome. Both the honor and the sharing of possessions express the natives' gratitude for what Paul meant to them. Their joyful response is expressed in their deeds. Again for Luke, sharing of possessions recalls Luke's summaries, in which life-together is marked by joy, sharing of resources, and gratitude (Acts 2:42-47; 4:32-37). Thus, Luke expresses the theme of mutual reciprocity. The natives and Publius are initially Paul's benefactors with their warm hospitality. Paul, in turn, becomes the benefactor of Publius, his father, and the natives with his extensive healings. In response, the natives with their "honor" and provisions become Paul's benefactors. Luke presents all of this in the context of joyous relationships.

Through the entire adventure, Luke intermingles charismatic power with emotional experiences and expressions of joy. The depressive conditions of abandoning hope of "salvation" (Acts 27:20) are countered through Paul's prophetic words and actions, which lead to the "salvation" of all. At the end, even Paul is saved from a poisonous viper and subsequently becomes both the recipient (kindness, honor, provision) and giver of benefaction (healings). Within the narrative, the reiterated admonition to "Cheer up" is positioned within a series of major life-threatening crises. Thus, the imperative carries great emotion. Paul himself models "cheer," "encouragement" and "thanksgiving" when he invites others to feel the same emotions.

Similarly, the people (Paul, Julius, the sailors, soldiers, the natives, Publius) discover more in their understanding, attitude, and behavior. In the very experience of crises, people can discover trust, joy, and even celebration. Even "pagan" natives grow in their understanding of Paul and their acceptance of divine visitation for their good, and they respond in kind.

Further, Luke pairs divine determination (decision) and human responsiveness. The divine "must" calls Paul to stand trial before Caesar. However, people make significant decisions. The initial bad decision to reject Paul's first prophecy allows nature to take its course, leading to disaster and loss. On the other hand, Julius' friendship with Paul allows him to learn from his mistake and make good decisions, to the extent that his saving action keeps the soldiers from killing all the prisoners, including Paul. When Paul warns Julius, "Unless these [sailors] remain in the ship, you (plural=all within the ship) cannot be saved" (Acts 27:31), the Centurion faces and makes a life-saving decision. Julius is no divine *pawn*, simply playing his part in a dramatic play. Along with others, he draws strength from Paul's repeated "encouragement" (27:33-34). Each person on the ship can choose to be encouraged by Paul's prophecies and prophetic actions.

Fittingly, Tannehill remarks, "Human actions that work toward the rescue of all are acceptable contributions to the realization of God's purpose, but actions that seek the safety of one's own group while abandoning others will block this purpose until corrected. When the parties in the ship work together cooperatively for the good of all, dangers are avoided and the ship's company is saved."[1185] When sailors seek to abandon ship or soldiers plan to kill prisoners, they act apart from the "salvation" of "all."

Within the broad framework of God's plan and human decisions, Luke combines miraculous events with emotional responses of joy for

God's saving activity, even in life-threatening crises. Even though Paul is under the looming prospect of death in Rome, it is important for Paul and Luke that their respective faith-communities feel encouragement, joy, and cheer in the midst of danger and threats to life.

Notes

1114 Keener, Vol. 2, 1208-1212, draws attention to other prison escapes, especially through angels.

1115 As Marshall notes, "Luke certainly regards the incident as miraculous." 124. *Contra* Dunn, "actually an early sympathizer with the new movement within the prison staff." 68.

1116 Compare "file leader and Savior" (ἀρχηγὸν καὶ σωτῆρα 5:31; "file leader of life" ἀρχηγὸν τῆς ζωῆς 3:15).

1117 In Pervo's words, "they are all dressed up and nowhere to go." 140.

1118 Pervo, 138.

1119 Barrett, Vol. 1, 287.

1120 See Richard A. Horsley, *Bandits, Prophets, and Messiahs* (Minneapolis: Winston Press, 1973), 165-167, 169.

1121 Barrett, Vol. 1, 284

1122 Pervo, 145.

1123 On the theme of "witness," see Acts 1:8; 2:11, 32-33; 4:8, 31.

1124 Similar thoughts in Barrett, Vol. 1, 291.

1125 Tannehill, Vol. Two, 152-155 links Stephen, Jesus, and the Exodus event; Barrett, *Commentary on Acts*, 577, argues for an Exodus allusion, suggesting "a night of messianic deliverance"; Johnson draws parallels with Jesus' trial, *The Acts of the Apostles*, 218; Pervo, 302, 309-311 alludes to Jesus and understands the Acts 12 story as another Passion story, and even a typological story, a "paradigm of Christian experience," including baptism. Susan Garrett argues convincingly for parallels between the Exodus, Jesus' passion and Peter's rescue, by highlighting shared vocabulary and themes. Susan R. Garrett, "Exodus from Bondage: Luke 9:31 and Acts 12:1-24," *Catholic Biblical Quarterly* 1 52 (1990), 656-680; Von Walter Radl similarly argues for connection between the Exodus and Peter's miraculous escape, Von Walter Radl, "Befreiung aus dem Gefängnis: Die Darstellung eines biblischen Grundthemas in Apg 12," *Biblische Zeitschrift*, 27 (1983), 81-96; Dunn, 162-163, counters such allusions.

1126 Luke provides little detail as to the issue surrounding Herod's dispute with his adjacent territories (12:20).

1127 Josephus also provides a story of Herod's death, *Antiquities*, 20:200 with both points of similarity and dissimilarity. Apparently, the prison guards are executed (12:19 "to be led away [to execution]"; ἀπαχθῆναι).

1128 Haenchen's argument that "James has taken over the leadership of the congregation" 391, is conjectural—to suggest that Peter's time is over. Luke doesn't say this. Dunn, *The Acts of the Apostles*, 159 follows Haenchen's position. Barrett, *Commentary on Acts*, 571, suggests only a hint, "It may go too far to suggest that Peter's message amounts to, 'Tell James it is now time for him to take over.'"

1129 Pervo, 301.

1130 Apparently Luke collapses the "feast of unleavened bread" (12:3) and "the Passover" (12:4).

1131 Saundra Schwartz draws interesting parallels between trial scenes in Greek novels and Acts. Relative to Acts 12, she notes, "The venue is different; it is set in the court of Herod, who is portrayed as a despot, a character type that appears repeatedly in the novels. The despot is violent, disregards due process, rules by whim and is driven by his (or her) appetites . . . The blameless apostle escapes and the tyrant pays the penalty." Saundra Schwartz, "The Trial Scene in the Greek Novels and in Acts," *Contextualizing Acts: Lukan Narrative and Greco-Roman Discourse,"* ed. Todd Penner and Caroline Vander Stichele, SBL Symposium Series 20 (2003), 123 (105-137).

1132 The Lukan verb, "I take away, do away with, destroy" (ἀναιρέω) is always used in a destructive manner.

1133 Keener, Vol. 2, 1877 points to the "morally disgusting behavior." Johnson, with other scholars point to the Jewish pleasure at the means of execution, "beheading" of Peter, based on *m. San.*7.2 as "the most shameful of deaths." Johnson, *The Acts of the Apostles*, 211.

1134 Pervo, 303.

1135 Barrett, *Commentary on Acts*, 577.

1136 E.g. "behold, two men stood by them" (Acts 1:10); "behold a man stood before him" (10:30). Elsewhere it is used by Luke for several divine "coincidences."

1137 Compare with the earlier angelic deliverance (5:19).

1138 BDAG, 330.

1139 As in Acts 9:3.

1140 BDAG, 122.

1141 See Josephus, *Wars*, VI, 293ff. for a reference to doors opening by themselves.

1142 Pervo, 304.

1143 συνοράω conveys the sense of "becoming aware" or "perceiving." BDAG, 791.

1144 Pervo, 306, highlights the various dangers of Peter out in the street or knocking at the gate, "an escaped convict under the sentence of death who must find somewhere to hide from the authorities who will soon raise an alarm." Since Luke says nothing about the danger motif, Pervo overstates his certainty.

1145 The verb, ὑπακούω is used of a doorkeeper "to listen for the signals of those who wish to enter, and to admit them if they are entitled to do so," BDAG, 837.

1146 Barrett, *Commentary on Acts*, 585.

1147 Keener, Vol. 2, 1943.

1148 Similar use of the verb in Acts 26:24-25.

1149 Luke also uses the verb, "I insist" (διϊσχυρίζομαι) in Lk 22:59, where another slave girl insists that Peter had been with Jesus—which Peter denies.

1150 For the idea of an individual and attendant angel, see Matt 18:10; LXX Gen 48:16; Tobit 5:22.

1151 See Lk 24:37—thinking they had seen a ghost—not the real Jesus.

1152 Pervo, 307.

1153 Oepke, *TDNT*, II, 460.

1154 Dunn, 161.

1155 See Josephus, *Antiquities*, 19:343-50, and Keener, vol. 2, 1967 for parallels.

1156 See Johnson, *The Acts of the Apostles*, 217.

1157 See Keener, vol. 2, 1957 for contrasts between Herod and Peter.

1158 Haenchen understands "the word of the Lord" (ὁ λόγος τοῦ θεοῦ) by, "the Christian missionary kerygma and the community living by it and for it." 387.

1159 The conservative position is taken up by Bruce, *The Book of Acts*, who bases much of his argument on James Smith, *The Voyage and Shipwreck of Paul* (London: 1848) 474-500. Others discount the historical aspects of the story by the argument that Luke has taken over Greco-Roman sea-voyage stories, replete with storms and shipwrecks (e.g., Homer's Odyssey) or Jonah, and inserted Pauline speeches into various episodes: Martin Dibelius, *Studies in the Acts of the Apostles* (London: 1956), 107; Hans Conzelmann, *Die Apostelgeschichte* (Tübingen: 1963), 140-147; Haenchen, 710. Pervo argues for a symbolic (not allegorical) approach to the narrative; however, he "sneaks in" extensive allegorical features into the narrative, e.g., "when it became day" (Acts 27:39) is interpreted as "the discovery of Jesus' resurrection," 664, and combines all sorts of allegorical details with existential language, e.g. 650, "sea travel becomes a common symbol for the 'course of human life.'" More moderate positions are taken by Dunn, *The Acts of the Apostles*, 334-348 and Johnson, *The Acts of the Apostles*, 450-452. Johnson states, "to move directly from the presence of literary motifs to the claim that Luke was simply fabricating the entire incidents is, as I have suggested, reckless," 452. The "we" passages also come into play (Acts 27:1, 2, 3 *et. al.* till the conclusion in Acts 28:1) may well suggest the presence of an eyewitness, which Barrett takes seriously. C. K. Barrett, "Paul Shipwrecked," *Scripture: Meaning and Method* (Pickering: Hull University Press, 1987), 52; Keener, Vol. 4, 3556-3564.

1160 The pejorative terms, "barbarians" (βάρβαροι) and "savages," need to be avoided. Although the natives are mistaken, Luke portrays them and Publius in a most positive light.

1161 The use of litotes, "not ordinary" (οὐ τὴν τυχοῦσαν) highlights their extraordinary kindness.

1162 Luke would have his readers connect the terms kindness and kindly.

1163 e.g., Bruce, *The Book of Acts*, 482. Also Dunn, *The Acts of the Apostles*, 338.

1164 Marshall, 406.

1165 Haenchen, 709. Similarly, Pervo, 657 remarks, "His words are inspired."

1166   Pervo, 656.

1167   See Tannehill, *Narrative Unity*, Vol. II, 336-337, for a double reading of "rescue" and "salvation." He notes, 337-338, "The emphasis on salvation in Luke-Acts gives to the emphasis on salvation in this sea voyage a second, symbolic sense ... a new boldness of hope that anticipates salvation (in some sense) for every individual of a pluralistic community and view persons such as Paul as mediators of this promise."

1168   Translation of Πολλῆς τε ἀσιτίας ὑπαρχούσης of Acts 27:21 by BDAG, 116.

1169   Conzelmann, *Acts*, 218, dismisses Paul's speech in the midst of hurricane force winds as "completely unreal."

1170   I am indebted to Aune for the headings, 268.

1171   See Acts 23:11 with a similar oracle of reassurance.

1172   See the extended treatment of δεῖ by Walter Grundmann, *TDNT*, Vol. II, 21-25. He states, "The usage of Luke has the widest implications. It gathers up all the relations within which δεῖ is found in the rest of the NT," 23.

1173   See Tannehill, *Narrative Unity*, Vol. II, 335 for a summary paragraph dealing with "all."

1174   Johnson, *The Acts of the Apostles*, 458. *Contra* Haenchen, 716, who argues that Paul is "a mighty superman."

1175   See Elizabeth's blessing upon Mary, (Lk 1:45); also Lk 2:20; 22:13.

1176   Keener, Vol. 4, 3641.

1177   Johnson, *The Acts of the Apostles*, 449.

1178   Perhaps a Lucan word play between, "God has *graciously given*" (κεχάρισται Acts 27:24) and Paul's action, "*he gave thanks* to God" (εὐχαρίστησεν) to God (27:35).

1179   It is beyond our scope to enter into detailed analysis of sacramental allusions.

1180   See earlier comment on "exceptional kindness" (οὐ τὴν φιλανθρωπίαν).

1181   The adverb πάντως is clearly emphatic.

1182   is used in the sense of retribution.

1183   See Peter's deflection in Acts 3:11-16.

1184   BDAG, 817-818.

1185   Tannehill, *Narrative Unity*, Vol. II, 338.

CHAPTER 10

THE GOD OF EMOTION

With the coming of Christ into this world,
his death and resurrection, and the outpouring
of the divine Spirit, the spring of eternal life begins for human
beings, all living beings and the earth. Mortal and earthly life
is taken up into the divine, eternal, and heavenly life.
—JÜRGEN MOLTMANN

This study reveals an approach to Luke-Acts that highlights Luke's important motif of joy as it bears upon charismatic experience. It has been shown that Luke is intentional in his paired-volumes, infusing his rich joy-vocabulary into the narratives to accentuate joy when people encounter charismatic incursions. A preponderance of his narratives climax with joy, indeed great joy. Luke also supplements his rich joy-vocabulary with other words that do not properly belong to the joy-vocabulary, e.g. "singing and dancing," or "with haste." Luke does not distinguish between inner joy and outer happiness, for he frequently alternates his terms.

Many implications emerge from Luke that directly bear upon the academy, interpretation and application of biblical texts, ministry, pastoral leadership, personal life, and the local and global witness of faith-communities:

1. God is a God of joy who wills joy for people. He has repeatedly encountered people through a plethora of charismatic experiences, from the very beginning of two miraculous conceptions in Luke, to Paul's

final ministry in Rome in Acts. Through the stories, faith-communities discover God's intention for joy in the person of Jesus and the Holy Spirit. Since God feels emotion, people likewise feel moved, and they prosper when they encounter supernatural dimensions. Divine visitations express God's compassion and his feeling-involvement with people. Jesus' agenda, stated in his inaugural address, is life-giving and joy-eliciting. That program finds fulfillment through the person, words, and works of Jesus as he embodies, preaches, and does the kingdom of God in concert with the Holy Spirit.

2. For Luke, Jesus is a man of great joy, attracting people to himself. He is winsome in his very person as he approaches people. Jesus is ecstatic when his people carry out his directions for their lives (Luke 10:21). His very ministry of joyous life reveals God's nature and God's will for humanity. In the person of Jesus, God brings "good news of great joy" for all the people. Luke highlights the joyous atmosphere, elated experiences, and jubilant expressions when people encounter Jesus through his preaching, healing, exorcisms, and other mighty works. Earthly joy for divine visitation is matched with simultaneous festive celebration in heaven. In a sense, earth and heaven meet. Luke's gospel begins with "good news of great joy" announced to the shepherds, and then it climaxes with "great joy" experienced and expressed by the disciples when they see the resurrected Jesus and learn of the anticipated Holy Spirit. His appearance to them is "too good to be true" (24:41), leading to "great joy" (24:52). Luke intends that his audience, then and now, experience the same emotions.

3. Luke introduces his readers to people who discover that, through Jesus, God acts with compassion and helpful visitation in the ambiguities of their broken lives. Jesus accepts people where they are, which leads to their related changes (repentance). For example, Jesus does not tell the marginalized toll-collectors and sinners to "get it right" before he engages them. Repentance often means a turn to God's new activity, *after* accepting grace. As such, Jesus flies in the face

of the Jewish paradigm that repentance leads to an experience of grace. Luke's paired volumes underscore the truth that people are "in process" as they discover more about Jesus, the Holy Spirit, and God. Believers are not ready-made, for they grow and mature as they learn about God and his joyous will for humanity. Peter is one such person who progressively works through his own "conversion," when he discovers God's impartiality and his desire for the inclusion of all people (Acts 10:34). Charismatic experiences feature large in Acts 10:1-11:18.

4. Luke's Book of Acts provides witness to God's will for joy for humanity, when people encounter God in a variety of charismatic experiences. The joyful nature of Jesus' ministry continues in Luke's second volume, in which the nascent Christian community continues to do "what Jesus began to do and teach" (Acts 1:1). Luke climaxes his stories with celebrations of joy, expressed when people experiences various Pentecosts, miracles, answered prayer, signs and wonders. Similar to his gospel, Luke continues to provide the joyous nature of the atmosphere, experiences, and expressions, when people encounter God's power.

5. In the paired-volumes, Luke also accentuates God's will for joyous inclusion, through the ministry of Jesus and the nascent church. God wills that people express acceptance without erecting boundaries in terms of "who's in" and "who's out." Joyous inclusion is demonstrated through stories of table-fellowship with the wrong kinds of people (toll-collectors and sinners), lepers, three Roman centurions, a vision of unclean animals, circumcision/uncircumcision, various Pentecosts in Acts, the Jerusalem Council, Paul's ministry to the Gentiles, and the concluding affirmation in Acts about the Gentiles, "they will listen" (Acts 28: 28). Various manifestations of the Holy Spirit are celebratory and inclusive in nature.

6. Interpreters of biblical texts need to notice the affective language of biblical stories without diminishing or ignoring emotions, since they are woven into the very fabric of a narrative-tapestry. This approach counters Western tendencies to favor propositional language and interpretation.

7. Jesus' ministry is holistic in nature, certainly touching the emotions. This is where people live. Readers discover that Jesus or the early Christians do not dampen joyous emotions as do the joy-less critics. This includes scholars who use pejorative language with respect to Christian emotions. Jesus interprets joy and joyous gratitude as "faith" (Luke 17:19). Jesus and the early Christians do not say that rationalism must take priority or trump human emotions of joy. Indeed, gratitude is inextricably paired with joy.

8. Luke's readers learn that joy belongs to the very nature of God's kingdom. Since the kingdom of God is both present and future, the joyful and powerful encounters with people also anticipate the *eschaton*. Through Jesus and through his disciples' short-term mission trips, and the ministry of the Early Church, God's kingdom is declared in both word and deed, as people experience the joy-eliciting "good news" through words, but also through healings and exorcisms. God's kingdom is fully present, and yet it also anticipates God's future reign, when all of the ambiguities of human experience will be eclipsed and will disappear.

9. Joy is but one element encased within the broader Christian emotions of God's kingdom. It can be both overemphasized and under-emphasized. The kingdom of God may be compared to a prism. Light passes through the prism, and in the process, it reveals a broad array of colors that are not noticeable otherwise. In God's kingdom, joy constitutes one such color, along with other Christian affections such as love, hope and peace. It is certainly one important ray, but not the whole. Joy is related to other emotions. For instance, when people encounter Jesus, they experience the emotion of love, often followed by the emotion of joy.

10. Luke doesn't only narrate stories, but he intends to draw his readership into the joyful expressions, experiences and atmosphere. In a vicarious way, Luke invites his readers to share experiences with attendant joy, not only in a personal way, but in a communal context. For Luke, receptivity means everything, not only for the people in his stories, but for his audience as well.

11. A lack of receptivity to joyful and miraculous events may indeed harden people, so they often express a spirit of meanness characterizing opponents (Lk 13:10-17). They cannot celebrate the good things that occur, which bring untold joy for recipients. In both volumes, Luke frequently highlights joy against the background of joy-less critics who are driven by fear, insecurity, jealousy, anger, and feelings of being threatened in some way. In many stories, opponents who seek to shame Jesus or the disciples are themselves shamed when they make futile attempts to suppress the truth. They cannot deny the reality of miraculous events. They can only accuse, attempt to suppress joy, physically attack, and discredit Jesus or the witness of the Early Church. Thus, a healed beggar stands as a living witness before the religious leaders (Acts 4:16). He is a physical parable of salvation, and the religious leaders can only issue a gag-order, due to their fear and insecurity.

12. In the narrative-summaries, Luke intends that his church-audience would reflect the same joyous life-together in a community characterized by miracles, a winsome witness, generosity, a sense of togetherness, and united prayer. Joyous life-together surely leads to an attractive witness to unbelievers. Joy also characterizes life-together, when God's people face difficult decisions (Acts 15).

13. Luke's readers, then and now, are to be receptive to the powerful baptism in the Spirit, in which people's lives will be transformed through experienced joy, a powerful verbal witness, miracles, and a boldness in speech to declare the wonder of the entire Jesus-story. The same baptism in the Spirit that Jesus experienced at the Jordan River carries over into the various Pentecostal receptions in the Book of Acts. It empowers his people to both speak and act for God with confidence and boldness of speech. There is absolutely no hint that miraculous experiences and spiritual gifts only belong to the apostolic era. The promise of the Holy Spirit by the risen Jesus (Luke 24:48-49 and Acts 1:8) doesn't only apply to the original disciples, but to Luke's readers, then and now. Correspondingly, Luke offers no patterned recipe or sequence for receiving the baptism in the Spirit.

Each person and each context reflect diversity. For Luke, the *how* is relatively insignificant, but the *fact* of reception of the Holy Spirit is pre-eminent, since the promise is guaranteed and the precious gift awaits eager reception.

14. Luke's readers learn that danger and threats can also be met with a paradoxical joy, a "joy notwithstanding."[1186] Whether people experience deliverance from prison, a shipwreck, or verbal or physical abuse, the call to joy remains constant, even to the extent that beaten apostles rejoice because they had been counted worthy to suffer for the name of Jesus (Acts 5:41). Luke does not generalize from these stories to say that God delivers all of his people from threats, danger, or even murder. Yet, at the same time, he does provide stories that affirm that God is on the side of his people, and he may demonstrate his advocacy through saving acts, such as angelic activity.

15. Joy reigns supreme even in confrontations with magicians and their magic. The Holy Spirit, who empowers God's people, trumps the power of magic. The "finger of God" (Luke 11:2; the Spirit of God in Matt 12:28) that Jesus uses in his exorcisms carries over in the Early Church in various clashes with magicians, and thereby render the magicians impotent, even expressed with Luke's humorous language (Acts 19:16).

16. Joy and miraculous power lead to God's glory, sung early in the annunciation and birth narratives. In frequent vignettes, when peoples' lives have been touched by God's power, joy is voiced in harmony with God's fame, his reputation, and his impressiveness. For example, Jews who object to Peter's table-fellowship with Gentiles are won over by Peter's story of how Cornelius and company were baptized in the Holy Spirit. Religious objections quickly turn to verbal expressions of God's fame, for they now testify to the new reality of "repentance unto life" (Acts 11:18), which is paired with the encounter of Cornelius and company with the Holy Spirit. The Jews who hear Peter's shared story are carried away with God's reputation voiced aloud in praise.

It is hoped that this journey into Luke's thought-world will impact readers, leading them to sympathetically engage the biblical narratives with receptivity. In visualizing the stories, readers are led to feel the joyous emotions of the text and thereby flourish. For people and churches, living a joy-less existence and expecting dour worship experiences, Luke's invitation to joy is clarion and real. This is how life is to be lived. People really live and blossom when they encounter God in one dimension or another. Dynamic living and blossoming lead to fruition with a natural progression of joyful encounter and bold witness to the entirety of the Jesus story and the extension of that testimony through the Early Church to the power of God, his relationality with people, and his joyful purpose for all of humanity.

Notes

1186 Thompson, 20.

ACKNOWLEDGMENTS

Ruth Ford who has edited my manuscript.

Rev. Robert Whitaker, who was a personal mentor to me in seminary.

Roy M. Carlisle, who was the editor at Harper & Row San Francisco, who invited me to co-author the Greek grammar, *Greek to Me*, with my father, Dr. Cullen I K Story; a fresh approach to learning biblical Greek. And who has acquired and championed this new book for The Crossroad Publishing Company. The late Dr. Robert Munger (Fuller Seminary), who believed in me, my leadership, and preaching, in faith-renewal efforts.

The late Dr. David Hubbard, as a model of a Christian scholar, teacher, mentor, leader, and a co-supervisor in my Ph.D. program; I remember well his invitation to come to personally talk with him about the power of the Holy Spirit.

The late Dr. J. Rodman Williams, who invited me to teach in a new school in Southern California; through that experience, I came to believe that God had gifted me to teach; it was a joy to teach with him in the School of Divinity of Regent University.

The late Dr. Cullen I K Story (Princeton Seminary), who was such a constant source of encouragement and communication during my pastoral and academic career, as well as my teaching; what a joyous experience to co-teach with him in the summer language program of Princeton.

Faculty colleagues in the School of Divinity of Regent University who have encouraged me in my writing effort.

Deans of the School of Divinity, who have been supportive of my writing thrust (Dr. Michael Palmer, Dr. Amos Yong, Dr. Corné Bekker).

Regent University that has offered me the immense privilege of teaching the Bible and biblical languages for 35 years. Daily I thank God for this pleasure.

The adult learners in the School of Divinity, with whom I share a common life; they constantly mean so much to me.

SELECTED BIBLIOGRAPHY

Bernadicou, Paulo J. *Joy in the Gospel of Luke*. Rome: Pontificiae Universitatis Gregoriannae, 1970.

Elliott, Matthew A. *Faithful Feelings: Rethinking Emotion in the New Testament*. Grand Rapids: Kregel, 2006.

Johnson, Luke Timothy. *Religious Experience in Early Christianity*. Minneapolis: Fortress Press, 1998.

Maitland, Sarah. *A Joyful Theology*. Minneapolis: Augsburg Books, 2002.

Moltmann, Jürgen. *Theology and Joy*. London: SCM Press LTD, 1973.

Morrice, William. *Joy in the New Testament*. Grand Rapids: William B. Eerdmans Publishing Company, 1984.

Volf, Miroslav and Crisp, Justin E., eds. *Joy and Human Flourishing*. Minneapolis: Fortress Press, 2015.

OTHER TITLES OF INTEREST:

Prophetic Witness: Catholic Women's Strategies for Reform
By Colleen M. Griffith

Presenting practical strategies for reform and renewal of the Church, this strikingly direct volume brings together the voices of leading Catholic theologians who offer ideas for change while still showing that feminist reflection can work in support of the Church.
978-0-8245-2526-2 paperback / 128 pages

Handing on the Faith: The Church's Mission and Challenge
By Robert P. Imbelli, Ed.

Renowned theologian and teacher Robert P. Imbelli introduces the work of leading Catholic theologians, writers, and scholars to discuss the challenges of handing on the faith and to rethink the essential core of Catholic identity.
978-0-8245-2409-8 paperback / 264 pages

Finding Beauty in the Other: Theological Reflections across Religious Traditions
Edited by Peter Casarella and Mun'im Sirry

This valuable collection of essays features a host of highly respected scholars, presenting a unique treatment of the concept of beauty as seen in a variety of religions and cultures. These include Catholicism, Hinduism, Buddhism, and Islam. In addition, beauty as seen in various African cultures is discussed.
978-0-8245-2336-7 paperback / 978-0-8245-2335-0 hard cover / 398 pages

Anatomy of Misremembering: Von Balthasar's Response to Philosophical Modernity

The most comprehensive account of the relationship between Hans Urs von Balthasar and Hegel. For the author, it is essential to engage and correct Hegel, whose thought is a comprehensive misremembering of the Christian thought, practices, and forms of life.
978-0-8245-2562-0 paperback / 688 pages